Evidence-Based Design
for
Interior Designers

Evidence-Based Design
for
Interior Designers

Linda L. Nussbaumer
South Dakota State University

Fairchild Books
An imprint of Bloomsbury Publishing Inc

BLOOMSBURY
NEW YORK · LONDON · OXFORD · NEW DELHI · SYDNEY

DRED COURT

Fairchild Books

An imprint of Bloomsbury Publishing Inc

1385 Broadway	50 Bedford Square
New York	London
NY 10018	WC1B 3DP
USA	UK

www.bloomsbury.com

FAIRCHILD BOOKS, BLOOMSBURY and the Diana logo are trademarks of Bloomsbury Publishing Plc

First published 2009
Reprinted 2017

Library of Congress Catalog Card Number
2008937706

ISBN: PB: 978-1-56367-759-5
ePDF: 978-1-6090-1397-4
ePub: 978-1-5013-1012-6

Printed and bound in the United States of America

To find out more about our authors and books visit www.bloomsbury.com. Here you will find extracts, author interviews, details of forthcoming events, and the option to sign up for our newsletters.

*To my husband, Jerry, who has always been
my greatest encourager and supporter.*

Contents

Extended Contents

EXTENDED CONTENTS

Preface

Research has become an important component throughout the design process. It provides evidence for better design solutions. Its application improves client, staff, and/or patient satisfaction. Knowledge and application of evidence-based research is required for healthcare designers to become certified and for students in accredited programs to apply to their projects. At the beginning of the twenty-first century, interior designers are faced with increasing challenges and opportunities that range from cultural diversity and globalization to sustainability and technology. Developing the best possible methods of research is vital to addressing these and other emerging design concerns.

Research includes collecting data through both fact finding and locating new evidence. Locating new evidence and applying that evidence to a design project is called evidence-based design (EBD). The purpose of EBD research is to conduct that research, report the findings, and apply the findings to the design solution. The quality of design solutions depends on the quality of research; therefore, understanding what and how to research topics relevant to a particular design project is vital.

EBD is discussed at conferences and reported in trade periodicals. In many design firms, designers are expected to conduct such research. If educators provide students with a format and basis for research that develops EBD, entry-level interior designers will bring greater knowledge to their employers.

EBD began in healthcare design. Drawing from the example of evidence-based medicine, designers in this field realized the importance of collecting new evidence to create safe, healthy environments for patients and staff. If applied in other types of design—such as office, hospitality, retail, and beyond—designs will improve employee satisfaction, increase productivity, increase sales, and benefit the field and their clients in an ever-growing variety of ways.

For these various types of design, this book will provide background information for fact finding and research of new evidence. Part One: Foundations of Evidence-Based Design provides background information on EBD, the design process, programming, resources, and design theories. Part Two: Data Collection explores methods of data collection along with the role of precedents in the design process. Part Three: Environmental Considerations examines the collection of facts and evidence on needs related to the physical structure and its components, sustainability, psychology, sociology, and diversity. Part Four: Commercial Spaces provides an overview of data collection for commercial projects and background information on various types of design—office, hospitality, retail, and others. Part Five: Residential Spaces examines family and housing structures as well as data collection. Finally, Part Six: Drawing Conclusions puts EBD into practice.

Although background information is provided on various needs and types of design, the book is not intended to be a comprehensive description in any way. What is most important is that students learn the *process* of exploring these areas.

A variety of sources are presented in this book that may engage the designer in EBD research. Some resources are available specifically for the designer, such as the InformeDesign database and the knowledge centers from ASID and IIDA. In my experience, I have found these sources to be valuable for data and ease of accessibility. These resources summarize or provide abstracts that help designers easily find data that can be applied to a design project. Students should not consider these particular sources to be the sole resources that designers use to research data; however, these resources are excellent examples to engage students in the process of EBD research. Again, it is of primary importance that students learn the *process* of research and apply it to their projects.

This book provides a basis for research and investigation prior to sketching or developing drawings. Its focus is research, which will take place in a library or through the Internet. Books, scholarly journals (hard copy and online), and trade magazines and other periodicals will also be important resources.

For students to learn what and how to conduct this research, various pedagogical approaches are used. At the beginning of each chapter, Objectives provide the learning focus, and at the end of each chapter, Key Terms—bolded throughout the text—aid in a better understanding of the material. A chapter-by-chapter list of resources for further research is provided at the end of this book to enhance the learning experience. These resources include books, periodical and journal articles, and online resources. A very important component within the chapters is the Ideas for Collecting New Evidence. These are designed as tips or suggestions for collecting evidence but should also initiate students to brainstorm new ideas of their own. An important component of any book is a case study. In this book, case studies demonstrate the application of EBD to office, hospitality, healthcare, and educational design as well as historic precedents.

Appendices offer examples of surveys, questionnaires, and other full-page documents. Throughout the book, tables, charts, illustrations, and photographs will provide a visual understanding of a topic. A glossary, bibliography, and index are also included at the end of the book.

Evidence-Based Design for Interior Designers is intended for use at all levels in higher education. Portions can be used at the freshman level to introduce students to EBD. Then, at subsequent levels, students can use the book for continued learning and as a resource into more detailed information for specific types of design. For example, if students are working on a healthcare design project, they would turn to the chapter on healthcare design along with the previous chapters and learning experiences in other courses. Also, practitioners must conduct EBD prior to placing the pen to paper (so to speak). They will find information on data collection, examples of questionnaires, and suggestions for fact finding and evidence to be excellent sources that will energize their design and carry their projects to a higher level.

Acknowledgments

Resources that students and practitioners may find helpful as they begin the process of fact finding and locating new evidence are numerous. Although the following resources—and many more—are referenced throughout the book, I'd like to offer a special note of appreciation to the following: *Architectural Programming: Information Management for Design,* by D. P. Duerk; *Problem Seeking: An Architectural Programming Primer,* by W. M. Pena and S. A. Parshall; *Environmental Psychology for Design* by Dak Kopek; *Architecture: Form, Space, Order* by Frank Ching; *Precedents in Architecture* by R. H. Clark and M. Pause; *Designing a Quality Lighting Environment* and *Fundamentals of Lighting,* by Susan Winchip; *Designing Commercial Interiors,* by Christine Piotrowski and Elizabeth Rogers; *The Not So Big House,* by Sarah Susanka; and *Residential Planning and Design* by Jeanne Ireland.

Condé Nast Publications and Fairchild Books are not only publishers but also mentors for authors. These professionals include Executive Editor Olga Kontzias; Sales Representative Stacey George; Senior Development Editor Jennifer Crane; and Development Editor Rob Phelps. A special thanks goes to Rob for his great work as a reviewer and editor. I would also like to thank the talented production and art team of Art Director Adam Bohannon; Production Director Ginger Hillman; Associate Production Editor Andrew Fargnoli; and Associate Art Director Erin Fitzsimmons. I am also grateful for the review and constructive criticism of Migette Kaup of Kansas State University and Caren Martin of University of Minnesota.

I would like to thank those who contributed to my book in a variety of ways:

For writing assistance in the Healthcare Design chapter, thank you: Charisse Oland, Oland Consulting in Sioux Falls, South Dakota; and CEO of Rehabilitation Hospital of Wisconsin in Wauskesha, Wisconsin; Nancy Fishman, Sharron van der Meulen, and Terri

Johnson, Principal Interior Designers, Zimmer Gunsul Frasca Architects LLP in Portland, Oregon; and Susan Zacharakis, Director of Clinical Planning, the Children's Hospital in Aurora, Colorado.

For providing interviews, reviews, information, and photographs of St. Elizabeth Ann Seton School/church and Las Vegas Chamber of Commerce offices, thank you to Rosemary D'Amato, registered interior designer, and Craig Galati, principal and architect from Lucchesi Galati.

For providing the case study and photographs of the Louis Kahn's Salk Institute, thank you to Lily Robinson, architect.

Thanks to my colleague Dean Isham, professor of interior design at South Dakota State University, who provided illustrations throughout the book. Thank you to student reviewers and South Dakota State University interior design students Emily Goeden and Michelle Ralston, who reviewed and edited the manuscript from a student's perspective. Michelle also assisted with information and photographs for the hospitality case study. Thank you also to Jane Hegland, department head, and Laurie Nichols, dean of the College of Family and Consumer Sciences, for their encouragement and support. Thank you also to my friends and family who supported this endeavor.

Evidence-Based Design
for
Interior Designers

Foundations of Evidence-Based Design

PART

ONE

Introduction to Evidence-Based Design

OBJECTIVES

After reading this chapter, you should be able to:

Describe general tasks and activities that take place during the design process

Describe specific tasks and activities that take place during the programming phase of the design process

Identify research topics within programming

Understand terminology that relates to research findings

Identify and apply resources to create evidence for evidence-based design

DRED COURT

design solution is only as good as the quality of its research. Identifying what is relevant to a particular design project and understanding how to research it are therefore essential. **Evidence-based design (EBD)** is the approach that designers take to attain the highest quality of research that leads them to the best possible design solutions.

EBD is defined as "a process for the conscientious, explicit, and judicious use of current best **evidence** from research and practice in making critical decisions, together with an informed client, about the design of each individual and unique project" (Stichler & Hamilton, 2008, p. 3). In other words, EBD is an informed approach to design where designers intentionally base their decisions on quantitative and qualitative research—two forms of systematic inquiry that will be defined and discussed further in this book. Systematic inquiry not only creates knowledge but also solves design problems. Thus, the purpose of EBD research is to conduct or locate research, report the findings, and apply the findings to the design solution. This research involves a thorough examination of precedents as well as future needs, both of which will result in a comprehensive design solution and will be covered in this book.

Before we can discuss the application of EBD we must first address basic information about the design process and then, more specifically, about **programming**, the first phase of EBD.

The Design Process

When designers are presented with a design problem, they use a systematic, logical method to solve the problem. The systematic, logical method ensures that both creative and comprehensive design solutions will satisfy and meet the needs of the client.

The **design process** involves **analysis** and **synthesis**. It is divided into phases: programming, schematic (or concept) development, design development, and contract administration (see Table 1.1).

The Programming Phase

Before designers begin the design process, they make initial contact with the client; this is the stage where designers recognize the problem. They then decide whether or not to commit to and accept the project. After accepted, a contract is prepared and the client pays a retainer to the designer. Now, the programming phase of the design process can begin.

The **programming phase** consists of information gathering. The designer begins by identifying the design problem. The next step is to identify the client's needs and desires. It is important at this stage to collect information regarding various components of the project such as the site and its structural and contextual needs, codes and regulations, socially responsible considerations, human factors, economic needs, diversity, and historic and design precedents. The designer must analyze and organize the gathered facts into the program document, which lists requirements for the design. Programming is all about collecting and analyzing new evidence. Data (i.e., facts and new evidence) are gathered and analyzed in a systematic way to inform the design process. Facts come from existing information or data,

Design Process Phases	Programming		Schematic (Concept) Development	Design Development	Contract Documentation	Contract Administration	
	Initial contact with client	Programming			Implementation Take action		
Scope of services and/or tasks	Recognize problem	Define problem	Continue to analyze facts	Select and refine	Bidding process	Order/ construction	Evaluate
	Commit to project	State the goals and objectives	Generate ideas and brainstorm	Develop drawings, details, specifications	Construction drawings	Ordering process	Create punch list during walkthrough
	Accept the project	Gather information: the facts	Sketching of ideas, plans, details, etc.		Specifications written	Construction	
	Contract written	Interview clients, use surveys, questionnaires, conduct observations, etc.	Develop preliminary plans			Supervision	After approximately three months, conduct POE
	Retainer obtained	Research to develop a strong evidence base					
		Analyze facts					
		Organize the information and develop program requirements					
		Continue to analyze facts					
	Analysis			Synthesis			

Table 1.1

Design Process

whereas evidence is produced from research or a new discovery. The designer will then use data in the decision-making process, which takes place during the programming and schematic design phases. Students learn to conduct research for an actual or hypothetical project (Figure 1.1), whereas interior designers or a design firm may conduct research for interior design projects (Figure 1.2).

The data that designers gather, analyze, and integrate into the process come from existing information, new evidence, or a combination of the two. This book focuses on gathering facts and collecting new evidence in the programming phase of the design process.

Figure 1.1 Students learn to conduct research for actual and/or hypothetical projects.

Figure 1.2 Research may be conducted by an interior designer or a group of interior designers in a firm.

The Schematic (or Concept) Development Phase

After designers have gathered information and completed the program, they begin the **schematic (or concept) development phase**. In this phase, designers continue to analyze the facts by generating ideas, brainstorming possibilities, and developing alternative solutions to the design problem. To analyze adjacencies, for example, designers develop matrices. Integrated into this phase is the development of the design concept, which drives the design and establishes the underlying principles that will result in the physical design. In other words, the design concept describes functional and aesthetic ideas that guide designers through subsequent phases and result in a successful solution. What happens now is the creation of schematics drawings, conceptual sketches such as bubble diagrams, plans, and illustrative sketches that are used to analyze the problem. These types of sketches help designers identify spatial and circulation relationships, functional requirements and relationships, and activities that take place in the spaces. This is the time to ideate many possibilities and not limit the possible solutions. These schematics are not drawn to scale because the purpose of ideation sketches is simply to efficiently convey the concepts. With several options at hand, the ones selected are typically those that meet the client's budget, needs, objectives, and desires. Schematics are developed into preliminary drawings by refining the sketches. Details evolve, and vertical spaces are defined through sections and elevations.

The Design Development Phase

Next, in the **design development phase**, designers synthesize the data and refine the best possible solution. From the preliminary drawings, designers develop final design drawings, details, sections, and elevations. Then they create schedules to determine who does what and when. These schedules include the major tasks, activities, people, materials, and time frames involved in the execution of the design.

The Contract Document Phase

In the **contract document phase**, the project is implemented. Here, designers prepare construction drawings (e.g., plans, elevations, and sections) and write specifications. Construction drawings must provide all necessary information to implement the project. This relates to structural, architectural, mechanical, and electrical aspects of the design as well as to finishes and furniture. Specifications are technical documents. They are written instructions to the general contractor and vendors for materials, performance standards, and methods of construction or installation.

The Contract Administration Phase

Finally, during the **contract administration phase**, the project is implemented. This includes the selection of the contractor and subcontractors, the placement of orders, construction and installation, and the supervision of work. Various methods of evaluation take place as the project nears or is at completion. First, a walk-through or site inspection determines if there are any omissions or errors. During this walk-through, notations are made on a form called a **punch list**. Often, the client will withhold final payment until these items are completed.

A short time after the client has moved in, a **post-occupancy evaluation (POE)** should also be completed. Preiser (1995) describes the POE as a diagnostic tool that designers use to identify and evaluate a completed project. A POE helps "to identify problem areas in existing buildings, to test new building prototypes and to develop design guidance and criteria for future facilities" (p. 19). The POE may also examine space utilization, evaluate data-gathering methods, and review conceptual development. The POE is a follow-up evaluation that is important to the client and the designer to improve present and future projects.

Programming

The programming phase is the most important step in the design process. Pena and Parshall (2001) state that programming is problem seeking. To successfully solve a problem, designers must first seek out as many aspects of that problem as possible; interior designers do this by learning about the client, site, type of design, and problems that may occur, and by researching evidence. (How researching evidence differs from finding facts will be discussed later in this chapter.) After designers have gathered facts and evidence, they must apply this knowledge to the design. Programming significantly improves the design outcome.

A methodology in which designers establish a plan of action to systematically collect data, programming begins as designers establish the basic goals and objectives for the project. Criteria to assist in determining goals and objectives include client and user needs as well as their expectations and decisions.

Programming involves the following six steps:

1. Establish goals and objectives—In establishing a goal or goals, the question to ask is: What does the client want to accomplish, and why? In establishing objectives, the question to ask is: How will the goal be achieved, and to what degree? In other words, the goal must be measurable. This is also the time to develop a mission statement and establish and state the purpose of the project. See Box 1.1 for an example of a programming goal and a programming objective.

2. Gather and analyze the facts—Gather information regarding the client and the needs of the client. Then analyze this information to determine its relevance to the project.

3. Specify needs—Determine and specify structural, contextual, and economic needs. Human factors such as anthropometrics, proxemics, and ergonomics are identified relative to psychological, physiological, and sociological needs.

4. Evaluate the collected data—Determine the importance and value of the program. Design theory—such as Gestalt, change, and interior ecosystem, to be discussed among others in Chapter 2—may be used to evaluate the research and program. Using these theories to evaluate data provides feedback regarding design decisions that may affect the project as a whole.

5. Organize and decide—Pull together the parts into a whole meaning (Gestalt); in other words, the designer determines the most relevant data that will ultimately deliver the best possible design solution.

6. Present conclusions—Findings are communicated, and feedback is ascertained to determine if the conclusions address the goals.

Data Collection

Designers collect data during the programming phase through **fact finding,** or **research,** or a combination of both. To help us understand the difference between fact finding and research, Wang (2007) defines fact finding as "dealing with facts that already exist (e.g., the number of chairs at the table), whereas research (e.g., placement of a chair or chairs related to psychological needs) seeks to produce new knowledge in recognizable ways that can usually be applied regardless of locale" (p. 35).

As information is gathered and analyzed, only facts and new evidence relating and pertaining to the project goal should be considered. Examples of data to be collected are listed as follows and in Table 1.2. The following summary will provide ideas for fact finding and collecting new evidence.

1. User needs and characteristics—Information is gathered in several ways, including interviews, user surveys, questionnaires, and observations. Data collection methods such as these and others, all of which will be discussed in Chapter 3, help the designer collect facts and possibly new evidence. As a designer you will examine organizational profiles, communication modes, and information about individual users and their needs. Using these components, your research for new evidence may examine how these will affect the design. You will consider present functional adjacencies and conduct a furniture, fixtures, and equipment (**FF&E**) inventory. It is also important when gathering information to visit the site or a similar site and to view blueprints.

2. Structural and contextual needs—Examine site, structural, and contextual needs and regulations, such as building and fire codes. Research the literature for ways that the site, structure (i.e., its construction materials and methods), and systems (e.g., HVAC and lighting) may affect the design. Is there new evidence regarding how code affects design?

3. Sustainability needs—Examine environmental concerns such as site, orientation, sustainability, and indoor air quality. Research literature for ways that other designers have applied such environmental concerns to the design. Consider and investigate the use of Leadership in Energy and Environmental Design (LEED) certification on the project. Investigate the application of universal design. Research the literature for ways that other designers have created universal design for their interiors. Research the literature for new evidence for ideas or solutions for socially responsible design.

4. Human factors—Examine the physiological, anthropometrics, ergonomics, psychological, and sociological needs. Research the literature for new ideas or solutions related to human factors.

5. Economic needs—Examine economic factors such as the cost to the client. Also examine the budget and life-cycle costing. Research the literature for ways that life-cycle costing can positively affect budget. Additionally, consider the effect of addressing various issues such as productivity in the workplace and its effect on the bottom line, etc. These may be specific to design types.

6. Functional needs—Determine the function of the space and the number of people that will occupy the space, and investigate the space requirements per person. Research the literature for new ways to create a better functioning space.

7. Appropriate FF&E—Determine the use of existing and/or purchasing of new FF&E. Research the literature for ways that other designers have used existing pieces in new and different ways.

8. Research design **typologies**—Review the basic information regarding the design type (e.g., hospitality design). Researching the literature for evidence may improve the design project.

9. Diversity aspects of design—Investigate various diverse design philosophies and their application to the design. For example, investigate how a diverse population can be accommodated within a space by the application of a different philosophy.

10. Historical and design **precedents**—Examine the literature on past projects (i.e., historical and design precedents) related to the type of architecture and design. Research the literature for ways other designers applied architecture and past designs into a project.

11. Develop the program document—Using the data gathered from the client, site, research, etc., develop research summaries and a program document.
    a. New evidence collected from research, observations, etc. is summarized in a narrative and listed in ways that this evidence will be applied to the design.
    b. Program requirements are developed into a program document. Examples of program documents are included in Appendices A: Program Document—Nonresidential and B: Program Document—Residential.

12. Use design theory to analyze and provide feedback—Using design theory such as Gestalt or interior ecosystems theory, the program can be analyzed for its importance and value. This will offer immediate feedback about decisions that may affect the entire project.

Sources for Evidence

According to Pena and Parshall (2001), "programming must be more than fact finding" (p. 71). Along with fact finding, research may be conducted to locate new evidence that may be applied to a design project. Sources that may be used to assist in the research include academic journals, trade publications, post-occupancy evaluations, and online databases as well as manufacturer's literature, product specifications, and past experience.

Academic Journals

Academic journals provide articles on research projects that will turn up new evidence. These types of journals are found in university libraries and online. The *Journal of Interior Design* is specific to interior design, and the *Journal of Facilities Management* is specific to facility management. A few examples of journals with articles relative to interior design include *Journal of Sociology, American Journal of Infection Control, Architecture and Behavior, Children and Schools, Building and Environment, Applied Ergonomics, Design Issues, Environment and Behavior, Occupational Ergonomics,* and *Urban Studies.* Many journals can be found through various search engines such as scholar.google.com and pubmed.gov. Additionally, InformeDesign, which is described later in this chapter, has summarized articles from many of these journals, drawing key points of interest to interior designers and omitting material irrelevant to design and technical jargon.

Trade Publications

Trade publications provide articles about completed projects. Examples of trade publications include *Interior Design, Interiors and Sources, Metropolis, I.D. (International Design),*

Table 1.2

Evidence-Based Design (Research within Programming)

No.	Programming Categories	Fact Finding	Research Literature for Evidence to Inform the Design
1.	User needs and characteristics	Collect organizational profiles, communication modes, and information about individual user and their needs.	How will these affect the design (layout—spatial relationships and organization)? Consider present function adjacencies.
		Conduct an FF&E inventory.	
		Conduct a site visit and view blueprints.	Examine the literature for similar sites and issues or problems.
2.	Structural and contextual needs	Examine site, structural and contextual needs.	Is there new evidence to support new ways the site and structure, and/or systems may affect the design?
		Conduct code search.	Is there new evidence regarding code affecting the design?
3.	Sustainability needs	Examine environmental concerns such as site, orientation, sustainability, and indoor air quality.	Research literature for new evidence for ideas or solutions regarding all aspects of socially responsible design.
			Research literature for ways that other designers have applied such environmental concerns to the design.
			Research studies conducted on indoor air quality
		Consider the use of LEED to the project.	Investigate how the results of other LEED projects affected the overall design.
4.	Human factors	Determine the physiological, anthropometrics, ergonomics, psychological, and sociological needs.	Research literature for new ideas or solutions related to human factors.
		Determine the physiological needs.	Research studies related to health concerns.
		Determine the psychological needs.	Research studies related to satisfaction.
		Determine the ergonomics concerns.	Research a specific client base to ergonomics.
		Determine the sociological needs.	Research socioeconomic group and a specific type of design.
		Apply universal design.	Research literature for ways other designers have created universal design or how it has affected similar designs.

(continued)

No.	Programming Categories	Fact Finding	Research Literature for Evidence to Inform the Design
5.	Economic needs	Budget and estimate costs.	Research a design type related to economic issues other designers have experienced (productivity, safety, etc.).
		Conduct a life-cycle cost analysis.	Research literature for ways that life-cycle costing can positively affect budget.
6.	Functional needs	Determine function(s) of spaces, number of people to occupy spaces, investigate space requirements per person.	Research literature for new ways to create better functioning spaces.
7.	Appropriate FF&E	Use existing and/or purchase new FF&E.	Research literature for ways that other designers have used existing pieces in new and different ways.
8.	Specific design types	Determine areas of concern.	Research literature for findings applicable to the design type.
9.	Diversity aspects of design	Investigate various diverse design philosophies and their application to the design.	Investigate how a diverse population can be accommodated within a space by the application of a different philosophy.
10.	Precedents in historical design	Examine the literature on past projects (historical design) related to the type of architecture and design.	Research literature for ways other designers applied architecture and past designs into a project.
11.	Develop program requirements	Using data gathered from client, site, research, and so on, program requirements are developed into a program document.	
12.	Use of design theory to analyze and provide feedback	Using design theory such as Gestalt, interior ecosystems theory, or others, the program can be analyzed for its importance and value. These will offer immediate feedback about decisions that may affect the entire project.	

Table 1.2 Evidence-Based Design (Research within Programming) *(continued)*

Visual Merchandising + Store Design (VM+SD), Fine Homebuilding, Lighting Dimensions, Walls and Ceilings, Home Furnishings News (HFN), The World of Interiors, InFurniture, Live Design, and *Frame Magazine.* The Web site www.i-d-i.com provides a list and description of these trade publications as well as other design magazines (www.i-d-d.com/interior_design_magazines/interior_designer_trade_magazines.htm). These publications include articles that describe design projects and may discuss ideas used to create their design as well as provide visuals.

Post-Occupancy Evaluations

The post-occupancy evaluation (POE) is a tool that identifies and evaluates completed projects. A POE should be conducted consistently. By doing so, important data may be retrieved regarding positive and/or negative effects of a design. It will also provide new evidence to improve future projects. Unfortunately, many designers find it difficult to return to a completed project to collect evidence on areas for improvement or successes. However, conducting a POE is one of the best ways to provide evidence for future projects and is highly recommended for all projects.

ASID or IIDA Knowledge Centers

The American Society of Interior Designers (ASID) and International Interior Design Association (IIDA) offer "knowledge centers" on their Web sites.

ASID (2005) (www.asid.org) provides a "gateway to professional interior design news, research and information on the Internet" through its Design Knowledge center. Within this Web site, resource sections include sustainable design, aging and accessibility, business and technology, industry and products news, publications, research, and codes and standards. Data particularly significant to developing new evidence can be found in the research section that includes industry research (e.g., Allsteel, Carpet and Rug Institute, and Greenguard) and academic research (e.g., Carnegie Mellon Green Design Institute and Center for Inclusive Design and Environmental Access).

The IIDA (IIDA, 2007) (http://knowledgecenter.iida.org) Knowledge Center provides new evidence through articles from many sources. Research may be conducted by resource type (e.g., academic journals, books, case studies, conference papers/presentations, exhibits, and industry reports), topic (e.g., accident prevention, acoustics, audiovisual), and client type (e.g., corporate, education, government, healthcare/senior living, and hospitality).

InformeDesign

As previously stated, research published in scholarly journals can provide evidence for designers to better understand today's issues. However, there are several concerns: (1) research findings are published in peer-reviewed academic journals, and are not easily accessed by designers; (2) if located, the keywords used to access this research are geared toward research and academics rather than practice; (3) access to these journals is costly; (4) research findings are seldom developed into design criteria that are understood by designers; (5) research is written from a research viewpoint and designers' education is not research based; and (6) academic journal articles use vocabulary and terms that are not user friendly.

Many designers have limited knowledge of research terminology. Moreover, they find it difficult to access. Nevertheless, designers who use evidence-based design do not necessary return to college and take courses in research methods. Instead, they use a tool created to provide evidence-based design criteria that is easily accessible to designers. This tool, called **InformeDesign** (www.informedesign.umn.edu), was created by Drs. Denise Guerin and Caren Martin from the University of Minnesota.

InformeDesign is ready for designers to use with a searchable database of more than 1,100 research summaries to which summaries are added almost weekly. Its monthly online and downloadable newsletter, *Implications*, focuses on design topics of interest such as design of learning environments for children, daylighting, indoor air quality, and many more. Many other components to this Web site will be discussed throughout this book.

InformeDesign Research Summaries

Within the InformeDesign Web site, **Research Summaries (RS)** are the most important part of how designers use the Web site in search of evidence to inform the design process. An RS is a summary of a refereed journal article. Articles come from more than 170 journals dealing with human behavior and the designed environment. InformeDesign staff members search the journals, read the articles, and write the research summaries. The summaries are more than synopses—the writers have drawn key points of specific interest to interior designers and omitted irrelevant material and research-based technical jargon. Each RS is two- to three-pages long and divided into standardized segments. Here the designer will find a transformation of the researcher's findings into design criteria. Each RS is divided into the following parts.

1. Design Issue
    *   Purpose of the study
    *   Rationale of the study

2. Design Criteria
    *   Criteria determined by author
    *   Criteria transformed by InformeDesign staff

3. Key Concepts
    *   Findings that address foundation issues of the topic or the research project that has been conducted. "For example: if you are looking into something for a design for Alzheimer's patients, the key findings may talk about the four or five stages of Alzheimer's and what the criteria are for each one of those stages. So, it really gives you some excellent background information" (Malkin & Guerin, 2005).

Key concepts may be used in the programming phase of the design process. They can provide user- and facility-based information about the issues and the basis or background. Their information can provide background to assist designers in composing better questions that will enrich discussions with clients/owners, staff, and users of the space as well as among the entire design team. These key concepts can also provide knowledge to aid the designer in speaking the language of the client/owner and other users.

The design criteria are often used in the schematic design and design development of the design process. Evidence-based criteria provide the evidence to inform solutions. Unlike the peer-review journal article, design criteria on InformeDesign allow quick and easy access to information. Thus, design criteria provide access to scientific studies and findings, verify the validity of the typical solution, and influence the status quo approach to design. It will move the design to a higher level of the design process.

A Valuable Tool

Using evidence from research summaries in InformeDesign allows designers to move beyond normative (i.e., typical design solutions) design. It moves designers into that stage in the design process where they question what has been done before and will have answers for potential new solutions that designers will propose. Using InformeDesign research summaries, designers examine the research evidence as well as consider their experience in conjunction with the new knowledge being acquired. The designer will analyze and synthesize the information in a new and different way. The results are that the designs become evidence-based with superior design solutions. This adds value to design solutions and to the design practice. By having this evidence available for your client, particularly for those clients who deal with evidence in their daily decision making, they will understand the validity of your solutions.

Martin and Guerin (2005) state the importance of this tool in developing successful, grounded, research-based design solutions:

> Designers can now be aware of design and human behavior research that has been conducted, the findings of that research, and how to use them to improve their practice through research-based solutions. Evidence-based design practice will improve the quality of life for all people and continue to allow designers to protect the public's health, safety, and welfare. (p. 179)

InformeDesign is a highly effective tool for designers and is changing the way design is being practiced. For this reason, it will be included as an integral part of this book not only as a resource, but also with suggested uses in various situations.

Research-Related Terminology

Knowledge of basic principles and terminology related to research is helpful in understanding research articles in various journals as well as the RS in InformeDesign. The following describes the various research methods used.

Researchers as well as designers use **observation** in a casual or methodical manner. Observations may be accomplished by walking through an existing space, or an instrument (check list, floor plan, map, or another type of instrument) may be used to record movement. Researchers use the **survey** method to examine attitudes, opinions, preferences, and needs. Questionnaires or face-to-face interviews are used in the survey method. **Experiments** are used to test hypotheses. Findings contribute to theory development. A **case study** involves an in-depth investigation into a single site, behavior, or individual (InformeDesign, 2005). **Content analysis** is a research technique used to analyze text (e.g., books, newspaper articles, and speeches) for the presence of a particular word(s); it systematically describes the form and content of written or spoken material (InformeDesign, 2005).

Researchers also use vocabulary that may not be familiar to practitioners. The InformeDesign glossary of terms provides clarification of terms not commonly used in the industry. (In this book, key terms are shown in bold and are listed in the Key Terms section at the end of each chapter.)

Research is a scholarly or scientific investigation or inquiry (Farlex, 2008), and in the development of the research project, the researcher determines goals for scientific discovery that will build **theory** (Farlex, 2008). Two types of research are commonly conducted. **Quantitative** research involves a numerical measurement of observations, whereas **qualitative** research is based on nonnumeric observations, which describe meaning and patterns of relationships (InformeDesign, 2005).

To conduct a research project, a **population**, or group of people, is selected from a **sample** or representative portion of the population. The **sample selection** is either a **randomized selection** (one that is chosen by chance), or a **convenience selection** (one that is easily accessed and available). The sample is then measured in a specific predetermined manner. Each **subject** within the sample is given a number in order to track the information; however, subject information is confidential. The **validity** of the instrument or procedure used to measure as well as the ability to generalize the results to another population are important to the significance of the project. In conducting and analyzing the data collected, **variables** are determined. Variables have different values (e.g., gender: male, female) and can be measured to determine the effect of one variable to another. Two common variables are the independent and dependent variables that are tested in an experiment (Guerin & Martin, 2006). Guerin and Martin (2006) further explain independent and dependent variables:

> The independent variable is a component that is changed by the researchers, such as the noise level in the workplace. The researcher can introduce the noise, increase the noise level, or decrease the noise level to determine its effect on employee performance, which is the dependent variable. (p. 179)

Application of New Evidence into a Project

To collect new evidence that will inform the design solution, the following approach will aid in the development of a research agenda:

1. Convert need(s) for information into answerable questions—example: what is the greatest concern within this type of space?

2. Locate best evidence with which to answer questions—example: what is the evidence regarding this issue(s)?

3. Critically evaluate the evidence—examples: Is it valid? Does it apply to my project? How relevant is the literature to the specific project and design concept?

4. Integrate new evidence with fact-finding data—example: determine how the evidence will be integrated with the facts.

5. Evaluate how effective and efficient the evidence is to the project.

6. Determine ways to improve the design (Malkin, 2008).

Throughout this text, you will find suggestions for research and ideas for gathering new evidence. You may or may not need these suggestions within your project. Thus, it is best to begin by considering the needs for your project and then track down the best evidence to answer your question. With evidence at hand, a decision must then be made regarding its validity and whether or not it applies to your project. To accomplish this, begin by writing a narrative summary of evidence followed by a list of evidence that applies to your project. The new evidence can then be integrated into the fact-finding data for further analysis. Here, evaluation should take place by considering how effective and efficient the evidence is to your project, and in what ways this evidence will improve your design. All facts and evidence can be inserted into a programming document (see Appendices A and B). Your program document will become the program requirements for your project.

Summary

This chapter provides background information on the design process with emphasis on the programming phase of design. This information includes a basic understanding of the design process. The process can be sorted into two categories: analysis and synthesis. Analysis takes place through the programming phase and part of the schematic phase. Synthesis is used to pull information together in the remaining phases. Phases of the process include: the programming phase, the schematic (or concept) development phase, the design development phase, the contract document phase, and the contract administration phase. Designers collect the majority of facts and new evidence during the programming phase; however, research for new evidence may be conducted throughout the design process. Books, periodicals, and online resources are available to collect new evidence. Particularly helpful is InformeDesign—a resource that provides research summaries to assist in understanding problems or issues as well as improve future designs for the built environment.

Key Terms

analysis

case study

concept (or schematic) development phase

content analysis

contract document phase

contract administration phase

convenience selection

design development phase

design process

evidence

evidence-based design (EBD)

experiment

fact finding

FF&E

InformeDesign

observation

population

post-occupancy evaluation (POE)

precedents

programming

programming phase

punch list

quantitative

qualitative

randomized selection

research

Research Summaries (RS)

sample

sample selection

schematic (or concept) development phase

subject

survey

synthesis

theory

typology (typologies)

validity

variable

Design Theories

OBJECTIVES

After reading this chapter, you should be able to:

Understand and research various design theories

Apply research of design theories into a written format

*Use knowledge gained in research to analyze
and/or apply to a design project*

Design theories are used to analyze the data collected for design projects. This analysis may occur at any stage within the design process; however, designers should put these theories to use during the programming phase. Analysis through a design theory can inform decisions that may affect the entire project.

Many of the numerous theories used by designers were derived from social sciences. These include the theories of Gestalt, functionalism, interior ecosystems, personal environment, social cognition, change, place, third place, Reggio, semiology, phenomenology, and rationalism, as well as normative and positive theories. But these are just to name a few. This chapter includes discussion of a few of the design theories most commonly used by interior designers.

Gestalt Theory

Early in the twentieth century, German and Austrian psychologists developed the **Gestalt theory** (Gestalt Psychology, 2008), which can be summed up with the phrase "the whole is greater than the sum of its parts" (Loustau, 1988, p. 4). These psychologists were studying mental processes and particularly the way people organize and make decisions when presented with visual stimuli (Gestalt Psychology, 2008; Lang, 1987; Kopec, 2006). They also believed that people tend to experience the whole as well as the individual part (Boeree, 2000). Therefore, the analysis of parts of a whole does not provide an understanding of the whole; rather, the meaning is revealed within the whole (Loustau, 1988).

For visual arts, Gestalt theory is especially important because it employs a visual system of organization or a system of putting components together. This theory is an abstract organization and a concept of visual perception that identifies patterns of behavior (Loustau, 1988). The theory's organizing principles are called Gestalt laws, which state that people experience things in an orderly, regular, simple manner. "For example, a set of dots outlining the shape of a star is likely to be perceived as a star, not as a set of dots" (Boeree, 2000, para. 23). Kopek (2006) summarized each Gestalt law as follows:

1. Law of Closure—Our minds fill in the missing areas in an incomplete figure.

2. Law of Similarity—We group similar items together within a large form to create some form of continuity.

3. Law of Proximity—When items are close together, they are seen as belonging together regardless of actual connection.

4. Law of Symmetry—We are compelled to group dissimilar items together so as to create symmetry.

5. Law of Continuation—We see things as a continuation or connection rather than as separate entries.

6. Law of Figure-Ground—We typically perceive only one aspect of an image when the image can be viewed in both positive-negative and foreground-background perspectives (pp. 52–53).

Figures 2.1 through 2.12 demonstrate an abstract organization and a design application for each principle.

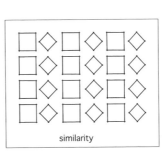 

Figure 2.1 *Left*: Gestalt Law of Closure: A circle is partially concealed in the background, which means it is incomplete. However, because our minds are capable of filling in the missing areas, we can easily identify a circle.

Figure 2.2 *Right*: Although there are missing areas of the sphere-shaped light fixture, our minds make the connections to form the sphere beyond the slatted gate.

Figure 2.3 *Left*: Gestalt Law of Similarity: In the alternating pattern of squares and diamonds, our minds see each type forming a line.

Figure 2.4 *Right*: In this image, similar chairs found on either side of the table form horizontal lines.

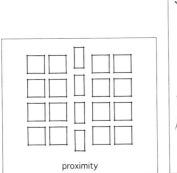 

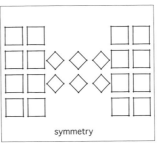 

Figure 2.5 *Left*: Gestalt Law of Proximity: Our minds see items with similar attributes forming a group.

Figure 2.6 *Right*: In this image, people see similar attributes of the picture frames and place these shapes into groups.

Figure 2.7 *Left*: Gestalt Law of Symmetry: When our minds see these objects, we see symmetry.

Figure 2.8 *Right*: When viewing this space, most people will see it as entirely symmetrical; however, the accessories are dissimilar in places, but as a whole the image portrays symmetry.

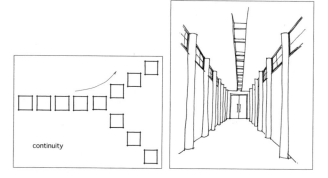

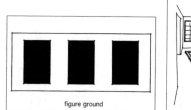

Figure 2.9 *Left*: Gestalt Law of Continuity: Our minds see a "Y," but few people will see two separate lines.
Figure 2.10 *Right*: In this example, most people will see decorative elements in this hallway, but few will see the individual pilasters.

Figure 2.11 *Left*: Gestalt Law of Figure-Ground: The positive image is darker in color. Some may see the rectangles while others may see the negative space that borders the rectangles.
Figure 2.12 *Right*: In this example the positive image is the sink area while the negative space is the open space around this sink area or the entire room.

Using Gestalt theory to analyze a project, the focus may be on the whole or the parts; however, the analysis of parts must reflect the whole design. To use Gestalt theory for analysis, it is recommended that the theory be further researched and then used to analyze and/or apply to a project.

Functionalism

Functionalism is important to the field of architecture and design because it had a great impact on modern architects such as LeCorbusier and Louis Sullivan and was reflected in their work. One of the guiding principles of the theory of functionalism is that "form follows function," a phrase that is usually attributed to Sullivan, the first modern architect of the twentieth century (1856–1924). This phrase is also associated with the Bauhaus school of design (Pile, 2000).

The three key concepts of functionalism are function, fitness, and utility. Beauty is an additional concept that is integrated into all of these concepts. Function relates to the purpose of the structure, space, or object (Bartuska & Young, 1994). Fitness relates to the suitability of the structure, space, or object relative to its purpose. Utility relates to the structure, space, or object's usefulness relative to the satisfaction of the user (Smith, 1911).

In Figure 2.13, the three circles represent the three functionalistic concepts (moving clockwise from the top right circle): function, fitness, and utility. The concept of beauty in functionalism, whether intrinsic or applied as ornamentation, is integrated within these three concepts; therefore, beauty is found at the center of the model where all three circles overlap. Additionally, a relationship exists between each pair of concepts (e.g., function and fitness are related by context; fitness and utility are related by quality; and utility and function are related by intent). The overlapping of circles represents each of these relationships. Each concept in the theory of functionalism has one or more descriptors, as shown in Figure 2.14. The framework helps organize analysis of a design, and the descriptors will be used in an example analysis.

Heuberger and Special's (1997) conceptual framework is based on essential skills within or aspects of interior design. The five categories are (1) space planning; (2) design elements and principles; (3) finish materials, decorative elements, and detailing; (4) lighting; and (5) furniture. Figure 2.13 lists these categories to the right of the functionalistic framework. For the purpose of analysis, these categories may be used in part or the whole along with functionalistic concepts.

In the following example, the conceptual framework is used to analyze the selection of an office chair (see Figure 2.14). Designers consider the following criteria when evaluating the appropriate selection of this chair. Descriptors are italicized in the following descriptions:

1. Function—The *purpose* of the chair is determined. What is the chair's purpose? How will it be *used*? Will it be *used* as a desk chair or as a guest chair? Does the *intended* purpose fulfill program requirements? To examine the relationship between function

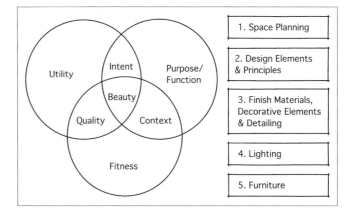

Figure 2.13 Functionalism: The circles show the three key concepts of functionalistic theory, the integration of beauty into all three concepts, and the relationship between pairs of concepts. The functionalism framework may be used for analysis along with Heuberger and Special's conceptual framework. The following are Heuberger and Special's five categories: (1) space planning; (2) design elements and principles; (3) finish materials, decorative elements, and detailing; (4) lighting; and (5) furniture. For analysis purposes, one or more of these categories may be used along with the functionalistic concepts.

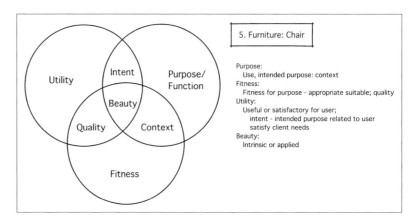

Figure 2.14 Illustration of functionalism using a chair with HS category #5 as the example and listing descriptors for each functionalistic concept. Each concept in functionalistic theory has one or more descriptors as shown in this figure. The descriptors for function are use, intention, and purpose. The descriptors for fitness are fitness for purpose and appropriateness. The descriptors for utility are usefulness and satisfactory for the user.

and the next concept, fitness, consider the issue of context. In what *context* will it be used, and is its *intended* purpose within that *context*? Is the concept reflected in the selection of the chair? What is the overall effect of the design to the *purpose*? Are the elements and principles applied *relative to the context*?

2. Fitness—*Fitness for purpose* is determined. Is the chair *appropriate* for its purpose? Will the chair be *suitable* for the location (executive office or reception area) and for the individual(s)? To examine the relationship between fitness and utility, consider the issue of quality. What is the *quality* of this chair? How is beauty integrated into the concept? Does the *fitness for purpose* meet code requirements?

3. Utility—The *useful* or *satisfactory for the user* nature of the chair is determined. Will the *user* require a sled base or a swivel base? Which is more *useful or satisfactory* in this location or for this individual? To examine the relationship between purpose/function and utility, consider the issue of *intent*. Is the chair useful for its *intended* purpose? Is the concept reflected appropriately through the design and material? Does the *intended purpose* fulfill the program requirements and *satisfy client needs*?

Beauty overlaps all three concepts. Therefore, in the example of a chair, extra chair features, the upholstery finish, and hard surface finish may be selected to add beauty—intrinsic or additional. For intrinsic, the question may be, does the chair function as intended for its purpose and the satisfaction of the user? For applied ornamentation, the question may be, does the application of ornamentation such as extra features, tufting, or trim add beauty to the chair?

The concepts of functionalism can be integrated into Heuberger and Special's framework to examine categories (one or all) and provide greater strength for analysis.

Interior Ecosystem Model

The **interior ecosystem model** is divided into three environments—natural, social or behavioral, and designed or built; all three of these environments are centered on the human organism. The left side of Figure 2.15 illustrates these theoretical concepts. The interior ecosystem model encompasses the relationship of the human to each environment—natural, social, and designed. It shows the human organism connected to and centered within the environmental circles. Environments are also connected and form a triangle. The representation of the human in the center means that humans can affect the environment and/ or each environment can affect the human. Lines between the environments denote an interface between environments and the human.

The interior ecosystem model can relate to macro (i.e., global) or micro (i.e., regional or individual) levels. Natural environments consider the geography or geographical location, climate, and natural resources. Social environments consider the behavior (e.g., activities, norms, values, and codes) and how behavior and culture affect design or how design affects culture. Designed environments consider the building (i.e., exteriors and/or interiors). This

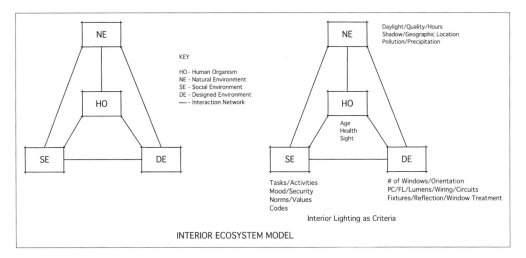

Figure 2.15 *Left*: The interior ecosystem model is divided into three environments—natural, social or behavioral, and designed or built—centered around the human organism. Environments are also connected and form a triangle. The representation of the human in the center means that humans can affect the environment and/or each environment can affect the human. Lines between the environments denote an interface between environments and the human. *Right*: Illustration of interior ecosystem for use in selection of appropriate lighting.

may include anything constructed by humans, including the building itself, clothing, products (e.g., lamps, cars, pens, desks, and chairs) that affect humans. The human organism in the center is affected by all or affects all environments.

The interior ecosystem model is used "to organize, select, or integrate variables (i.e., criteria) that measure a specific construct (i.e., concept or thing) such as interior lighting" (Guerin, 1992, p. 256). The analysis can begin with research questions such as, how will lighting in a space positively impact the human and all environments? The right side of Figure 2.15 illustrates the application of the interior ecosystem model for the selection of lighting into an interior environment.

In analyzing aspects of the design through this query, designers can manipulate or control criteria to improve the design. Guerin (1992) provides an example of the model's use by first identifying components of the model that are most reflective of the research issue:

1. The human organism (HO) must be identified. Is the user of the interior environment a resident of a house, an office employee, or a hospital patient?

2. Is the lighting design in contract or residential environments?

3. The user-based design decisions are made relative to lighting such as age, health, or sight.

4. The user interacts with all three environments: the natural environment (NE), the social environment (SE), and the designed environment (DE). This could be singly or concurrently through the network.

"Because lighting is more reflective of the built environment, interaction may also occur within the environment, between or among variables (criteria). As is true of any system, the interaction of variables may impact other parts of the system" (p. 257).

The interior ecosystem model can examine the whole or parts. However, the important aspect is the effect on the human as well as all environments. This could involve the selection of one or all materials, lighting, color, furniture, or it may relate to sustainability or the age of the occupants.

Person-Environment Theory

The **person-environment theory** connects the individual and his or her environment and person-to-person relationships within the environment (Lang 1987). Particularly important is a person's behavior (positive or negative) that results in the interaction of the individual and the environment (Lewin, 1951). Figure 2.16 illustrates a basic graphical representation of person-environment theory.

The factors include function, competence, and congruence. The individual must be able to function in the environment (Lawton, 1986), to be competent to handle the demands of the environment, and to have congruence (harmonious) environment (Schaie & Willis, 1999). For example, an older adult who has cognitive limitations may seem capable of handling daily activities when they function in a supportive environment with all resources available. In contrast, even the most competent and capable individual may seem incompetent when functioning in an environment that is very demanding with limited resources. "A loss of competence resulting from incongruence (i.e., lacking harmony) between the individual and the environment may reflect decreases in the abilities of the individual, changes in environmental demands or resources, or a combination of these" (Schaie & Willis, 1999, p. 181).

Other factors in person-environment theory that affect a person's competency outcome are emotion and temperament—genetic, biological, and environmental; these can affect **environmental press,** or pressure, either positively or negatively (Lawton, 1998). Figure 2.17 illustrates environmental press theory.

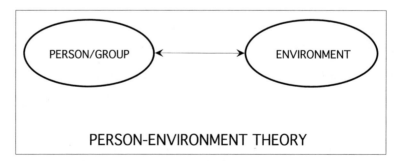

Figure 2.16 The graphical representation of person-environment theory shows that the connection between an environment and a person/group affect each other.

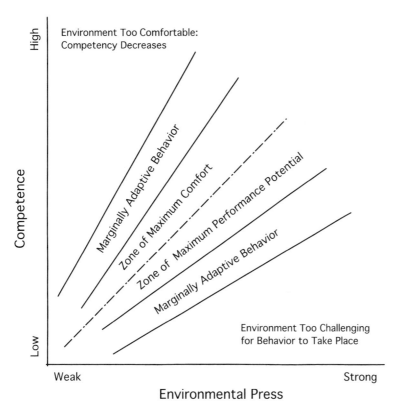

Figure 2.17 The illustration of environmental press relates to the positive and negative pressure that affect the person in the environment. This provides a graphical representation of these pressures.

As people age, they may decide to move to different housing—whether a smaller house, a retirement community, or a nursing home. Because they may have spent most of their lives in one location, moving can be difficult. The pressure of change is difficult (Lawton, 1986). Consequently, many older people change some aspect of their current residence (Golant, 1998). They also may find many other reasons not to move. For example, even though their present location may be difficult, they have adapted and become familiar with the problems and have had practice in coping with them. They have also learned how to live with what they have, and they neither want to part with possessions nor learn new traffic patterns, modes of use, and avoidance patterns in new surroundings (Lawton, 1986). Therefore, Lawton continues, as time draws nearer for the elderly to leave what is familiar, their competence level relative to the move will make a difference in the adaptation level. Golant (1998) states that change in residence can have a negative or positive outcome on the older population. In some cases, there has been a high mortality and morbidity rate, poorer health, great dissatisfaction with housing, and decline in morale. And yet, some older people have benefited from the move because of living in more supportive (i.e., physical, social, and organizational) settings. Moving into a positive living environment will make this move easier.

Howell's (1980) study provides usable information to analyze a design that may become "well rounded." The information gathered helped to determine what were the enablers and barriers in using the environments and to understand the multiple needs of this age group. Howell suggested that older adults be involved in decision making for their environment as follows:

- Be given the opportunity to share their ideas about features within their environment in open discussions.

- Be observed to understand how they use public spaces within their housing environments.

- Have the opportunity to preview and appraise the design in terms of its suitability for meeting current needs of occupants.

This theory is especially useful for analysis in the design of facilities that accommodate similar culture backgrounds or experiences, groups such as people who are mentally challenged, or age groups such as the older adult with physical or mental impairments. It is most useful for analyzing healthcare facilities for all ages but particularly the older adult. Most importantly, using person-environment theory is more than analyzing a space; it is observing the potential occupants and allowing them to appraise the design based on experience. Thus, results from a well-rounded analysis will provide recommendations for a design that will (1) modify or change an environment to accommodate occupants, (2) improve quality of life, (3) allow for autonomy, and (4) lessen injury.

Symbolic Interactionism

Symbolic interactionism relates to symbols—objects or things—that are used for the purpose of communication. Blumer (1986) points out that there are three basic premises:

1. People act toward objects or things based on the meanings for individuals. Objects may be physical (e.g., chairs, art, photographs); social (e.g., roles); and abstract (e.g., concepts, ideas, or values).

2. Meaning of the objects relates to the social interaction with others.

3. Interpretative process is used to deal with objects that individuals encounter.

With step one, the designer may be able to determine during an interview or observation what object or objects are symbolic to the occupant. Step two is symbolic self-completion. At this point, it must be clear that the object is used for impression management and self-definition. Step three is presentation of self. At this point, the object or objects become part of a performance that communicates who we are and what we are about. There is a performer—person with the object—and an audience—the observer (Goffman, 1959).

Figure 2.18 illustrates these three components of symbolic interactionism and their interconnectedness. Clearly, the symbolic interactionism uses a symbol for symbolic self-

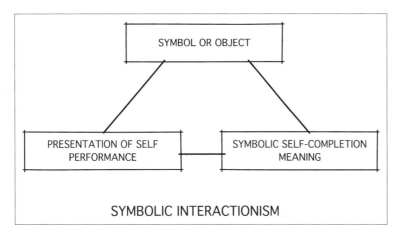

Figure 2.18 People acquire possessions that become important to them. The possession or object becomes a symbol or symbolic of who they are (symbolic self-completion—meaning) and how they want to present themselves to others (presentation of self—performance).

completion and presentation of self. In other words, every individual has objects that are meaningful to him/her. These objects may be located in a home, an office, or a personal space—bedroom or dorm room. These objects are not only important to the individual, but the individual also uses the object as a means to define him- or herself or to impress others. Thus, it communicates to others what is important to the individual, who he/she is, and what he/she is all about.

Most commonly, the home is considered the place that symbolizes the occupants. However, offices or other areas in which one works may include objects that also define the individual. For the designer, it is important to look for clues that identify important objects.

Change Theory

"Change is everywhere" (Holbeche, 2006, p. 3), and change can occur on a continuum both over a long period of time as well as very rapidly. With today's globalization and technological advances, change occurs more rapidly (Holbeche, 2006). Factors affecting change in design are sociology (including globalization), economy, technology, resources, information, consumer preferences, and time. For example, designers may specify a specific product for several years; then, suddenly, new technological advances make previous products obsolete, and a new product might be specified. As the new information is distributed, consumers become aware and may prefer the new product; this may increase sales. If the cost is higher, the economy is affected. The factor that affects all others is time and, particularly, the rate of change over time.

The most effective way to use **change theory** in design is to examine the overall

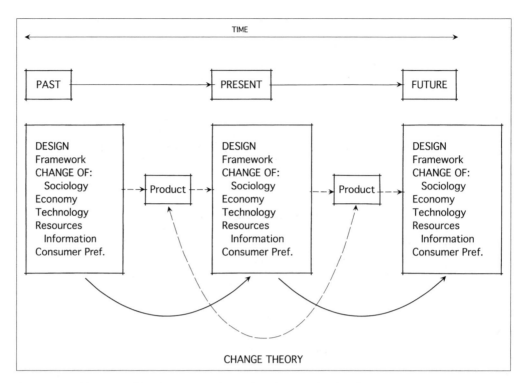

Figure 2.19 Change is affected by various factors (e.g., economy, technology, resources, information, and consumer preferences) and occurs over a period of time or rapidly. Changes that have or may occur to products can be examined using factors from change theory.

design program and consider which aspects of the design may be affected most rapidly by change and the way it will affect design decisions. For example, take designers' concern for the environment and their determination to create sustainable designs. The designer might choose to investigate the sustainable aspect of products that have been specified in the past by asking the following questions: Have changes been made to a product or group of products that will improve indoor air quality (IAQ)? If there are issues that affect IAQ, will changes be made to this product(s) in the near future? If so, they may conduct a follow-up investigation in a specific period of time; if not, they remove it from their product list and resource room. Using change theory, products can be examined relative to change in various factors listed previously and in Figure 2.19.

Meaning of Place

Every individual has a different concept of place. **Meaning of place** is often associated with the terms place identity, sense of place, and place attachment. Each is filled with a variety of emotions related to meaning of place. However, with the increase in globalization and use of technology, the various associations with place have become blurred or more difficult to identify (Kopec, 2006).

Place Identity

"**Place identity** refers to how people incorporate a place into the larger concept of their own identities or sense of self" (Kopec, 2006, p. 62). Often people identify themselves with a larger type of identification. In other words, their identification may be related to either who they are or who they want to be. For example, a Texan often incorporates his or her state's identity as one's own; this may also include a display of the state symbol, the Lone Star; similarly, people often identify themselves with their workplace environment (Kopec, 2006).

Sense of Place

A **sense of place** occurs for a person "when a level of comfort and feelings of safety associated with a place . . . translates to a sense of belonging" (Kopec, 2006, p. 62). This sense of place may be on a cultural or personal level. For example, cultural identification for a Muslim is the city of Mecca (Kopec, 2006) and for a Roman Catholic is the Vatican in Rome. Personal identification may be an individual's home or a favorite location—a store, school, or coffee shop, for example. Some have a sense of place through their cultural identity. In Donald Worster's (1982) book, *Dust Bowl: The Southern Plains in the 1930s,* Worster recalls memories of his childhood during the dust bowl era. These memories and personal history include features of a place and illustrates the author's sense of place.

Place Attachment

When individuals form an emotional bond with their immediate social and physical environment, it is called **place attachment**. People become attached to place because these (1) settings have deep meaning, (2) settings and identities are interlaced, and/or (3) settings provide a restorative environment. According to Kopec (2006), there are three elements that can connect people to a setting and influence their physical and emotional well-being: (1) "their personal characteristics and behaviors; (2) the availability of facilities, opportunities, and resources; and (3) a sense of belonging" (p. 62). Most often, people become attached to places that match who they are and provide emotional security—a sense of belonging and/or freedom. Additionally, attachment to a specific place can change through time and life.

An InformeDesign RS, "Place Attachment of Residents of All-Black Towns" (2003, November 1), examined a study about feelings of place attachment of older residents in 12 Oklahoma towns. A criterion suggests that awareness of social-historical factors, race, personal history, and position in the community were influential in place attachment among elderly individuals in the community. This study suggests that place attachment was affected by various factors that included history, social integration, racial issues, and personal histories. Thus, the setting had deep meaning, the setting and their identities were woven together, and most likely, the setting was a restorative environment because of their attachment.

Third Place Theory

As a general rule, people's first attachment is their home, second is their workplace, and third is a place within the community. **Third place theory** is place attachment that considers the concept of community building such as a social place, meeting place, or public space. Third place locations may also include a store, library, restaurant, bar, mall, sacred space, or even a street corner. Coffee shops have been and are still important third places for many people.

An InformeDesign RS, "Religious Symbolism and Place Attachment" (2005, December 14), examined a discussion of the role of religion in place attachment and used examples from various religious traditions. The position paper suggests that individuals may develop place attachment through an actual setting or emotional interaction with a space deemed sacred. This study supports the role of religion in place attachment either real or emotional. It also may be considered third place theory.

An InformeDesign RS, "Physical and Social Aspects of Coffee Shops" (2007, March 14), summarized a study that described the coffee shops' physical and social qualities that influence gathering and place attachment. Because the number of coffee shops have greatly increased, they have become places to gather and for community activities. Be aware that these spaces are important third place spaces, and designs must provide comfortable gathering spaces.

Meaning of place—place identity, sense of place, place attachment or third place theory—must be considered in any design type. Individuals become identified with and attached to places that are important to them.

Application

Selecting the appropriate design theory for application to a design project will depend on various factors. For example, client needs that relate to self-image may suggest social cognition theory. Client needs that relate to attachment may suggest a meaning of place theory. Specific issues such as sustainability or function may suggest interior ecosystems theory or functionalism. Design type such as long-term healthcare might suggest person-environment theory. To aid the selection, Table 2.1 provides application suggestion. One or more theories may be used for analysis.

With one or two theories selected for the purpose of analysis, further investigation of the theory should be conducted. This will provide greater background prior to its use. This information should be written in narrative with bulleted points that may be used for analysis. Then these points may be used to analyze a design project or determine how this information will be applied to the design. This also may be presented in a combination of narrative and bulleted points.

Summary

The use of theory to analyze design projects improves and strengthens design solutions. The theory chosen may depend upon the type of design project. For example, Gestalt theory can be applied to all projects, and particularly relates to elements and principles of design. Functionalism is most useful to examine basic function relative to its fit in the environment and to satisfy users' needs. Interior ecosystem theory has many applications,

Table 2.1

Design Theory: Application for Client Needs, Specific Issues, Design Types, or Other Individual Purposes

Design Theory	Application Suggestions
Gestalt	Examine parts to whole with focus on aesthetic concepts: • Space planning • Design elements and principles • Finish materials, decorative elements, and details • Lighting • Furniture
Functionalism	Examine the following areas relative to functional concerns: purpose, fitness for purpose, useful and satisfactory for user: • Space planning • Design elements and principles • Finish materials, decorative elements, and details • Lighting • FF&E
Interior Ecosystems Model	Consideration for all environments to human: • Sustainability • Site • Structure materials and systems • Contextual, i.e., HVAC, plumbing, lighting • Interior materials to all environments and human

Person-Environment and Environmental Press	Application for the following design types:
	• Environments for older adults:
	  ◦ Long-term care, assisted living, congregate living, aging-in-place
	• Environment for groups with similar needs, abilities, experiences:
	  ◦ Detention centers, prisons, physical or mental challenges, group homes

Symbolic Interaction	Application for individuals, families, organizations with a need to communicate an image and who they are
Change Theory	Examination of change over time: past, present, future: • Sociology: globalization, socioeconomics status • Economy • Technology • Resources • Information • Consumer preferences
Meaning of Place	Concept of place is individual: • Meaning may be filled with emotions • Decreasing with increase in globalization and use of technology • Research and application must be one or more of the following: place identity, sense of place, place attachment, and third place theory
Place Identity	Connection between individual and larger type of identification: • State • Town • Workplace • Sacred place • Other larger types of identification

(continued)

	Table 2.1	
	Design Theory: Application for Client Needs, Specific Issues, Design Types, or Other Individual Purposes (*continued*)	
Design Theory	**Application Suggestions**	
Sense of Place	Application relates to a person's level of comfort and sense of safety: • Cultural identification • Religious identification • Personal identification: home, childhood memories, etc. • Favorite location: store, school, coffee shop	
Place Attachment	Application is individual: • Home • Gathering spaces such as in third place theory	
Third Place Theory	Application appropriate for gathering spaces: • Sacred spaces • Malls • Stores • Coffee shops • Restaurants • Bars • Other public spaces	
Other Possible Theories to Research	Educational design: • Reggio theory • Kolb's learning style theory • Gardner's multi-intelligence theory • Various design types • Cognitive wayfinding theory • Semiology (study of signs and signs related to behavior)	

particularly in consideration of sustainability with all environments. Person-environment theory is useful in designs for space for groups of people who are similar—elderly, mentally challenged, prison inmates, and detention center residents. Symbolic interactionism will help the designer consider what is important to individuals within their personal spaces and what is needed to communicate who they are. It is also important for organizations to communicate their image and who they are to clients, customers, and public. Change theory is particularly important in the workplace with constant changes to organizational structures as well as globalization and technology. Meaning of place may also become personal to individuals, but when designing spaces that are "third place," these spaces must be inviting and comfortable to become an important third place.

Though various theories and applications were presented, the list of theories is too lengthy for this chapter. To name only a few, there are many learning theories that may be investigated and can affect educational design: Kolb's learning style theory, Gardner's multi-intelligence theory, and Reggio theory. Others may be applicable to various design types: cognitive wayfinding theory and semiology. Investigation of other theories through suggested sources may provide basis for analysis.

Key Terms

change theory

Gestalt theory

environmental press

functionalism

interior ecosystem model

meaning of place

person-environment theory

place attachment

place identity

sense of place

symbolic interactionism

third place theory

Data Collection

PART
TWO

Methods of Data Collection

OBJECTIVES

After reading this chapter, you should be able to:

Describe the different methods of data collection

Understand how data collection is applied to a project

Utilize resources such as IIDA Knowledge Center and InformeDesign that lead to and/or provide evidence to inform and improve the design

Collect data using various methods of data collection

Develop documents that summarize new evidence collected

Develop a program document that will incorporate all collected data—both facts and evidence

DRED COURT

Designers use various methods of data collection to learn about their clients and their client's needs. These methods fall into two categories: quantitative and qualitative. A quantitative method, for example, may identify the number of people who use a particular space, whereas a qualitative method may define the type of activities that the people who use that space would perform there. This chapter examines the various methods of data collection that can be found in both categories. It also provides sample questionnaires for you to modify to suit various types of design situations.

Program Development

Designers begin a design project by collecting facts and researching for new evidence. After they collect the data, they organize the information into a program document. A **program document** is the tool that designers use to guide them in solving their design problems. The program document begins with a problem statement, which is then followed by an identification of goals and objectives. Even with a small project, such as a living room, kitchen, office, or bathroom, program documents must be developed to meet all requirements. Thus, whether the project is large or small, the development of its program document ensures that the client and designer share the same goals and objectives for the project (Pile, 2003).

According to Pile (2003), when the design problem is clearly stated, the solution may become self-evident. Objectives and requirements that are unclear typically cause confusion, and even delays that can lead to disappointing and unsatisfactory results. Thus, as designers gather data—both facts and evidence—they clarify, step by step, each project's problem statement, goals, and objectives.

Designer as Researcher

As data are collected, designers become researchers. Even when designers use research data from various sources that may seem like simple fact gathering (e.g., InformeDesign RS), they are researching information to apply to their project and, thus, have taken on the role of a researcher.

Data Collection Methods

To learn about client needs and requirements, designers collect data using a variety of methods. More than one method may be used for a project, and the method chosen will depend on the type of project. For example, when working on a residential project, a designer may ask questions of the client using a questionnaire, take the physical measurement of space and existing furnishings, and interview each family member. With a nonresidential project such as healthcare design, designers collect data through many different methods such as written questionnaires, physical measurements of space and existing furnishings, interviews with those who use the space, focus groups in the community, and observations of people using the space.

Methods of data collection for fact finding and researching evidence include:

- **User surveys**, or (written) **questionnaires** with pre-designed questions

- **Interviews** with open-ended questions for one-on-one interviews or focus groups

- Surveys conducted by taking physical measurements of all objects in the space, including existing conditions and furniture, fixtures, and equipment (FF&E)

- Observation of behavior, both structured (i.e., recording only what the researcher has planned to observe) and unstructured (i.e., recording whatever the researcher happens to see while making his or her observations) (Sommer & Sommer, 2001; Scott-Webber, 1998)
  - Casual Observation
  - Participant Observation
  - Trace Observation
  - Systematic Observation
  - Behavior Mapping (Guerin & Dohr, 2005)

- Visual and Content Analysis
  - Recording through use of photography or a video camera (Pile, 2003; Scott-Webber, 1998; Slotkis, 2006)
  - Examine written or visual documents for content analysis (Guerin & Dohr, 2005)

- Case Studies
  - Examining results of past projects through post-occupancy evaluations (POEs)

- Experimentation
  - **Pre-test/treatment/post-test** (Guerin & Dohr, 2005)
  - **Mock-ups** or models (Scott-Webber, 1998)

There are specialized and pre-designed forms that may be used as guides to aid in the development of an assessment tool specific for a project (Piotrowski, 2002). Appendices C–L and N–U in this book provide examples of these forms for data collection.

Surveys and Interviews

Designers conduct surveys and interviews in order to clarify clients' goals and objectives (Pile, 2003).

Participants in Surveys and Interviews

Design projects typically fall into two categories: residential and commercial, both of which will be discussed in detail in Chapters 11 through 18. Generally, when designers conduct interviews for residential spaces, they interview the occupants and owner of the space. For commercial spaces, designers collect data from individuals from the following groups:

- Management—executives, managers, department heads, and others in managerial position (Pile, 2003; Rayfield, 1994)

- Other personnel—workers: staff, laborers, and those in supportive positions, e.g., clerical workers and administrative assistants

- Typical users—patients, hotel guests, customers, and other users (Pile, 2003)

Conducting Surveys—Written Questionnaires

A written questionnaire (e.g., paper or electronic survey) is frequently used to collect data. Questionnaires are filled out by users of the space and are useful tools to gather information because they provide information for individual users needs. For large commercial projects, having employees complete written questionnaires is efficient because it saves time (Piotrowski, 2002; Rayfield, 1994). When conducting large projects, designers administer written questionnaires to a cross section of the organization. For example, with an organization with more than 10,000 square feet of building space, the designers might give written questionnaires to 10 percent of its employees. In doing so, it is important that they accurately select a representative from each department within the organization (Rayfield, 1994).

Survey questions typically include information about the following:

1. Client's goals and objectives for the project

2. Organization's past, present, and future directions
    a. Organization's mission statement and strategic plan (Cama, 1997)
    b. Organization's history, structure, and culture

3. Existing conditions

4. User's needs, wants, desires, values, and issues

5. Functional and operational issues (Scott-Webber, 1998)

6. Current and future plans—growth projections (Rayfield, 1994; Scott-Webber, 1998)

7. Spatial requirements
    a. Kinds and number of spaces
    b. Relationship between spaces (Pile, 2003)
    c. Staff numbers and positions
    d. Support space requirements
    e. Adjacency requirements
    f. FF&E needs (Rayfield, 1994)

Some survey questions are more appropriate for management; these may include questions about a company's goals and objectives (See Appendix C). Others may be more appropriate for other personnel. Surveys for workers, for example, may include questions about their positions, the manner in which the firm works, physical conditions of the space, or function of the space. Written questionnaires are more formal and may include multiple-choice questionnaires with rank-order questions and/or fill-in-the-blank questions. Some surveys may have only one type of question or all three types. Sample multiple-choices and rank-order questions with a few spaces to fill in the blank are found in Appendix D. Appendix E is an example of a written questionnaire that is a fill-in-the-blank type of survey. Each design firm may have its own method that has been used and tested.

Designers also include FF&E inventories in their surveys. FF&E inventories will be discussed further in Chapter 11.

Conducting Surveys of Existing Conditions and FF&E

The survey of **existing conditions** begins by reviewing existing plans (if available) and then touring the existing facility. During the tour, physical measurements of the space and all objects in the space must be taken (Piotrowski, 2002). The tour will further define existing conditions, identify operating procedures, locate support requirements, and determine deficiencies as well as identify effectiveness of the present space. Additionally, this information will identify discrepancies in information from questionnaires and interviews (Rayfield, 1994). Discrepancies between original plans and actual space are frequently due to construction that has taken place since original plans were drawn (see Appendix F). Thus, a tour and physical measurements are essential (Pile, 2003). As site surveys are conducted, designers:

1. Determine the orientation of windows relative to natural light. How will the orientation change during various times of day and seasons of the year? Do nearby buildings or the potential for future buildings obstruct natural light?

2. Locate views or obstructions from windows. Are the present views good, or are improvements needed? Are there obstructions to the view? What are obstructions that may occur in the future?

3. Examine the quality of the present layout. What are the present shapes of spaces, and where are they located? Are the adjacencies organized appropriately, or is change needed? Are the storage areas and/or closets adequate, or is more space needed? Are the bathrooms and kitchen adequate? Are the elevators and stairs adequate in the building (commercial and/or apartment)?

4. Note any problems (exterior and interior) related to noise. Are there noise issues from outside the building, the elevator, staircase, and/or adjacent spaces? Within the spaces, are there noise and/or privacy issues for the users?

5. Examine elements that should be changed. This could include the possibility of changing the location of walls, windows, doors; the adequacy of storage and/or closets; and improvements needed for bathrooms and kitchens (Pile, 2003).

A great deal of care should be taken while surveying a space. Any problems or discrepancies found during the site survey must be noted in detail. These notes will aid in solving the issues. Though a time-consuming process, this is crucial to design and to prepare documentation for completing the project (Piotrowski, 2002).

Another aspect of a site survey deals with FF&E. Frequently, clients prefer to reuse existing FF&E (Piotrowski, 2002). Therefore, an inventory and analysis of existing FF&E is conducted. More information about the inventory of FF&E is discussed in Chapter 6.

Conducting Interviews

The disadvantage of survey questionnaires is that they are entirely written, allowing no verbal input. Therefore, live interviews are also conducted. Particularly, live interviews are conducted with management in order to learn more about the organization's structure and culture as well as the goals and objectives for the new facility to be designed.

Interviews are similar to conversations or discussions based on questions. The purpose of these questions is to assess individuals' emotions, attitudes, beliefs, and opinions about the space. Responses to direct questions are called **direct data**. Responses that are less obvious, such as body language, gestures, and eye contact, are called **indirect data** (Guerin & Dohr, 2005).

Structured or **focused interviews** use questions that are pre-designed; these are called **interviewer-administered** interviews. Unstructured interviews allow for unplanned questions. Here, the researcher expects alternative opinions, attitudes, or beliefs. Unstructured interviews allow the subject to contribute more and may bring out information that had not been considered (Guerin & Dohr, 2005).

Open-ended questions are written or verbal responses that encourage broader responses. Such questions are used when the researcher cannot anticipate all the possible answers. Basically, the range of possible answers would be too large for a multiple-choice question. Additionally, the researcher does not want to suggest answers and prefers the answer be in the subject's own words (Sommer & Sommer, 2001).

Closed-ended questions are frequently multiple-choice questions and most frequently used in paper surveys. Such questions are used when more specific answers are expected, the number of subjects is large, answers can easily be computer scored, and group responses may be compared (Sommer & Sommer, 2001).

Interviewing users of the space is an extremely useful tool to gather information about individual and group requirements. For small projects, all users may be interviewed. However, in larger firms, interviews are conducted among key personnel (Pile, 2003). Management can provide answers to questions similar to those found in surveys, or written questionnaires. However, interview questions must be open ended to provide greater insight (see Appendix E).

Personnel, or workers, should be asked questions related to their spatial requirements, including spatial, adjacency, and FF&E needs. This group will also provide information on employee attitudes that may not be apparent to management (Pile, 2003; Rayfield, 1994).

Interviews should include not only management and other personnel, but also typical users; customers, patients, guests, and so on should also be interviewed to evaluate their needs. These users' involvement will provide data that goes beyond what managers and personnel can provide or may have even forgotten (Pile, 2003). Typical users may be chosen at random at various intervals during a day, week, or month. However, the interview process should be conducted in a short timeline, if possible.

To accurately obtain data from interviews, two types of training sessions should be conducted for interviewers and interviewees. For the interviewers, training sessions will clarify survey objectives and questions to be asked, and for the interviewees, training sessions will prepare them to accurately respond to questions. These sessions will not only ensure accurate responses but also accelerate the interview process and are particularly important for interviews within large firms (Rayfield, 1994).

The advantage of interviews is the opportunity for users to provide a verbal response. The disadvantages are that interviews take time, and responses may lack full disclosure or

Figure 3.1 A researcher takes notes as she observes the behavior of students to determine circulation patterns.

Figure 3.2 A researcher's observation notes.

may even be embellished. Therefore, proper training and preparation for interviews may eliminate such response issues.

Observation of Behavior

In the method of data collection known as observation of behaviors, the researcher views behaviors of users. This method is advantageous in providing useful information about the routine, circulation, interactions, and much more (see Figure 3.1). It also provides valuable evidence about the users as they go through their daily routine. Analysis of data includes looking for patterns of behavior during observation (see Figure 3.2).

There are also disadvantages. Observations are time consuming, day-to-day routines may change, and users are typically aware that they are being observed and may behave differently. Clearly, more than one day of observation is recommended.

Observations may be unstructured or structured. The **unstructured observation** identifies tangible evidence that links interaction between people and their environment. This observation of evidence supplies additional data beyond surveys and interviews. Observations may occur in an existing or a similar site. For example, if an interior designer is involved in designing a new nursing home, observations could be made in an existing facility. The unstructured observation will identify general characteristics, problem areas, and unusual conditions in the space (Scott-Webber, 1998).

Unstructured Observations

Unstructured observations may be **casual observations, participant observations,** or **trace observations** (Sommer & Sommer, 2001).

Casual Observations Casual observations are visual inspections that are quick with no predetermined categories. For example, the researcher may be shopping to locate a specific item, and in that process finds it difficult to locate the area where the product is displayed (Guerin & Dohr, 2005). This information may be used later to develop a structured observation to design another retail space. In other words, life experiences can also play a part in collecting evidence for future projects.

Participant Observations In participant observations, the observer role-plays or becomes a user and part of the environment being observed. This type of observation helps the designer to understand other viewpoints (learn from another's perspective). However, according to Guerin and Dohr (2005), there are risks associated with "this type of observation . . . as the observer can become biased by accidental involvement in people's activities" (p. 4). For this reason, this method is less frequently used.

Trace Observations Trace observations involve observing or looking for physical traces of evidence. With this type of observation, the researcher looks for evidence of earlier activity or indications of how people use the space. A comparison would be the collection of trace in a crime investigation, which can be described as *leaving a trail* of evidence (Sommer & Sommer, 2001, pg 75). Within design, there are two types of trace observations: **erosion trace** (wearing down or away) and **accretion trace** (indicating an accumulation or buildup) (Berg, 1989; Guerin & Dohr, 2005; Sommer & Sommer, 2001).

Erosion trace observations indicate patterns of usages in which wear indicates how the space or an object is used (Guerin & Dohr, 2005). For example, during an observation, the designer may notice that the carpet is worn in a different area along a pathway from one space to another. This may indicate an obstruction or that a redesign of the pathway is necessary.

Designers use accretion trace observations to look for buildups of residue or interactions. This type of trace shows the way users have changed their environment. Examples of accretion trace observations are papers stacked may indicate an inadequate filing system, "people may move chairs closer together in a study area so they can interact as a group, or may leave trash on the floor if there are no waste cans" (Guerin & Dohr, 2005, p. 5).

Trace observations have several advantages:

- Observations do not take place while people are using the space and there is no obtrusion.

- The space can be observed at any time and over several days.

- Observers can return to the space several times and bring others to also observe the space.

- Photographs or videos can document the trace observation.

- Trace observations are inexpensive and can provide interesting evidence.

- It is an excellent method to examine a research problem (Guerin & Dohr, 2005; Sommer & Sommer, 2001).

There are also disadvantages to trace observations. Too much can be read into the trace observation. For example, a one-time-only occurrence may happen during a visit;

therefore, repeat visits may confirm or negate the trace (Guerin & Dohr, 2005). Another disadvantage is that an enormous quantity of evidence can be collected; this can slow the process of solving the design problem.

Trace observations are frequently used to work through various problems related to behavioral patterns. Particularly, contradictions may surface between trace observations and surveys and/or interviews. The following are examples of such contradictions:

- Wayfinding issues were not indicated in surveys or interviews. Trace observation indicates that signage is not permanent (handwritten).

- Organizational structure does not fit management's description of its structure. Survey provides a description of a flat or level organization, whereas trace observations indicate a hierarchical organization (Guerin & Dohr, 2005).

In the structured observation, behaviors are mapped within a specific setting during a specified period of time. Through structured observations of the individuals who use the space, designers learn what users actually do rather than assuming what they do in their spaces. Thus, behavioral mapping is observing the users within their environment. The following are a few basic questions to be considered during behavioral mapping:

- What is important to learn about the users of the space?

- Is the behavior active or passive?

- What are indicators of interaction between the user and the environment?

- What is important to know about the environment?

- What procedure should be taken to observe (Scott-Webber, 1998)?

Structured Observations
Structured observations are either **systematic observations** or **behavioral mapping**.

Systematic Observations Systematic observations are designed with specific research questions to be answered. The observation is carefully planned, and a predesigned score sheet is developed to record the data. With such observations, another researcher can easily repeat the process within the same or another environment; this allows several researchers to collect data for the same project. However, training is crucial so that all observers understand and record the behaviors in the same way. This increases the reliability of the data collected by all observers (Guerin & Dohr, 2005; Sommer & Sommer, 2001).

Behavioral Mapping Behavioral mapping is the creation of a map or drawing—similar to a floor plan (Berg, 1989; Guerin & Dohr, 2005). As with a floor plan, the behavioral map should include all structure elements—outside and inside—such as access ways, streetlights, trees and shrubbery, the building, walls, doors, windows, and permanent fixtures and equipment. The map must be duplicated so that each time an observation is conducted, a fresh map can be used (Berg, 1989). During the observations, the maps are used to indicate the people who use the space, their activities, and the location of those activities. During the observations, notations are made on the map to indicate locations of the people and the activities in which they are engaged. Frequently, observations may show spaces are actually used in a different manner than their intent. This is best observed over several days and at various times of the day to obtain accurate data (Guerin & Dohr, 2005).

There are two types of behavioral maps: **place centered** or **person centered**. Place-centered maps focus on how people use the space. This type of data collection method is less obtrusive and is particularly good for public spaces. An observer watches the actions in a particular space or setting such as a hotel, nursing home, or school, and the diagram or plan is used to record actions (Guerin & Dohr, 1989, p. 4). Person-centered maps study people's tasks, activities, and how they move through the space. Charting a group's activities throughout the day helps a researcher learn about a particular group. This type of observation is conducted on only a few individuals at a time and can be obtrusive (Guerin & Dohr, 2005; Sommer & Sommer, 2001).

Visual and Content Analysis

Visual and content analysis consists of visual and/or written material as well as the spoken word (Sommer & Sommer, 2001). Visual material is the recording of existing spaces through use of photography or a video camera (Scott-Webber, 1998). It also provides visual documentation of the interior as well as the small details that are used for analysis. Visual materials may be photographs that already exist and/or those that are taken by the researcher. Existing photographs provide historical data about what existed in the past. Photographs can also assist in the interview process with interviewees describing changes and needs for the future (Berg, 1989). Researchers may also take photographs or videos. This provides documentation, which presently exists. It will eliminate the need to revisit the project site (Pile, 2003) and is also unobtrusive (Berg, 1989).

Written materials such as a mission statement, a strategic plan, and lists of policies and procedures should also be analyzed. This type of data provides insight into the direction the firm would like to head as well as how they operate (Cama, 1997). Additionally, existing tapes or videos as well as recordings of the spoken word provide connections to the visual and written material.

Case Studies

The **case study** method is used to systematically solve a problem and is an in-depth investigation of a single occurrence involving an individual, a group, or an entire community. It can involve a variety of data collection methods such as various types of observations, and visual and written analysis. In design as in other disciplines, the case study method is unique to a particular situation and setting. Case studies may also be comparative; in this case, the researcher looks for variables or characteristics that are common to both occurrences rather those that are different (Guerin & Dohr, 2005; Sommer & Sommer, 2001). At times, designers develop and publish case studies of their projects so that others may learn from their experience. Case studies from which readers may learn are included in this textbook.

There are also other case study methods. A post-occupancy evaluation (POE) will help to fine-tune a completed project, test how well the program was met, and evaluate the project as a model for future projects. For example, after conducting a POE, the evaluation will assess how well the space performs for the occupants relative to various predetermined criteria such as functions and circulation. This method can help identify good and poor performance of the building or space. Feedback can be utilized and improve future projects of a similar size and type (Piotrowski, 2002). A POE will also provide new evidence for future projects. (For an example of a POE, see Appendix M.)

Durek (1993) states that the most frequent POE topics are one or more of the following: (1) users' perceptions of satisfaction; (2) users' behavior in specific building conditions; (3) building support for activities; (4) safety requirements; (5) life-cycle costs; (6) comfort levels related to mechanical systems; and (7) design issues related to privacy, security, and circulation. To conduct a successful POE, Durek (1993) suggests the following steps:

1. Brief the current building managers about the purpose and the content of the evaluation.

2. Conduct a tour to orient the research team members and to introduce the participants.

3. Conduct specific research studies from interviews and surveys to observation studies and photo documentation.

4. Analyze the data.

5. Debrief the research team.

6. Debrief the client participants.

7. Document and present the results of the process (pp. 215–216).

A POE is an excellent research study from which designers can learn what was successful and what needs to improve. Though many are not published, it would be advantageous to all designers to publish these evaluations.

Experimentation

Experimentation is systematically testing ideas (or hypotheses). In others words, the researcher is trying to discover "what causes what" (Sommer & Sommer, 2001, p. 83). In an experiment, variables are elements that are manipulated and compared. One of the most common methods of experimentation includes a pre-test, treatment, and post-test. With this type of experiment, the subject is given a pre-test followed by the treatment; then a post-test is administered (Guerin & Dohr, 2005; Martin & Guerin, 2006).

The treatment may be an activity, a learning situation, a condition, or an event. Groups may also be compared. In this case, one group is the experimental group and the other is the control group. The difference is that the control group does not receive the treatment. The test will determine if the treatment had an effect on the experimental group (Vockell & Asher, 1995).

This type of study is often conducted in higher education (Guerin & Dohr, 2005). For example, a pre-test may be taken on the first day of class. Then a new instruction method is used to teach students. After the instruction is completed, a post-test is given to students. This experiment allows the teacher to determine the amount of learning that has

Figure 3.3 Students are able to see possibilities by exploring three-dimensional process models, such as this interior design graduate student's "rip-n-tear model" for a Native American Cultural Center.

taken place. If the instruction method is new, one section may be taught by the old method while another section is taught using the new method. The post-test will help the instructor determine the effect of the new teaching method.

Another example of an experiment may be used to determine the effect of the independent variable(s) upon the dependent variable—for example, the type of lamp upon a subject's eyes. To conduct the experiment, a treatment may have a subject work at a desk for a specified period of time, and after that period of time, the subject rates how his or her eyes feel.

Experimentation through mock-ups is another way of testing an idea. Testing is conducted by using either the physical (e.g., new product mock-ups) or the visual (e.g., concept maps or mathematical forms). Such models can bring out what may have been invisible or hidden (Goat & Wang, 2002). Particularly, some models may be created to experiment with design ideas (Scott-Webber, 1998). These may be process models of an idea (see Figure 3.3). Other models are used to conduct experiments in a laboratory such as those used to test interior materials and/or products for flame resistant testing (Goat & Wang, 2002). Concept maps in design may be bubble diagrams that test ideas during the schematic development phase.

The Program Document

The program document provides a systematic method of recording information from data collection. Designers begin assembling their program documents by writing their problem statement, goals, and objectives. As designers collect information through fact finding and researching for new evidence, their program documents are gradually completed.

Problem Statement

According to Pena et al. (2001), "problem definition should be the first step in the design process" (p. 52). Thus, the designer needs to write a problem statement. "Problem statements must be clear and concise—in the designer's own words so there is no doubt that he or she understands. When writing a problem statement, the designer should focus on the obvious—which is often overlooked" (p. 92). Additionally, the designer should stress the uniqueness of the project.

A problem statement should include significant and specific conditions while establishing a general direction for the design project, preferably in terms of performance. However, this statement should be ambiguous enough to eliminate the sense that there is only one solution. Designers write problem statements in the past tense. Additionally, some resources (Duerk, 1993; Kilmer and Kilmer, 1992) suggest a mission statement that states the purpose of the project. However, a problem statement helps the designer focus on what the "problem is." Thus, a short statement of purpose may be the first sentence of a problem statement. The following is an example of a problem statement:

> The insurance firm has grown from a two-person office to a four-person office that includes the owner, two insurance agents, and one receptionist. The firm will be moving into a new open space that has not been divided.

Goals

According to Durek (1993), "goals are statements that move us to take action. They are vehicles for making design decisions" (p. 36). Thus, goals state the intentions—what the client wants to accomplish—so that when the project is complete, the stated goals will be attained. The opposite of a problem statement, goal statements should be precise and clearly stated so that they can be realized. "A goal is a statement of what the future state should be" (p. 36). Thus, goals are written in the present tense that is preceded by an intent verb; for example, "The facility should provide stimulating environment that promotes teamwork." Additionally, a goal statement should be developed for each design issue that has been revealed during programming as well as during the entire design process.

According to Kilmer & Kilmer (1992), the following questions may be asked that will assist in writing goals:

1. What is to be achieved?

2. Why is it to be achieved?

3. What are the client goals?

4. What are the design goals?

5. Prioritize the goals (p. 182).

Objectives

Under each goal, one or more objectives must be written. "Objectives indicate how to achieve the goal and to what degree" (Kilmer & Kilmer, 1992, p. 1981). An example of an objective is: "Incorporate team spaces into each department" and "Provide areas for interaction between workstations as well as team areas within each department." As noted in these examples, the goal statement is general whereas the objective is specific.

Application

Most often, the practitioner will collect evidence in one or several of the methods discussed in this chapter. Data collection methods used by practitioners are listed in Appendices C through L as well as in Q and R. Seldom will the practitioner conduct the traditional research that is conducted by academic researchers, which is disseminated through media such as journals, periodicals, and online resources. However, many of these sources are available through the IIDA Knowledge Center and InformeDesign. As discussed in Chapter 1, the IIDA Knowledge Center provides academic and/or industry research. InformeDesign provides research summaries (RS) of academic research. Evidence from both sources informs design solutions.

The InformeDesign Web site provides research tutorials to help designers better understand the research process. The tutorials offer information on research basics—concepts, vocabulary, and examples. Guerin and Dohr (2005) state that the purpose of the tutorial is for designers to:

- Understand the importance of research in design, especially EBD.

- Recall research vocabulary.

- Increase their understanding of research methods.

- Develop a rationale for the use of research-based findings in design solutions.

Additionally, the tutorial, which is divided into three parts, will provide information on how to use results of RS and what differences the summaries can make to the design solution. Ultimately, InformeDesign RS from academic studies and/or product information from manufacturer's studies will provide evidence throughout the design process.

Summary

A variety of data collection methods provide facts and evidence for a design project. The Appendices in this book contain examples of both commercial and residential questionnaires. For residential spaces, Appendices N through U may be used to collect data. Using these forms, data can be collected from all occupants of the space. For commercial spaces, Appendices C through M as well as Q through U may be used to collect data.

Designers collect data from management, other personnel, and typical users through written surveys and/or interviews. It is crucial to carefully select representation and craft questions (Rayfield, 1994). The effectiveness of written surveys and interviews depends upon several factors relative to: (1) the appropriate selection of representatives; (2) their knowledge; (3) the caliber of questions; and (4) the accuracy of their responses. Chapters will aid in the development of questions and areas to consider for research. These areas include structural and contextual needs, sustainability, human factors, diversity, commercial and residential spaces, precedents, and design theories.

Additionally, designers use other methods such as observations, experiments, visual and content analysis, case studies, and evidence from POEs. Journal articles, trade publications, online resources such as InformeDesign, and other sources will provide important background from research and other projects. New evidence found in the research should be summarized. A narrative and/or list should then be developed that will be applied to the design project. After designers have collected facts and new evidence, they begin the program document by stating the problem, identifying the goals, and determining the objectives for the project. Then they list the program requirements, which include data collected of both facts and evidence that apply to the design project.

Key Terms

accretion trace

behavioral mapping

case study

casual observation

closed-ended questions

direct data

erosion trace

existing conditions

indirect data

interview

interviewer-administered

mock-ups

open-ended questions

participant observation

person-centered maps

place-centered maps

post-test

pre-test

program document

questionnaire

structured (focused)
  interview

systematic observation

trace observation

treatment

unstructured interview

user survey

visual and content analysis

THEODORE

Historic Precedents

OBJECTIVES

After reading this chapter, you should be able to:

Locate examples of historic precedents

Determine and use criteria for analyzing historic precedents

*Analyze an example of historic precedents that
may become evidence for a design project*

DRED COURT

Designers conduct evidence-based design (EBD) not only through research summaries and journal articles, but also through examination and analysis of **precedents**.

To understand the meaning of precedent in the context of design, a look at other disciplines will provide a basis. In law, decisions made by the court often cite a case or an example that is similar. The U.S. legal system relies heavily on the body of known, or established, precedents. Though precedents in the court system have great strength, earlier precedents may be reviewed and overturned in some situations (Precedents, 2007).

In design, research of precedents provides inspiration and development of new ideas for exterior and interior components of a project as well as for the entire project. As in the court system, past precedents may also change the direction and improve new and future projects.

Thus, research of precedents in design involves the examination of **historic precedents**—architecture and interior designs from the past. It also involves the examination of **design precedents**, which looks at various design types such as retail, office, hospitality, healthcare, and retail. We will discuss design precedents in Chapter 5.

Historic precedents—architectural and interior—provide inspiration often needed to develop new and innovative ideas. For example, Palladio applied Vitruvius' proportioning system to his design of Villa Capra (La Rotonda). Thomas Jefferson was inspired by and applied concepts from Palladio's designs to Monticello. In the case study in this chapter, Louis Kahn applied features and concepts from historic precedents—the Alhambra and St. Francis of Assisi monastery—to the Salk Institute in La Jolla, California. From the legendary to the ordinary, one can find architectural features and theories from historic precedents applied in past projects practically everywhere, and all of these can apply to today's designs as well. With an appropriate example determined, criteria can be developed and used to analyze architecture and interiors. Research and analysis of historic precedents provide grounded evidence, inspiration for new ideas, and improvement in present and future projects.

The best sources for historic precedent may be found through using one or more of the following methods: (1) reading history books—architectural and interiors; (2) traveling to and visiting specific historic sites; and/or (3) reviewing articles found in periodicals such as the *Journal of Interior Design*, or summarized on databases such as InformeDesign that critically analyze architecture and interiors. All of these methods provide excellent sources to locate ideas for and/or evidence from an analysis.

Criteria for Analysis

When investigating historic precedents, a framework can be developed from which to conduct research. The College of William and Mary (WM) (2008) has developed an architectural framework (i.e., design guidelines) that encourages unity in the design of its campus. The guidelines are divided into two areas with several criteria within each: architectural order (e.g., plan, geometry, scale, massing, proportions, site and orientation, symmetry, and hierarchy) and architectural elements (e.g., doors, windows, and roofs). Many of these criteria are specific to WM's needs. Ching (2007) and Clark and Pause (2004) also examine historic precedents using architectural criteria (i.e., entrance, structure, repetitive to unique, circulation, views, materials, and details) and theoretical criteria (i.e., elements and principles). Through a combination of these sources, the following criteria will be used as the basic research and analysis of historic precedents.

- Architectural and interior criteria
  - Site and orientation
  - Entrance
  - Structure
  - Repetitive to unique
  - Circulation: horizontal and vertical
  - Views
  - Materials and details

- Theoretical criteria
  - Line
  - Planes
  - Shape and form
  - Mass or volume
  - Scale and proportion
  - Balance
  - Light

The list of architectural and interior and theoretical criteria is not all-inclusive; criteria may be added or deleted to best analyze historic precedents. In this chapter, each criterion will be described, examples provided, and questions posed to be used in analyzing an historic building and/or space. Some criteria will be interrelated and, therefore, reinforced.

Criteria for Architectural and Interior Design

Table 4.1 lists and explains each architectural and interior criterion that may be used to analyze architecture and interiors. Table 4.2 offers questions for analysis of architectural and interior criteria. A narrative description of each architectural and interior criterion, along with examples and questions for analysis, follows.

Site and Orientation

The site location for a design project is often chosen before an interior designer becomes involved; however, in some firms, determining the site location may be part of the process. Past cultures carefully chose the location of architectural sites. For example, the placement of the infamous Greek temple called the Parthenon is the focal point of all buildings on the Acropolis, a hill outside ancient Athens. Its architectural beauty can be viewed from a distance for all to see. During the Middle Ages, fortified castles were strategically located

Criteria	Explanation
Site and Orientation	View or seclusion, geography, topography
Entrance	• Entrance door on the façade penetrates plane • An approach is perpendicular, oblique, hidden, or spiral • Portals or gateways: orients visitor into area, space, and/or building • Approach to building and entrance may vary in duration: few paces to series of spaces Entrances can be visually reinforced: • Lower, wider, narrower; deep or circuitous; articulated with or without ornamentation • Scale of entrance: building and human
Structure	• Connection between section and elevation to floor plan • Geometry in plan and elevation • Hierarchy: rank ordering of attributes • Patterns, scale configuration, geometry, articulation • Quality, richness, detail, ornamentation, special materials used as indicator of importance • Interior to exterior: connect to nature—open gardens connected to view or entrance, etc.
Repetitive to Unique	• Relationship between the repetitive and unique elements: unique elements dominate
Circulation	• Represents movement and stationary components • Relates to function and circulation • Focus on dominant relationship
Path	• Perceptual thread linking a series of interior and exterior spaces • Moving in time through and experiencing sequence of spaces, space • Paths of movement are linear in nature (for people, cares, goods, services) • Form and scale of entrance and/or path convey the functional and symbolic distinction • Enclosed path: public galleria or private corridor • Open path: open on one or both sides and form a gallery or balcony • Promenade, pause, rest, or viewing area along a path must accommodate movement of people
Staircase	• Going up: conveys privacy, aloofness, or detachment; going down: secure, protected, or stable • Shallow and/or side steps convey an invitation to public spaces • Width provides a visual cue: public or private • Narrow and/or steep to private spaces; shallow and/or wide steps to public spaces • Slope of staircase—proportioned to fit the body movement and capability • Path of movement: reinforce, interrupt, accommodates change, or terminate • Pitch of stairs and location of landings determine rhythmic movements: ascending, descending • Space for staircase: run along room's edge, wrap around a space, or can rise between walls • Three-dimensional forms moving up or down

Table 4.1

Historic Precedents: Architectural and Interior Criteria

Table 4.1
Historic Precedents: Architectural and Interior Criteria (continued)

Criteria	Explanation
	• Three-dimensional experience and quality: treat as sculpture, freestanding, or attached to wall plane • Space can become an oversized, elaborate staircase • Organizing element weaves a series of spaces

Views	• Interior to exterior views: vistas, gardens, fountains, etc.
	• Openings to provide light and establish visual relationships: windows, skylights
	• Small opening:
	  • Grouped windows sequenced to fragment view
	  • Encourages movement through space
	• Long, narrow openings (vertical or horizontal):
	  • Larger openings provide larger, broader vistas
	  • Bay window provides view from different directions
	• Interior views:
	  • Focal gatherings
	  • Degrees of public viewing

Materials and Details	• Contrast of surfaces and edges using different colors, shapes, tonal value, etc. • Openings punctuate the surface • Corners define or diminish • Changes in floor and ceiling heights • Flooring: step down, visual change • Ceilings: tray, shed, vaulted, beamed, etc. • Attention to detail: moldings, trim, hardware, sculpture, etc.

to view and prepare for an approaching enemy (Kostof, 1985). Today, as in the past, a site location needs to be strategically located to meet client needs and desires, whether it is the capability to be viewed, secluded, or connected to nature.

In analyzing site and orientation, designers ask the following questions:

- What is the geography and topography?

- How does the geography and topography affect the design?

- Is there a view or is the building secluded?

- If there is a view, is the building appropriately sited for best advantage?

Entrance

The entrance is an opening that penetrates a vertical plane—the façade—and gives an impression of what is beyond the entrance doors. The approach to this entrance is the beginning of that impression. The approach may be perpendicular, oblique (i.e., to the side), hidden, or spiraling. For example, a perpendicular approach is employed for some plantation homes with a drive through a grove of trees directly to the entrance door. An oblique approach is used for many homes today with the driveway to the side and the entrance

Table 4.2	
Questions for Analysis: Architectural and Interior Criteria	
Criteria	**Questions**
Site and Orientation	• What is the geography and topography? • How do the geography and topography affect the design? • Is there a view or is the building secluded? • If there is a view, is the building appropriately sited for best advantage?
Entrance	• Is the approach and entrance an appropriate precursor to the experience on the inside? • Is the entrance at the building scale and/or human scale? • If a connection to nature is important in the design, does the landscape provide a precursor to the visual experience beyond the entrance?
Structure	When determining the geometric two-dimensional forms found in plan view to elevations and/or section: • Is there a relationship between the geometric forms found on the plan to elevations and/or the sections? • What is the relationship between the dominant to the subordinate parts?
Repetitive to Unique	• What is repetitive and what is unique? • How do the repetitive and unique relate to one another? • Does the unique element dominate? • Does the entire plan focus on the dominant concept?
Circulation	• Does the path move through a logical sequence of spaces? • Does the movement relate to function? • Do paths and staircases meet the following guidelines: Is path unobstructed? Is public or private paths indicated? Are ADA guidelines met?
Views	When considering the relationship between the interior spaces to the exterior: • Are the vistas, gardens, fountains, and so on easily viewed from the interior? • Is there a connection between the exterior view and interior spaces? • What is the interior focal point? • Is there a connection between an exterior view and an interior focal point?
Materials and Details	• Do materials and details coordinate? • What colors, shapes, tonal values, materials are used? • Is the concept fully realized through materials and details?

at an angle to the approach. A hidden approach makes guests look for the entrance; the entrance to Frank Lloyd Wright's Meyer May House in Grand Rapids, Michigan, is an example of this. A spiraling approach winds toward the entrance, such as that of the Hearst Castle, which spirals up a hill toward its entrance.

In more expensive homes and/or gated communities, portals or gateways are the traditional means of orienting visitors into an area, space, and/or building. The impression of what may be located beyond these gates or entrance doors either welcomes or guards against entry. The approach to a building and its entrance may vary in duration from a few paces to a series of spaces. After reaching the entrance, the visitor will find a variety of designs. These designs may be low, wide, narrow, or deep. They may also be articulated with ornamentation or decoration (Ching, 2007).

In analyzing the architecture and interior, designers ask the following questions:

• Are the approach and entrance appropriate precursors to the experience on the inside?

• Is the entrance at the building scale and/or human scale?

• If a connection to nature is important in the design, does the landscape provide a precursor to the visual experience beyond the entrance?

Structure

Structure is synonymous with support—columns, planes, or a combination of the two. Therefore, it is important for interior designers to understand the connection between the section and elevation to the floor plan. Spatial relationships, in both past or present projects, can be analyzed by sketching parts (i.e., elevations and sections) relative to the structure to gain a better understanding of their relationship. In this process, rooms can be identified in both plan as well as in elevation and section. This leads to the examination of units, or parts, to the whole. Also, in examining both the elevation and a floor plan, the geometric two-dimensional forms may be determined. A relationship between the forms may be found on the plan and in elevation. By analyzing the geometric relationships, a stronger connection is made between the parts of the architecture or space to the whole. Hierarchy is an indicator of importance or rank order. The plan, elevations, and/or sections help determine the relationship between the dominant to subordinate parts (Clark & Pause, 2004). An example is Taliesin West in Scottsdale, Arizona, where rectangular shapes, some manipulated and placed at 60-degree angles, make an interesting design.

In analyzing shapes and forms, begin by determining the geometric two-dimensional forms found in plan view to elevations and/or section. Then the following questions may be asked:

• Is there a relationship between the geometric forms found on the plan to elevations and/or sections?

• What is the relationship between the dominant to the subordinate parts?

Repetitive to Unique

In examining this criteria, note that there is a continuing relationship to the architectural criteria. Additionally, the concept of repetitive to unique relates to theoretical criteria—specifically to the principles of basic design theory, rhythm, emphasis, and harmony (Clark & Pause, 2004). This may be seen in the basic elements of line, shape, and/or form (i.e., theoretical criteria).

For example, a Gothic cathedral has many repetitive forms, such as ribbed **groin vaults** on the ceiling and piers supporting the structure. However, when the transept and nave cross is capped with a **dome** and the space opens wider between piers, these components render this section of the building unique from the previous, repetitive sections.

Continuing beyond the crossing to the choir and apse, the shape changes from rectangles to the semicircle, which renders this section unique and dominant. As a floor plan and elevations are examined, there will be repetitive and unique shapes. Repetitive shapes will be overshadowed by the unique, which should dominate (Clark & Pause, 2004).

In analyzing repetitive to unique, designers ask the following questions:

- What is repetitive and what is unique?

- How do the repetitive and unique aspects relate to one another?

- Does the unique element dominate?

- Does the entire plan focus on the dominant concept?

Circulation

Circulation represents movement and stationary components that relate to the function of the space (Clark & Pause, 2004). Circulation is horizontal (e.g., the path) and vertical movement (e.g., the staircase, elevator, and escalator). Movement is the thread that links interior and exterior space and moves the occupant through a sequence of spaces. The path is linear; it provides both a functional and symbolic distinction that represents the design concept. A circulation space may be enclosed public or private hallways or corridors, or the space may be open on one or both sides, such as a gallery or balcony. This provides visual and spatial links to other areas. Whether closed or open, there may be areas along the path to pause, rest, or view without obstructing the movement of others along the path (Ching, 2007). Examining the paths relative to the movement through the space as well as sequencing of space will reveal circulation patterns.

The staircase provides vertical movement between levels in a building or outdoor spaces. When moving upward, a sense of privacy, aloofness, or detachment may be felt. When moving downward, a sense of moving toward a more secure, protected, or stable environment may occur. These spaces may convey visual cues that the staircase is private or open to the public. For example, a narrow and/or steep staircase will lead to private spaces, whereas shallow and/or wide steps convey an invitation to the public. The slope of the staircase should be in proportion to body movement. For example, a steep climb causes fatigue and gives a sense of insecurity; shallow steps may be too deep for the natural stride easiness. Following the Americans with Disabilities Act (ADA) guidelines will avoid these problems. Interruptions along the vertical path reinforce movement and indicate changes in direction or termination. The vertical path can be treated as an additive form or a volumetric solid. The pitch of a stair and location of landings also create rhythmic movements —ascending and descending through space.

Space occupied by a staircase may be located along the edge of a room, wrap around the space, rise between walls, or open in the center of the space. The staircase can also become a three-dimensional experience whether treated as a sculptural, freestanding form, or attached to a wall plane. The space taken up by the staircase may even be oversized to emphasis an elaborate three-dimensional form. It can also become an element that organizes and weaves together a series of varied levels—inside and/or outside the building (Ching, 2007). An example of vertical circulation is the steps that lead to the San Miniato Cathedral outside Florence, Italy. These steps are important in both moving toward the entrance as well as providing an experience along the path of circulation. The long flights of steps allow one to see and view the church as well as look back and view Florence in the distance. Consideration for movement and circulation may provide experiences for the user. The circulation methods (path and staircases) found in historic spaces can provide examples of moving through a space that can inform a design project.

In analyzing movement, designers ask the following questions:

- Does the path move through a logical sequence of spaces?

- Does the movement relate to function?

- Do paths and staircases meet the following guidelines: Are paths unobstructed? Are public or private paths indicated? Are ADA guidelines met?

Views

The view or views outside the space can provide emphasis to many interior spaces. Views may include vistas, gardens, and fountains. Openings are needed to establish a relationship between the view and the interior. For example, windows, skylights, and glass doors provide that relationship as well as lighting the interior. Openings may be small and/or grouped to fragment the view, or may be long and narrow or large to allow larger and broader views.

Within the interior, focal points are important and provide a gathering space or area for public viewing such as an art gallery. For example, the tokonoma (or raised alcove) in a Japanese house becomes the internal focal point (Ching, 2007). Opening between spaces can provide a visual relationship. From the interior of Philip Johnson's Glass House, the occupant has a 360-degree view of his surroundings; however, the fireplace is the focal point of the interior. Light comes through the glass that walls the house, and placement of furniture is the only separation between spaces.

To analyze the view or views, the designer may begin by considering the relationship between the interior spaces to the exterior, and ask the following questions:

- Are the vistas, gardens, fountains, or other exterior focal points easily viewed from the interior?

- Is there a connection between the exterior view and interior spaces?

- What is the interior focal point?

- Is there a connection between an exterior view and an interior focal point?

Materials and Details

On the exterior and interior, surfaces and edges can be accentuated or diminished by material and/or detail application. The surface and edges (i.e., corners) of a façade may be contrasted with different colors, shapes, tonal value, or other elements, which may provide interest and may also provide emphasis. For example, the corners of a Georgian-style brick house are defined with stone quoins—different material and color. To diminish corners, Frank Lloyd Wright employed rounded corners on the Johnson Wax Building in Racine, Wisconsin. On the interior, a wall finish may be contrasted with different colors or tonal values, and edge treatments may be moldings for windows, archways, doorways, and other placements. These finishes may emphasis or punctuate the surface; however, the edges or corners may define or even diminish.

In analyzing materials and details, designers may ask the following questions:

- Do materials and details coordinate?

- What colors, shapes, tonal values, and materials are used?

- Is the concept fully realized through materials and details?

Theoretical Criteria

Table 4.3 lists and explains theoretical criteria (i.e., elements and principles) used to analyze architecture and interiors. Table 4.4 offers questions for analysis of architecture and interiors using theoretical criteria. The following provides a narrative description of each criterion along with examples and questions for analysis.

Line

Line on an exterior or in an interior provides: (1) visual expression of direction, movement, and growth; (2) articulates or defines edges or corners; and/or (3) an organizational device to align and order forms and space (Ching, 2007). As with the criteria—materials and details—line can also be used to articulate the form (e.g., corners or planes) and surfaces by changing materials, colors, texture, and light.

In analyzing line, designers ask the following questions:

- How does line provide the visual expression, direction, and movement?

- How does line articulate and define aspects of the exterior and interior?

- How does line become an organizing device?

- How is line used to articulate the form and/or surfaces?

Planes

Planes define boundaries of volumes that may be implied or actual. Planes are analyzed by examining how well the planes define each of the following:

- The façade and the organization of openings

- The implied planes for gathering spaces (e.g., markets, parks, and atriums)

- The exterior walls that mold interior spaces

- Overhead ceilings, walls, or floors that create the volume

- Interior wall planes that determine size and shape of the interior spaces

Ultimately, planes, whether implied or actual, determine the quality of space and the relationship of one space to another. Planes that are out of reach frequently symbolize sky

Table 4.3
Historic Precedents: Theoretical Criteria

Criteria	Explanation
Line	• Visual expression of direction, movement, growth • Segmentation of line (parallel or crossing) • Movement through space • Supporting as with post and beam • Articulates and defines: different material used on edges or corners (exterior or interior)
Planes	• Organizational: the device aligns and orders forms and space • Defines open or gathering space; forms define open volume • Exterior wall: defines and molds interior spaces • Interior wall planes: size and shape of spaces or rooms determined by wall plane • Out-of-reach planes: symbolize sky, shelter; unify different parts of space
Shape and Form	• Inseparable: triangle to pyramid; circle to sphere or cylinder • Additive: transform the form by adding a form • Subtractive: transform the form by taking away a portion • Form types: centralized; clustered or interlocking; grid • Change the form: rotate the grid • Articulate corners or planes: lines, shapes, forms; change materials, colors, texture, light
Mass or Volume	• Creates volume: three-dimensional element; defined by boundaries/planes—walls, floors, ceiling, roof • Massing defines, articulates: creates emphasis or image of total building
Scale and Proportion	• Scale and proportion interrelated • Golden mean, section, rectangle • Human scale: human body dimensions of (our pace, reach, or grasp) • Building scale: small versus large relative to psychology (emotions)
Balance	• Balance: perceptual and conceptual equilibrium: symmetry, asymmetry, radial • Symmetry: specialized form of balance • Both impact all other analysis issues
Light	• Natural light: daylight enters building • Light affects perceptions of mass and volume • Reinforces structure that may be articulated or diminished • Radiant energy of light reveals shape, color, textures of forms in space • Light penetrates windows (wall plane) or skylights (roof plane) • Sun's energy on room's surface affects space: enlivens colors of materials, textiles, etc. • Light—ever changing: changes during day; creates patterns of light, shade, shadows • Direct sunlight affects pattern

	Table 4.4
	Questions for Analysis: Theoretical Criteria
Criteria	**Questions**
Line	• How does line provide the visual expression, direction, and movement? • How does line articulate and define aspects of the exterior and interior? • How does line become an organizing device? • How is line used to articulate the form and/or surfaces?
Planes	How will the planes define the following applicable points: • The façade • The organization of openings • The implied planes for gather spaces (markets, squares, etc.) • The exterior walls that mold interior spaces • Overhead ceilings, walls, or floors that create the volume • Interior wall planes that determine size and shape of the interior spaces
Shape and Form	• Is the form transformed in plan view? • Is the change effective to the overall design?
Mass and Volume	• What areas are emphasized and how is this accomplished? • Does it provide a perceived image of the total architecture or space?
Scale and Proportion	• Was human scale considered? • In what ways does the space visually appear small scaled and vice versa—large scaled? • How are the golden mean, golden section, and golden rectangle used to examine the appropriateness of scale and proportion of the architecture and interior?
Balance	Do the following indicate balance and provide actual or visual equilibrium? • Line, shape, form • Structure • Entrance • Movement through the space
Light	Analyze how natural light will affect the space; analyze how light will change, reveal, or even diminish various elements within the interior during different times of the day as well as seasons of the year
Final Analysis	To complete the analysis, the following questions should be answered: • What is consistently found in this design? • What can be applied from this analysis to another (or a present) project? • What problems were found that can be avoided? • How could the problems found improve another project? • How will this information be applied and improve your project?

and/or shelter. They also unify different parts of space, become a means for artistic expression, such as Michelangelo's Sistine Chapel, or become a passive and receding surface without ornamentation or decoration (Ching, 2007).

In analyzing planes, designers ask the following question:

• How will the planes define the previously listed applicable points?

Shape and Form

Shape, both regular and irregular, and form coexist. Therefore, the analysis of shapes and forms are inseparable, such as a triangle to the pyramidal form or the circle to the sphere or cylinder (Ching, 2007). Especially important is the ability to change or change the form through a subtractive or additive method, depending on what is to become dominant. Subtractive refers to removal from the form and is used when the whole is dominant. Additive refers to attachment to the form, which renders the parts of the building as dominant (Clark & Pause, 2004). Transformation—subtractive or additive—provides variety and makes the architecture or interior unique. There are different types of forms: centralized (e.g., La Rotonda by Palladio), clustered or interlocking (e.g., Taos Pueblo, New Mexico), linear (e.g., Mies van der Rohe's apartment block, Weissenhof Siedlung), or grid form (e.g., El Escorial, near Madrid, Spain). Using other examples, Figure 4.1a–d illustrates examples of these different forms: centralized, clustered or interlocking, linear, or grid form.

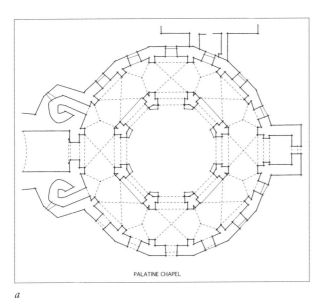

PALATINE CHAPEL

a

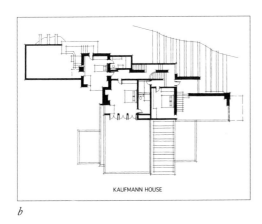

KAUFMANN HOUSE

b

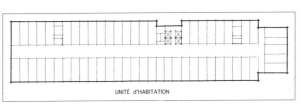

UNITÉ d'HABITATION

c

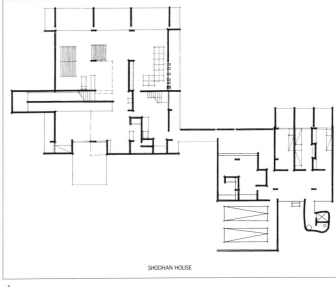

SHODHAN HOUSE

d

Figure 4.1 The following forms illustrate centralized, clustered or interlocking, linear, and grid forms. The plan view of (a) Palatine Chapel in Aachen, Germany, shows a centralized organization. The plan view of (b) Kaufmann House, Falling Waters, by Frank Lloyd Wright, shows a clustered or interlocking organization. The plan views of (c) Le Corbusier's Unité d'Habitation show linear organization. The plan view of (d) Shodhan House in Ahmedabad, India, by Le Corbusier shows a grid organization.

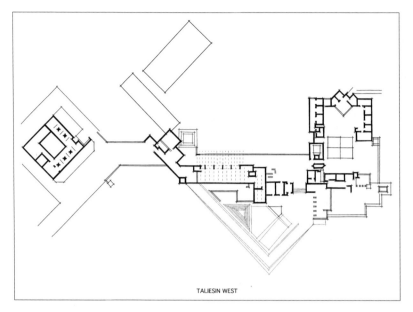

TALIESIN WEST

Figure 4.2 The plan view of Frank Lloyd Wright's Taliesin West illustrates a rotating grid.

Grid forms may be manipulated by rotating parts of the grid, which create a more interesting spatial layout. Wright's Taliesin West begins as a grid form with portions rotated. Figure 4.2 illustrates the grid form with rotated portions.

In the analysis of shape and form, designers ask the following questions:

• Is the form transformed in plan view?

• Is the change effective to the overall design?

Mass and Volume

Three-dimensional elements—mass and volume—include the building, space, or a void. These are defined by boundaries (e.g., walls, floors, ceiling, and roof planes). Often, elements are massed together to create emphasis. For example, elements may be massed together to articulate or define a façade. The façade, then, becomes a point of emphasis and an image of the total building (Ching, 2007).

In the analysis of mass or volume, designers address the following questions:

• What areas are emphasized, and how is this accomplished?

• Does it provide a perceived image of the total architecture or space?

Scale and Proportion

Human scale in architecture is based on dimensions of human body—dimensions of elements related to dimensions of our pace, reach, or grasp. Small-scaled spaces provide an intimate feeling, whereas large-scaled space makes one feel small and insignificant (Ching, 2007). Scale and proportion are interrelated. For example, the size of an object may seem standard, but an object placed alongside another material or form will indicate whether one part is proportionally correct to the other or the whole (Ching, 2007; Kilmer & Kilmer, 1992).

In analyzing scale and proportion, designers address the following questions:

- Was human scale considered?

- In what ways does the space visually appear small scaled and vice versa—large scaled?

- How are the **golden mean, golden section,** and **golden rectangle** used to examine the appropriateness of scale and proportion of the architecture and interior?

Balance

Balance is a principle of design that is important to create either a perceived or conceptual equilibrium. Symmetrical balance and radial balance are more formal, whereas asymmetrical tends to be informal. Thus, both impact all other analysis issues such as line, shape, and form as well as the structure, entrance, and movement through the space (Clark & Pause, 2004).

In analyzing balance, actual or visual equilibrium is essential in good design; therefore, designers examine the following question:

- Do line, shape, and form; structure and entrance; and movement through space indicate balance and provide actual or visual equilibrium?

Light

Light in this analysis will focus on natural light as it penetrates the space. Because daylighting is an important method of lighting and energy savings, how it affects the interior is crucial. When daylight enters a building it affects the viewer's perceptions of mass and volume. It may also reinforce the structure (Clark & Pause, 2004) as well as reveal shapes, colors, and textures in the space. Light penetrates space through windows in a wall plane or through skylights in overhead roof planes. The sun's energy falls upon the room's surface, which enlivens elements such as the colors of materials and textiles. Light also changes throughout the day and creates patterns of light, shade, and shadow; direct sunlight creates sharp patterns (Ching, 2007).

In analyzing how natural light will affect the space, it is important to look at how light will change, reveal, or even diminish various elements within the interior during different times of the day as well as seasons of the year.

Final Analysis

After locating and analyzing various historic precedents, some final questions should be addressed to determine what has been gained from the analysis. The last section of Table 4.4 lists possible questions for the final analysis:

- What is consistently found in this design?

- What can be applied from this analysis to another (or a present) project?

- What problems were found that can be avoided?

- How could the problems found improve another project?

- How will this information be applied and inform another project?

Many suggestions for analysis have been provided; however, the list is not all inclusive. Other criteria may be added, some deleted, or some melded together. Additionally, some criteria interrelate, and thus, some answers to the questions within the analysis may be repetitive. In a thorough analysis, the repetition will bring forth the important aspects of a design. Clearly, through analysis, lessons can be learned from the past. The intent is to use this method as an analysis of past and present architecture and interiors and, with an analysis, inspire new innovative design solutions. Ching (2007) and Clark and Pause (2004) used many of these components in a graphical analysis. These books provide excellent resources to coincide with a written analysis such as the following example.

Application

To best understand the application of historic precedents, consider the following two examples: the Villa Capra (La Rotonda), and an analysis of sacred spaces by Watson and Kucko (2001), to which both of the proposed criteria are applied.

Villa Capra (La Rotonda) Analysis

As an example, imagine that classical concepts are important for a design project. Though the Parthenon and the Pantheon are options for analysis, the Villa Capra (or La Rotonda) was chosen for analysis because it incorporates classical elements—a portico, columns, and a dome. Additionally, because the architect Palladio is well known, his work and inspiration are important to the analysis. The following is an example of a brief analysis. Figure 4.3 provides plans, elevations, and other details of the Villa Capra (La Rotonda) to better understand the analysis.

Architectural and Interior Criteria

Designers apply the following architectural and interior criteria in the applications of historic precedents:

- Site and orientation—A connection to nature is not found; however, it is located on a hill for viewing by others.

- Entrance—The portico entrance is at building scale, but the entrance door is at human scale.

- Structure (exterior and interior)—The plan can be developed into various geometric shapes on the façade and the plan: rectangles, circle, and triangle (exterior triangle: bottom left corner to peak of dome to bottom right corner).

- Repetitive to unique—There are repetitive rectangular shapes with a unique circular shape. The circle is the nucleus with rectangular shapes surrounding the center.

- Circulation (horizontal)—Circulation is on an axis and moves straight ahead or perpendicular to the major line of traffic. The central space is the focal point, and movement of the path is directed to the focal point. The path is unobstructed as it moves to the central space and is not closed by doors, whereas private space may be closed from other areas. Because the central space is the focal point, the circulation fits the conceptual design of the space.

Case Study 4.1

The Role of Historic Precedents in Contemporary Design

By Lily Robinson, RA, ASID, IDEC

Shortly after the success of his breakthrough polio vaccine in 1955, Dr. Jonas Salk set out to build a research facility where top scientists from around the world could live, work, and meet in a sort of monastic environment (Carter, 1966). The Salk Institute for Biological Studies represents a unique collaborative effort between a forward-thinking scientist and a top architect, Louis Kahn. The program of areas for the institute was not dictated by the client, but rather grew out of research; particularly, research of historic precedents (Ronner & Jhaveri, 1987). Kahn collected data through informal interviews and observations. However, to develop form, he searched images of historic precedents.

In interviews from a previous project, Kahn learned that the scientists were so dedicated to their work that at lunchtime they moved test tubes from benches to sit and eat and disregarded the noise around them. Kahn realized that the wants of the scientists did not necessarily match their needs. "I realized that there should be 'a clean air and stainless steel' area, and 'a rug and oak table' area. From this realization, form became" (Ronner et al. 1987, p. 138). The data informed Kahn that spaces needed to be separated by function—(1) experimentation, (2) private contemplation, and (3) social interaction—in order to accomplish the goal of moving knowledge forward. Kahn also included a new type of space, the "unnamed space," which was not ascribed to any one function, but would accommodate unknown uses, allow for inspiration and, as Kahn stated "for the glory of the fuller environment" (Ronner et al. 1987, p. 131).

With an innovative program of areas in place, Kahn scoured for ideas for form from historic prec-

edents, imagery, readings of the site, and personal observations. These were essential to develop the physical aspects—size and shape of spaces. In fact, Kahn was so inspired by historic monuments that he would often "leave illustrated architectural books on the employees' drafting tables" for their inspiration (Wiseman, 2007, p. 104). Kahn often looked to historic precedents in search of classical, iconographic forms on which to base new uses and modernistic principles.

For the main concept of the facility, Kahn derived form from the monastery, St. Francis of Assisi—a historic precedent. Kahn and Salk had visited this historic place at different times: Kahn in 1928 and Salk in 1954. Salk was influenced by the life of the monks, their dedication to something higher than their own lives. Kahn saw a perfect building type that matched the function and needs of a research facility; particularly, the specialized spaces for silent contemplation, and the social plaza and an arcade for circulation. Kahn was also attracted to the quality of light produced by the interaction of the columns of the arcade and the openness of the plaza. Figure Case Study 4.1.1 illustrates the plaza of St. Francis of Assisi.

One of the controversies, or mysteries, that surrounds the Salk Institute is the source for the inspiration for the water feature dividing the plaza. From one historical account, a design by Luis Barragan inspired the open plaza between the two mirror image lab buildings. Another source of inspiration may have been the Mughal gardens in India and Pakistan. However, a Kahn employee and supervisor of Salk Institute construction, Jack McAllister stated in an interview that the Alham-

Figure Case Study 4.1.1 The St. Francis of Assisi monastery influenced Salk and inspired architect Louis Kahn in the design of the Salk Center. For Salk, it was the monks' dedication to a higher power. For Kahn, it was the combination of functions into one building. *(iStockPhoto)*

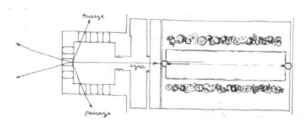

Figure Case Study 4.1.2 To provide an understanding of the Alhambra water feature, Kahn created this sketch of the Alhambra.

Figure Case Study 4.1.3 A photograph illustrates the Alhambra water feature that inspired Kahn's design. *(© David Sutherland/Getty Images)*

bra, a Moorish landmark, might have inspired the water feature (Wiseman, 2007). Figures Case Study 4.1.2 and 4.1.3 illustrate the water feature at the Alhambra in a sketch and photograph, respectively.

A look at Kahn's sketches (Figure Case Study 4.1.4) and early models indicate not only research of historic precedents but also site research and analysis that included climate, land formations, the site's proximity to the ocean, personal observation of the ocean view, the path of the sun, and solar orientation of the buildings. Site maps were all researched and analyzed in sketches and model form. Kahn used the similar climates to draw a parallel between La Jolla and the Greco-Roman world and the Middle East, further supporting his use of formal historical references to ancient monuments, plazas,

Figure Case Study 4.1.4 Having been inspired by the Alhambra water feature, Kahn sketched his concept for the Salk Institute with the ocean as a focal point. Kahn's sketches indicate research of historic precedents and site analysis.

Figure Case Study 4.1.5 The completed building at the Salk Institute reflects the inspiration from the Alhambra with the view of the ocean from the plaza. *(Photo by Lily Robinson)*

Figure Case Study 4.1.7 Photographs of the study areas near the plaza allow natural light and a view of the ocean into the space. *(Photo by Lily Robinson)*

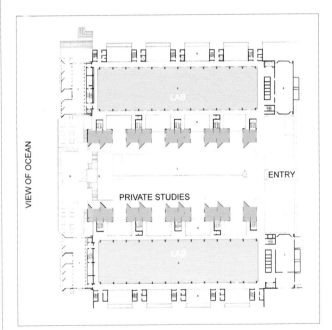

Figure Case Study 4.1.6 The diagrammatic plan of the Salk Institute identifies the various functions of the building. *(Photo by Lily Robinson)*

and water features. Figure Case Study 4.1.5 shows the concepts from water feature at the Alhambra, the plaza at St. Francis of Assisi monastary, and the connection to the ocean and natural light. As is illustrated in Figure Case Study 4.1.6, the labs—areas of experimentation are in the center of each building section, whereas the study areas are near the plaza. Natural light and view—are allowed into the study area (see Figure Case Study 4.1.7). The plaza, on the other hand, is the social area that provides the necessary connection between people and nature—the ocean view. Clearly, this case study illustrates a successful use of historic precedents, seamlessly incorporating specific architectural concepts from antiquity into contemporary design.

Case Study 4.2

Application of Criteria and Questions to Kimbell Art Museum

As you read through this case study, focus your attention on historic precedents,
criteria from these precedents to apply to the design of the Kimbell Art Museum,
and Key Terms discussed in Chapter 4.

For centuries, designers have examined historic precedents. Renaissance architect Palladio studied writings of Vitruvius and adapted concepts from Roman temples. Thomas Jefferson, the third U.S. president, studied work by the Renaissance architects as well as the Romans, particularly the Roman temple Maison Carrée in Mîmes, France. In the 1800s, an architectural school—Ecole des Beaux-Art in Paris—established goals to bring back the earlier concepts of Roman and Renaissance buildings. More recently, the architect Robert Venturi adapted ideas from the past not only in architecture but also the Federal style in furniture. Clearly, the examination of historic precedents provides insight into contemporary designs whether in architecture, interiors, or other design disciplines.

Hypothetically, let's assume that a design team made up of architects, interior designers, engineers, and landscape designers are designing a museum that will focus on sustainability. Various aspects of the design warrant the examination of historic precedents. Using various criteria discussed in this chapter, Louis Kahn's Kimbell Art Museum in Fort Worth, Texas, will be used as precedents.

In working through this analysis, Table Case Study 4.2.1 lists criteria on the left. Then, using the criteria and questions from Tables 4.1 through 4.4, the center column is a brief description or statement that analyzes Kahn's design—the historic precedents. After this list was compiled, key words that emerged consistently were italicized. Then, in the third column, these key words were used to apply to the new design. In the next step, the designer would use the analysis to sketch conceptual diagrams.

Within this example, all criteria were used; however, it is not necessary for all criteria to be used and applied. For example, the case study by Lily Robinson that describes Kahn's use of historic precedents for the Salk Institute uses some of the criteria such as daylighting and view. However, additional criteria were applied such as types of spaces, which Kahn used to examine historic use of spaces. Thus, though all criteria were used in the example, not all need to be applied to a project; however, additional criteria may be developed.

Criteria and analysis of historic precedents allow key terms to emerge that may be applied to a contemporary design. The conceptual diagrams may then incorporate ideas that have developed through an historic precedents analysis.

	Table Case Study 4.2.1 **Application of Architectural and Interior Criteria and Theoretical Criteria**	
	Historic Precedent: Museum Design	
	Louis Kahn's Kimbell Art Museum Fort Worth, Texas	**Hypothetical Plan: Museum with a focus on sustainability Springfield, Missouri**
Criteria	Analysis of historic precedents	Analysis applied to a contemporary design
	Site and Orientation	
	Gradual slope	Location should have gradual slope
	Building is open to view of open spaces	Building location in botanical gardens and arboretum
	Water feature *connects design to nature*	*Connect to nature in the design*
	Entrance	
	Perpendicular approach	*Perpendicular* approach
	Open space invites guest to entrance	Entrance must be inviting to guests
	Entrance is appropriate to building scale *Entrance is appropriate to human scale*	*Entrance is appropriate to human scale*
	Structure	
	Connection of *rectangular shapes*	*Connection of shapes*
	Semicircular arch/vaults seen only in elevation	Examine plan to elevation carefully
	Connection to nature with open space and water	*Connection to nature*
	Repetitive and Unique	
	Repetitive rectangular shape	*Repetitive shapes*
	Repetitive semicircular arch/vaults and vaulted ceiling	*Repetitive architectural features*
	Open space with implied planes lead toward entrance: unique	*A unique shape for emphasis*
	Circulation	
	Grid pattern of movement	*Grid as a possible plan, pattern, and path*
	Grid *path* on interior	*Use a grid path on interior*
	Open path in open exterior space	*Open path from exterior to interior*
	Views	
	Urban park setting	Significant *views* to exterior
	Some areas *view to open spaces*	*View* to open space
	Artwork is focal point of interior	*View* related to a focal point
	Materials and Details	
	Brick, poured-in-place concrete masonry	Sustainable material must be used
	Vaulted ceilings with *daylighting*	*Daylighting to be incorporated into plan*
	Simple, monumental	*Simple form, structure*

(Table continued on next page)

Table Case Study 4.2.1		
Application of Architectural and Interior Criteria and Theoretical Criteria		
Historic Precedent: Museum Design		
	Louis Kahn's Kimbell Art Museum Fort Worth, Texas	**Hypothetical Plan: Museum with a focus on sustainability Springfield, Missouri**
Criteria	Analysis of historic precedents	Analysis applied to a contemporary design
	Line	
	Straight and curved lines	*Line types dependent on shape*
	Straight and curved line defines the form	*Lines to define the form*
	Lines create the *grid form*	*Possible use of grid form*
	Planes	
	Open spaces contain implied planes	Location *implied planes*
	Exterior *rectangular and semicircular shapes* mold interior	Exteriors *shapes* must mold interior
	Shape and Form	
	Rectangular shapes transform the interior into rectangular plan view	*Shapes transform* interior plan
	Grid form complements exterior form	*Plan form complements exterior form*
	Mass and Volume	
	Emphasis to repetitive forms	*Emphasis to repetitive forms*
	Forms provides a perceived image of the total architecture and space	*Forms* provides sense of total architecture and space
	Scale and Proportion	
	Entrance and interior at *human scale*	Entrance and interior at *human scale*
	Spaces within gallery appear larger than they are with the use of *natural daylight*	*Sense of space affected by daylighting*
	Balance	
	Symmetrical balance found through shapes, form, and placement of entrances	*Type of balance must be repetitive*
	With a symmetrical entrance, movement through space begins on one side and must cross over to the opposite side	*Balance* related to movement through space
	Light	
	Indirect *natural daylight* streams into space from the ceiling and from windows facing the part and/or open spaces	Indirect *natural daylight important in design to create a positive, warm environment*
	Natural daylight provide warmth to space	*Natural daylight* providing warmth
	Daylight is indirect: eliminates glare—light has a positive effect on spaces	*Indirect daylight* to eliminate glare

(Table continued on next page)

	Table Case Study 4.2.1 **Application of Architectural and Interior Criteria and Theoretical Criteria**	
	Historic Precedent: Museum Design	
	Louis Kahn's Kimbell Art Museum Fort Worth, Texas	**Hypothetical Plan: Museum with a focus on sustainability Springfield, Missouri**
Criteria	Analysis of historic precedents	Analysis applied to a contemporary design
	Final Analysis	
	Important terminology and phrases italicized	Most important key terms from analysis listed below with essential terms italicized
	• *Rectangle, rectangular forms* • *Curves, semicircle affect shape of form* • *Repetition of shape and form* • *Symmetrical placement of shapes and forms* • *Grid plan, pattern, and paths* • *Daylight affects space: warm and visually enlarger*	• *Incorporate a grid pattern and paths* • *Grid form* will provide *simplicity* • *Repetition of shapes and form with a unique shape and form* • *Unique shape and form that will determine the connection to nature* • *Balance to emphasize shapes and form* • *Use of daylight essential for space* • *Use indirect daylighting*

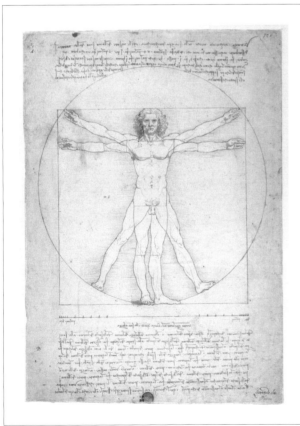

Figure Case Study 4.2.1 Leonardo Da Vinci's "Vitruvian Man" was based on writings by Vitruvius—a Roman Architect (1 BCE) and author of *De Architectura*—whose work became an authority and influence from the Roman period through the Renaissance, and continues to be influential into the twenty-first century. Though Vitruvius used the human body as a measurement to create proportion into a harmonious whole, Da Vinci took this description and created the diagram of the "Vitruvian Man." *(© Cameraphoto Arte, Venice/Art Resource)*

Figure Case Study 4.2.2 Roman temples were designed using the Vitruvian man's proportions to create a harmonious whole. *(iStockPhoto)*

Figure Case Study 4.2.3 The sixteenth-century Italian architect Palladio created porticoes for the Villa Rotunda—a concept adapted from Roman temples. *(iStockPhoto)*

Figure Case Study 4.2.4 Thomas Jefferson observed and employed ideas and concepts from the Roman temple Maison Carée and the architecture of Palladio, such as the Villa Rotunda, to his architectural work (e.g., Monticello and the University of Virginia). *(iStockPhoto)*

Figure Case Study 4.2.5 Venturi's postmodernist designs reflect the use of symbolic architectural forms of antiquity while manipulating and often reinventing forms, as is seen in the façade of the Vanna Venturi House. *(GreatBuildings.com)*

Figure Case Study 4.2.6 The perpendicular approach into the open space invites guests to the Kimbell Art Museum building entrance. *(© Kimbell Art Museum, Fort Worth, Texas/Art Resource)*

Figure Case Study 4.2.7 The semicircular arch and rectangular shapes provide repetitive movement that leads to the entrance of the Kimbell Art Museum. An example of the unique as opposed to the repetitive, the entrance is an open space with implied planes. *(© Kimbell Art Museum, Fort Worth, Texas/Art Resource)*

Figure Case Study 4.2.8 Indirect natural light flows into the interior of the Kimbell Art Museum. Natural indirect daylight provides warmth as well as a positive effect on the interior spaces. *(© Dennis Marsico/CORBIS)*

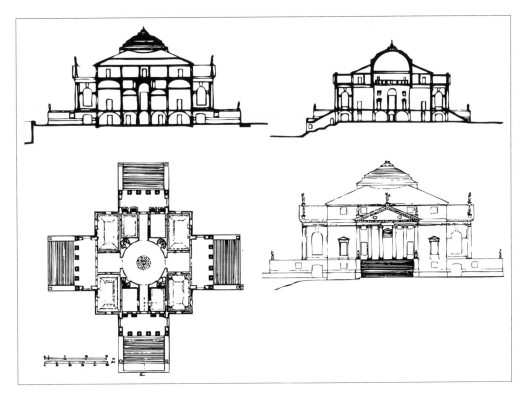

Figure 4.3 Various illustrations of Villa Capra, La Rotunda.

- Views—There are no external views indicated. Rather, views are internal and toward the central space—the focal point.

- Materials and details—This information was not available.

Theoretical Criteria

Designers apply the following theoretical criteria in the applications of historic precedents:

- Line—The visual expression of line: lines that form the plan meet and cross, they are not crossing diagonally, but rather vertically or horizontally. For that reason, line denotes formality. Line is used to articulate the exterior and define the proportions (golden mean). Line also organizes spaces into various shapes and forms.

- Planes—The façade is an organization of openings; doors and windows are placed symmetrically, defining a formal, symmetrical balance. The columns create implied walls before reaching the entrance. The symmetry of the exterior walls (i.e., façade) molds the symmetry of the interior.

- Shape and form—The rectangular shapes become forms repeated in a symmetrical manner with the circle at the center. The circle forms a center radius.

- Mass or volume—The circle shape that becomes a cylindrical form is emphasized because it lies at the center and contains the largest volume.

- Scale and proportion: In plan view, the scale of each space is in proportion to each other and the whole.

- Balance—Symmetrical balance is prevalent through the design: on the façade, entrance, plan view, shapes, forms, and movement.

- Light—Light comes through windows at the highest point of the center space. As light moves throughout the day and seasons of the year, various parts of the center space will be emphasized. Light, both direct and indirect, comes through each of the windows on the façade. Light will affect the space differently at various times of the day and seasons of the year.

- Final analysis—Consistent findings include repetitive forms with a unique cylinder in the center. There are repetitive rectangular geometric shapes and a unique circular shape in the center that provide the emphasis for the entire space. This brings harmony through unity and variety of shapes as well as emphasis of a unique circular shape. This reinforces the symmetry, balance, and geometry as well as parts to the whole. The exterior and interior are placed in symmetrical balance, and the proportioning of the façade is consistent with the golden mean proportions. The symmetrical balance connects the exterior to the interior. Though the site and orientation are not part of this study, the lack of connection to nature may be addressed in another project. Classical proportions of the exterior and interior will be connected, and particularly, the golden mean will be applied to the exterior façade and to the interior structural details. Symmetry will be applied with spatial organization. A connection to nature will be incorporated into the design.

A graphical analysis may be included with the narrative, which will provide a solid, grounded analysis. From the process (i.e., review and analysis), designers learn about the components, including classical elements, proportion, and the architect's inspiration. The strength of the analysis was found in Palladio's application of proportions. Also learned from the analysis was unexpected: a lack of connection with nature. This information then can be applied to the project. Using precedents to inform the design begins by locating one or two buildings and/or interior that will provide needed information. Then the building and/or interior may be reviewed and analyzed.

Sacred Spaces Analysis

Drs. Stephanie Watson and Jane Kucko (2001) are professors of interior design at the University of Minnesota and Texas Christian University, respectively. In their article, "Thorncrown and the Mildred B. Cooper Chapels: Sacred Structures Designed by Fay Jones," published in the *Journal of Interior Design*, they analyzed these two chapels. The criteria used were architecture and the cosmos; number symbolism; and natural rhythms, patterns, and materials. Using these criteria, the following recaps the analysis of the sacred architectural examples:

1. Architecture and the Cosmos
   a. The structure is integrated into surroundings.
   b. Observers' experience coalesces through senses.
   c. Natural environment accented by use of water and light.

2. Number Symbolism
   a. Proportioning system used as framework—golden section, double square, and **vesica piscis**—the intersection of two circles of the same radius.

b. Primary shapes—square, circle, and triangle; and their equivalent forms—cube, sphere, and pyramid used in the environment.
3. Natural rhythms, patterns, and materials
    a. Form and pattern create the relationship of the parts to the whole.
    b. Patterns that embody life-forms should dominate.
    c. Patterns and forms must be repeated.
    d. Materials convey strength and quality by the method used; each material expresses basic nature (pp. 24–25).

The architect of these sacred structures created environments that have become precedents not only for sacred spaces but also for structures that merge into their environment.

From viewing both examples, it is clear that criteria can be manipulated and analysis of historic precedents provides important evidence to inform a design project.

Use of Precedents Reinforced

Reinforcing the research of precedents, an InformeDesign RS, "Meaning and Identity behind Egyptian Architecture" (2008, May 7), summarizes a study that explains the importance of precedents research in the design of Egyptian architecture. Mediterranean and Middle Eastern cultures have influenced Egyptian contemporary architecture, and the influences have created a great opportunity for innovative designs. The author suggests that designers understand the intrinsic meaning of a building's design and the architectural symbolism of the past. These meanings can be reinterpreted into a design project.

Summary

EBD goes beyond research summaries or journal articles. It also includes the examination and analysis of precedents. Learning from past designs provides inspirations for new and innovative ideas for today's designs. This chapter provides a method by which architecture and interior design can be examined and analyzed as well as examples to guide your analysis. From viewing these examples, it is clear that criteria can be manipulated, and analysis of historic precedents provides important evidence to inform a design project. When conducting your examination, the combination of a written narrative and graphics will provide solid, grounded analysis that can then be applied to your project. Clearly, the examination of historic precedents has occurred through the centuries, and will continue to inspire and improve design projects.

Key Terms

design precedents	golden section	historic precedents
dome	golden rectangle	precedents
golden mean	groin vault	vesica piscis

THEODORE

Design Precedents

OBJECTIVES

After reading this chapter, you should be able to:

Locate examples of design precedents

Determine aspects of the design precedents project that can be analyzed

*Analyze aspects of the design precedents project that
may become evidence for a design project*

- DRED COURT -

Design precedents (also called precedents studies or case studies) include completed design projects of various types such as office, hospitality, healthcare, and retail. The process of examining design precedents involves the research of parts of a design or the whole design from which designers gain and apply ideas to other projects. This could also be described as learning from your firm's or another firm's post-occupancy evaluation (POE) project. To accomplish this, designers consult fellow professionals as well as publications. Most often, articles in publications such as trade magazines, books, and online resources provide background on a firm's projects.

At this point, designers have collected the facts and evidence for a particular design project, but the research must come together with a design concept or conceptual ideas that will drive the design. Thus, examining design precedents may identify changes or trends, conceptual design ideas, images, and many more ideas that will inspire and provide information for a design project. Often, design precedents research will identify emerging trends affecting design. It will identify design concepts and ways the concept was implemented, and will also identify new innovative ideas that can be applied to pull a project together. Clearly, learning from others' design situations will aid in solving new design problems or issues that may occur and, ultimately, provide new evidence to inform a design project.

In examining precedents, designers research categories broadly, and then narrow the research to more specific types. For example, design precedents categories, such as retail, may be researched broadly and then within a specific typology, such as boutique or department store. In this example, retail design precedents may also coincide with shopping mall types, such as mega mall, strip mall, or other types.

To learn about successful projects completed by other designers, the following methods can be used:

- Locate past projects found through written sources:
  - Trade magazines—traditional or online
  - Online resources—a specific building or site
  - Design firm's online portfolio
  - POEs from past projects
  - Books of successful design projects

- Interview the design firm or a specific space in your community. The design firm may provide information on aspects of the design (particularly conceptual ideas) that may inform your design—successes and failures.

- Examine the articles and/or actual project:
  - Determine conceptual ideas used and how they were implemented.
  - How did these ideas affect spatial organization, design, materials, lighting, or other aspects of the design?
  - Examine trends or new innovative ideas that may be significant in future design projects.

- Determine what was learned that could be applied to another project.

Additional suggestions for research may be found within the various categories such as branding, images, target market, and new methods for selling. Office design and each of the following design types will also be discussed in greater length in forthcoming chapters.

Office Design

A concept that conveys a firm's image—often called branding—is important. A firm's clientele and the public should be able to see the concept developed by the designers and that the concept portrays the company's image. Conveying of an image tells others, such as clientele and the public, why the firm exists and demonstrates its purpose. The following example is by the HOK group, a globally renowned architectural and design firm with 26 regional offices on four continents. It describes how HOK's design of MediaCom's interiors convey their image (Tisch, 2008).

MediaCom is a multinational strategic planning and buying agency in Toronto, Canada. MediaCom's wish was to have their creative spirit and innovative business style reflected in their interior spaces. This meant that the space needed to be a people-oriented space with an open plan and plenty of light. To encourage the creative spirit, neighborhoods were incorporated into an open plan that included executive offices. Figure 5.1 shows the open plan.

Examining office design precedents involves not only reading but also observing completed examples. While conducting this research, the following questions may be asked:

- Did the concept portray the firm's image or brand?

- How was it portrayed and was it successfully portrayed?

- Was the design concept clearly demonstrated?

- How successful is the design concept?

- Could it have improved and in what ways?

- What was learned that could be applied to another project?

Figure 5.1 Open plan with conference room located within neighborhoods.

Hospitality: Hotel Design

Frequently, hotels are designed to either relate to a corporation's image or to the local outdoor environment such as the hotels at Disney World in Orlando. Therefore, research of ideas on portraying an image may also be conducted. Also, the hotel's image may relate to its design concept.

The hotel's façade, entrance, and lobby create the first impression and showcase its uniqueness. Depending on the design, exclusive or casual and simple, the design concept will also encourage the public to enter or to keep unwanted people away. The design concept of the hotel begins in the entrance and lobby and then continues on to guest rooms as well as other areas for guests such as restaurants and bars (Kilmer & Kilmer, 1992).

Developing innovative ideas in hotel design may improve a traveler's time away from home. David Rockwell, founder and CEO of the Rockwell Group, New York, developed two new conceptual ideas in designing hotels: (1) the creation of a full-scale mock-up, and (2) the invention of the **luxe-oriented** chain hotel—a small luxury **chain**, or franchise, **boutique hotel**. His full-scale mock-up helps potential developers determine whether they want in on the concept. The luxe-oriented chain is the first chain that weds the luxury boutique into a franchise. The design of this hotel also caters to the well-educated business traveler who has higher expectations for design (Hagberg, 2008). Figure 5.2 shows the floor plan of this luxe-oriented boutique hotel, which is generally compact, purposeful, and meets the needs of a specific clientele.

Other research may include current and leisure trends that will reveal desires and needs of vacationers as well as the business traveler. Marketing must identify the ideal consumer, or the target market, and attract that consumer to the hotel. Additionally, with knowledge of the target market, marketing to that particular consumer through branding will increase the number of customers and produce income. Looking ahead to determine future trends is also important, such as the example by the Rockwell Group. Will the **baby boomers** be trendsetters? If the baby boomers are filling the hotels, what will their needs be? Will universal design be crucial? Will there be greater issues with mobility, hearing, and vision that will affect the design relative to materials and color as well as light? Or will the millennial age group be trendsetters? If so, what are their expectations and needs? What design concepts and images will they expect? Examining precedents in trade publication will provide insightful concept ideas to apply to other design projects.

Hospitality: Restaurant Design

In examining design concepts for restaurants, many are thematic, whereas others portray a concept. For example, Rain Forest restaurants, located throughout the United States, are thematic with design and materials that appropriately follow a tropical theme with jungle animals, plants, and intermittent rain. McDonald's portrays a conceptual image of fun and excitement through the design and materials.

Design concepts should be appropriate to the target market, and materials, spaces,

Figure 5.2 A boutique hotel caters to a specific client. This luxe-oriented boutique hotel is compact and meets the needs of its clientele—the business traveler—one who does not need the frills of a great restaurant, shoe shine, or laundry service. The traveler only needs a place to check in, access e-mail, get some sleep, wake to natural light, grab a quick breakfast in the morning, and be on the road. However, it is a traveler who is aware of and expects good design.

Figure 5.3 Bluprint is a restaurant located in the Merchandise Mart in Chicago. The color palette, materials, and lighting are used to shape the varied moods and purposes for the dining experience.

and finishes must be supportive of the dining experience. The following is an example in which the concept meets the needs of the target market, and is expressed in materials, lighting, and color.

Bluprint is a new restaurant in Chicago's Merchandise Mart designed by VOA Associates. With its location, VOA realized that the restaurant design needed to cater to its target market—other designers. The concept was "dining in style," whether for lunch or dinner, or a large group meeting or an individual client meeting. The restaurant was divided into different areas related to moods and purposes. Figure 5.3 illustrates the change in moods and purposes from a dining area to the bar area. Rich color palette, leather and walnut materials, and various lighting applications shape the varied moods and purposes as well as bring style to the dining experience (Lincoln, 2007). Therefore, what can be learned from this example would be to not only fulfill the design concept but also provide ways (e.g., design of layout, materials, colors, lighting) of separating the dining experience.

Research of precedents in restaurant design will often focus on the concept that meets the target market and projects an image or brand. The following questions should be considered:

- How was the image portrayed in the design concept?

- Is there a connection between food served and the design concept?

- Do the interior materials support the concept and image?

- What has been learned that can be applied to another project?

Healthcare Design

For a healthcare facility, the design concept must relate to the design intent and to patient typology. Clearly, a children's hospital will have a different concept than a heart hospital. However, though not obvious to the casual visitor, healthcare facilities must create a welcoming, healing image and environment with an emphasis on the safety of patients and staff.

Hospitals have changed over the years from an institutional feel to a welcoming environment. Tisch (2008a) describes the Children's Healthcare in Atlanta as a joyful, nature-inspired interior. She states that the healthcare facility promotes an uplifting message that "inspires a sense of wonder for children of all ages" (p. 40). Nature and nature-learning areas can be found throughout the facility. This is evident in the floor-to-ceiling iris graphic featuring a nature-learning wall, which is located in an elevator lobby of the Children's Intensive Care Unit (CICU). Figure 5.4 is a photograph of the CICU elevator lobby. Certainly, the concept was carried throughout the entire facility. But most importantly, the concept was based on research that determined the appropriate color selection and supported the use of EBD.

Viewing a hospital project from the patients', visitors', and doctors' perspectives provides surprising information. The design team from NBBJ put the human factor first when they worked on the hospital design for the E. W. and Mary Firstenburg Tower—Phase I of a renewal project at Southwest Washington Medical Center in Vancouver, British Columbia. NBBJ Partner Richard Dallam and his team observed and analyzed the hospital experience from the perspective of the patient, visitor, and medical professional. From their experience, the team learned that the hospital experience could be frightening for the patient and tiring for doctors and nurses. To alleviate the stress and create a "beacon of healing," they needed to consider how to remove the fear factor. So, they started at the entry, a parking lot, and created a garden that included a waterfall. To accomplish this, the parking area was relocated underground. In the lobby, which looks like a five-star hotel, the reception area is behind a wall of glass. Also within the lobby, there are ribbons of luminous copper-painted drywall, and a travertine floor inset with mahogany-colored carpet. Patient floors provide a light, bright, and calming feeling; and rather than antiseptic white or green, the hallways are painted in pale teal and soft cream (Benshneider, 2008). The lobby window wall features painted aluminum frames, limestone-clad columns, and an undulating copper-painted ceiling to soften the space. The feeling the space projects is definitely not hospital-like, but truly like a five-star hotel—a beacon of healing.

Figure 5.4 The design concept for the CICU elevator was based on research, which determined the color selection.

Research of design precedents in healthcare design should begin with a general overview and then focus on the various design types, such as children's hospital, medical office building, and dental office. Articles may be found in trade magazines such as *Interiors and Sources* or *Healthcare Design*. These articles may also provide successes related to conceptual ideas as well as work experience, communication, technology, the patient experience, patient and family involvement in care, safety and infection control, privacy, branding, aesthetics, and sustainability. Additionally, examples of newly designed facilities can be found on Web sites. Such is the case with the Children's Hospital in Aurora, Colorado, which displays images and information about their facility (www.thechildrenhospital.org).

Retail Design

Design concepts for retail spaces are similar to hospitality design in that they reflect the image and/or brand of the establishment. Some may relate to the target market, and others to the product being sold. However, design concepts used for retail design must meet the needs of today's shopper.

Designing an upscale retail space will have an entirely different concept than traditional department stores, such as Macy's or Sears. Holt Renfrew is an upscale, high-end chic Canadian department store. The use of glossy finishes and fixtures, sleek lines, and neutral color palette exemplifies the high-end look (Cannon, 2007). Figure 5.5 shows Holt Renfrew's high-end chic look.

Figure 5.5 The design of the Canadian department store Holt Renfrew creates a high-end look with glossy finishes and fixtures, sleek lines, and a neutral color palette.

Figure 5.6 "Island Jewel" fruit section of the Landmark supermarket emphasizes a clean, bright environment through various design elements— line, planes, and shapes.

Supermarkets

For designers, walking into most supermarkets is almost a design-numbing experience. Generally, determining a design concept for such space is less important than moving people through the space. However, the design of Landmark, a sleek new supermarket in the Philippines, is a design experience. Often in Asia, groceries are purchased at the farmer's market with the traditional stands. But in Landmark, the concept is the opposite with a clean, bright environment accentuated with "swooping curves, floating planes, oval-shaped pods, and a cut-out ceiling that serpentines through the entire space" (Kaufman, 2008, p. 53). The fruit section, "Island Jewel," accentuates the island's specialty and emphasizes the clean and bright concept with the perfect arrangement and sleek finishes. Figure 5.6 illustrates the concept within the "Island Jewel" fruit section.

Research in retail design examines precedents in appropriate use of lighting, display of merchandise, and appropriate colors as well as projecting an image, branding, and conceptual ideas. Ultimately, the design must promote the selling of merchandise to the appropriate client (Kilmer & Kilmer, 1992).

Educational Design

Designs of educational environments must emphasize and promote learning; therefore, design concepts are following that trend. A review of trade magazines, such as *Architecture Minnesota*, may help locate design concepts that have been successful. Some may not only promote learning but also promote a style and regional connection.

The style Abstract Regionalism was applied to the design of the new student center at Tulane University in New Orleans. Abstract Regionalism combines minimalism with the regional environment. The architectural firm VJAA from Minneapolis, Minnesota, designed the new center. Abstract is clearly found in the minimalistic use of products and materials with structural elements visible. Regionalism relates to the clues taken from the New Orleans environment. Some of these clues were to wrap "the building with shading devices—trellised porches, horizontal louvers, canopies, and deep-set balconies—while inserting a series of inventive cooling elements inside: rotating and pendulum fans, solar vents, and radiant chilled-water walls" (Fisher, 2008, p. 31). The design also considered the community; the wrap-around porches enable social mixing that is an important part of the culture in New Orleans. These designs blend abstract design with the tradition-inspired wrap feature on the exterior. What has been learned from this project is not just the application of style but also regional or community concepts so that the building and interiors are integral to the community.

The previous example is a design on a university campus. Educational design precedents research may also include other types—preschool, elementary education, secondary education, libraries, and laboratories. However, research of precedents should begin by examining overall educational design and then focusing on a specific type. Particularly, research of conceptual ideas from other design projects can be applied to another project.

Public and Government Design

Frequently, the concept for public and government offices is to portray the historicism of a community or demonstrate strength. However, some design concepts can still demonstrate strength and also display a modern twist by projecting a forward-looking image. That is the case with the design of a police stationhouse in New York.

The New York Police Department (NYPD) stationhouse will soon be "a little greener" with the first LEED-rated (Leadership in Energy and Environmental Design) police station in New York. It will not only be greener but will also display a modern rather than historic design. The concept for this building is a "linear structure," which will be positioned on an irregular landscape. Its cantilevered canopies will extend over the entrance steps toward the street (Tamarin, 2008a). The building's modern design will fit well into the landscape and bring a modern twist to the concept of governmental buildings. Figure 5.7 shows the modern design of the NYPD stationhouse.

Examination of past and present examples (and even future, such as the stationhouse) will provide evidence for successful applications of the design concept.

Museum Design

The concept for museum design generally relates to the specific typology. For example, the design concept for a modern art museum will be very different from a botanical garden.

The Wing Luke Asian Museum is located in the East Kong Yick Building, Seattle, Washington, which is a restored 1910 social center for Asian immigrants, specifically those

Figure 5.7 The 121st Police Precinct stationhouse will be the first LEED-rated police facility in New York City. The linear structure design makes the site's irregular landscape more welcoming.

of Chinese, Japanese, and Filipino origins. Restoration is the key, which includes preservation and renovation as well as restoration. A major portion of the original building was preserved, including the narrow doorways and corridors. On the upper floors, the smaller rooms were preserved that presently house the museum exhibits. Other elements were repaired and reinstalled while others were recycled. Particularly important is the connection of the museum to the community. Therefore, spaces for meetings, events, performance, and presentation were provided along with "exhibit areas for local artists and emerging Asian Pacific Americans" (Tamarin, 2008b). What seems most important in this design is the connection of the building design and the Asian Pacific American community.

Research of precedents in museum design must look at past designs relative to conceptual ideas that have been applied by other designers. Examine how the concept draws you into the museum. Is it the entrance, or is the type of exhibit that draws the viewer? What is the entrance experience—staircase, façade, and entrances into individual spaces? Do they relate to the concept and the museum type? Examine the circulation path of other designs—what worked, and what needs to improve?

Residential Design

Residential design precedents should focus on conceptual ideas, updating ideas, current trends, or other lifestyles such as the vacation home, second homes, etc. Some examples may be found in *Interior Design, Architecture Minnesota* and other regional architecture magazines, as well as *Kitchens and Baths* and other magazines with residential projects. The following example is a kitchen and bath redesign that updates as well as connects the interior to the exterior.

The master bathroom and kitchen in a 1960s Los Angeles home were redesigned. The new designs were minimalistic, employing simple, clean lines. The original bath and kitchen did not support the views; so, in the remodel, the bath design was not only trendy with clean lines but also took advantage of its windows. As with the bathroom, the kitchen was refocused toward a view through the dining room to the canyons and the Pacific Ocean (Clean Lines, 2007). From this example, the lesson learned may be that updating is not just purchasing new cabinetry, appliances, and/or fixtures but also determining the focus, whether it is on the interior or exterior.

A house, vacation home, or even a cabin on a lake is often a dream for many Americans. Featured on Home & Garden Television (HGTV) was one such example. Rehkamp Larson Architects removed a former seasonal cabin and replaced it with a year-round home and, in the process, salvaged timber beams and siding (LeFevre, 2008). An important aspect of this project was the sustainable aspect—salvaging materials for reuse.

Research of precedents for residential design may include trade publications, designers' online portfolios, or visiting model homes that can provide ideas to drive the design.

Application

This chapter has provided examples within the various design types. In conducting the design precedents research, begin broadly and then narrow to the specifics. For example, when designing a museum for a specific culture (e.g., Chinese), research must begin broad with museums in general, to art museums, and museums related to a variety of cultures. Then, in this process, the focus will gradually narrow to that specific culture.

Summary

Locating information about conceptual ideas and more from the projects of other designers provides evidence for design precedents. In this chapter, we've explored ideas for research to demonstrate where evidence was found in trade publications. Many of these trade publications are also online and help to simplify the search process. These resources as well as interviewing designers or observing their projects will provide evidence from past projects —design precedents—that will improve future design projects. In a forthcoming chapter, you'll find suggestions for collection data that will build your knowledge of evidence-based design for specific design types.

Key Terms

baby boomers   chain   luxe-oriented

boutique hotel

Environmental Considerations

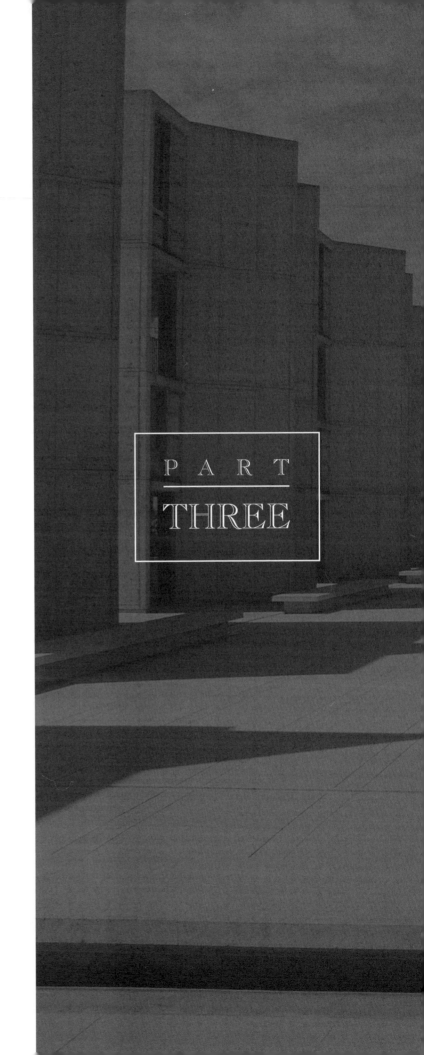

PART

THREE

Structural Needs

OBJECTIVES

After reading this chapter, you should be able to:

Understand zoning regulations and structural needs

Identify and examine evidence regarding structural systems and materials that will improve the design

Understand the importance of the Americans with Disabilities Act, describe its regulations, and examine evidence that will improve the design in accordance with these regulations

Understand the importance of a code search, apply it to projects, and examine evidence regarding regulations that will improve the design

DRED COURT

As you engage in the process of data collection for your design project, consider the larger picture. This includes the zoning, structural and contextual, and sustainability needs of your site. Throughout this book, you will find research noted and ideas for evidence listed that will help you come up with new possibilities for research of your own. This chapter gives you background information related to the larger picture along with examples of related research that has been conducted and ideas for locating new evidence.

Site Zoning

Zoning laws and site location affect many aspects of a building's structure. The designer must consider the entire structure—not only the interior. Building, flooring, ceiling, and mechanical and electrical systems all impact interior design. Additionally, the location of windows, doors, heat registers, and many other features also impact interior design. The design of an interior must be integrated into all systems; it is an integral part of the built environment.

Design must also incorporate regulations for fire and building codes and comply with Americans with Disability Act (ADA) codes for accessibility. These regulations create a safe, healthy, comfortable, and accessible environment for all users; this is called **universal design**. Though the ADA meets regulations for accessibility, environments must extend beyond meeting regulations and become universally accessible. Universal designs are well-planned spaces that meet the needs of every user without attracting attention to people with disabilities. For example, a ramp makes an entrance accessible to meet ADA requirements, but it suggests that those with disabilities must use this method of entering. However, with universal design, an approach is sloped but has a non-institutional, aesthetically pleasing design for all users. Data acquired through fact finding and research for new evidence on structural and contextual needs, building and fire codes, and ADA is important in the development of evidence-based design (EBD). This data will be important in setting foundations for the project.

Designers must understand zoning laws and their effects on the types of buildings that can be built. These laws, for example, may influence growth of an area. After complying with zoning laws and the site chosen, a site analysis will help orient the building to take advantage of environmental conditions that affect the design of the interior.

Zoning Laws

Prior to determining the appropriate location for a building site, designers must complete an investigation of the zoning laws and regulations. Zoning laws control growth of states, counties, and cities as well as subdivisions and urban areas. Land is divided into areas called **zoning districts**. Each zoning district has specific conditions by which land as well as buildings are legally developed and used (Kilmer & Kilmer, 1992; Zoning, 2007). There are zones for commercial, industrial, and residential areas (Kilmer & Kilmer, 1992; Pile, 2003).

Commercial Zones

Commercial zones may also be broken down into Highway Business (HB), Central Business (CB), or Local Business (LB). Within these zones, there may be small shopping areas, small neighborhood grocery stores, large shopping malls, or offices in a downtown district.

Industrial Zones

Industrial zones are divided into light and heavy industrial districts. In light industrial districts, noise, fumes, traffic, or other intrusions are minimal, whereas in heavy industrial districts, these intrusions into the surrounding environment are prevalent. Frequently, industrial facilities are located within industrial parks with their related offices interspersed within or near these facilities.

Residential Zones

Residential zones are separated into low-density, single-family, medium-density, two-family dwellings, and multi-family dwellings. Within some residential zones, housing types and minimum square footages are required (Kilmer & Kilmer, 1992).

A community's zoning regulations are created to separate areas that may be in conflict related to noise, fumes, traffic, etc. However, variances can be filed to the community's zoning commission to allow exceptions. These exceptions may be accepted or denied based on information provided to the requesting party (Kilmer & Kilmer, 1992; Pile 2003).

Zoning Laws and the Interior Designer

Interior designers may be part of a design team that investigates the project location. Therefore, it is important for interior designers to understand zoning and be able to determine an appropriate location for a business or resident relative to zoning laws. Regardless of their participation in choosing a site's location, interior designers should understand zoning laws and reasons for such laws. Zoning may affect the success, security, and comfort of employees or family members because of the location of a business or home. For this reason, the location is an extremely important consideration (Slotkis, 2007).

Other concerns related to zoning can be found in literature. For example, an InformeDesign RS, "Legal Issues and Managed Growth" (2006, May 10), summarizes a study that cited influences on growth management and suggested that conventional zoning may break up areas instead of promoting the preservation of natural environments. Additionally, the InformeDesign RS "Alternative Suburbs for Desert Metropolitan Area" (2006, April 26) notes that some issues may arise that related to a specific region that is growing exponentially (e.g., desert areas in Phoenix). Such growth has affected the development of suburbs. Therefore, in selecting a location, consideration for the environment, infrastructure, landscapes, density, and more must be taken into account.

Another issue relates zoning to diversity. An InformeDesign RS, "Can Zoning Facilitate Diversity?" (2006, December 6), summarizes a study that assessed the impact of land-use zoning on human diversity such as socioeconomic status and race. This study determined that zoning for diverse housing types in residential areas could possibly be linked to diverse incomes. For designers, awareness of various issues may affect decision making in locating commercial or residential structures.

Site and Orientation

After the location has been determined, geography plays a role in the building's design (Slotkis, 2007). The design and placement of a building for a specific site affect the design of interior spaces; therefore, interior designers must understand and have knowledge of the site and a buildings orientation.

Prior to placing a building on a specific site, site plans must be developed. This process involves various professions from urban planning, engineering, and architecture to landscape architecture. **Site planning** not only includes the building within a site but also consideration for parks, highways, and other elements of the environment within the vicinity of the building. "Site planning is the process of harmoniously relating buildings and other structures to the environment and to one another" (Kilmer & Kilmer, 1992, p. 272). Thus, architects and interior designers use these relationships to create an idea or concept that encompasses all three: site, building, and interiors. Therefore, interior designers must relate the interior of the building to its exterior and surrounding site.

Site Analysis

After the site has been selected, a site analysis must be conducted to determine the relationship of the site to the proposed or remodeled building (Kilmer & Kilmer, 1992). The location of the building within the site can influence many factors. For example, consider the effectiveness of passive solar strategies. In summer months and in southern climates, the building's orientation must minimize the sun's rays upon the structure and the interiors and maximize cooling breezes. In the winter and in northern climates, the building's orientation must maximize the sun's rays. Trees shade the summer sun on the south and west, and windbreaks minimize the effects of prevailing winter winds on the north. This also indicates the best location of windows and doors (Site Analysis & Building Placement, 2007). See Figure 6.1 for a graphical representation of the sun's orientation at different seasons.

Figure 6.1 Orientation of the sun to the building affects the decisions made on the interior.

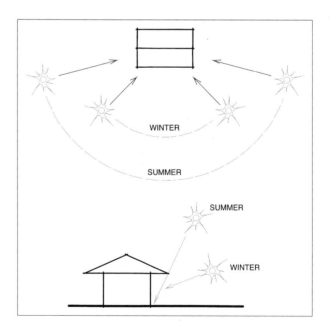

ENVIRONMENTAL CONSIDERATIONS

Table 6.1
Site Analysis Checklist

Use this table to help you analyze all aspects that influence a site design.

Item	Positive or Negative Determinants
Climate	• Wind, precipitation, temperature, solar availability and orientation • Possibilities for energy efficiency and outdoor use
Historic Implications	• Historic or archaeological features to be presented
Social Context	• Relationships and impact of people and their activities to the site or adjacent to it
Zoning and Land Use	• Exiting, proposed, and possible variances needed for any development • Restrictions on building height, setbacks, lot coverage
Topography	• Ground surface changes, slopes, geology, and hydrology resources
Vegetation and Animal Life	• Species, number, location, size, and age of existing trees and implications of site development to these
Utilities	• Existing and new electricity, gas, water, sewer, communication, and other utility needs
Sensory Impacts	• Sounds, smells, and views generated on and adjacent to the site
Access	• Transportation onto the site for pedestrians, vehicles, and goods • Circulation patterns within the site
Man-Made Structures	• Existing buildings and other structures to be removed, left, or remodeled
Legal	• Existing and proposed ownership, leases, rights-of-way, uses, taxes

Source: Kilmer & Kilmer (1992).

Thus, physical characteristics to consider are the topography of the site and lot, its possible view, the prevailing winds, its solar exposure, the noise and/or traffic, and any environmental hazards or pollution. Additionally, the designer must consider social characteristics that relate to the culture of the area where the building will be located. Conflict between the area's cultural values, lifestyles, and expectations should be avoided.

After investigating the site and analyzing compatibility between the building and the site, the building's orientation can be determined. Refer to the Site Analysis Checklist in Table 6.1 and the following questions concerning site analysis:

- What features exist on the site?

- How might a development be oriented to best preserve natural features?

- Is the restoration of existing ecosystems possible?

- What are the characteristics of trees located on the site? Include their location, age, and species.

- Complete a site analysis with a topographic map or survey of the site and make notes (University of Florida, 2007).

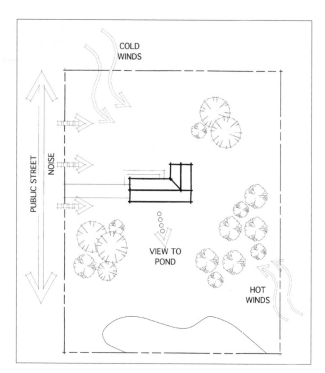

Figure 6.2 An analysis aids the building placement on the site to take advantage of the positive qualities, such as the view, and de-emphasis the negative qualities, such as the prevailing winds and noise.

These questions as well as the checklist in Table 6.1 will help you analyze all aspects that influence site design. Figure 6.2 graphically represents a site analysis and shows the advantages and disadvantages of that site.

Literature may provide evidence regarding issues related to site planning and analysis. For example, an InformeDesign RS, "Trees Improve Neighborhoods near Retail Environments" (2007, August 21) summarizes a study that investigates the effects of retail land use on homeowner satisfaction, and ways to avoid or lessen negative effects, such as traffic and increased noise. Findings from this study are particularly helpful for any project where residential and retail developments may be located near or adjacent to each other.

Structural Needs

Designers consider the health, safety, and welfare of users for the space of any building. The structure must provide for the basic need for shelter—safety and protection from climactic elements, such as solar and other heat, coldness, moisture, and humidity (DeVido, 1996; Kilmer & Kilmer, 1992). The structure must also be sound and be designed to promote a safe environment. Additionally, various structural aspects that provide protection are (1) the pitch or slope of the building's roof to shed rain and/or snow, (2) windows that provide light on the interior during the day, and (3) the overhang that protects the interior from the heat of the summer sun and allows for warmth from the winter sun (DeVido, 1996).

The design of the building should provide convenient and logical entrances and safety in exiting the building. Within the building, the distribution of energy affects health, safety, and welfare of the users. This includes the controlling the interior environment to provide comfort through appropriate lighting, comfortable temperatures and humidity, adequate air, and circulation as well as appropriate selection of materials and equipment that promotes safety (Kilmer & Kilmer, 1992). Reviewing the literature will provide new evidence related to site and structure to inform the design.

Structural Materials

In early civilizations, local materials were used for construction; these included stones in mountainous regions, timber in forests, and ice in arctic regions. When transportation systems were developed, materials could be purchased and delivered from greater distances. Technology also changed materials from heavy timbers and stones to lightweight yet stronger materials that could span greater distances, allow greater height, and unusual shapes. For example, precast concrete or steel beams allow for greater spans and heights. Though new technology allows for limitless possibilities for the design of an interior, cost and inefficiency may render the idea prohibitive. Construction must be cost effective, and materials must be ecologically sound and environmentally safe (DeVido, 1996).

Structural Systems

A variety of structural systems support buildings, including the foundation, walls, floors, and roof. Foundation systems support loads and can be made from precast concrete, masonry, poured concrete, or **concrete masonry units** (**CMUs**) (Bingelli, 2007; Rupp & Friedmann, 1989; Kicklighter, 2000; Spence, 1993). Wood foundations are sometimes designed for below-grade use in light wood-frame construction (Spence, 1993).

Some walls are load bearing while others are not. Walls enclose the building with light wood-frame construction; steel framing; and masonry—brick, stone, CMUs, or other materials. Brick or stone veneers may be applied to wood frame or CMUs. Stone may also be decorative, create openings, and so on (Bingelli, 2007; Rupp & Friedmann, 1989; Kicklighter, 2000; Spence, 1993).

Sheltering the interior, roof systems are constructed of various materials and in various shapes. A reinforced concrete roof may be flat, folded, domed, or shell shaped. Structural steel may be flat, or assembled into a truss system. Space frames are three-dimensional steel structures with triangular steel-support decking (Bingelli, 2007; Rupp & Friedmann, 1989). Buckminster Fuller's **geodesic dome** allows for a great span. Its prefabricated interlocking system eliminated the need for columns and allowed for open interior spaces (Harwood et al., 2008). Air-supported structures are used for winter covers for pools, tennis courts, stadiums, and pavilions for events such as world fairs (Rupp & Friedmann, 1989). An innovative roof and wall system was developed using steel cables in fabric sleeves that are supported by steel or aluminum masts and allow for a great span (Spence, 1993). Günter Behnisch and Partner used this method to design the tent-like structure for the 1972 Olympic Stadium in Munich (Olympiapark München, 2008).

Supporting furnishings as well as people, floor systems may be constructed of various materials such as wood, concrete, precast concrete, structural steel, and steel decking (Bingelli, 2007; Rupp & Friedmann, 1989; Kicklighter, 2000; Spence, 1993).

Ideas for Collecting New Evidence

Examples of research topics into site and structure include building sites in rural areas, affordable housing effects on nearby property values, anchor stores influence on the shopping center, business adjacent to rail lines, and retail development in suburban areas.

Designers need to know the type of materials used in construction because this affects application of interior materials and products. To learn about new products, their application, and the issues related to various structural materials, designers must research (fact finding) the materials in an existing building or on the materials to be used for the new building. Two good sources would be *Architectural Graphic Standards*, by Charles Ramsey and Harold Sleeper, and *Architectural Working Drawings: Residential and Commercial Buildings*, by William Perkins Spence. Both are listed under Resources at the back of this book. You could also look at other books on architectural standards, construction, and/or working drawings.

Research of new evidence on structural materials may be conducted from various sources. The InformeDesign RS, "Strawbales Can Make Good Wall Building Material" (2007, October 31), for example, summarizes the exploration of straw bales as a building material, and lists design criteria to provide benefits, risks, and concerns with the use of straw bales. An InformeDesign RS, "Moisture Permeability in Building Materials" (2007, August 8), summarizes a study of temperature effects on moisture permeability of building materials such as plywood, medium-density fiberboard (MDF), plasterboard, and phenolic foam insulation. An important criterion was identified that altered the moisture permeability rates of wood-based materials: rates are higher when the relative humidity exceeds 60 percent.

Local, State, and Federal Regulations

Building codes set minimum performance and standards for design, materials, and methods of construction. The purpose of these codes is to protect and preserve the environment as well as protect and promote the health, safety, and welfare of people. National building codes were established in 1905. Building codes are set at the federal level; however, state and local codes may be more stringent and must be followed. Clearly, a survey and review of applicable codes is necessary to be sure that all legal restraints are considered (Piotrowski, 2002).

Fire and Building Codes

Fire codes were developed in response to fires that took many lives. The greatest danger in fires is toxicity and smoke inhalation. Thus, building codes govern toxicity levels and smoke development in addition to flame spread. Appendix W offers information about code research for interior spaces. Refer to the following two lists for basic areas of code research for commercial and residential spaces.

Basic areas of code research for commercial spaces include:

- Occupancy type and requirements

- Number of people and concentration of floor loads for specific groups

- Setbacks of a structure: relates to the spread of fire from one structure to another

- Type of construction: fire-resistant materials and construction methods

- Fire-resistant construction: specially constructed walls, doors, ceilings, or floors are placed through a building to slow the spread of fire (given ratings of one hour or more)

ENVIRONMENTAL CONSIDERATIONS

- Major codes deal with
  - Exits and stairs
  - Fire detection
  - Fire suppression: fire extinguishers, sprinklers, hoses

- Barrier-free access
  Basic areas of code research for residential spaces include:

- Egress windows

- Minimum height of ceilings

- Fire-resistant materials as required (depending on type of occupancy)

- Single-family dwelling is different from an apartment complex

Consult the International Building Code (IBC) book to conduct a code search. A code search may be produced using a spreadsheet and later inserted into construction documents. Beyond fact finding, new evidence can be found in literature reviews relative to codes and regulations. For example, Carlson (2008) found that interior elements are contributing factors to tragic fires. In some cases, the lack of extinguishing systems and flammable finish materials were major contributing factors, which means that a thorough code search is essential. This article can help identify criteria that will provide greater safety for a building's occupants.

Americans with Disabilities Act

Universal design is defined as design that has well-planned spaces that meet the needs of every user without drawing attention to people with disabilities. To create a universally designed space, designers must begin with the minimum requirements of the ADA. Bringing ADA requirements into the renovation or preservation of older buildings is called adaptive reuse and can pose greater problems to the designer than new building projects.
The following are examples of minimum requirements for ADA accessibility.

- Parking, walkways—ramps with slopes of 1-foot rise to 12-foot run

- Building entry—3-foot-wide door, low threshold

- Corridors and doors—32-inch-minimum door clearance; 24-inch clearance on pull side

- Restrooms—5-foot-diameter clearance; 3-foot-wide clearance in stall

- Stairs—rise/run 7-inches/11-inches; handrails

- Toilet stall—full clearance

- Special features—water fountain accessibility, signage, telephones, counters, emergency devices

When designing a residential space that must be accessible, the following concerns should be addressed:

- Main entrance and entrance through garage
- Width of hallways
- Kitchens
- Bathrooms
- Vertical movement (e.g., first floor to basement or to upper level)

To complete an ADA search for a specific project, consult an ADA compliance textbook. To emphasize the importance of complying with ADA law, Mazundar and Geis (2002) conducted a case study to examine designers' liability relative to the law. The study states that meeting accessibility guidelines allows for better environments. However, designers must realize that people with disabilities are all different—each has different needs that may vary or change. This makes a strong case for creating universal design.

Application

This chapter's applications, into structural needs, include a list for choosing a construction system. They also include articles that can provide evidence related to structural needs to inform a design project. Though the articles come from the InformeDesign database, other sources may be investigated. These sources include IIDA Knowledge Center Web site, academic journals related to architecture, housing, or interior design.

Bingelli (2007) provides a list for "choosing a construction system where architects and engineers select a building construction system based on" the following criteria:

- Compatibility, safety, and movement
- Ability to resist fire
- Thickness of construction assemblies and building height limits
- Ability to control heat
- Air flow, water migration, and condensation concerns
- Acoustic issues
- Durability and maintenance
- Safety in use
- Aesthetic qualities
- Compliance with building codes and zoning ordinances
- Initial cost: materials, transportation, equipment, and labor
- Life-cycle cost: initial cost plus maintenance and energy consumption over the building's useful lifetime, replacement costs, and interest on investment

- Energy and resource conservation, efficiency of mechanical and electrical systems, health impact of materials used

- Construction safety, industry standards, location of construction, construction equipment requirements

- Construction budgets, schedules, and weather conditions (p. 344)

Though some items on this list are not explored in this book, this list provides a starting point to collect facts and locate new evidence in your research. This may include areas related to zoning, various buildings systems and materials, IBC fire codes, and ADA codes.

InformeDesign contains several RS that pertain to the zoning, site, structures, etc. One RS, "Using Neighborhood History to Shape Neighborhood Future," examines a framework developed to explore the neighborhood environmental history (NEH) of urban areas and applied the framework to improve neighborhood planning, in Cleveland, Ohio (InformeDesign; 2006, February 22).

Additionally, new evidence can be found that will improve the design solution and particularly important are the use of POEs to locate new evidence that can impact future decisions. The InformeDesign RS "Strawbales Can Make Good Wall Building Material" (2007, October 3) states that POEs should not only evaluate circulation and environmental comfort, but also fire safety and accessibility. Design criteria identified include (1) utilizing POEs to assess accessibility and fire safety, (2) using external methods to improve post-occupancy evaluation (POE) process and create ways to routinely evaluate facilities, (3) creating discovery maps from the POE results, and (4) using the results to continue communication with the users and the design solution. Additionally, a very important criterion is to educate staff and crew on proper maintenance of fire protection equipment, which will encourage fire safety. With these criteria in mind, safe interior environments will be designed.

Summary

Information about a project's site provides important background material for its design. Begin by obtaining knowledge about regional or city zoning laws and all other site issues that may affect the project. After a site is selected, a site analysis helps designers determine the orientation and factors that may affect the interior design. Structural materials and specific needs may be determined based on the building type and location as well as sustainability issues—ways to conserve the environment. Refer to this chapter's suggestions for data collection, analysis, and research of new evidence to apply to and inform your design project.

Key Terms

concrete masonry unit (CMU)

geodesic dome

site planning

universal design

zoning districts

zoning law

THEODORE

Contextual Needs

OBJECTIVES

After reading this chapter, you should be able to:

Define contextual needs for a site in terms of the cultural and physical requirements of the surrounding environment

Recognize contextual needs that relate to interior environmental systems such as mechanical, electrical, plumbing, sprinkler, acoustical, and other concealed systems

Examine evidence regarding contextual systems that will improve the design

DRED COURT

To create a space that harmoniously coexists with its surroundings, designers must contemplate a myriad of interrelated conditions between the space and its surroundings. These interrelated conditions are called contextual needs.

Contextual needs stem from both cultural and physical components. Cultural components include historical, religious, and political aspects within the surroundings of a site (Kilmer & Kilmer, 1992). When designing an interior to be used by a particular culture, elements of that culture would be included in the design in order to match the contextual needs of its environs (Nielson & Taylor, 2007). Physical components, on the other hand, include mechanical systems; electrical power sources; communication modes; and water, sewer, and transportation units.

Designers determine and list contextual needs of the site into the program document (Kilmer & Kilmer, 1992). For the site's cultural requirements, designers may note family history, ethnic background, or local culture that may affect decisions related to the design of the interior spaces. How members of a specific culture may use a space is crucial in data collection. For the site's physical requirements, designers integrate acoustics, safety, and security into the building's systems (Pile, 2003). The need for noise control, for example, would be considered as data are collected.

As you read through this chapter, think about the places that you've been. What were the cultural and physical conditions of these environments? How well did the sites meet their contextual needs? How might their designers have done better to meet these needs, and what did they do especially well?

Cultural Requirements

Every culture possesses different needs and requirements, and designers need to be sensitive to them. For example, families with Asian backgrounds may prefer to incorporate more open, flexible spaces. For Muslim families where only family members may view the faces of the women, privacy becomes an important aspect of the design. Chapter 10 further explores this subject.

Physical Requirements: Mechanical Systems

The purpose of mechanical systems is to condition the interior (Bingelli, 2007; Kilmer & Kilmer, 1992; Nielson & Taylor, 2007; Pile, 2004; Spence, 1993). Mechanical systems include heating, ventilation, and air conditioning (HVAC); plumbing; electrical; and communication modes such as telephone and other electronic cables. Mechanical systems such as electrical wiring and HVAC ductwork are usually concealed vertically and horizontally, and are integrated and parallel to one another. In other words, two types of components running together concealed in the walls and flooring systems.

Heating, Ventilation, and Air Conditioning (HVAC)

Mechanical systems create a livable environment by affecting comfort and function (or its use) as well as the appearance of interior space and furnishings (Bingelli, 2007). For example, HVAC controls surrounding air temperature that includes surrounding surfaces, the relative humidity of the air, the air movement, and the air quality or purity (i.e., the absence of odors, dust, and pollen) (Kilmer & Kilmer, 1992). Mechanical systems create noise in the interiors. Studying or sleeping areas should be located to avoid noise from a furnace or air conditioner. In more humid climates, mechanical systems without humidity control affect the appearance of materials in the space; therefore, materials and furnishings must be selected with this in mind.

Sources of Energy

Some buildings use a variety of energy sources. Others get their power from just one source. But almost every building must use energy to operate and to create livable environments. These sources include fossil fuels; natural materials such as wood; geothermal; solar energy; water; nuclear; and wind.

Fossil fuels such as coal, oil, and gas are natural resources with a limited supply. Natural materials such as wood are often secondary heat sources and are usually used to create an ambience rather than for heat. The disadvantage of burning fossil fuels—or wood—is that they can add to both outdoor and indoor air pollution.

Geothermal energy is a renewable source that comes from the earth. To produce geothermal energy, trapped heat in the earth is tapped to create steam and hot water. **Solar energy** is the collection of energy from the sun—a renewable energy source. Electricity is also developed from water (hydroelectric), fossil fuel, wind, solar (photoelectric), and nuclear plants (Kilmer & Kilmer, 1992). "Nuclear energy results from the fusion (joining together) or the fission (tearing apart) of atoms" (Ireland, 2007, p. 39). Though controversial, producing nuclear power is less expensive than other large-scale forms of energy production (e.g., oil refineries). Wind energy has become a major energy source to produce electricity. Using the windmill concept, turbines collect energy from the wind, which is converted into electricity and sold to local power companies. New energy sources continue to be developed such as bioconversion that uses organic materials—crops, algae and seaweed, waste from crops, and waste products—from various sources such as industries and cities (Ireland, 2007).

Heating and Cooling Interiors

The choice of fuel is typically based on local availability and cost. For example, natural gas may be more available in some parts of the country, whereas wind turbines make more sense in others. Residential heating systems include forced air, hot water or steam, and radiant and solar heating. Residential cooling systems work through compressive refrigeration, which is powered by electricity. Large commercial heating systems often use boilers to force air or hot water and, for cooling, chilled water-cooling systems (Spence, 1993). With the water-cooling system, water is chilled and "pumped through cooling coils in an air handler. The cool air in the air handler is moved through ducts into rooms" (Spence, 1993, p. 438). Both methods use compressed refrigeration; however, with the residential method, the electric cooling system is mounted on a forced-air furnace, whereas the commercial system chills water. Energy-saving heating and cooling methods will be discussed in Chapter 8.

Electrical Systems

Electrical systems supply power for illumination and as energy to operate appliances, furnaces, and other electrical equipment. Requirements vary from one building to another; therefore, careful analysis of each building's requirements is vital (Spence, 1993). Communication lines, including those for telephones and other data, are included with the electrical system. One of the most important electrical systems that affect interior environments is lighting.

Lighting

Lighting is an essential element that illuminates the space and affects the design of interiors. It affects users both psychologically and physiologically. The type of lamp, as well as its fixture, affects the quantity and quality of the space (Allen et al., 2004). The following is a list of criteria in selection of appropriate lighting:

- Quantity of light: a measurable amount of light used within the space. This can be accomplished by referring to a chart or through calculation. (Refer to Susan M. Winchip's *Designing a Quality Lighting Environment* or *Fundamentals of Lighting* for calculations.)

- Quality lighting

- Light sources: natural and artificial

- Lighting fixtures (also called "luminaires"), selection, and placement

- Lighting selected for specific areas and activities

- Lighting related to human health and behavior (Winchip, 2005, 2008)

Within these criteria, designers thread various methods of energy conservation. These methods will be further discussed in this chapter and addressed in Chapter 8.

Quality of Light

Quality lighting provides users with an interior that functions comfortably, feels safe, and creates an aesthetically pleasing environment. It also reduces energy costs and conserves natural resources. Clearly, the design of a quality lighting environment applies design theory, human factors, and conservation. This is achieved when designers have complete control over the lighting system, and that includes layered lighting or from both natural and multiple artificial light sources. Natural light sources come from fire, the sun, and daylight, whereas artificial light sources include general ambient (overall lighting), task, and accent lighting (Winchip, 2005, 2008).

Interior designers calculate the quantity of light for new construction and remodeling projects; therefore, it is important for interior designers to learn to measure the quantity

Ideas for Collecting New Evidence

Examples for research into mechanical systems include use of performance of under-floor ventilation systems, bioclimatic housing prototypes, air flow and comfort, conservation of water in hotels, improved ventilation improves job performance, and concern for crawl space air leaks into interiors.

Table 7.1		
Color Rendering Index		
Lamp	CRI Index	Location
Incandescent	95	Residential
Premium cool white compact fluorescent light (CFL)	88	Residential/Retail
Premium 4-foot fluorescent	85	Retail
Premium warm white CFL	84	Residential
Common warm white CFL	80	Residential
Common 4-foot fluorescent lamp	62	Office
Common high-pressure sodium	22	Street lighting

Source: Color Rendering (2007).

of light. The quantity of light in a space is determined through one of two calculation methods: lumen or point-by-point. For calculating the quantity of light, refer to Winchip's books, *Fundamentals of Lighting* (2005) and *Designing a Quality Lighting Environment* (2008).

Quality lighting is enhanced by color rendition and temperature of the light source. The **color rendering index (CRI)** number ranges from 0 to 100 and relates to the way an object appears under a light source. "The higher the number, the better the color rendering ability of the lamp" (Winchip, 2008). For example, an incandescent lamp is approximately 95 compared to the common 4-foot fluorescent lamp, which is 62 (see Table 7.1). Lamps with 80 or more CRIs are generally considered high and closer to natural light. "CRI values should only be compared when the light sources being compared have similar color temperature ratings" (Color Rendering, 2007).

Color temperature, or chromaticity, indicates the degree of red or blue from both natural and artificial light sources and is measured in **kelvins (K)**. If the number of kelvins is lower, the apparent color of a light source is warmer and appears as a tone of red. Conversely, if the number is higher, the apparent color of a light source is cooler and appears as a tone of blue. For example, measured in kelvins, the warm color from a candle is approximately 2000K, whereas the cool daylight is 5000K. Also, measured in kelvins, lamps range from 3000K to 4100K (Winchip, 2004). Clearly, quantity of light and quality lighting in spaces is important in an effective design of an interior.

Selecting and Placing a Lighting Fixture
The choice and placement of a fixture affects the function, aesthetics, and economics of the interior. First, consider the direction of light—direct, indirect, semi-direct, semi-indirect, or diffused. Next, determine the appropriate type of mounting. Luminaires, for example, may be recessed, surface mounted, suspended, tract, structural, portable, or furniture integrated. Lamps used in luminaires include incandescent, fluorescent, and high-intensity discharge (HID). All of these lamps are available in a variety of sizes, shapes, and materials. These lamps or light sources can be categorized as general/ambient, task, and accent lighting (Winchip, 2005, 2008).

Within this process of selecting the fixture and lamp, the designer must make some decisions about energy conservation and economics. Government agencies and professional organizations have established standards and codes to promote energy conservation. Designers must research for local, state, and national regulations to gather information on energy-efficient lighting systems. Goals for specifying energy-efficient lighting systems include reduction of nonrenewable resources, control of the consumption of renewable products, minimization of pollution to air, water, and soil, protection of natural habitats, elimination of toxic substances, and reduction of light pollution (Winchip, 2008).

Lighting is selected for specific areas and activities. To obtain quality lighting, designers must keep in mind the type of area (e.g., kitchen) and human activity taking place (e.g., preparing meals). Additionally, the interior elements—materials, colors, texture, and furniture, as well as the architectural elements—shape, details, and more—affect the quality of light. Careful consideration must, therefore, be taken to select and layer lighting for the best results (Winchip, 2008). Research for new evidence on the quality of lighting will inform the design solution. For example, Winchip (2005, 2008) provides examples of such integrations.

The Physiological and Psychological Effects of Lighting

Lighting affects human health and behavior (i.e., the physiological and the psychological) both positively and negatively. For example, poor lighting can cause eyestrain, headaches, skin cancer, premature aging, and other conditions. Flickering lights may trigger seizures for individuals with epilepsy. Similarly, lighting affects human emotions. Sunshine may generate cheerful feelings, whereas gloomy conditions can generate "feelings of depression and sadness" (Winchip, 2005, p. 325). Artificial lighting can create perceptions of cheerfulness or encourage gloom. More information on lighting can be found in Winchip's books from 2005 and 2008. Research of new evidence to inform the design can include studies on how lighting may affect human health and/or behaviors.

Researching Lighting

During the programming phase, designers collect data on lighting and must address a variety of issues in order "to design a quality lighting environment" (Winchip, 2005, p. 608). Methods of data collection include interviews, surveys, field observations, research, and interior assessments (Winchip, 2005). Interview and survey questions for residential interiors focus on needs and specific activities that occur in each space. Interview and survey questions for commercial interiors focus on client and end-user perceptions of lighting design, and human behavior (i.e., activities and tasks) in the space. Through interviews and observations, interior designers identify the role of lighting activities, and anticipate changes to alleviate future problems (Winchip, 2005, 2008). See Table 7.2 to help you assess interior spaces relative to lighting.

Examples of additional interior lighting assessments are found in Appendices T and U. These methods of data collection will inform the design with facts and new evidence and lead the designer toward areas of research. Additionally, a review of literature relative to lighting will provide insight and inform the design solution.

One topic for research may be the evaluation of the quality of lighting in various types of interior environments. An InformeDesign RS, "Researching Lighting Quality in Offices with Images" (2006, August 23), summarizes a study that investigated the quality

			Luminaire Style/ Color/ Finish	Light Distribution[c]	Location	Lamp	Wattage/ Code CRI CCT	Ballast/ Transformer	Controls	Location of Windows/ Other Apertures for Daylight	Problems/ Remarks
Room	Lighting Method[a]	Lighting Layer[b]									

Table 7.2

Interior Assessment

Client: Location: Date:

Lighting Inventory:

[a] Daylight, recessed, surface mounted, suspended, track/cable, structural, furniture integrated, portable
[b] General, task, accent, decorative
[c] Indirect, direct, semi-direct, semi-indirect, diffused

Source: Winchip (2005).

of office lighting by using rendered images, which were adapted depending on the user's preference. Three suggested criteria of which to be aware include: (1) great variation of light levels may be perceived brighter than uniform light levels; (2) medium brightness and variation in light levels may be more attractive to the majority of users; and (3) color images that are high quality and computer rendered can be used for lighting quality research and identifying optimal lighting design based on users' preferences.

An InformeDesign RS, "Evaluating the Quality of the Office Environment" (2005, March 1), summarizes a study that compared spatial characteristics and the indoor air climate in offices to evaluate the work environment. Design criteria gleaned from this research suggested (1) providing daylight into the workspaces as well as visual access to the outdoors, (2) providing informal meeting spaces to promote communications, and (3) allowing staff to control temperature and create an individual comfort.

Communication Lines

Drawings that indicate power outlets also show telephone and communication systems. This means that interior designers must indicate the location of lines and outlets for equipment such as telephones, computer terminals, intercommunication systems, public address speakers, and buzzers. Through interviews and observations, designers collect data regarding clients' needs and desires for locating telephone and communication systems.

It is also important to review the literature with attention particularly paid to periodicals for new evidence regarding communication within today's interiors such as the use of cell phones and other electronic devices that may enhance as well as disrupt the office or other environments.

Plumbing Systems

Plumbing systems relate to water intake, conditioning, heating, and disposal (Nielson & Taylor, 2007). Water is supplied to fixtures through pipes, whereas drains and sewer lines dispose of waste. A trained plumber is required to install the plumbing system (Spence, 1993). In nonresidential spaces, a plumbing chase (i.e., a larger plumbing wall area) is needed to carry the water to and waste from the building. In residential spaces, plumbing runs vertically and horizontally through the structure's framework (Nielson & Taylor, 2007).

Plumbing codes specify the minimum number and type of fixtures required in residential and nonresidential buildings (Spence, 1993). Fixtures include lavatories, water closets, bidets, and sinks, and porcelain is the most common material with the widest color selection. Today's residential bathrooms have become larger, and some fixtures have even become sculptural, furniture-like, or pedestal forms. Showers and bathtubs are frequently made of fiberglass with curved corners and devoid of crevices for easy cleaning (Allen et al., 2004). Specific design standards are required for handicap accessibility (Spence, 1993).

The number of stalls in women's restrooms is a concern and, in designing such spaces, evidence from observation and literature review may improve future restroom designs. An InformeDesign RS, "Unequal Restroom Waiting" (2005, December 21), for example, summarizes a study on the issue of inequality in men's and women's use of toileting fixtures in public restrooms. The authors suggest that standards for the number of fixtures be determine based on user needs rather than type.

Sprinkler Systems

Sprinkler systems, which include piping and water supply, provide fire protection to the interior (Spence, 1993). They are designed for and installed in high-rise buildings, hotels, and public buildings (Allen et al., 2004). Though interior designers must understand sprinkler systems, specialists, who understand the correct uses of features such as the pipe size and location of sprinkler heads, are required to design them (Spence, 1993). However, the interior designer works with the specialist to verify the location of sprinkler heads and provide appropriate clearance at each location (Bingelli, 2007). An InformeDesign RS, "Post-Occupancy Evaluation of Hospital Accessibility and Fire Safety" (2007, October 3), not only points out the importance of post-occupancy evaluations (POEs) but also the concern for proper maintenance of fire protection equipment—such as sprinkler systems.

Acoustics

Ideas for Collecting New Evidence

When researching commercial spaces, examine ways of increasing hotel profits through planning related to guest-room floors, the relationship between appliance life and water quality, and energy use in residential buildings.

Excessive noise is disruptive. To control sound, sound-absorbing materials can be applied in construction. Sound-absorbing materials may be installed or applied on the interior floors, walls, and ceilings as well as furniture (Nielson & Taylor, 2007; Pile, 2003). During the selection process, designers consider sound-absorbing material especially in nonresidential spaces where there are greater numbers and movement of people (Nielson & Taylor, 2007).

The noise reduction coefficient (NRC) for materials provides information on the amount of sound absorption. For example, concrete or terrazzo is .02; wood is .03; carpeting on concrete is .45; and carpeting with pad is .70 (NRCs, 1998). Web sites, such as that of the Norlite Corporation, are good resources to find lists of materials and their NRC ratings.

Articles from research or trade publications can provide ideas to improve acoustical qualities with the interior environment. Madsen (2006) discusses ways to achieve a balanced acoustical design. Suggestions include using sound-masking technology as well as installing interior products that have acoustical properties. Also suggested is the hiring of an acoustician who can give advice to optimize acoustics through the layout and the design.

Other Concealed Systems

Designers must also consider various other systems. Some of these systems are designed for convenience, such as central vacuum systems, whereas others are designed for protection, such as security systems and fire alarms.

Central Vacuum Systems

Central vacuum systems are installed in the walls of many residential interiors. These systems are especially convenient for the multi-story house occupant who might otherwise have to carry a portable vacuum cleaner up and down stairs (Allen et al., 2004). However, these systems are very difficult to retrofit unless the existing building is gutted.

Security Systems

Security systems are also concealed within the walls in both residential and nonresidential buildings. Their sensing devices trigger alarms and turn on lights as well as alert a security company and/or local law enforcement (Allen et al., 2004). Security is more important than in the past, and research is continually being conducted on ways to make our buildings secure. Suttell (2006) suggests that the elements of a good security plan will vary from building to building; however, all plans should focus on the physical systems, operation, and education and training.

Transportation Units

Transportation units include elevators, platform lifts, escalators, and dumbwaiters. Designers may be consulted to select finishes for elevator cabs as well as elevator lobbies at each level. "Building codes heavily regulate elevator design, installation, and signals, and

... ADA mandates minimum dimensions for wheelchair accessibility" (Binggeli, 2007). Some interiors are retrofitted with vertical platform lifts. Lifts take up less space and are more economical than an elevator. Escalators are frequently used in retail establishments to allow customers to view merchandise as they move from level to level. However, escalators take up a great deal of space and require additional adequate space at loading and unloading points. Dumbwaiters are used to move products from one level to another. In hospitals, dumbwaiters move linens, pharmaceuticals, and food. In department stores, dumbwaiters move merchandise. In multilevel restaurants, dumbwaiters transport food and return dirty dishes (Bingelli, 2007).

Fire Alarms

Fire alarms include smoke- and heat-sensing devices. These devices set off an audible and visual alarm and are required by code in commercial buildings (Allen et al., 2004). Sprinkler systems are fire safety devices, and were discussed earlier in this chapter.

Application

A variety of articles provide evidence related to contextual needs. These articles come from various sources such as the International Interior Design Association (IIDA) Knowledge Center, American Society of Interior Designers (ASID) Knowledge Center, and InformeDesign databases. The following are examples of articles that provide evidence to inform a design project.

The IIDA Knowledge Center Web site contains articles relative to energy within a case study section. The article, *Cold-Climate Case Study for Affordable Zero Energy Homes*, by Norton and Christensen (2006), discusses the application of zero energy methods for affordable housing. Another case study, *Exit Signs*, discusses how the change to Energy Star–labeled light-emitting diode (LED) exit signs will reduce energy and re-lamping costs as well as pollution power that plants produce (Brons & Koltai, 2000). Another article, *The Performance of Remodeling Contractors in an Era of Industry Growth and Specialization* by Will and Baker (2007), analyzes the structure, performance, and survivorship trends of professional remodeling contractors.

The ASID Knowledge Center also provides several articles in its Universal Design section. An article, *Universal Design: A Commitment to Accommodate All*, shares information on renovating for universal design. ASID also provides other Universal Design links (ASID, 2008).

InformeDesign contains several RS that pertain to contextual needs. RS examples include "Beach-Going Habits of Coastal Residents" (InformeDesign, 2005, April 2), "Emotional Reactions to Threatening Natural Encounters" (InformeDesign, 2006, September 20), and "Mechanical Lifts in Healthcare Facilities" (InformeDesign, 2005, July 15). RS examples that focus on fire safety and fire alarms include "Fire Alarm Levels in Senior Care Facilities" (InformeDesign, 2005, March 10), "Hospitality Building Design and Materials Impact Fire Safety" (InformeDesign, 2003, July 22), and "Fire Exits and Instruction Facilitate Safe Evacuation" (InformeDesign, 2003, June 3).

Summary

This chapter provides background information related to contextual needs—cultural and physical. Cultural contextual needs relate to family history, ethnic background, or a local culture. Such needs are important to lifestyle, religious beliefs, or customs of individuals or groups of people. This topic will be further discussed in Chapter 10. Physical contextual needs relate to various systems in a building such as mechanical, electrical, plumbing, sprinkler, acoustical, and other concealed systems.

Mechanical systems are designed to condition the interior for comfort and allow the user to function in the space as it was intended. These systems are powered through energy sources, both renewable, such as sun and wind, and nonrenewable, such as fossil fuels. New sources are continually being developed that will be energy efficient and capable of bioconversion.

Electrical systems supply power for illumination and energy for various types of equipment. Lighting is essential to illuminate spaces and affect the design of interiors and the user—psychologically and physiologically. Therefore, choosing appropriate lighting using criteria listed in the text is crucial. During the programming phase, data collection must focus on specific needs of the occupants. Additionally, research provides new evidence that will inform and improve the design.

Plumbing codes specify the minimum number and type of fixtures required in residential and nonresidential buildings. Within nonresidential public buildings, the number of stalls in women's restrooms has been inadequate. Studies suggest standards in equality for men's and women's use of toileting fixtures in public restrooms.

Because contextual needs address both building and space, they must coexist harmoniously to provide a comfortable interior environment. Additionally, the various systems discussed relate to users' needs—human factors: physiological, anthropometrics, ergonomics, psychological, and sociological; these will be further addressed in Chapter 9. These various needs affect the health, safety, and welfare of occupants; therefore, it is important to conduct research for new evidence that will inform and improve your design.

Key Terms

color rendering index (CRI)   kelvins (K)   solar energy

THEODORE

Sustainability Needs

OBJECTIVES

After reading this chapter, you should be able to:

Explain how the term sustainable design relates to preservation, restoration, renovation, and adaptive reuse

Implement cost-saving and environmentally friendly methods of using energy

Observe how products and materials selected for projects affect the global environment

Select materials and products that promote good indoor air quality; then develop a list of these materials and products that are appropriate to the project at hand

List the basics of LEED requirements for improving global and interior environments

Develop areas for research of new evidence in all of the previously mentioned areas to inform and improve the design

DRED COURT

Environmental issues are at the forefront of design, and the term most frequently used that relates to the environment is **sustainable design**. This chapter addresses various issues related to our environment and provides examples of evidence that can inform designs. This topic includes issues such as a global approach to design; **preservation, restoration, renovation,** and **adaptive reuse**; sources of energy and energy-saving methods, **indoor air quality (IAQ)**, and selection of materials based on sustainable practices.

Sustainable Design

Various terms have been used to represent sustainable design: **green design, environmental design, cradle to cradle (c2c),** and **eco-effectiveness**. All represent a concern for the environment. But what exactly is sustainable design? The National Park Service's Guiding Principles of Sustainable Design (n.d.) offers a very good definition:

> The concept of sustainable design has come to the forefront in the last 20 years. It is a concept that recognizes that human civilization is an integral part of the natural world and that nature must be preserved and perpetuated if the human community itself is to survive. Sustainable design articulates this idea through developments that exemplify the principles of conservation and encourage the application of those principles in our daily lives. (para. 6)

For design fields, the process of sustainable design uses products, materials, and methods that impact humans and the global environment in the least possible way; this type of design also includes a **life-cycle assessment** of a designed environment or product from raw material to disposal.

Global Approach to Environmental Conservation

Industrial practices have negatively affected the ecological balance, and as limited **nonrenewable resources** are being depleted, new ideas and practices are being developed to use **renewable resources** as well as to conserve resources. In the past, design decisions were based on function, need, aesthetics, and style; however, today, environmental issues that affect our global environment as well as the interior environment have changed the decision-making process. Designers are concerned about how materials are extracted or produced (i.e., the manufacturing process) from creation through end of use. The following provides the basic steps of the life cycle of a product with concerns for sustainability noted:

1. Extraction—What is the method of extraction and the type of resources used (e.g., limited or sustainable)?

2. Production—How does the manufacturing process impact the environment?

3. Finishes—How do toxic finishes impact the air quality of interiors?

4. Packaging—Are the packaging materials nonrenewable and so become waste at the destination?

5. Transportation—Is the transportation fueled by nonrenewable energy (i.e., raw material to installation)?

6. Installation and use stage—Do harmful vapors and dust impact the air quality of interiors?

7. Maintenance—Do toxic products impact the air quality of interiors?

8. End of product life—Is the product's life cycle cradle to cradle (i.e., renewable, recyclable, or otherwise reclaimable) or **cradle to grave** (i.e., waste after current use)?

This list covers the basics of what designers must consider when moving toward sustainable design.

Preservation, Restoration, Renovation, and Adaptive Reuse

Preservation, restoration, renovation, and adaptive reuse of buildings and related materials are related to sustainable design. In the United States, many buildings are constructed and then, as they become obsolete, demolished (Pile, 2003). Many buildings, however, have historical attributes that spare them from the wrecking ball and must then, of course, be considered in the redesign. There are several methods of eliminating the demolition of our buildings. These methods are preservation, restoration, renovation, and adaptive reuse—all of which create sustainability.

Preservation refers to the maintenance of the original structure, materials, and form so that none deteriorate or are demolished. The process of preservation generally begins when the building is constructed, but can occur at any point during its life. Preservation is a joint effort by many professions, including archeologists, historians, museologists, architects, and experienced craftsman (Kilmer & Kilmer, 1992). Figure 8.1 is an example of the preservation of Drayton Hall. Built in 1738, Drayton Hall is the oldest surviving example of Georgian Palladian architecture and is located outside Charleston, South Carolina. The National Trust for Historic Preservation has preserved this southern plantation house.

Restoration means returning a structure to its original appearance and integrity by removing later additions and modifications. Often, missing details are replaced with the same original type of material and/or repaired. Restoration is not limited to the structure or exterior. Interior features (e.g., woodwork, wall and window treatments, floor coverings, and light fixtures), furniture, and other objects or accessories can be included as part of a restoration (Kilmer & Kilmer, 1992). A true restoration will restore or replace using original materials.

Renovation or rehabilitation refers to upgrading or altering existing buildings to increase their useful life and function. Historical, cultural, or architectural features of a building can be preserved in the process (Kilmer & Kilmer, 1992). In other words, not all of the building needs to be preserved, but features may be preserved and reused in the design.

Figure 8.1 The Drayton Hall interior has been preserved and reflects its original time period.

Designers identify features of the building that will be preserved and/or renovated. Figures 8.2 and 8.3 are before and after photos, respectively, that illustrate the renovating or rehabilitating of a space for today's use.

According to Slotkis (2007), "over time, buildings become obsolete" (p. 107). Thus, to preserve a building shell or structure, buildings can be adapted for reuse to meet today's needs. Therefore, rather than demolishing the building, an existing structure is modified to serve a useful purpose while the character of the original structure remains. Though the structure is preserved or restored, the use of the interior can become entirely different from the original interior (Kilmer & Kilmer, 1992).

Preservation, restoration, renovation and adaptive reuse are forms of sustainable design. It is becoming more important to sustain buildings and eliminate waste during construction and redesign in order to preserve and protect our environment for future generations. This must include the reusing, reducing, and recycling of materials and products from the construction to completion and, when built, in maintaining the building.

There are many research summaries or articles in journals and/or trade publications that address these issues. A couple examples are included here. An InformeDesign RS, "Architecture in Historic Districts" (2006, July 17), summarizes a study that examined perceptions and attitudes of imitation historic architecture and historic preservation. Often, imitation historic architecture can be found in tourist areas as well as in new developments in order to create identity. In fact, some review boards require specific imitation styles. However, this may detract from the historic districts within a city. Therefore, the designer should understand the community's history and determine whether or not to imitate historic architecture.

An InformeDesign RS, "Preserving Traditional Housing in Beijing" (2004, August 31), summarized a study that examined challenges of preserving the traditional Chinese courtyard in Beijing's redevelopment. Results from this study may be applied to the preservation of American traditional housing. Design criteria provide areas of awareness as well as considerations. Some criteria relate to financial resources that may be limited or regulated. Some criteria consider the native residents and suggest that consequences may result from the displacement of residents by such factors as luxury housing. Criteria also indicate the benefits of a wide range of local residents becoming involved in the process. To maintain a sense of historicism among the residents, the vernacular of their housing must be preserved. Sometimes, however, a variety of styles exists in a particular district; this can bring up additional challenges for historic preservation. The uniqueness of the district and its culture base is an important consideration.

Sustainable Design in Interiors

Not only is it important to preserve, restore, reuse, and recycle, it is also important to save or conserve energy and reduce our use of resources. To understand these issues, a brief discussion describes various sources of energy and ways to improve energy, i.e, solar. Suggested research topics will provide new evidence related to energy.

Sources of Energy

Fossil fuels such as coal, oil, and gas are natural resources with a limited supply. Natural materials such as wood are often secondary heat sources; these are typically used to create an ambience rather than as a source of heat. Their disadvantage, along with being a natural resource, is that they add to both outdoor and indoor air pollution.

Figure 8.2 *Above*: This 1924 photo shows women at sewing machines in the former Munsingwear plant. Renovation of the interior began in the 1980s.
Figure 8.3 *Right*: The interior of the former Munsingwear plant was renovated into a design center, the International Market Square. Design showrooms, offices, and multistory residential housing occupy Minnesota's largest renovated building. This is an example of adaptive reuse in which the interior has been renovated and the exterior preserved.

Electricity is a source of energy developed from water (hydroelectric), fossil fuels, geothermal, wind, solar (**photoelectric** and **photovoltaic**), and nuclear plants. Of these, wind and solar are renewable sources.

Geothermal energy comes from the earth. To produce geothermal energy, heat trapped in the earth is tapped to produce steam and hot water. Solar energy is the collection of energy from the sun; this is a renewable energy source.

Solar Energy

Solar energy can be used for heating and cooling, and for generating electricity. However, the greatest concern in using sunlight is that it can cause overheating and fading of colors. Therefore, the design of solar energy will affect interior comfort and aesthetics (Kilmer & Kilmer, 1992; Nielson & Taylor, 2007).

There are two types of solar energy: active methods and passive methods. **Active solar energy** uses technology and mechanical equipment to collect solar radiation and convert it to thermal energy (see Figure 8.4). Active solar uses collectors, a transport unit, storage container, and ductwork. Collectors are used to capture the sun's rays through a panel facing south. The transport unit moves the heat from the collectors into storage. The distribution system, or ductwork, distributes heat from storage to spaces throughout the building. The system also requires controls such as a thermostat, sensors, and other monitoring devices to control the amount of heat, as do other heating methods (Kilmer & Kilmer, 1992; Nielson & Taylor, 2007; Spence, 1993).

The disadvantages are that a backup heating source is needed if the system cannot produce enough energy on cloudy days or at night. Other sources, such as wood-burning stoves, fireplaces, or other conventional methods are needed for such situations (Kilmer & Kilmer, 1992; Nielson & Taylor, 2007; Spence, 1993).

Active solar systems are more expensive than passive solar. Passive systems use natural, or "passive," means to transfer energy from the sun, but there is little or no mechanical equipment. Passive solar takes advantage of physical laws of heat transfer and is an integral part of a building's design. This type of system requires that the user be an active participant in order to control the temperature variation (Kilmer & Kilmer, 1992; Nielson & Taylor, 2007).

There are various ways to collect **passive solar energy**. The simplest method is direct, which requires that an occupied space serve as the collector. This would include a large expanse of south-facing glass. However, shading, roof overhangs, and vents are needed to restrict sunlight or exhaust heat. Additionally, to prevent major heat loss, windows must be insulated with appropriate glass or window treatments (Kilmer & Kilmer, 1992; Nielson & Taylor, 2007; Spence, 1993).

To design such a space, thermal mass is needed to absorb heat. Concrete, brick, and other dense materials trap the sun's heat and release it later into the space. The drawback is that excessive amounts of direct sunlight can fade/damage the interior (Kilmer & Kilmer, 1992; Nielson & Taylor, 2007; Spence, 1993).

With the indirect method, a separate space receives the sun's energy and heat. Two ways used in this method are the **Trombe wall** and **roof pond**. Trombe walls are created using large expanses of south-facing glass with a dark-colored thermal mass set only a few inches behind the glass. The mass receives the sun's heat and stores it and then slowly releases it into adjacent occupied space. Vents placed low and high in Trombe walls take

ENVIRONMENTAL CONSIDERATIONS

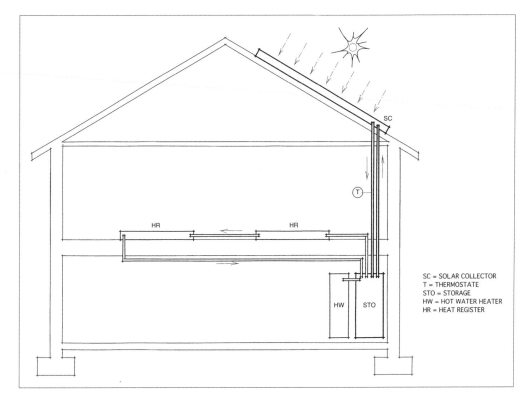

Figure 8.4 The components of an active solar collection system include: collector, transport, distribution, storage, backup source, and controls.

advantage of the natural convection loop with hot air rising and cool air falling (Kilmer & Kilmer, 1992; Nielson & Taylor, 2007; Spence, 1993). The roof pond also requires thermal mass but is located on a roof. Because the liquid medium must not be subjected to extreme heat and freezing temperatures, this method can only be used in more moderate year round temperatures (Kilmer & Kilmer, 1992).

Isolated gain can occur in two conditions: sunrooms or greenhouses, and **thermosiphoning.** Sunrooms or greenhouses are frequently used in both residential and commercial buildings. These types of spaces work efficiently when coupled with thermal mass storage and movable insulation devices. Thermosiphoning uses convection, the system and collector that are independent of the occupied space. Heat collected is transferred and rises to an occupied space (Kilmer & Kilmer, 1992; Nielson & Taylor, 2007).

Energy Losses

Interiors are heated directly by burning fuels in the space or indirectly by transferring a heated medium to the space from a central plant. Kilmer and Kilmer (1992) describe the four ways that heat is lost or transferred into the interior.

- **Convection**—heat transfer through the atmosphere by motion of cool or warm air currents across a surface (metaphor: blowing wind)

- **Radiation**—heat transfer through space, such as heat radiated from the sun, a fire, or a person (metaphor: sun, fire, or people)

- **Conduction**—heat transfers directly through matter, as from a warm material to a cooler material (metaphor: flat pan to cooktop)

- **Evaporation**—heat is lost through the process of moisture turning into vapor (metaphor: fog) (p. 290)

There are three ways to conserve energy and reduce heat transfer or loss. The first is to insulate—the greater the resistance to heat (R value), the better the insulation. The second is to caulk around windows and doors that can leak cold air into the building. The third is to lower the thermostat in the winter—68 degrees is a reasonable recommendation—and to raise it in the summer (78 degrees is an efficient setting) (Kilmer & Kilmer, 1992).

Indoor Air Quality

Poor IAQ is a health issue. Though often odors are associated with poor IAQ, many toxic chemicals do not give off odors. Thus, interior designers must be knowledgeable about ways that IAQ can affect the well-being of clients.

In the 1940s, concerns surfaced related to outdoor air pollution; however, though indoor air contaminants were present and causing illness as early as the 1940s, concerns were not addressed until the 1980s and today, IAQ is still often compromised with various toxic chemicals.

Problems developed due to IAQ can be attributed to modern technology, synthetic materials and fibers, newer cheaper products (i.e., plastic, chemical by-products), and the energy crisis of the 1970s, which led to the tightening of buildings.

The Environmental Protection Agency (EPA) has defined factors affecting IAQ; these include temperature, relative humidity, contaminant source, and air exchange rate. They also suggest the following ways to positively affect IAQ: (1) an acceptable temperature must be maintained; (2) an acceptable relative humidity must be maintained; (3) airborne and contaminant sources must be controlled; and (4) air must be adequately ventilated. Interior designers must be particularly concerned about the sources of indoor air contaminants.

Sources of Indoor Air Pollution

Indoor air quality is affected by various sources from poor outdoor air quality to indoor activities; these include:

- Outdoor air, soil, and water

- Building materials, structure, envelope

- Building system, HVAC, plumbing

- Indoor finishes and furnishings

- Equipment, appliances, office machines

- Maintenance, cleaning products

- Personal hygiene products, cosmetics

- Occupants' activities

Many of these various sources emit gases into the air that may be from **volatile organic compounds (VOCs)**, formaldehyde, or other chemicals. **Toxins** from various chemicals found in products and materials are absorbed into other materials and later desorbed back into the interior; this is called the **sink** effect. Of particular concern is the level of toxicity from chemicals found in the materials and products used in an interior space. Therefore, materials must be carefully researched, selected, and specified to minimize indoor air pollution.

Emissions from VOCs as well as microbial contamination can affect IAQ, which affects human health. Illness may be acute (temporary) or chronic (ongoing). To evaluate toxins in an interior, three methods may be used. One is a sensory response—smelling an odor; however, not all toxins give off an odor. Second is a bio-response, which means that the human body responds negatively by becoming ill—headache, running nose, etc. The last method is to use test equipment that electronically analyzes the amount of toxins emitted from a material or product.

Chemicals emitting toxins in our interior space can affect human health. Illnesses such as asthma, **multiple chemical sensitivity (MCS)**, and even neurological health have occurred or been heightened by toxins that affect IAQ. For example, MCS symptoms may begin as cold to flu-like and headaches and then **synergize** into allergic reactions that increase symptoms to dizziness, nausea, fatigue, lethargy, inability to concentrate, and even death. There are a plethora of chemicals in our environment—outdoor and inside—and research indicates that the number of offending chemicals is increasing (Nash, 2001). Designers must stay abreast of the evidence related to chemicals in interior materials.

Creating a Healthy Environment

Healthy environments can be created for individuals with asthma or MCS. To begin, all toxic materials must be removed and replaced with nontoxic materials. A chemical-free space, or **oasis**, can be created in the home or workplace to provide a safe, cleansing environment (Nussbaumer, 2005).

Often individuals with MCS will avoid areas such as cosmetic departments, leather stores, or any stores during the change of seasons, and may take medication to become desensitized to chemicals so they are able to handle some of the toxins in an environment. Especially important for an interior designer is that all materials and products selected must be free of chemicals. Lastly, spaces must be continuously clean to avoid the buildup of chemical odors, microbial contamination, and dust particles—all of which may affect the individual with asthma, MCS, or allergies. Thus, to control IAQ, the source of pollution must be eliminated, removed, and/or diluted.

Plants' Effect on Indoor Air Pollution

Plants are great aesthetic additions to an interior, and they can also reduce air pollution. An InformeDesign RS, "Plants Reduce Air Pollution" (2005, November 2), summarizes an experiment conducted to examine the ability of plants to remove urban air pollutants —carbon dioxide and nitrogen oxide. These two common urban pollutants contribute to global warming as well as affect human health. Results determined that plants purify the air in two ways: (1) absorption through photosynthesis, and (2) adsorption on leaves, which collect pollutants on the surface. This research also indicated that nitrogen oxide decreased significantly when plants were present in the experiment—the pollutant was removed by both absorption and adsorption methods. Additionally, carbon dioxide was removed only by absorption, and when temperatures increased (up to 40 degrees Celsius or 104 degrees Fahrenheit) even more carbon dioxide was absorbed. In other words, more absorption will take place during warmer months than in the winter. The design criteria identified was that interior designers should consider incorporating plants into the interiors, which may improve IAQ (InfomeDesign, 2005, November 2). One cautionary measure would be to make sure that mold does not develop in the soil, which would increase rather than decrease indoor air pollution.

Application

Applying sustainable design principles into design projects is essential. This section addresses ways to apply these principles. Additionally, there are a variety of articles from various sources that can provide evidence related to sustainable design. Examples included are from the International Interior Design Association (IIDA) Knowledge Center Web site, and InformeDesign database.

Because sustainable design is intrinsic to interior design, the application of **Leadership in Energy and Environmental Design (LEED)** is important to all interior design projects—whether in coursework or in the field, i.e., architectural, interior design, and residential design firms. Working toward a LEED-certified project encourages the adoption of sustainable building practices that promote energy efficiency and healthier environments for the occupants (USGBC, 2008). The research and process of making decisions related to obtaining LEED points does involve in-depth research of all aspects of a design project as well as the materials intended for specification. Thus, it is suggested that LEED criteria be examined and applied. LEED rating systems may be found on the United States Green Building Council Web site (USGBC, 2008).

To locate new evidence, consider the IIDA Knowledge Center and InformeDesign, which provide a variety of articles and research summaries that apply to sustainable design. In the IIDA Knowledge Center, for example, a case study provides information about an adaptive reuse project. This case study, *Creating Schools and Strengthening Communities through Adaptive Reuse* by Stephen Spector, focuses on the benefits of adaptive reuse in four schools, which are located in Arizona, North Carolina, California, and New Jersey.

The following two RS examples from InformeDesign can be reviewed and criteria found where applicable: "Achieving Sustainability by Reusing Buildings" is a position paper that examines how sustainability can be improved through adaptive reuse (InformeDesign, 2007, November 7), and "Bringing Daylight into Underground Spaces" is a study that determined an approach for calculating the width of light shafts needed to illuminate underground open spaces (InformeDesign, 2007, May 24). Research topics related to indoor air quality may relate to childcare centers, classrooms, or building materials (InformeDesign, 2005).

Summary

This chapter explored the process of sustainable design uses related to products, materials, and methods. The goal of each is to impact humans and the global environment in the least possible way. Industrial practices have negatively affected the ecological balance and depleted limited nonrenewable resources. However, with the implementation of sustainable design, industrial practices can positively affect the ecological balance. New ideas and practices are being developed to use renewable resources and to conserve resources. Conserving resources also includes conserving energy, such as the use of solar energy with photoelectric or photovoltaic cells.

Sustainable design also relates to the preservation of buildings and interiors. Waste is produced in the process of building. Therefore, it is necessary to reuse, recycle, and reduce the amount of waste in the process of building and renovation.

Designers are concerned about the life-cycle assessment of a designed environment or product from raw material to disposal. Thus, the investigation of a product's life cycle is the first step toward improving our global environment.

Additionally, human health has been affected by poor IAQ. Therefore, interior designers must research toxicity prior to selecting and specifying products and materials. Using the various databases, articles and research summaries will provide new evidence that will inform the design.

Key Terms

active solar energy

adaptive reuse

convection

conduction

cradle to cradle (c2c)

cradle to grave

eco-effectiveness

emissions

environmental design

evaporation

geothermal

green design

indoor air quality (IAQ)

Leadership in Energy and Environmental Design (LEED)

life-cycle assessment

multiple chemical sensitivity (MCS)

nonrenewable resources

oasis

passive solar energy

photoelectric

photovoltaic

preservation

radiation

renewable resources

renovation

restoration

roof pond

synergize

sink

sustainable design

thermosiphoning

toxins

Trombe wall

volatile organic compounds (VOCs)

THEODORE

Human Factors

OBJECTIVES

After reading this chapter, you should be able to:

Examine and research evidence of physiological needs such as anthropometrics and ergonomics in various situations

Examine and research evidence of psychological needs and the emotional well-being of clients

Examine and research evidence of sociological needs related to diverse populations and situations

Explain the importance of universal design and examine evidence to inform the design

Apply research from evidence to develop EBD

DRED COURT

Often, the economic needs of a client seem most important. Although cost, budget, and other financial concerns are key, the users of a space also have varying needs that go beyond these economic factors. A design impacts the health, safety, and welfare of users, and this involves both physiological and psychological concerns. For example, design stimulates emotional reactions in users; thus, privacy versus interaction is one factor to consider.

Designers must also consider sociological needs. Sociological needs refer to the interrelationship of humans to their environment relative to a diverse population. Creating a design that is universal to all, regardless of ability, meets not only the sociological but also the physiological and psychological needs of every user.

Previous chapters explored how data collected from the client helped designers understand the structure and function of the organization or the home. Research that relates to **human factors** is essential to the well-being of the client and users of the space. This includes physiological, psychological, and sociological needs. Research into these needs is central to the development of evidence-based design.

Physiological Needs

Physiological needs relate to physical requirements for the human body and how the body functions within the environment. This includes **anthropometrics** and **ergonomics** as well as the effect of the environment (e.g., noise, light, temperature, humidity, and ventilation) on human senses (Kilmer & Kilmer, 1992).

Table 9.1
Anthropometric Chart with Select Anthropometric Feature for Average Adults

(Relates to measurements on Figure 9.1)

Body features	Male			Female		
	5%	50%	95%	5%	50%	95%
Standing height	63.6	68.3	72.3	59.0	62.9	67.1
Sitting height: erect	33.2	35.7	38.0	30.9	33.4	35.7
Sitting height: normal	31.6	34.1	36.6	29.6	32.3	34.7
Knee height	19.3	21.4	23.4	17.9	19.6	21.5
Popliteal height	15.5	17.3	19.3	14.0	15.7	17.7
Elbow-rest height	7.4	9.5	11.6	7.1	9.2	11.0
Thigh clearance height	4.3	5.7	6.9	4.1	5.4	6.9
Buttock-knee height	21.3	23.3	25.2	20.4	22.4	24.6
Buttock-popliteal length	17.3	19.5	21.6	17.0	18.9	21.0
Elbow to elbow breadth	13.7	16.5	19.9	12.3	15.1	19.3
Seat breath	12.2	14.0	15.9	12.3	14.3	17.1
Weight, pounds	126.0	166.0	217.0	104.0	137.0	199.0

Source: Slotkis (2006).

ENVIRONMENTAL CONSIDERATIONS

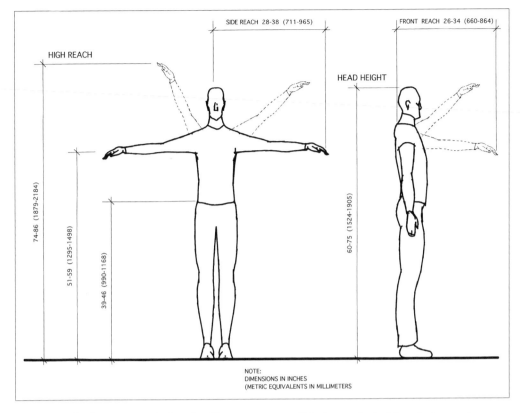

Figure 9.1 Anthropometrics is the scientific measurement of the human body. Here the human is standing and/or reaching.

Anthropometrics

Anthropometrics is the scientific measurement of the human body. Measurements of body size and stature determine the amount of space required by the human physical form. A range of measurements is relevant to various age groups regarding movement of the body in space. These movements include standing, sitting, interacting with others, and performing a variety of activities (Allen et al., 2004; Dreyfuss, 2002; Kilmer & Kilmer, 1992; Panero & Zelnik, 1979Pile, 2003; Slotkis, 2006).

Anthropometrics data are crucial in determining spatial needs for the clients as well as end users' needs related to mobility and physical strength (Allen et al. 2004). Additionally, anthropometrics data establish standard sizes (height and width) for many products, such as chair seats, doors, bathroom fixtures, countertops, and tabletops. From this information, designers are able to determine how clients relate to their environment and objects within the environment. Designers also pay special attention to physical problems that the client may face (Binggeli, 2007).

Table 9.1 lists standard measurements for men and women, and Figure 9.1 shows a graphical representation of standard measurements. However, it is important to keep in mind that not everyone is average and, therefore, furniture and equipment should have adjustability to accommodate everyone. This is the basic principle of universal design. Universal design is the creation of well-planned spaces that meet the needs of every user without drawing attention to people with disabilities. The goal of **universal design** is to improve features of furnishings that provide adjustability (Slotkis, 2007) and allow everyone with and without physical impairments to use the furnishings.

Ergonomics

Ergonomics is defined as an applied science that studies the relationship between human beings and their functions within their environment—the way bodies work efficiently in space (Allen et al. 2004; Human-factors Engineering, 2007; Kilmer & Kilmer, 1992). Ergonomics applies anthropometric data to provide comfort and efficiency in performing tasks while sitting, standing, or walking. Originally, studies were conducted to examine the work situations in military applications such as cockpits and space capsules. Today, studies involve the human body and the use of equipment within all types of interior environments. Data from such studies have affected the design of computers, workstations, furniture design, automobile design, and more (Kilmer & Kilmer, 1992).

During the data collection process, designers must pay particular attention to ergonomics. The application of ergonomics will vary depending on the users' physical stature and the task being performed (Kilmer & Kilmer, 1992). In other words, each situation is different and knowledge about the user and their tasks will provide background for the appropriate furniture, equipment, and other components of the space. The individual's stature and furniture are measurable components that will lead to design that provides comfort and efficiency. In addition, it is important to plan for adjustability that will also allow for flexibility. For example, an adjustable desk chair provides flexibility for varied tasks such as working on a computer, doing paperwork, or reading.

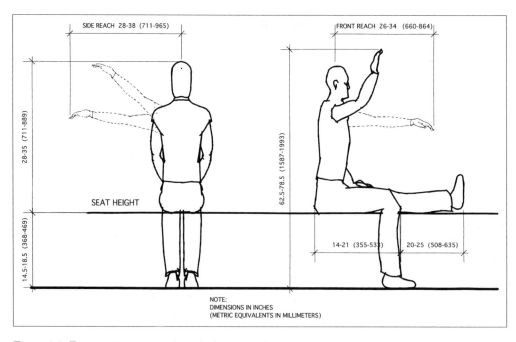

Figure 9.2 Ergonomics examines how the human body relates to the function or task performed.

ENVIRONMENTAL CONSIDERATIONS

Box 9.1 provides a checklist to evaluation ergonomics to aid in the appropriate furniture design for individuals in an office situation. Figure 9.2 shows the application of ergonomics using a computer workstation.

Box 9.1

Ergonomic Evaluation Checklist

Desk/Workstation

1. Do you have enough room on your work surface for all your computer accessories?
2. Is your desk surface deep enough to provide at least 18 inches between your eyes and the computer screen?
3. Are your most frequently accessed items (e.g., phone and manuals) easy to reach?
4. If your desk has a fixed height, is the keyboard tray adjustable?
5. Have you removed all under-desk obstructions?
6. Do you have a document holder to hold paper for prolonged computer inputting?
7. Do your arms rest upon or contact any sharp or square edges on your work surfaces?
8. If a large percentage of your time involves using a phone, do you use a phone headset?
9. Is your source light out of your line of sight?

Chair

1. Is your chair height adjustable?
2. Is your chair back adjustable up and down?
3. Is your chair back contoured to support the lower back?
4. Is your backrest large enough to support your entire back, but not interfere with the use of your arms?
5. Is your lumbar support a minimum of 12 inches wide?
6. Is there room (2 to 4 inches) between the front edge of the seat pan and the back of your knees?
7. If your feet do not rest flat on the floor when your chair is properly adjusted, do you use a footrest?
8. Is the top of your footrest covered with a non-skid material to reduce slippage?
9. Do your chair arms interfere with you getting close to your work?
10. Do your chair arms allow you to sit with your shoulders relaxed and not elevated?
11. Does your chair have removable armrests?
12. Is the distance between your armrests adjustable?
13. Are your knees bent, forming approximately a 90-degree or greater angle?
14. Does the chair have a stable base supported by five legs with casters?

Monitor

1. Is the viewing distance to your computer monitor somewhere between 18 and 30 inches?
2. Is the top of your computer screen at or just below eye level?
3. If you wear bifocals or trifocals, can you see the computer monitor without having to tilt your head back to read the screen or other items in your work area?
4. Is your computer monitor free of glare or reflections?
5. Is the monitor screen clean?
6. Is character size easy to read?
7. Do you have blinds on the windows near your computer?
8. Do you use a glare screen to reduce glare on your monitor?

(continued)

Box 9.1

Ergonomic Evaluation Checklist *(continued)*

Keyboard

1. With your chair adjusted properly, is your work surface at approximately elbow level?
2. Are your shoulders relaxed and not elevated when you work at your work surface?
3. Is the height of your keyboard low enough so your arms are relaxed at your sides?
4. When you address your work surface to type or write, is there approximately a 90-degree angle between your forearms and upper arms and are your elbows close to your body?
5. When you address your work surface to type, are your wrists in line with your forearms and not bent upward, downward, or side to side?
6. Do you have a wrist rest to support your wrists in a straight and neutral position?

Mouse, Trackball, or Other Input Device

1. Is your mouse, trackball, or other input device (e.g., touchpad) located directly in your immediate reach zone?
2. Is your mouse or trackball positioned next to your keyboard?
3. Is your mouse or trackball placed together with your keyboard on an adjustable work surface or tray?
4. Is your mouse work surface stable?
5. Is the mouse or trackball at the same level as your keyboard?

Work Habits

1. Do you take short and frequent breaks every 20 to 30 minutes?
2. Do you frequently change body positions while working?
3. Do you provide your eyes with vision breaks every half hour?
4. Are you free from experiencing any pain or discomfort while working?

Source: Center for Disease Control and Prevention (CDC). (2000b). *Ergonomic checklist*. Retrieved on November 2, 2007, from www.cdc.gov/od/ohs/Ergonomics/compergo.htm

---

Psychological and Sociological Needs

Unlike physiological needs, psychological needs are immeasurable. They relate to the user's feelings and interactions with other users. For example, some people require more privacy, whereas others prefer interaction, even with strangers. The area around a person is referred to as that person's "personal space." It is like a bubble that surrounds each of us. Some people have smaller personal bubbles than others. These bubbles are shaped by cultural or background experiences. When a friend moves into one's personal space, one usually feels comfortable; however, if a stranger enters one's personal space, one often feels discomfort (Kilmer & Kilmer, 1992; Nielsen & Taylor, 2007). These interactions refer to proxemics.

Proxemics

Proxemics is the study of the relationship between humans in a particular culture and their use and perceptions of space (Hall, 1966).

ENVIRONMENTAL CONSIDERATIONS

Anthropology of Space

Because proxemics is used to define the relationships of humans within a space, space can be organized to encourage or even discourage human interaction. There are three kinds of spaces in which to organize activities; **fixed-feature, semifixed-feature,** and **informal** or **nonfixed space.** Each way not only affects activities but also interaction of humans (Hall, 1966).

Fixed-Feature Space Fixed-feature spaces are the fixed material elements that control human behavior; these include the building itself, the permanent walls within buildings, and equipment or fixed furnishings. Creating a fixed-feature space is the basic method of organizing activities in which people engage—individually or in groups, and thus, the activities become static and immovable. For example, in American culture, an invisible boundary separates one yard from another; this is considered a fixed-feature space. Another example is a kitchen is designed for food preparation, and thus is a fixed-feature space (Hall, 1966).

In many Western homes, fixed-feature spaces are needed for specific functions such as socializing and entertaining, eating, food preparation, sleeping, sanitation, and so on. So, if an object or activity associated with a space is moved to a different space, a room could be considered "a mess" because the activities and/or objects are inconsistent with the function of the space. Office work taking place in a bedroom, for example, would render the space messy (Hall, 1966).

The relationship of fixed-feature space to personality and to culture is also important. Individuals, families, and/or cultures may choose to use spaces differently than others. Americans use spaces for specific purposes as already noted. However, spaces within homes are changing because activities are changing due to changes in human behavior. For example, in some American homes, the separate dining room melded into the food preparation and entertaining/social areas (Hall, 1966). For middle- and lower-class homes, this space is called the "Great Room."

Semifixed-Feature Space Semifixed-feature spaces include areas with movable objects/furniture, furniture arrangement, or the ability to move furniture from place to place. The way furniture is arranged affects interactions of humans. If the intent is to keep them apart, the furniture will be arranged in a row or far apart—this is called a **sociofugal** space. If the intent is to bring people together, the furniture will be arranged perpendicular to each other, which will encourage interaction—this is called a **sociopetal** space (Hall, 1966). Figures 9.3 and 9.4 provide examples of sociofugal and sociopetal.

Examples of sociofugal spaces are found in medical waiting rooms and lecture halls where interaction is frequently discouraged. Examples of sociopetal spaces are found in living rooms, hotel lobbies, and other spaces where conversation and interaction are encouraged.

Anthropologist Edward T. Hall (1966) cites an example that clearly demonstrates how the manipulation of semifixed-feature space affects human behavior in a hospital in Saskatchewan:

> [Doctor] Osmond had noticed that some spaces, like railway waiting rooms, tend to keep people apart. . . . The hospital of which he was in charge was replete with sociofugal spaces.

. . . Furthermore, the custodial staff and nurses tended to prefer (separating the patients) because they were easier to maintain. Chairs in the halls, which would be found in little circles after visiting hours, would soon be lined up neatly in military fashion, in rows along the walls (p. 101). There were no tables in the space. So, magazines were not read or briefly viewed and dropped to the floor and quickly swept up by staff members (p. 103).

One situation, which attracted Osmond's attention, was the newly built "model" female geriatrics ward. Everything was new and shiny, neat and clean. There was enough space, and the colors were cheerful (p. 101). The only trouble was that the longer the patients stayed in the ward, the less they seemed to talk to each other. Gradually, they were becoming like the furniture, permanently and silently glued to the walls at regular intervals between the beds. In addition, they all seemed depressed (p. 102).

Dr. Osmond made changes with the assistance of the staff to create a sociopetal space. Tables were added and furniture placed at right angles. When patients became accustomed to the new arrangement, the number of conversations doubled and reading tripled. The conclusions drawn from this experiment were threefold. (1) These observations are not always applicable in all situations. Placing furniture at right angles is limited to certain types of conversations between individuals in certain relationships within restricted cultural settings. (2) A sociofugal space in one culture may be a sociopetal space in another. (3) Sociofugal are not always bad arrangements and sociopetal spaces are not always good arrangements. What is most important is to create "flexibility and congruence between

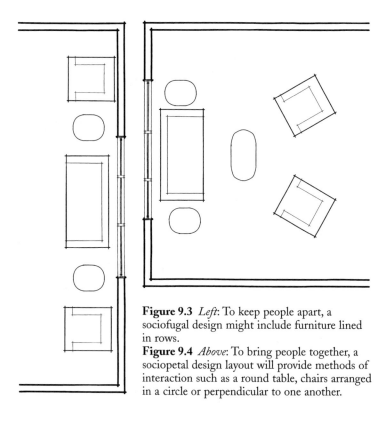

Figure 9.3 *Left*: To keep people apart, a sociofugal design might include furniture lined in rows.
Figure 9.4 *Above*: To bring people together, a sociopetal design layout will provide methods of interaction such as a round table, chairs arranged in a circle or perpendicular to one another.

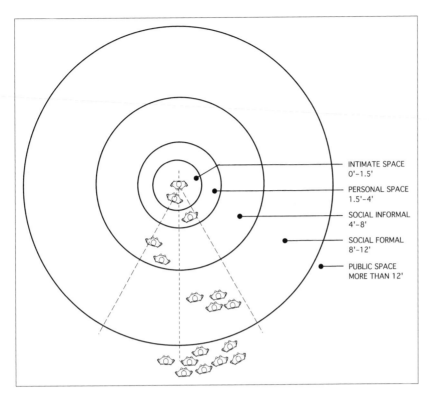

INTIMATE SPACE
0'–1.5'

PERSONAL SPACE
1.5'–4'

SOCIAL INFORMAL
4'–8'

SOCIAL FORMAL
8'–12'

PUBLIC SPACE
MORE THAN 12'

Figure 9.5 The four distance zones of proxemics are concerned with distance between people.

design and function so that there is a variety of spaces, and people can be involved or not, as the occasion and mood demand" (pp. 103–4). Clearly, the way an interior is created affects interaction between humans within the space.

Informal, or Nonfixed, Space Lastly, informal, or nonfixed, space relates to human interaction within the spatial experience (e.g., people to people). This relates to distance zones or the distance between two people that will affect placement of furniture.

Distance Zones

Hall (1966) developed four spatial zones—intimate, personal, social, and public. These consider the distance between two people and are particularly important to understand when designing a space. Figure 9.5 provides a graphical representation of proxemics and the spatial zones.

The intimate zone, or bubble, spans between the point of contact to 18 inches out and is reserved for those with whom a person feels close. This zone relates to affection, protection, and comfort as well as aggressive behavior. A stranger penetrating an individual's intimate space may cause both parties to feel discomfort. Voice levels range from a whisper to a very low volume (Hall, 1966). Therefore, designers must avoid creating environments that penetrate the intimate space.

Research topics for proxemics include cultural barriers in the workplace to improve the design (see July 25, 2005, InformeDesign RS "Breaking Cultural Barriers in the Workplace,"), and design of office space for both older and middle-aged employees (see June 2, 2003, InformeDesign RS "Age Affects Perceptions of Workplace Design").

Ideas for Collecting New Evidence

The personal zone or bubble stretches from 18 inches to 4 feet out from the individual. Friends are allowed in the personal zone at arms' length and do not penetrate the inner or intimate zone with few exceptions such as a handshake. Other cultures view this space as smaller. For example, people from the Middle East, South America, and southern Europe have a smaller personal space bubble. Customarily, they may comfortably embrace or touch in an appropriate manner. Voice levels are at a modified range with casual conversation (Hall, 1966).

The knowledge of how and who will use the space affects furniture arrangement. Placing furniture at right angles to one another allows penetration into the personal space (Kilmer & Kilmer, 1992; Nielsen & Taylor, 2007). People need personal spaces even in shared spaces. For example, in a shared children's bedroom, each child will create his or her own private space within the room. This need for a private area for one's own belongings carries over into adult life within the home as well as in the workplace. Thus, designers must be sensitive to this as data are collected (Allen et al., 2004).

The social zone ranges from 4 to 12 feet and can be either informal or formal. It could be in a social or business situation. Mandatory recognition begins at 8 feet or closer, making it possible to converse easily with voice levels are at a normal range (Hall, 1966). As closeness and interaction increases, the less formal the situation becomes. Placing furniture so that two people sit opposite from each other is an arrangement that exists within the social zone—informal or formal (Kilmer & Kilmer, 1992; Nielsen & Taylor, 2007).

The public zone stretches from 12 feet and beyond. In this zone, there is little or no interaction. One example is the relationship between a speaker and the audience where voice levels are loud or at full volume, or the speaking voice (Hall, 1966). In waiting rooms or reception areas, chairs are chosen rather than sofas so that no individual feels that his or her personal space has been invaded. These situations are generally public zones (Kilmer & Kilmer, 1992; Nielsen & Taylor, 2007).

America's population has become diverse with many varied cultures, and people of these varied cultures are now working in offices and moving into various dwelling types. Therefore, the ability to understand the various distance zones related to cultures, activities, and relationships as well as emotions is extremely important (Hall, 1966). Keep in mind that distances are approximate as the use of space and preferences vary from culture to culture and person to person. Thus, because personal space requirements will vary, the data and research on the client's preferences along with approximate zonal distance will aid in planning interior spaces.

Crowding

Crowding can also bring psychological feelings of insecurity and confinement or provide security and stability. When animals are crowded into small spaces, they exhibit stress, abnormal behavior, illness, and sometimes death. However, in dimensionally crowded situations, humans generally do not exhibit such behaviors. Rather, crowding in humans generally relates to culture and personality as well as the desire for involvement with other people. Some people enjoy interaction and involvement with others in crowded situations. Others feel overstimulated from crowding and need areas of solitude, or areas of retreat from others.

Interiors can be designed to accommodate preferences. For example, some individuals like to be surrounded by objects, furniture, and more, whereas others prefer open spaces —visual or actual (Neilson & Taylor, 2007). Thus, during the data collection process, it is important to learn the preferences of clients and users of the space. However, crowding issues may also relate to different design typologies, such as casino or residential design.

An InformeDesign RS, "Individual Responses to Casino Design" (2007, June 13), summarizes a study that revealed design strategies used for casino design that may create a psychologically revitalizing environment for the users. For example, the design may incorporate features such as sunlight, moving water, high ceilings, and open spaces to provide a sense of security and pleasure. In contrast, other features such as low ceilings and winding pathways through the compact gambling layout focus on gambling equipment. These concepts may be applied to other types of design by creating areas that are calming and others that are stimulating.

Territoriality

Territoriality, another aspect of proxemics, is the need to have a sense of one's own space. This can be achieved with one's own items, colors, and other physical manifestations of personal self. For example, many individuals have their own seat in a classroom, sit in the same pew in church, or occupy a favorite chair in the family room. If one's seat is taken, he or she may feel annoyed and even displaced (Nielson & Taylor, 2007). Territoriality is a basic need to have a space; therefore, if spaces are shared, areas must be provided for individual, private space.

Data collection will reveal territoriality needs of individuals within the space. For example, an InformeDesign RS, "Hospital Spaces Affect Nurses" (2005, September 30), summarizes a study that examined gender roles in hospitals and nurses' work environment with particular concern for privacy, mobility, and opportunities for personalization, e.g., personal memorabilia such as photographs. This reinforced the idea that designers should investigate how territoriality can be achieved.

Universal Design

As stated earlier in this chapter, universal design is the creation of well-planned spaces that meet the needs of every user without drawing attention to people with disabilities. It must provide access to usable products and environments for all people, to the greatest extent possible and without the need for adaptation or specialized design (Center for Universal Design, 1997). When planning for universal design, a designer must consider many issues, including human factors, Americans with Disability Act (ADA) requirements, eyesight challenges such as poor vision and blindness, and hearing problems (Center for Universal Design, 1997).

Seven principles of universal design were developed by the Center for Universal Design (CUD) for a wide range of disciplines that relate to the environment, products, and communication. Using these principles, products and environments may be evaluated for their universality. Why is universal design important in commercial spaces? It is important to accommodate everyone in all aspects of our interior spaces, so that all users of a space may move through and work in all spaces comfortably. The seven priniciples identified by CUD (1997) are as follows:

- Equitable Use—The design is useful and marketable to people with diverse abilities.

- Flexibility in Use—The design accommodates a wide range of individual preferences and abilities.

- Simple and Intuitive—Use of the design is easy to understand, regardless of the user's experience, knowledge, language skills, or current concentration level.

- Perceptible Information—The design communicates necessary information effectively to the user, regardless of ambient conditions or the user's sensory abilities.

- Tolerance for Error—The design minimizes hazards and the adverse consequences of accidental or unintended actions.

- Low Physical Effort—The design can be used efficiently and comfortably and with a minimum of fatigue.

- Size and Space for Approach and Use—Appropriate size and space is provided for approach, reach, manipulation, and use regardless of user's body size, posture, or mobility (p. 2).

Although it is important to apply ADA regulations, it is even better to apply universal design principles in order to meet the needs of every user without drawing attention to people with disabilities. A review of literature will locate new evidence from research projects and applications by other designers. For example, an InformeDesign RS, "Kitchens for Older People" (2004, February 9), summarized a study that supports and provides evidence for universal design concepts. Observations of older people's use of kitchens provided recommendations for future kitchen designs to accommodate physical disabilities as well as for a wide range of users.

Wayfinding

Wayfinding is a process by which individuals navigate through unfamiliar territory (Clark, 2007; Salmi, 2007). You may think of wayfinding as signage that leads you to a destination. The purpose of wayfinding is to direct people through a primary circulation path, such as corridors and aisles, that lead to a variety of destinations. However, successful wayfinding also provides everyone access to the same products and activities within an interior and throughout a community. Universal design, therefore, presents additional challenges to wayfinding (Salmi, 2007).

Inseparable from wayfinding, cognitive mapping (mental map of a three-dimensional space) provides individuals with a spatial representation to orient wayfinding (Salmi, 2007). Wayfinding should include a variety of ways to move users through a space.

Wayfinding Methods

Designers create wayfinding using several methods; these include:

- Examining the circulation path through spatial organization or building layout

- Providing visual cues such as landmarks

- Providing direction through signage

- Providing directories to assist in wayfinding

- Designing maps that are easy to read

- Using color and lighting to reinforce the pathway (Salmi, 2007)

Locating Evidence on Wayfinding

To locate evidence to inform the design, designers may ask:

- How can children, the elderly, the visually impaired, AIDS patients, people of a particular gender, and others be affected by wayfinding?

- What wayfinding methods used in various commercial spaces are successful or unsuccessful, and why?

Casinos, for example, seem to be complicated, particularly in circulation and wayfinding. Often, we ask, "What are the wayfinding methods used in casino design, and are they meant to be complicated?" Research indicates that the confusing layout creates stress and often stimulates gambling. To eliminate this problem, the combination of visually rich materials and easy-to-understand layouts would support wayfinding and provide a sense of security (InformeDesign, 2007, June 13).

Application

Information about the application of human factors can be found in a variety of resources such as books, periodicals, and the Internet. The International Interior Design Association (IIDA) Knowledge Center and InformeDesign provide a wealth of information and a variety of studies related to human factors. The following examples of research studies relate to various design typologies.

A study by Cocci and Bordi (2005) investigated if the ergonomically designed worktables affected productivity. An experimental research method was used to collect data from two groups of students—an experimental group and a control group. Students were randomly selected and assigned a special task for the day. These students were informed about the experiment and that it would take about 40 minutes. They were taken to a special research kitchen that was set up for the experiment. Students in the control group worked at a table of the standard 34-inch height. Students in the experimental group worked at tables that were adjusted based on the participant's elbow height. All participants worked for 40 minutes. Observations revealed that participants in the control group became more fidgety and voiced greater discomfort before the experiment ended. Thus, findings supported the fact that ergonomically designed tables contribute to the improvement of productivity and support the value of ergonomically designed workplaces.

A study by Winchip, Inman, and Dunn (1989) examined multifamily residential design and crowding. It revealed that "the stage of family life cycle shows a relationship with perceived residential stress and behavioral attitudes toward the residential setting in the married-student housing units. Specifically, crowded-stage families (families in crowded conditions) viewed their current dwelling as more crowded and more stressful; thus, their overall rating was lower than for early-stage families (families in less crowded conditions)" (p. 186).

A third study relates to nursing home design. Often, nursing home facilities have affected their residents negatively; the challenge, then, is to create a psychologically positive environment. An InformeDesign RS, "Evaluating Nursing Home Environments" (2007, July 6), summarizes a study that assessed and compared physical environments of nursing home residents. This study developed a series of checklists to assess these environments and also determined the criteria that would promote a positive environment and quality of life for the nursing home residents. For example, private or single-occupancy bathrooms could be provided not only for privacy but also to maintain the dignity and comfort of a resident.

Summary

Human factors—anthropometrics, ergonomics, and proxemics—affect physical, emotional, and cultural needs of occupants. First, the physical or physiological needs relate to anthropometrics and ergonomics. With anthropometrics, scientific measurements of the human body, we are able to determine spatial needs for clients. However, these measurements are standard for the average person. It is, therefore, important to consider ergonomics for each individual to be comfortable and efficienct in performing tasks.

Emotional or psychological needs are immeasurable and relate to the user's feelings and interactions with other users. Proxemics, the study of relationships between humans in a particular culture, help designers consider the emotional feelings of users and, through research, realize that our designs can impact emotions and behavior. Additionally, designers must also understand the cultural aspects that may affect design decisions.

An important aspect of human factors is to create space using universal design. Spaces must be accessible to everyone, and this includes applying good wayfinding methods to the design. Research to locate evidence related to universal design and wayfinding will inform and improve the design.

With knowledge of human factors, the designer can meet users' specific needs and positively affect their health, safety, and welfare. Most importantly, research studies will provide new evidence to aid understanding of human factors and inform the design.

Key Terms

anthropometrics

crowding

ergonomics

fixed-feature space

human factors

informal (nonfixed) space

proxemics

semifixed-feature space

sociofugal

sociopetal

territoriality

universal design

wayfinding

THEODORE

Diversity in Design

OBJECTIVES

After reading this chapter, you should be able to:

Understand the meaning of diversity

Recognize different types of philosophy

Explain how diverse philosophies relate to design

Locate evidence related to diversity

DRED COURT

iversity means more than differences in ethnicity. According to Anthony (2001), "diversity is a set of human traits that have an impact on individuals' values, opportunities, and perceptions of self and others" (p. 22). Anthony (2001) identifies six core dimensions of diversity that apply to the greater population and 10 subcategories within these categories. These six core dimensions are ethnicity, age, gender, mental or physical abilities, race, and sexual orientation. Subcategories include religion, income, education, first language, geographic location, military experience, communication style, organizational level, work experience, and work style (Anthony, 2001).

Designers work with clients from diverse backgrounds; therefore, knowledge and understanding of diversity is essential. Designers may have clients who want to incorporate a diverse design philosophy within a home or workplace. In such cases, research into diversity is important both in fact finding and in the development of evidence for specific situations. Findings will result in appropriately designing spaces and accommodating individual needs.

Ethnicity and Religion

Today's global society allows designers easier access to knowledge and observance of facts about various ethnic cultures including these cultures' philosophical differences that affect the design. Some design philosophies relate to Eastern and/or religious cultures such as **feng shui**, **shibui**, and **Vaastu Shastra**. Some relate to many cultural and/or spiritual backgrounds such as African and various Native American cultures. Others, such as Islam, relate to specific religious cultures that are steeped in tradition and affect lifestyle as well as design.

Chinese Design

Chinese art and architecture are governed by unity, harmony, and balance. These concepts have been influenced by various religions: Confucianism, Buddhism, Taoism, and Christianity. Each aids the development of inner character and affects rituals, symbols, and spatial arrangements (Harwood, May, & Sherman, 2002). Chinese style of architecture is as unique as its up-swinging roof.

Chinese architecture and interiors are based on a Confucian order of symmetry, axial balance, and finiteness. In contrast, Chinese artistic designs and landscapes are also unique and use the Taoist religious qualities of empty space, infinity, and asymmetrical composition (Harwood et al., 2002). In the seventeenth century, Eastern art and design began influencing European interiors, which later influenced French and American interiors. When Eastern artistic design concepts are incorporated into furniture, it is called the **Chinoiserie** style—a style of art and design that reflect Chinese influence—(Allen et al., 2004). But the most intriguing theory in Eastern design is the concept of feng shui.

Feng Shui

Feng shui has become a popular concept in the Western world; however, many designers have little knowledge of its background and concepts. To understand feng shui, the terms

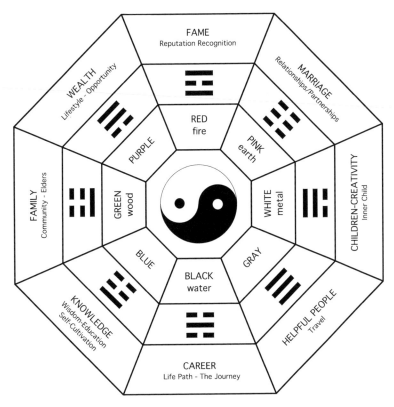

Figure 10.1 The feng shui philosophy uses the earth's natural forces (chi) to balance the yin and yang that achieve harmony. Feng shui affects all aspects of design—architecture, interiors, furnishings, and accessories—that includes color, form, pattern, arrangement, and relationship.

chi, yin, and yang must be defined. According to Harwood et al. (2002), the concept of **chi** relates to energy or the "duality of **yin** (negative, feminine, dark) and **yang** (positive, masculine, and light) guide universal life. The laws of the five elements of wood, fire, earth, metal, and water govern relationships in the natural environment" (p. 17). The feng shui philosophy is a system of orientation that "uses the earth's natural forces to balance the yin and yang to achieve harmony" (p. 17). Feng shui literally means wind and water. It affects all aspects of design—architecture, interiors, furnishings, and accessories—that includes color, form, pattern, arrangement, and relationship (see Figure 10.1).

Allen et al. (2004) state that the feng shui color schemes are based on the various Chinese philosophies and practices. One example uses compass mythology, which is an eight-sided symbol corresponding to the four compass points and midpoints, and depending upon an individual's birth year, the feng shui color scheme is interpreted differently. Each birth year is related to the basic element of earth, water, wood, fire, and metal. For example, if someone was born in the year of wood, green may be used for the color scheme as green represents wood. Red would, then, need to be avoided in the color scheme because it is associated with fire—fire destroys wood. Additionally, white is associated with light and is highly valued. Black is highly valuable and represents water and money; however, it is used carefully as it is the opposite of light. Finally, after colors are chosen, one must create harmony and balance the yin and yang to make the design successful.

Binggeli (2007) states that to produce harmony with an interior, feng shui may be used as a guide to spatial arrangement. It can be applied to different interior spaces from restaurants and homes to office buildings and airports in order to enhance and complement the interior design. In particular, the rules and resolutions of feng shui are suggestions that can guide individual interpretations and preferences. "Feng shui guidelines help guide judgments about each space under consideration. The breadth of choice in feng shui solutions leaves room for individual taste and ingenuity" (p. 245). One uniform aspect of this theory, however, is the space left between furniture to allow the free flow of chi to circulate through the space.

If the feng shui philosophy is to be used in a design project, designers must not only study the philosophy but also examine evidence that may provide a deeper understanding of the theories and practices. For example, an InformeDesign RS, "Beliefs that Underlie Feng Shui" (2006, September 20), summarizes a study that explored the ancient theories and practices of feng shui and discussed its popularity in the West. One of the greatest concerns expressed was that the Western version of feng shui may not be appropriately reflected. Therefore, designers must thoroughly research the underlying beliefs and values of the feng shui philosophy before using in a different culture (e.g., Western). This article does provide some basic concepts of feng shui and may provide appropriate background for the designer from which the research of feng shui may begin.

Japanese Design

Similar to Chinese, Japanese art and architecture are governed by unity, harmony, and balance. Daily Japanese life has been shaped by various religions such as Buddhism, Shinto, Zen Buddhism, Neo-Confucianism, and Christianity—each with differing influences and one sometimes combined with another (Harwood et al., 2002).

Japanese design demonstrates a strong relationship to nature. Interior spaces emphasize simplicity, horizontality, and informality—all aspects of nature. Rooms are open, as in nature, and are designed and arranged around the **tatami** mat, which measures 3 feet by 6 feet. To keep an open feeling, screens rather than walls are used to separate rooms. **Fusuma** screens are used to separate rooms. **Shoji** screens are used at the window and, at times, as room dividers. The simplicity found in interiors is also revealed in art display (Allen et al. 2004). For example, an **ikebana**, or special floral arrangement, stands alone in alcoves called **tokonoma**; this provides color in a simplistic manner (Harwood et al. 2002). The concepts of Japanese design influence architects such as Frank Lloyd Wright, who had great admiration for Japanese design. Wright's applications can be seen with the connection to nature and horizontality (Allen et al., 2004). This reflects one of the most intriguing Japanese concepts that expresses the connection to nature—shibui.

Shibui

"Shibui (pronounced shih BOO ee), or shibusa, expresses in one word the Japanese approach to beauty as well as the intrinsic nature of Japanese culture" (Allen et al., 2004, p. 106). It is a theoretical concept that harmonizes color by combining hues that are appealing for a long period of time. Based on nature, colors harmonize in a subtle manner and are close in value and intensity with a small amount of a sharp accent color. It also incorporates subtle patterns and/or slight variations of textures (Nielsen & Taylor, 2007). The following explains how to achieve a shibui effect by remembering that color is based on nature:

- Colors in the largest areas are quiet and undemanding (neutralized).

- Bright, vibrant colors are found in a small proportion.

- The darker and more solid colors are under the feet.

- Colors become lighter and more delicate as they move upward.

- Natural landscape has a matte finish with only a little shininess—similar to the "sun sparkling on a ripple in a stream" (p. 106).

- Pattern and texture in nature are everywhere; however, they are subtle and visible with close inspection.

- "No two patterns are identical, yet unity prevails" (p. 106).

- The natural colors, textures, and patterns may appear simple but with close inspection are very complex.

The American architect Wright not only applied Japanese design concepts to his architecture but he also appreciated and incorporated the shibui design philosophy into many of his works (Allen et al., 2004). When shibui is used in an interior, it creates a sense of peace and relaxation (Nielsen & Taylor, 2007). It is serene but is powerfully understated and unobtrusive (Allen et al., 2004). Young and Young, authors of *The Art of Japanese Architecture,* have spent many years researching Japanese architecture and shibui. Chapter 3 of their online book, *Spontaneity of Japanese Art and Culture,* is an excellent source of information that reinforces the idea of simplicity (Young & Young, 2006). Prior to using the shibui theoretical concept, designers should research the background to understand it; then they can apply the concept to their design projects. Additionally, research of nature into design can also provide evidence and insight for methods of informing a design project. Figure 10.2 includes a nature inspiration and an interior photograph that applies the shibui theoretical concept.

Figure 10.2 As in nature, darker colors begin at the base and lighten as color moves upward. Shown in the nature image, neutralized colors dominate with bright, vibrant colored accents. Textures are subtle and found everywhere. Shibui uses nature as its inspiration to create an environment that can be comfortable for a long period of time.

Indian Design

India's culture has been influenced by various religions: Hinduism, Judaism, Buddhism, Jainism, Christianity, Islam, and many others (India, 2008). However, Hinduism is the most dominant and influences the daily life of its followers. Hinduism is a way of life rather than a religion; its concepts are tolerance and peacefulness (Hinduism, 2008). Religious temples are uniquely designed depending on the region in which they are located. Temples in Northern India look like towers with curving sides. They resemble trees growing near each other with their tops tied together. Temples in Southern India are rectangular pyramids made of steplike blocks of stone. Each step tells a story about the Hindu God in a sculptural form (Kannikeswaran, 2008). Also, an important part of Hindu life is the theory called Vaastu Shastra.

Vaastu Shastra

Vaastu Shastra is an ancient Hindu theory that is similar to the feng shui belief system (Binggeli, 2007). Vaastu (sometimes spelled Vastu) means *dwelling* or *site*. Originally, it was applied to the design of traditional Indian architecture—city planning, temples for gods, palaces, forts, and residences for the upper class; today it is applied to any dwelling type —palaces to apartments to office buildings (Cox, 2000). Its design is intended to integrate the inner self with the outer environment. Vaastu Shastra uses positive powers of the earth, water, and fire, or sun (Figure 10.3). "It suggests ways to live in tune with the laws of nature to enhance health and prosperity" (Binggeli, 2007, p. 246). Like the chi in feng shui, Vaastu is the energy (Arya, 2000).

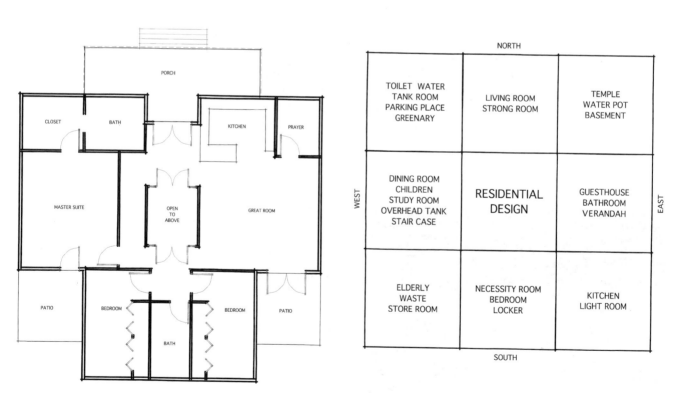

Figure 10.3 Similar to feng shui, Vaastu Shastra philosophy uses positive energy from the earth.

Also, like feng shui, Vaastu governs the site and building orientation and placement of every detail including the proportions of all spaces, including ceilings and roofs, entrances, doors, windows, staircases, kitchens, bedrooms, and toilets. To design the interior spaces, this ancient Hindu theory advocates great amounts of light as well as natural ventilation; however, furniture is at a minimum (Arya, 2000; Binggeli, 2007; Vaastu International, 2000).

In Vaastu architecture, square and rectangular shapes are used because these shapes indicate safety, stability, and completeness. There are also guidelines for each room in the house. The kitchen, for example, is the most loved and lived in by family members. Two characteristics of the kitchen are warmth and strength; therefore, the materials need to express warmth and strength. This may be interpreted and applied as the warmth of wood combined with the strong character of stone—marble or granite.

Dining rooms are generally positioned on the east, south, or west portion of the house, and may be either an independent room or in continuation of the kitchen. To stimulate your appetite, shades of pink or orange are recommended for the walls. A rectangular dining table is the preferred shape. A verandah should be positioned in the east or north portion of the house. East is considered the best choice because it is believed to bring more positive energy from the morning sun into the house (Vaastu International, 2000).

Vaastu Shastra is a complex method by which a home or business may be designed. Because it is complex, books or experts in the field should be used as resources to fully understand and apply the guidelines. It would also be wise to work with an expert who has designed architecture and interiors in the Vaastu Shastra manner. Knowledge will be gained in several ways: (1) learn about the concepts; (2) learn to apply concepts; (3) observe how the design affected the client; and (4) use the previous three points to develop evidence and inform another design project. This method of understanding diversity of ethnicity and religion can be applied to both feng shui and Vaastu Shastra.

African Design

African architecture and design is steeped in ceremonial traditions as well as Christian and Islamic influences (Binggeli, 2007). African visual arts refer to works from areas of the continent's sub-Saharan regions—all areas except the Caucasian North African region. Because the regions are different in climate, topography, and natural resources, the customs are also as diverse as is the art (African Art Museum, 1999).

Regardless of the diverse customs and art style, African architecture and design has been particularly influenced by religion. For example, art was used to resolve conflicts and educate and, especially, to symbolize worship. Their designs are rich in visual literacy with extensive use of geometric patterns that contain cultural meanings (Allen et al., 2004). According to the Smithsonian Institution (n.d.), African art is a fusion of spiritual beliefs and social purpose with visual imagery. The artistic expression is found in ceremonial masks and fertility figures that are created for ceremonial purposes and in utilitarian objects used for daily living. Typically, materials used are woods, metals, ceramic, textiles, and beads (Allen et al., 2004).

The Aduma tribe, for example, is located in the Ogooue River region in Gabon. The tribesmen are the great boatmen of the region and had a belief in God, the creator, and in

Ideas for Collecting New Evidence

Research into space planning for Eastern design includes examples of the use of feng shui, shibui, and/ or Vaastu Shastra and issues related their use.

an immortal soul. They also believed in retribution for evil and, therefore, worshipped spirits and ghosts. Masks were used for celebratory dances for major social rituals.

Architecture of sub-Saharan Africa is linked to Islam and Christianity. Mosques as well as churches have been built in various regions. In parts of Western and Eastern Africa, magnificent mosques have been built of mud. In Ethiopia, rock-hewn churches have been constructed. For the most part, domestic African architecture is reflective of the interaction between natural resources, the climate, and vegetation as well as the economy and dense population in some regions. The most durable material is stone while other materials deteriorate from rain, rot, and termites. For the majority of Africans, buildings are constructed of light materials—grasses, wood, and clay—that are easy to transport (African Architecture, 2008). Additionally, furniture is mobile and has special meaning. For example, "the chair or stool is a very personal item—historically carried with the individual and not shared with others" (Allen et al., 2004, p. 39).

The application of African design may be to accessorize with art or create a thematic interior incorporating furniture and artifacts. Regardless, it is important to research African design, locate and interview an expert on African design, locate and observe an interior with an application of African art and design, and then apply this knowledge to inform a design project.

Native American Design

There are many different Native American tribes, and there are similarities and differences among them. However, their connections among cultural beliefs, nature, and family are very strong.

The design of Native American architecture must begin with thorough research and, ultimately, understanding of their culture and natural environment. The concepts of their buildings are interconnected with a "balance of values between cultural beliefs and a . . . relationship to the land and its abundant resources" (Begay, 2004a). The material character of their architecture is best described as "simple in appearance yet communicates a sense of place between nature and people" (Begay, 2004a).

Former Native American housing varied from one part of the country to another, and houses were generally communal with several closely related families living in one house. Some houses were rectangular; some were round, some were a teepee shape, and others were stacked as in the Pueblo style (Finney, n.d.). For the Navajo, an early structure with a round or octagonal footprint was called the hogan. The hogan was a ritual structure and important as: (1) a shelter to protect the body; (2) the heart of family values; (3) the host for social functions; and (4) a setting for ceremonies, such as weddings (Begay, 2004a).

The longhouses were used in various tribes, but especially by the Iroquois Indians. Longhouses were nearly 100 feet long and divided into 10-foot-square compartments that opened into a central area where the fire warmed the house and offered a place for families to congregate. Generally, only two families were centered around each fireplace. Along the sides, raised platforms were covered with skins, which provided seating and beds for sleeping (Kinney, n.d.). Figure 10.4 represents an interior space divided into sections.

Reinforcing the purpose of structure, the dominant element is the family. In fact, the size of housing structures is based on the number of individuals who would live in a hogan or other types of house (e.g., longhouse). Structures are never larger than what can

Figure 10.4 The longhouse used by some Native Americans. The longhouse interior space is divided into compartments so that several families can live in one house. The design philosophy of Native Americans is represented by color and direction.

accommodate a moderately sized family. Other elements associated with the four directions, or cardinal points, may include spatial adjacency design, cosmology, stones, colors, and values (Begay, 2004b).

For the Dakota Indians, or Sioux, the four directions are a very important part of worship. When praying with the Sacred Pipe, which is used only for a spiritual celebration, the Native American will face each direction in succession, beginning with the west. Each direction—west, north, east, and south—represents a color—black, red, white, and yellow. West is black and stands for evil, danger, and the condition of man. North is red and stands for conflict, tension, decision, and man's decision whether or not to revert back to black or go to white. East is white and stands for victory, purity, life, and the rising sun that eliminates red and brings forth a clear sky. South is yellow and stands for peace, fruitfulness, warmth, and the notion that regardless of the danger, tension, or conflict that once existed, all of that is now in the past (American Indian Culture Research Center, n.d.). Figure 10.5 illustrates the Native American design philosophy.

Though color is important in the ceremony, natural colors of the earth dominate the building. Natural colors—browns, tans, reds, buffs, yellows—are preferred for the exterior facades because of the relations with the earth. Materials such as concrete block, stones, stucco, and wood provide the natural texture. In essence, the natural materials are used to "paint the building" (Baley, 2004c).

Shapes, colors, directions, and symbols are important in the design of spaces for Native Americans. Therefore, designers who have the opportunity to work on a design project that relate to a Native American culture must not only thoroughly research the culture but also learn from it. This may mean visiting the reservations, listening to the stories, and other forms of interaction and observation in order to gain insight into these beliefs and customs and, ultimately, to gain evidence to inform the design.

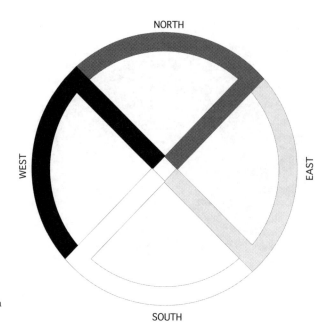

Figure 10.5 Diagram of Navajo design philosophy.

Islamic Design

Islamic art and architecture are unique and highly decorative. Their design is influenced by religion, which involves both traditions and lifestyle. Islamic art and architecture are especially characterized by their intricate geometric design (Harwood, May, & Sherman, 2002). Islamic designs were particularly influential in Spain during the Moorish occupation. Moorish interiors were highly decorated in geometric designs, and the horseshoe arch was frequently employed (Allen et al., 2004). Most importantly, religion impacts on the design of houses and workplaces. Thus, if designing for a Muslim family, research must be conducted on the design of the house.

An InformeDesign RS, "Religion and Climate Impact Traditional Housing in Iran" (2005, October 27), examined the impact of religion as well as climate on traditional courtyard houses located in Iran. Iran's dominant religion is **Islam** but in the past, Zoroastrianism dominated. Thus, the study compared and contrasted houses built by Muslims and Zoroastrians. Its authors determined that the houses in Iran were influence by religion, culture, climate, and topography. Because designers may work with Muslim families, they must understand their special housing design needs. The following are a few of the concepts applicable to homes for a Muslim family.

- Private and public space must be distinct with the separation of males and females who are not related by blood or marriage.

- Hospitality is a key factor of Islam that influences the design.

- Adobe and mud brick are traditional materials used in the arid climate.

Particularly important is designing culturally sensitive housing that promotes privacy for Muslim women. One study suggests the Japanese screen design for privacy and beauty

(Gelil, 2006). Another study, summarized in the InformeDesign RS "Housing Design for Somali Immigrants" (2008, May 7), analyzes the experience of Somali immigrants in the United States. The study looked at ways that designers could create culturally sensitive housing for this ethnic group. Their summary states that many housing units in the United States are not suitable to fulfill the immigrant's cultural requirements and, therefore, can create emotional and physical stress. Additionally, culturally sensitive design strategies have typically been limited to the exterior and ignore the interior spaces. Because Somali immigrants are most often Muslims, there are special needs that relate to their religion. Design criteria were identified for house design to accommodate a Somali family; these include:

- A minimum of four bedrooms should be provided for a large Somali family and visitors.

- Outdoor play spaces should be designed for children so that the women can supervise children from indoors and also be screened from neighbors.

- Separate kitchen areas should be designed not only to allow women to remove veils while preparing food and accommodate multiple cooks but also to prevent cooking smells from permeating into other areas.

Other criteria were provided, which can be found in the InformeDesign RS "Housing Design for Somali Immigrants" (2008, May 7). The exterior view in Figure 10.6 illustrate the areas that can easily allow women to have privacy and remove their veils.

Interiors for Muslim families must adhere to their traditions. An RS found on InformeDesign, "Meaning and Symbolism in Arab-American Muslim Home Interiors" (2007, September 12), states that interiors of Arab-American Muslim homes are influenced by the cultural forces from their homeland; however, there is a growing indifference to these ideals as families undergo a generational, social, and cultural change. Even with these changes, many families still adhere to the cultural practices. Therefore, these studies provide some basic information related to the design of houses for a family who practice Islam. When designing for a Muslim family, further research into their traditions and their concerns for a proper design is important to provide evidence that will inform the design.

Ideas for Collecting New Evidence

Research into space planning for the Muslim home includes privacy issues.

Figure 10.6 Muslim women need areas where they may remove their veils while maintaining privacy and be able to view children or others from outside their homes. In this example, a privacy fence and louvered areas allow women to view or be outside and still maintain privacy from the public when unveiled.

Other Types of Diversity

Diversity includes more than ethnicity and religion. Diversity of age also affects design. For example, needs are diverse for children in preschool versus primary, secondary, or higher educational facilities. These include color, furniture type and size, and spatial needs. Older adults, especially the elderly, have different needs. In the workplace, aspects of a design affect each user. The aging eye, for example, needs more light and begins to see color differently. Many of these concerns have been discussed in earlier chapters, but clearly, research of literature for diversity of age can inform a design project.

Other concerns for diversity may also be gender, familial structural types, physical abilities, mental abilities, and socioeconomic status, all of which can affect the design of interior spaces. Each of the following questions should be considered and researched to inform the design:

- Gender—What are different needs of each gender in a particular situation? Will gender difference affect the design outcome?

- Familial structural types—In designing a multifamily unit, have different family structures been considered for future occupancy?

- Physical abilities—Has or will universal design be applied?

- Mental abilities—Is signage clear? Is the wayfinding method clear for different abilities? Is color applied for clarity? Is the product easy to use?

Socioeconomic Status

Socioeconomic status is defined by differences in household income level, household type, race, age, and housing ownership. Diversity in income can affect social status. As noted in Chapter 6, the InformeDesign RS "Can Zoning Facilitate Diversity?" (2006, December 6) summarized a study that assessed the impact of land-use zoning on human diversity such as socioeconomic status and race. The study determined that zoning for diverse housing types in residential areas could possibly be linked to diverse incomes. It is suggested that diversity may be necessary and is supported by building types, public services, recreational facilities, traffic noise, or even tree-lined streets. The organization of many urban environments are separated by zoning (e.g., residential, commercial, and industrial). Some areas of socioeconomic diversity need to be concentrated, some may be scattered through a city, and others are separated with or without zoning regulations. Though not advocated, a designer should understand that zoning could increase and accentuate the difference in socioeconomic status.

Application

Research of diverse cultures provides awareness and realization of other cultures that will inform the design in a variety of ways. Its impact goes far beyond the aesthetic. For example, the InformeDesign RS "Beliefs that Underlie Feng Shui" (2006, September 20) summarized a study conducted to investigate traditional color use and its meanings to diverse cultures. As pointed out in InformeDesign RS "Cultural Stability in Design" (2005, July 26), designers must be aware of and realize how the visual traditions affect design, which include folklore in this case. From feng shui to folklore, all aspects of a culture must be examined and taken into consideration.

In the case of the feng shui study, the author learned that color is an important aspect of human existence and is used to define our environment and experiences. Frequently, people modify their surroundings for the following reasons: (1) to signify meaning or even emotions; (2) to define and regulate space as well as behavior; (3) to commemorate events; and (4) to define political or national affiliation. Therefore, it is important for designers to be aware of meanings or use of color that varies and is often based on ritual, religion, literature, folklore, and history. Additionally, for some cultures, colors have curative or protective power and/or positive or negative associations. Therefore, when designing for a different or integration of ethnic groups, research of facts is crucial to a successful design.

An InformeDesign RS, "Color, Meaning, Culture, and Design" (2003, February 10), summarizes a study that developed a series of interior color palettes and used them to determine color meaning and preferences of subjects of European-based cultures (e.g., United States and England) and Asian-based cultures (e.g., Japan and Korea). From the results of the study, color palettes were suggested for each of the cultures, including Japanese, Korean, English, and American. For example, a color palette for a Korean client includes neutral hues, middle values, weak chroma (or intensity or saturation), and medium to high contrast, whereas a color palette for an English client includes warm hues, middle values, moderate chroma, and medium to low contrast. The study was limited to college students in residential spaces and misinterpretations may have occurred when translating words into Korean and Japanese; nevertheless, the study does provide a tested method related to color meaning and preferences.

Additionally, as will be discussed in Chapter 11, color affects people differently in different spaces such as hospitals, homes, restaurants, offices, and other commercial spaces.

Interpretation of Culture into Design

The application of a culture into a design can be difficult; it takes **cultural intelligence**, which means the ability to interpret a culture other than one's own (InformeDesign, 2005, July 27). Therefore, it is important to know how to acquire and apply cultural intelligence. For example, as cultural intelligence is acquired in a workplace setting, designers need to know that a company's or a global culture may affect how actions, gestures, and speech are interpreted. Avoiding misunderstandings is important. For this reason, the following design criteria have been developed for designing corporate settings (this can also apply to other settings or situations):

• Observe client's or coworker's behavior to understand the firm's or individual's culture.

• Understand that some people are uncomfortable analyzing their own culture and may have difficulty explaining their customs.

- Understand that some cultures have different personal boundaries, or distance zones.

- Understand that cultural difference might be influenced by various backgrounds (e.g., ethnicity such as Asian, Middle Eastern, German, Native American, African, or American), or by knowledge, or by profession (e.g., designer, engineer, architect, or accountant).

- Understand that the use of gesture and/or phrase may be appropriate in one culture or setting, and not in another.

Whether it is an organizational or ethnic culture, understanding its diversity will better inform the design. *The Power of Color: Creating Healing Spaces* by Sara Mayberry and Laurie Zargon (1995) provides some background information that will consider color for diverse design types, and serves as a good example for learning about any area of design and its meaning relative to culture.

Summary

Diversity means more than differences in ethnicity. It can be divided into six core dimensions and many categories within each dimension. In a diverse society such as that of the United States, clients expect designers to be knowledgeable, understanding, and ready to incorporate diverse design philosophies into the design of a home or workplace. To prepare for these situations, examination into diversity must include both fact finding and research of evidence. Findings will then result in appropriately designing spaces and accommodating individual needs for diverse clients.

Key Terms

cultural intelligence	ikebana	tatami
chi	Islam	tokonoma
chinoiserie	shibui	Vaastu Shastra
feng shui	shoji	yin
fusuma	socioeconomic status	yang

Commercial Spaces

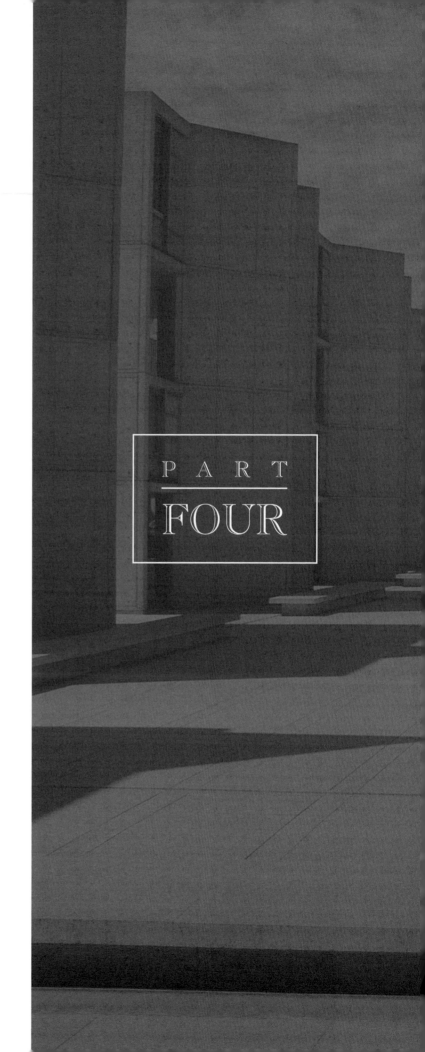

P A R T

FOUR

THEODORE

Data Collection for Commercial Spaces

OBJECTIVES

After reading this chapter, you should be able to:

Explain what is involved in data collection for commercial spaces

Identify the commercial space client

Describe the organization through its organization documents and how the organization's communication modes affect spatial arrangement

Examine spatial relationships, spatial organization, functional needs, and adjacencies

Conduct research into possible areas that will provide additional evidence

DRED COURT

This chapter provides a step-by-step approach to data collection for commercial interiors. First, designers must identify the client and users of the space as well as the **target market**. Next, they review existing documents related to spatial organization and **organizational profiles,** and determine appropriate data collection methods. Finally, they examine communication modes and space allocations, including functional needs and adjacencies; inventory **furniture, fixtures, and equipment (FF&E)**; and collect economic data.

But before any of this can begin, interior designers must understand the client for the commercial design project.

Client for Commercial Interiors

The client of a commercial interior may be one individual or a large group. For small commercial spaces, the client is generally the owner and an occupant of the space. In larger corporations, the owner may be a board of directors that includes a CEO and the company's management team along with investors who are not employed with the firm. Some of these may only be involved in the economics rather than the design of the space. The occupants of the space include users—staff or employees—and end users—the public and other visitors (Slotkis, 2006).

Data Collection

Data are collected from the client and occupants of the space by various methods. (Review Chapter 3 for details on these methods.) Various methods of data collection for commercial spaces include:

- User survey questionnaires

- Interviews

- Surveying existing conditions and FF&E

- Observation of behavior

- Visual and content analysis

- Experimentation

- Case studies

As data are collected, the designer looks at communication interaction, analyses of activity and equipment, and comments about the existing space.

The organization's management and staff are the primary sources of the organization's current and future requirements. The combination of individual surveys and interviews is the most effective method of collecting data from those who use the space; however, individual interviews in large corporations can be difficult and time consuming. Of course, the effectiveness of the data received is dependent on the reliability of survey questions being asked, validity of the answers, and the interviewer's interpretation (Rayfield, 1994). Therefore, questions must be written thoughtfully to provide valid answers that cannot be misinterpreted.

The survey should include current and space requirements: staffing numbers, support space requirements such as reception areas, conference rooms, filing, storage (Rayfield, 1994), and others related to specific design categories, such as healthcare.

Organizational Documents

To understand more about a particular commercial environment, **desk audits** are conducted. This is the review and/or analysis of an organization's documents (Slotkis, 2006). These documents include the organization's profiles and culture, charts, brochures, business and management plans, policies and procedures, records of growth patterns, mission statement, and strategic plan (Cama, 1996, Rayfield, 1994; Slotkis, 2006).

Analyzing organizational documents provides insight into the firm. The **organizational profiles** will show the manner in which management leads the firm. The **organizational chart** lists the names, titles, and positions of personnel within the company (Farren, 1988). If the firm does not have an organizational chart, the designer should draft a chart. The organizational profiles and charts along with observation and interviews are important to the designer because these documents will provide background into the organization's culture, i.e., the attitudes that characterize the firm (Rayfield, 1994). The different types of organizational profiles and cultures will be discussed later in this chapter.

"The day-to-day work relationships that keep the enterprise going [may] not strictly adhere to this chart" (Piotrowski & Rogers, 2007, p. 37); however, one-on-one interviews and on-site inspections will provide a clearer picture of the more informal channels of communications (Piotrowski & Rogers, 2007).

Brochures provide information about the purpose of the organization (i.e., the reason for its existence) and the way it projects its image to others. Business and management plans provide background on ownership, legal structure, services performed, marketing and operational plans, and financial information (Piotrowski, 2002, 2007). Policies and procedures show the firm's guiding principles as well as the day-to-day business operation. Records of growth show where the firm has been and the direction it is going (Rayfield, 1994). A **mission statement** also states the firm's purpose, whereas the **strategic plan** shows the direction that the company plans to go (Cama, 1996). Thus, the examination of the organization's documents helps the designer understand the organization's past, present, and future needs for the facility.

A literature review may provide new evidence on how an organization's culture, mission, or a strategic plan may inform the design. Additionally, conducting a content analysis of written documents (i.e., mission statement and strategic plan) will provide evidence about the firm's purpose and plans for the future and the type of organization. These will inform the development of the design project.

Organizational Profiles or Cultural Types

To understand how the organization works, designers identify organization profiles or culture types—the four **organizational culture** types are hierarchy, market, clan, and

Ideas for Collecting New Evidence

An example of a research topic into an organization's mission statement is the connection between mission and design for a company.

adhocracy. Figure 11.1 depicts hierarchical- and market-type cultures. Figure 11.2 represents the clan and adhocracy-type cultures.

Hierarchical Organizational Culture This type of culture is arranged in a hierarchy (Hierarchical, 2007) with power moving from the top down. Some characteristics of this organization are:

- Highly structured, formal system with an inward focus

- Stereotypically considered a bureaucratic corporation

- Formal policies and procedures

- Goals of stability, performance, and efficient operations

- Dependable delivery, smooth scheduling, and low cost signifying success (Tharp, 2005)

Its graphical diagram would be a pyramidal shape with the CEO at the top and many layers of management positioned below (see Figure 11.1).

Market Organizational Culture This type of organizational culture is similar to a hierarchical organization and has an external orientation. Some characteristics of this organization are:

- Result-driven attitude with an emphasis on job completion

- Competitive and goal-oriented people

- Demanding, hard-driven, and productive leaders

- Reputation and success highly valued

- Market share and penetration, competitive pricing, and market leadership signifying success (Tharp, 2005)

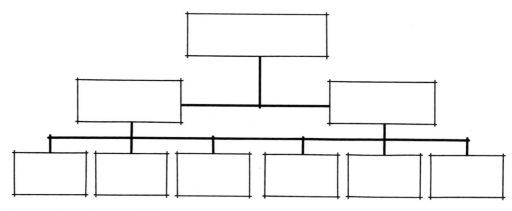

Figure 11.1 This pyramidal chart represents the hierarchical and market organizational cultures that represent power moving from the top down.

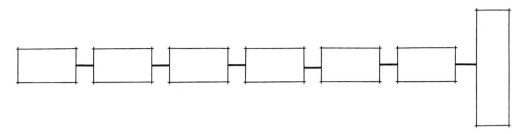

Figure 11.2 The linear chart of a level or flat organization represents the clan or adhocracy organizational cultures with greater flexibility and discretion for teamwork.

Clan Organizational Culture This type of organizational culture has similar values of the hierarchical organization with an inward focus. However, the clan organizational culture emphasizes flexibility and discretion. Some characteristics of this organization are:

- Open, friendly workplace

- Extended family atmosphere where people share of themselves

- Leaders as mentors—even as parental figures

- Group loyalty and sense of tradition

- Group cohesion highly respected

- Teamwork, participation, and consensus as high priorities (Tharp, 2005)

Because of the focus on teamwork and cohesiveness, the clan organization may be referred to as a flat or level organization. In such an organization, the manager works within the teams as is indicated by the large square. The principal or owner may also have team involvement, as is indicated at the side of the chart in Figure 11.2. A graphical diagram would look like a level playing field with everyone working together (see Figure 11.2).

Adhocractic Organizational Culture An adhocractic organizational culture is similar to the clan organization in flexibility and discretion; however, it has an external focus. Some characteristics of this organization are:

- A dynamic, entrepreneurial, and creative workplace

- Development of innovative ideas; experimentation, thinking differently, and risk taking encouraged

- Leading edge is a goal

- Focus on growth and acquisition of new resources

- Industry leadership highly valued

- Encourage individual freedom and initiative (Tharp, 2005)

Figure 11.3a–d shows the work culture of the four organizational types. Figure 11.4a–d demonstrates four work styles (Haworth, 2007).

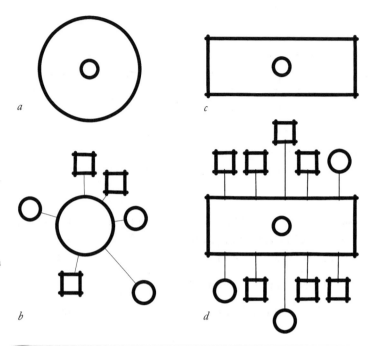

Figure 11.3a–d Within an organization, a network or pattern of communication is found that effectively promotes the exchange of ideas and information within an organization. Work culture types include (a) clan, (b) adhocracy, (c) hierarchy, and (d) market.

Figure 11.4a–d Work styles within an organization include (a) technical, (b) transactional, (c) consultative, and (d) collaborative.

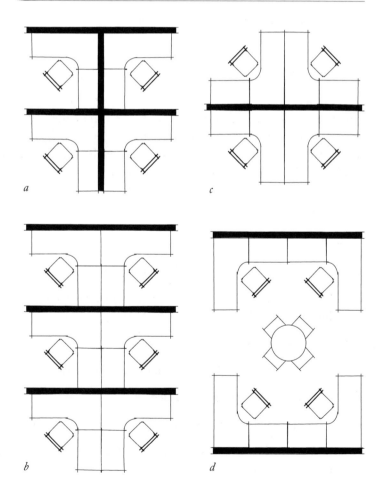

Spatial Relationships to Organization Structure

Offices designed with executive offices located around the perimeter of the building often indicate a hierarchical or market type of organization. Frequently, corridors and permeable boundaries also mark these types of organizations. In contrast, the clan (i.e., level or flat) and, possibly, adhocracy organizations are arranged with management interspersed with their teams. Teamwork is encouraged through flexible and open layout, flexible and open corridors, open circulation through spaces, team gathering places, as well as flexible furniture systems (Kilmer & Kilmer, 1992).

Designers must research ways that organizational profiles or culture affect spatial layout to find information that may inform the design. Research may be conducted through observations, interviews, and written surveys. Next, a review of literature should be conducted to determine spatial relationships and organization to best fit the firm's organizational profile. Additionally, a firm with a hierarchical or market type of organization may want to change from a traditional structure to that of a level or flat organization. For instance, the organization may have observed other firms and realize that the level or flat organization really does work, or the firm may work as a level or flat organization but the spatial organization is hierarchical and does not allow for the desired teamwork approach. In such cases, the observations, interviews, and written surveys will provide evidence to organize the spaces.

Communication Modes

To understand the **communication modes** within a firm, researchers ask pertinent questions during interviews and surveys. The purpose of these questions is to examine whether communication is formal, informal, or a combination of both. Are there face-to-face communications and/or paper communications? Are these interactions formal or informal? What, if any, are the other forms of interaction used by the firm, and are these other forms of communication formal or informal (Kilmer & Kilmer, 1992)? Personal interviews and on-site observations will provide a better understanding of a firm's communication modes (Binggeli, 2007).

Additionally, interviews with management and reviews of the organization profiles (hierarchy, market, clan, and adhocracy) will also provide cues to an organization's communications. For example, the interviewer and/or observer should notice whether or not there is a need for privacy in phone and face-to-face conversations, or if open office planning is best for a team approach to communication. Even with a team approach, spaces for private conversations may still need to be included in the planning process. The data collected regarding communication modes will affect spatial layout. Figure 11.5 illustrates a network or pattern of communication that effectively promotes the exchange of ideas and information within an organization. This illustration will assist in answering the questions "Who communicates with whom, how, and how often?" (Pena & Parshall, 2001, p. 80). With data collected that answer these questions, a diagram can be drawn that explains communication modes in a graphic format.

Technology has also changed methods of communication and storage. Paper storage may lessen while storage for electronic media increase. Electronic media storage may include computer hard drives and other electronic equipment such as printers, a server,

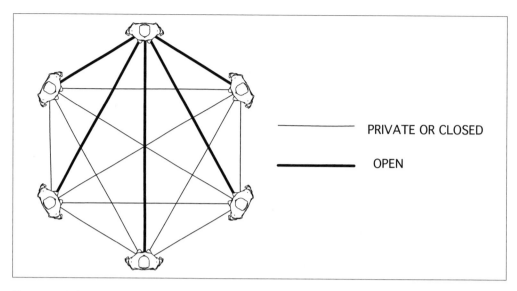

PRIVATE OR CLOSED

OPEN

Figure 11.5 Communication modes may be mandatory, secondary, or none required.

and electronic archival storage (Kilmer & Kilmer, 1992). The information from interviews, a walk-through, and observations will determine types of technology and storage needed that will affect spatial layout.

A review of literature may provide evidence for problems or solutions to obtain privacy in an open-office system or the effects of technological communication on interpersonal relationships or on effective communication. Such research can inform the design and improve design solutions.

Space Allocation: Functional Needs and Adjacencies

Designers examine existing conditions of spatial relationships and organization by reviewing existing space plans, drawings, and documents concerning architectural, engineering, electrical, and other factors. They tour existing facilities to provide additional information and verify and determine discrepancies in data collected from interviews and surveys. Tours provide opportunities to not only examine existing conditions and operating procedures but also to gain insight into support requirements and deficiencies (Binggeli, 2007; Pile, 2003; Rayfield, 1994). Tours also help determine what is working well within the office environment and what needs to be improved (Rayfield, 1994). If a tour of an existing facility is not possible, touring a similar facility can be a viable substitute.

Functional needs and adjacencies for commercial interiors relate to the operation of the firm and the physical and spatial needs of individuals and departments as a whole. In other words, how does the organization operate? How many users are there? What are their requirements? What is the physical proximity of its parts (e.g., individuals and departments)?

By observing a space, designers determine the function of the space, the number of people to occupy the space, and their basic requirements. They identify the activities that occur in the facility and work to accommodate them. Designers determine the required usable square footage based on the number of people, their needs, and their activities (Rayfield, 1994).

Designers also must research support spatial requirements. These include reception areas, conference rooms, filing spaces, and storage facilities (Rayfield, 1994). What is needed in these spaces and what square footage is required?

Next, they determine the users' adjacency requirements (mandatory, secondary, or none), type of support function areas, and individuals. They examine the working relationship of user groups or departments. They examine those who work in close proximity to one another to accomplish their tasks or job responsibilities (Rayfield, 1994).

Along with the function, spatial requirements, and adjacencies, designers also perform the following:

- Examine circulation—horizontal and vertical

- Examine reporting and communication procedures (Rayfield, 1994)

- Determine technological, equipment, and furniture requirements (Rayfield, 1994)

- Determine requirements for the design of **heating, ventilation, and air conditioning (HVAC)**, power supply, and distribution to the space (Rayfield, 1994)

- Investigate expected growth and/or other kinds of change and its rate

- Determine aesthetic requirements for the space (Rayfield, 1994)

- Investigate common or shared spaces and the location

- Determine wayfinding methods (Salmi, 2007)

- Determine requirements of the Americans with Disabilities Act **(ADA)** requirements

- Determine fire and building codes requirements (Rayfield, 1994)

All of these are important in determining space allocation and should be considered as the spatial requirements are developed. An example of a space-planning program is shown in Appendix V. Additionally, a review of literature should be conducted to collect new evidence on space allocation and productivity.

FF&E Inventory for Commercial Interiors

Scott-Webber (1998) states "the documentation of all of the existing . . . FF&E is an extremely important task" (p. 46). Whether a design project is a remodel or a new build, FF&E must be included in the plans. It will be important to determine whether the client will be reusing existing, replacing, purchasing new, or a combination of all three. If the client needs to use existing equipment, a complete inventory to analyze and inventory the furniture and equipment that the client owns must be conducted (Kilmer & Kilmer, 1992; Piotrowski, 2002 & 2007). The inventory will also include product specifications and condition (Kilmer & Kilmer, 1992; Piotrowski, 2002 & 2007), and while conducting the

Ideas for Collecting New Evidence

Examples of research topics into function, spatial requirements, and adjacencies include productivity or flexibility; function and accessibility; arrangement relative to age of worker; arrangement relative to client type; appropriate adjacencies by design type; connection between organizational design and employees; and optimizing retail space allocations.

inventory, pieces may be evaluated for reuse. The evaluation should also "include recommendations for possible refinishing or reupholstering as well as evaluations to determine the best future location and use of the existing furniture" (Rayfield, 1994, p. 61). It will also identify sizes to aid in determining square-footage requirements. Inventory of existing FF&E can be a tedious process; however, in a large firm if conducted by department, the process will be more efficient (Rayfield, 1994).

Included in a furniture inventory are such items as desks, chairs, sofas, tables, credenzas, and **casegoods** that are found in the workplace (Kilmer & Kilmer, 1992). The inventory of each piece of furniture should include the following specifications as well as its condition:

- Item number

- Type

- Size: height, width, and depth

- Color

- Finish

- Condition

- Refinishing

- Reupholstering

Included in the fixtures inventory are lighting, mechanical, and electrical items (Scott-Webber, 1998). Included in an equipment inventory are such items as telephones, computers, video equipment, copy machines, and other nonfurniture items (Kilmer & Kilmer, 1992). The inventory should provide information for each piece of equipment for space planning as well as mechanical and electrical engineering as follows:

- Item number

- Type

- Size

- Built-in, freestanding, or work surface

- Power requirements

- Heat release

- Acoustic constraints

- Cabling requirements

- Special requirements such as special HVAC or plumbing

To record existing FF&E, designers may create a spreadsheet. Tables 11.1 through 11.3 are examples of spreadsheets for each area.

Item No.	Type	Size W × L × D	Color	Finish	Condition	Refinishing	Reupholstering

Table 11.1
Existing Furniture Inventory

Item No.	Type	Size W × L × D	Color	Finish	Condition	Refinishing	Other Information

Table 11.2
Existing Fixtures Inventory 2

Item No.	Type	Size W × L × D	Built-in Freestanding Work Surface	Finish	Power Req.	Heat Release	Acoustic	Cabling	Special Req.

Table 11.3
Existing Equipment Inventory 3

Ideas for Collecting New Evidence

Examples of research topics into FF&E include selection of furniture and accommodating needs of children in daycare; patients in healthcare; varied ages in offices; adolescents in dormitories; customers in restaurants and/or retail; and elderly and/or bariatric in senior housing facilities.

New pieces of furniture and equipment are continually being designed and brought to market. For this reason, designers must investigate these new products. To collect new evidence, it is important to examine periodicals not only on these new products but also for issues related to new various age groups or situations, i.e., retail or nursing homes.

Bariatric Furniture

Because of the increase in obesity, bariatric furniture has become important in the appropriate selection of furniture. The InformeDesign RS "Obesity and the Designed Environment" (2007, August 29) summarizes an article that suggests areas of possible research for obesity and the designed environment as well as suggestions to provide healthy alternatives such as promoting the use of stairs and placing them in a more convenient location to encourage physical activity.

Color

Color, as it relates to lighting, was mentioned earlier in Chapter 4. Because color affects people psychologically, it also plays a part in data collection for commercial spaces. As stated by Marberry and Zagon (1995), color for commercial spaces should be analyzed by beginning with the identification of those who interact within these spaces—offices, hospitality, healthcare, education, and others. Marberry and Zagon provide the following suggestion for choosing color in the following interior environments.

- Offices—Workers should have an environment that is supportive and encourages interaction. Using the full spectrum of color, a balanced palette is suggested with the avoidance of large expanses of bright colors, particularly, vibrating and strong contrasting colors.

- Hospitality—Hotels and restaurants: People should feel comfortable and relaxed so they can rest or enjoy being entertained. Using the full spectrum of color, stronger, brighter colors with great contrast provide an atmosphere that is uplifting.

- Healthcare—There are many types of healthcare to consider; these include hospitals (e.g., general and pediatric), ambulatory or outpatient care centers, daycare, and long-term care. Generally, creating a healing environment is the goal for healthcare. Marberry and Zagon (1995) note that mind/body research indicates that when patients feel less stress, they recover faster than if they were in a more stressful environment. A balanced color palette is recommended and will eliminate the jaundiced-look associated with too much yellow. Using green—the opposite of red—in operating rooms lessens eyestrain. In facilities for the elderly, hues that are similar in saturation and value should not be placed side by side because it would be difficult to interpret important information about their environment such as depth and contrast of objects.

- Education—Elementary school classrooms, for example, should be fun places that encourage learning. Using the full spectrum of color creates an energetic, uplifting, and positive environment. However, it is not limited to primary colors. High-reflective color can be applied in corridors and stairways with an accent color on railings and doors. The color palette in the classroom should not distract but promote concentration; therefore, a neutral palette with bright accents is a good solution. However, review of literature for neurologically challenged children, i.e., the autistic, may need different and less stimulating environments. This topic is discussed in Chapter 12 with ideas for research.

Marberry and Zagon (1995) provide other suggestion in their book, *The Power of Color: Creating Healthy Interior Spaces*. Additionally, information can be located in RS from InformeDesign, which can provide new evidence from research.

Economics

Economic factors involving initial cost, budget, price range, and life-cycle costing for commercial spaces will be specific for each design type. Many choices related to design affect the economics or bottom line—whether short term or long term.

Application

Research topics related to commercial spaces can be researched from a variety of sources. These sources include American Society of Interior Designers (ASID) Knowledge Center and International Interior Design Association (IIDA) Knowledge Center. Linked through ASID and IIDA, office systems manufacturers such as Allsteel, Herman Miller, Steelcase, and Haworth conduct research and publish articles on their Web sites. Research articles may also be accessed from academic journals through a database such as InformeDesign, Ingentaconnect, or Blackwell Publishing. The following provides specific locations and examples of research studies related to commercial spaces.

Both ASID and IIDA's Knowledge Centers have articles that provide research, case studies, and industry and academic resources. The ASID Knowledge Center Web site contains a research section, with links to Allsteel, Herman Miller, Steelcase, and Haworth. The Allsteel link connects to ergonomics, seating adjustments, workplace trends, and more. Herman Miller contains a research section that will provide information about cultural change, open environments, new ways of working, and much more. Steelcase contains resources on learning and working, environment for discovery, etc. Haworth also contains research articles on human performance—ergonomics, lifestyle—physical space and productivity, motivation—productivity, and others.

The IIDA Knowledge Center Web site contains a variety of research articles. Some look at current trends, work performance, healthcare facility evaluation to inform future design decisions, space planning, and more. The following are articles under space planning that may be helpful in collecting new evidence. For example, Veitch, Farley, and Newsham (2002) conducted a field study that determined the effects of open-plan office design on indoor environment and human satisfaction.

Other Web site articles provide additional evidence. Tharp's (2005) article, "Four Organizational Culture Types," explains organizational cultural types. Zhao and Tseng's (2007) article, "Flexible Facility Interior Layout: A Real Options Approach," explores flexible facility layouts that can be used in a dynamic manner and respond to changing demands.

Examples of RS on organizational culture, organizational structures, FF&E, and more can be found on InformeDesign. The InformeDesign RS "Organizational Culture Influences Employee Performance" (2004, July 20) examines a case study that analyzes the way environment design, communication, and organizational culture affect human performance at work. "Job Analysis in Organizations Without Boundaries," another InformeDesign RS (2004, March 30), references a position paper that addresses the human resource issues of job analysis, recruitment, and selection in organizations without boundaries. The InformeDesign RS "Specifying Seating for the Elderly" (2004, March 15) features an experiment that analyzed the varied abilities of the elderly in getting up out of a chair, whereas the InformeDesign RS "Task Chair Preferences" (2005, July 15) is a study that compares users' preferences for two types of task chairs.

Summary

This chapter provides background information that will aid in the collection of data as well as research for commercial interiors. First, we examined how the client in commercial spaces is very different from residential. That client could be one person or a large group of people who have a major stake in the design. We also explored the organization documents that provide insight into the organizational profile or culture.

Spatial organization is affected by the four organizational profiles or culture: hierarchy, market, clan, and adhocracy. Executive offices located around the perimeter of the building generally indicates a hierarchical or market type of organization. Conversely, management is interspersed with the teams within the clan (i.e., level or flat) and, sometimes, adhocracy organizations. Here, teamwork is encouraged with a flexible and open layout. This information will also be obtained through interviews, surveys, and/or observations.

Understanding communication modes within a firm is also important and affects the design layout. Some firms prefer communication that is formal, informal, or a combination of both. Some firms use face-to-face and/or paper communication methods. Communication preferences become clear through the interviews and surveys. Additionally, the function, spatial requirements, and adjacencies for the firm and individuals also become clear through interviews, surveys, and inventories. FF&E inventories provide data on existing fixtures as well as what needs to be replaced or purchased.

Beyond gathering fact-finding data, researching new evidence is important. Research studies may provide evidence to improve productivity and employee satisfaction whether through the design layout, FF&E selected, or color choices. Many of the ideas provided in this chapter are a great place to start, but new research studies are continually published and should be investigated.

Key Terms

ADA

casegoods

communication modes

desk audit

furniture, fixtures, and
    equipment (FF&E)

heating, ventilating, and air
    conditioning (HVAC)

mission statement

organizational culture

organizational profile

organizational chart

strategic plan

target market

CHAPTER

12

Office Design

OBJECTIVES

After reading this chapter, you should be able to:

List the areas for data collection and special needs relative to office design categories

Develop EBD for office spaces

Commercial interiors vary greatly. Categories include offices, retail, hospitality, healthcare, and education, just to name a few. Spatial needs and functions within office design also vary widely. The previous chapter provided areas for general data collection. This chapter provides additional information regarding data collection specifically for office design. Subsequent chapters will discuss hospitality, healthcare, retail, and other design categories.

Office Design

A list of office design **typology** can be quite large. Office design types may include the insurance office, the accounting office, the corporate office, the law office, and financial institutions. Within each type, there are other specific types, or sub-types. For example, specific types of financial institutions may include banks, savings and loans, investment firms, credit unions, and trading centers. Each type of office has its own set of concerns. With financial institutions, for example, there are similar concerns for office design, but with a specific need for security. Within these specific types, there are specialized areas. For example, a financial institution may be a large banking firm or the small-town bank; although some aspects of both may be similar, each have different needs and desires.

History of Office Design

Offices began as one-person operations with the owner conducting all aspects of the business. Then, as businesses grew and employees were hired, the arrangement of the office changed from one room to several rooms; offices were segregated into closed offices—one person per office. As businesses continued to grow, so did the size and configuration of the office. In most offices, administrators were strategically located on the perimeter of the building that signified status within the firm. Such offices were provided with windows to the outside for natural light and to the inside to oversee the workforce. The main workforce was located in the center of the building, and desks were placed in rigid rows; this area was called the "**bullpen**" (Kilmer & Kilmer, 1992; Piotrowski & Rogers, 2007).

In the 1950s, administrative offices shifted near the center of the building and the workforce was arranged with windows facing open spaces located around the building's perimeter. This brought about the development of modular wall constructed systems. The layout of these modular systems brought more light into the interior and allowed for flexibility in relocating offices. Eventually, this gave birth to **open planning**; walled offices were removed, and executives and staff strategically scattered around the building floor. It also brought a reemergence of executive status with executives being placed closest to windows or corners of the building; this reflected the pyramidal, or hierarchical, organization. This type of spatial arrangement made it easier and cheaper to move furniture than to tear down in order to reconfigure according to business needs. This was also the beginning of the "team" structure, which increased work productivity (Kilmer & Kilmer, 1992; Piotrowski & Rogers, 2007). The advantages of open planning promoted communications and teamwork within a level or flat organization. The disadvantages were the loss of privacy as well as noisy people and machines (Kilmer & Kilmer, 1992). Changes from traditional office

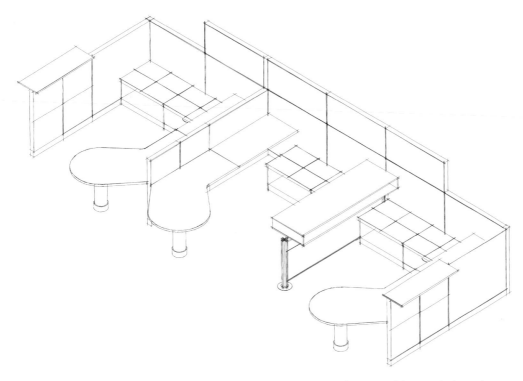

Figure 12.1 Today, most office space configurations include systems furniture with acoustical panels.

structure to open office planning took place because research was conducted on organizational structure and productivity (Piotrowski & Rogers, 2007). Today, office systems furniture with acoustical panels allow for teamwork and sound control. Figure 12.1 illustrates an open office plan.

In offices today, technology has also affected office designs and changed the way business is conducted. Work environments have also improved over those from the past. However, because of technology, many offices have downsized and some employees are working from home offices (Piotrowski & Rogers, 2007). Thus, there are many alternative office arrangements: hoteling, telecommuting, loosely coupled office, and virtual office.

Technology has also created **hoteling**—an unassigned office approach in which the individual employee has no dedicated personally assigned office, workstation, or desk. Real estate offices commonly operate using this approach. In hoteling, an organization's system is specific to each office. However, most commonly, the worker calls ahead to reserve for an office or workstation and, upon arrival, takes an available workplace that suits his or her needs (Becker & Steele, 1994; Piotrowski & Rogers, 2007). Other terminology is given to the unassigned office approach such as **free-address, guesting, just-in-time**, and **hot-desk** (Piotrowski & Rogers, 2007).

Home-based **telecommuting** began as a means of assisting women wanting to work at home. However, more recently, corporations have found this type of work cost effective for the employer and employee. Companies vary in what they provide employees and needs for these types of offices (Becker & Steele, 1994).

Loosely coupled office has no one particular office setting. The setting could be at home, in a neighborhood work center, in a car or on an airplane, or at the central office; the setting varies from week to week or even day to day. Settings are linked physically by the movement of employees who work in these settings over the course of a day, a week, or the life of a project; and by the electronic movement of information through e-mail, voicemail, videoconferencing, telephone, and fax (Becker & Steele, 1994).

The **virtual office** may be the office of the future—one that has a mind of its own. It's an office that instantly responds to the occupant's arrival by adjusting the temperature, lighting, and airflow to the preferred settings. It unlocks sealed personal information folders on the computer. Overhead lights visibly announce one's entrance and alerts a "buddy list" of coworkers. It also signals through an exterior electronic message board when the occupant is ready for visitors, the day's agenda, and anything else that would need to be announced (Levitch, 2003). According to Piotrowski and Rogers (2007), the virtual office is one in which everything needed to conduct business is in a briefcase or car, i.e., cell phone, laptop computer, fax, printer, etc. Thus, work can be done anywhere at any time—a description similar to the loosely coupled office.

Most often, present office design utilizes the open plan office. Future office design may be similar or different. Some say that the office of tomorrow may become obsolete because more computers and communication means a decentralized workforce. Others say that face-to-face communication is very important, and offices will need to be adaptable to the virtual and real combined. Thus, design research on ideas for office designs will develop evidence to inform the design.

Spatial Relationships and Organization

The design of a commercial office spaces involves extensive space planning and design of office environments—small to large (Allen et al. 2004). Offices are separated into zones: public and private. Public zones are areas where the public (clients and guests) is allowed to enter. These areas include the entry and/or reception areas, and conference or presentation rooms. Private zones are areas where the public is excluded. These areas include offices—walled and open, training areas, employee conference rooms, open offices, support staff areas, work centers, break rooms, and restrooms (Allen et al., 2004; Kilmer & Kilmer, 1992).

Public Zone

The design of the reception or entry area is extremely important for two reasons. First, the purpose of this area is to immediately impress the visitor. Second, the design of the space must immediately convey the image of the firm to the client. The design concept for the space must be clearly seen upon entrance to convey the image (Allen et al., 2004; Kilmer & Kilmer, 1992).

The reception areas include two activities—the office workspace for a receptionist and waiting/conversation area for guests. The reception area must be adjacent to the main entrance, near the conference or presentation rooms, and with easy access to the private offices. The reception areas should also be near a break room or have a coffee break area that will serve guest refreshments while waiting. A storage area for outerwear (e.g., coats, umbrellas, boots) should also be located in the reception area (Allen et al., 2004).

Public conference or presentation rooms are necessary for meetings either among staff or with visitors and/or clients, and should be welcoming to visitors. The conference room may be located in one central space that is directly connected to the reception or entry area (Allen et al., 2004). Depending on the type of firm or the purpose of the conference room, this space may be formal or informal, and it may be an open, a closed, or a combination of open and closed space (Kilmer & Kilmer, 1992). Audiovisual equipment and presentation materials should be stored in an adjacent and concealed area (Allen et al., 2004).

Training areas may be intended for employee training or for training of the public and employees. Therefore, it would be important to determine who will use the space, how often, how many trainees, and then determine the best location within the firm—in a public or private zone. The type of furniture will depend on the type of training session(s), and a storage area will be needed for the audiovisual equipment.

Private Zone

Offices are arranged by department (or division) or, in large corporations, an entire floor may be dedicated to a department (or division).

The location and arrangement will depend on variables, including organizational profile, function, and communication. For example, in an organization that is structured as a hierarchy, executives or other management personnel generally occupy walled offices. These offices may be located throughout the space or grouped together in a spatial arrangement. Additionally, depending on the size or type of firm, executive offices may be grouped in a suite of rooms with a private administrative assistant's office, a private office, conference room, bathroom, and storage area (Allen et al., 2004; Kilmer & Kilmer, 1992). There may also be a bar as well as dining and entertainment facilities (Kilmer & Kilmer, 1992).

Many commercial firms provide open office or systems furniture for employees. They are generally grouped by department or division, and are shielded from the noise but located adjacent to the support staff (Allen et al., 2004). A literature review will provide evidence on issues related to noise and productivity that may inform the design layout.

Support staff (i.e., secretaries and administrative assistants) who serve one or a number of employees and/or management are generally located in open offices. Such offices are placed near those they serve and near work centers. In a smaller firm, the receptionist serves as support staff as well as meeting the public. In a larger firm, support staff may be located in a **pool** or **secretarial bay** (Allen et al., 2004). Here the staff may be given some degree of control over their environment and a sense of personalization or territoriality (Steelcase.com; knoll.com). Further research for evidence on creating a sense of personalization or territoriality will inform the design.

Office personnel often use private conference rooms, which may be an informal open space or a formal conference room and may be adjacent to the executive offices. Some offices have shared conference spaces interspersed throughout the plan that provide a teamwork setting. Training rooms in private areas are intended to train employees and, thus, clients and/or guests are not allowed in this area. Conference and training rooms in private areas will have the similar needs for audiovisual equipment and storage as those in the public area. Facts relating to the use and needs for the conference room are gathered from the client; however, a literature review may provide evidence that may improve spatial layout and, thus, inform the design.

Ideas for Collecting New Evidence

An example of a research topic into literature on space allocation is employee satisfaction and/or productivity. Observations of employee behavior or interviews will also provide evidence that may improve the design.

Work centers are typically closed off because they are frequently cluttered and/or noisy. These centers contain central files, paper, other office equipment and supplies (Allen et al., 2004; Kilmer & Kilmer, 1992). In smaller firms, the workroom may become the employee lounge and, thus, a sink will require the space be located near plumbing lines (Allen et al., 2004). Research from literature and observations will provide evidence to inform and locate work centers.

Some firms require an area for resources—library or communications room. This area in architectural and interior design firms requires a resource library for materials used for the design projects. This space must be located for easy access by employees who will need these resources (Kilmer & Kilmer, 1992). With the change from traditional resources to Internet resources, research on the advantages and disadvantages of each may be helpful to inform and then develop the appropriate design.

In the larger firms, amenities may be provided. These may include a break room or lunchroom room or space, a child-care facility on the premises, and fitness rooms. Each of these spaces will have special needs and need to be located near plumbing lines. Often the amenities provided are intended to improve both the health and productivity of employees (Kilmer & Kilmer, 1992). A review of literature on various amenities and ways they improve health and productivity will inform the design.

In large corporations, restrooms must be located near plumbing lines, which will determine placement of restrooms. In high-rise buildings, plumbing lines may be located in the central core of the building. In small corporations, restrooms will be located for access by guests and/or visitors and employees between the public and private areas. In commercial interiors, restrooms are required to be Americans with Disability Act (ADA) accessible (Allen et al., 2004). Restrooms vary in size depending upon the number of employees on one level of the firm. A review of literature or observations may help determine the number of stalls needed to eliminate this problem and inform the design.

Departments

Depending upon the type and size of an office, the type and size of departments will vary. However, departments are generally the basic planning units within the office and are organized spatially according to a systems analysis: workflow, communications, proximity (i.e., adjacency), and people relationships.

Data Collection for Office Design

Today's offices are designed to increase employee satisfaction and productivity. Some of the amenities are helpful, such as exercise areas and cafeterias, but the primary goal is to enhance productivity. Therefore, this is an area for research that is crucial to all office design projects.

Designers collect data from employees using predesigned questionnaires that have open-ended questions, one-answer questions, or a combination of the two. When collecting data for a design, all those who use the space—executives, management, and employees —must be involved.

Space requirements are specific to each organization; however, there are standard square footages. Managerial or private offices are approximately 120 to 140 square feet for traditional furniture, or 80 to 100 square feet for systems furniture (Piotrowski & Rogers, 2007). Clerical, keyboard, and customer service require approximately 36 square feet (Allen et al., 2004).

The focus of security for offices and office buildings is "on the safety of the employees in the facility" (Piotrowski & Rogers, 2007, pg. 85). Security needs are dependent upon the client's particular security issues—some have few issues while others need complicated monitoring and access systems. The most appropriate method of security for a client will be determined through interviews as well as observations (Piotrowski & Rogers, 2007). Through a review of literature, research may provide evidence to improve security and safety of employees in offices and office buildings.

Code research must be conducted. Designers search and analyze building and fire code as well as ADA codes relative to the specific building and occupant of the space. These topics were discussed in Chapter 6. Although code research refers to fact gathering, it is also useful to look at studies that have been conducted to examine fire safety issues; these studies provide evidence to inform and improve design.

Financial Institutions

Let's look at financial institutions, one of the office design types. The requirements of financial institutions—banking, savings and loans, investment firms, credit unions, and trading centers—are similar to and yet different from other office types. First, the design of each institution should convey in its image to the customer both a sense of monetary security for the money and a progressive outlook. In the past, a formal, traditional image was most common and gave a sense of security; but today, a contemporary image often gives a sense of a new and progressive approach to business (Kilmer & Kilmer, 1992).

The greatest concern for financial institutions is to convey not only a sense of security in business practices but also a sense of security in the physical space that business is conducted, i.e., a secured space. Therefore, research into spatial organization relative to security is crucial.

Space allocation of public, semi-public, and private areas must be secure. Adjacencies and circulation for financial institutions are related to the public versus private zones. The public zone begins at the bank's entrance with the lobby, teller windows, and loan offices. Adjacent to this area is generally a semi-public zone, the safety deposit area. Then, behind these are private behind-the-scenes workings of the bank. The public is seldom allowed in these secure spaces that include the main bank vault and armored car delivery area. Banks will also have clerical areas, an employee lounge, central files, and storage (Kilmer & Kilmer, 1992). Figure 12.2 illustrates a financial institution's floor plan.

As in many businesses, bank operations and workflow are computerized. Even though transactions are electronic, money and other legal tender are still exchanged and stored. Data are stored on the bank's computer—onsite or at the main terminal. Banking today is electronic and can be accessed by physically going to the bank, using a computer from any location (e.g., home, work, or even a hotel room), or when traveling via automatic teller machines (ATMs). To maintain security at remote locations such as ATMs, security cameras monitor transactions.

For financial institutions, suggested literature reviews might relate to the design of

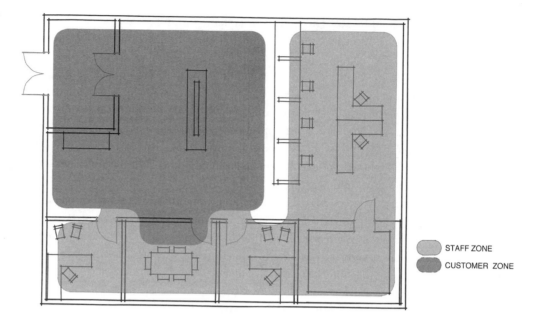

STAFF ZONE

CUSTOMER ZONE

Figure 12.2 This diagram illustrates space allocation for a financial institution.

office projects that convey a sense of security, improve work process and communications as well as productivity, create a flexible environment, and increase building value for future resale. These types of research will inform the design.

Application

Topics for research into commercial spaces were suggested in the previous chapter. Of course research can also be specifically conducted within specific design typologies. The Las Vegas Chamber of Commerce case study exemplifies research conducted for an office design project.

The International Interior Design Association (IIDA) Knowledge Center has sections that relate to specific office design types such as corporate or government. It also has sections listed by topic such as FF&E, space planning, or computer technology. The American Society of Interior Designers (ASID) Knowledge Center links to other industry sources such as Steelcase, which has research on higher education, open plan and private offices, ergonomics, work style and culture, and ergonomics.

InformeDesign's (2008, April 30) RS "Designing Workplaces for Flexibility" provides evidence related to the flexibility in the workplace and creativity. Criteria were identified to improve the workplace environment.

In reviewing the InformeDesign RS, it is important to review its Key Concepts and Design Criteria and then use those criteria in informing the design.

Summary

Office design has changed greatly over the years. In part, technology has caused these changes. For example, technology allows work to take place from multiple locations such as a home office, library, airport, and regional office. Nevertheless, many large commercial office spaces are still in need of design services, and their design involves extensive space planning to create productive office environments. Financial institutions, for example, must convey an image to the customer of both a sense of monetary security for the money and a progressive outlook.

Whether a corporate office or financial institution, the spatial layout is separated into zones—public and private. Public zones allow the public (clients and guests) to enter, whereas private zones are excluded from the public. Relating to the organizational culture, some offices or financial institutions are walled into private offices, whereas others contain the open office or systems furniture.

Using various methods, data collected from the client and the space will assist in design. Additionally, research for new evidence is necessary; research areas for office design should include noise and productivity, spatial requirements, and security. Thus, research will provide evidence on these issues to inform and improve the design layout.

Key Terms

bullpen

free-address

guesting

hot-desk

hoteling

just-in-time

loosely coupled office

open planning

pool

secretarial bay

telecommuting

typology

virtual office

Hospitality Design

OBJECTIVES

After reading this chapter, you should be able to:

Examine the areas for data collection and special needs relative to hospitality design categories

Develop evidence-based design (EBD) for hospitality design

DRED COURT

Hospitality design blends commercial design with aspects of residential design that includes guest rooms, dining, and other aspects of the residence (Allen, et al., 2004). Hospitality design includes hotels, or lodging, and restaurants, or food and beverage facilities. The large, worldwide hospitality industry provides places for socializing, entertainment, information, nutritional nourishment, and overnight and longer-stay accommodation (Baucom, 1996; Kilmer & Kilmer, 1992).

There are many types of lodging and food and beverage facilities. Typing hospitality design can be difficult—not only because of the variety of types, but also due to the variety of needs that may be specialized. A few examples of hotel typology include **luxury hotels, resort hotels, conference centers, casinos, limited-service hotels** (i.e., **motels**) (McDonough et al., 2001; Piotrowski & Rogers, 2007), **bed-and-breakfast inns, extended-stay or all-suite facilities**, and **hostels** (Piotrowski & Rogers, 2007). Restaurant types may include fast food, coffee shop, hotel dining, family restaurant, gathering place, and cafeteria (Baraban & Burocher, 2001).

This chapter explores areas of data collection for hospitality design, first for lodging and then for food and beverage facilities.

Hotel Design

Whether a hotel guest's stay is for work, pleasure, or a combination of the two, "hotels are in the business of memories, and thus, owners, architects (and interior designers) must be diligent in the design of a hotel to ensure a good and lasting memory" (McDonough et al., 2001, p. 1). The design must not only aid in that experience but also ensure a return of the guest. This is possible through data collection of facts and evidence that support good design.

Since the 1950s and during the 1960s, an increase in tourism took place among the Western nations, and travel occurred both domestically and internationally. The industrial revolution laid the groundwork for affluence. The industrial revolution also increased the spending power of the middle class and provided them with the means to travel. During this time, travel was mostly for business and educational purposes. Men traveled on business, and middle- and upper-class families traveled to historic sites and other cultures in order to further their education. Travel on an ever-broadening scale was made possible with the invention of the steam locomotive and the internal combustion engine, improved and extended road systems, and increased mobility of the population. Thus, hotel accommodations improved, particularly to accommodate upper-class desires. From the 1960s to the 1980s, the tourist industry was booming (Huffadine, 1993). Since then, the industry has continued to boom with a constantly changing market that depends upon economics and the needs of customers (Baucom, 1996).

Needs and expectations for lodging have varied and changed through time. Today, hotels are larger and cleaner with a greater need for security and amenities such as Internet services (Piotrowski & Rogers, 2007). Amenities provided by hotels depend upon typology and the target market. A list of hotel design typology might include:

- Airport hotel

- Travel lodge

- Motel

- Resort

- Convention-oriented hotel

- Urban hotel

- Bed-and-breakfast

Client

Traditionally, clients for hospitality design projects have been the sponsors, investors, and other decision makers. However, a hospitality design client also includes hotel management groups as well as participants who are involved in the development and promotion of a facility (Huffadine, 1993).

Target Market

Hotel guests are diverse, representing, for example, many different nationalities and a variety of age groups (Huffadine, 1993). They travel for different reasons, whether for business or pleasure (McDonough et al., 2001). Hotels are typically in metropolitan areas, whereas limited-service hotels or motels are more frequently found in the suburbs and in smaller cities (Kilmer & Kilmer, 1992). The design focus of limited-service hotels is on guest rooms (McDonough et al., 2001) with quick, easy-to-reach services, and convenient parking spots that guests now expect. Often, when travelers are at the end point of a destination, they are more interested in activities outside of the facility, such as sightseeing and other entertainment or recreation, than in the facility itself; however, guests do expect comfort and conveniences such as restaurants, lounges, game rooms, and/or kitchenettes (Kilmer & Kilmer, 1992).

A feasibility study, or market analysis, determines whether or not a project will be successful before construction. A consultant who specialized in conducting such work often prepares this type of study. Though expensive, it may save a developer time, money, and effort by avoiding costly mistakes. More information on feasibility studies is included in Christine Piotrowski and Elisabeth Rogers (2007) book, *Designing Commercial Interiors*. Important to the designer is the direct connection between the feasibility study and concept statements; the concept statements must reflect the results of the feasibility study to ensure the accuracy of the target market, the services offered, the mix of accommodations, and the ambience (Piotrowski & Rogers, 2007). Thus, when the feasibility study is complete, the interior designer must carefully consider the target market in developing an appropriate concept.

The designer must research the locale in which the projected hotel will be located. As stated by McDonough et al. (2001), the selected target market must be "compatible with the intended location" (p. 15). Additionally, providing appropriate services that will accommodate visitors to a particular destination ensures good design and satisfies guests.

To determine the target market, guest profile, and location, designers must gather facts through written surveys, observations, interviews, and/or focus groups within the community. By these means, they gather evidence to inform the design regarding the market in the community. Along with these data collection methods, research summaries (RS) from InformeDesign will also provide evidence to inform the design. For example, one study compared and contrasted hotel selection criteria and leisure travelers. Such criteria will help identify amenities and design solutions for a design project (InformeDesign, 2006, July 12). Another example identified innovative design elements and amenities for hotels to distinguish themselves in the hotel market and increase the profit margin (InformeDesign, 2002, December 4a).

Spatial Relationships and Organization

In all hotels, spatial relationships and organization include three basic areas: public spaces, guest rooms, and **back of house** (McDonough et al., 2001). Note that guest rooms and back of house are private zones. Some facilities need space for eating, exercising, and entertaining to accommodate their overnight guests. What makes a hotel distinctive are the guest and the staff, and the design must cater to guests' expectations and staff must provide services to meet those needs (Kilmer & Kilmer, 1992).

It is particularly important for the hotel to function efficiently and consistently (McDonough et al., 2001). For example, the entrance and lobby serve as multifunctional spaces where employees oversee the arrival and departure of guests. A reception area controls movement in and out of the hotel. It becomes a central clearinghouse for baggage handling and corridors and elevators that move traffic (Kilmer & Kilmer, 1992). Careful examination and planning of circulation movement will alleviate congestion. However, observations of people moving in and around the entrance and lobby will provide evidence to improve or develop better circulation and inform the design.

Fig. 13.1 Hotel reception area in Sardinia, Italy

Hotels are generally multilevel buildings because of cost of property that limits building areas; thus, vertical circulation provides for compacting of services (Kilmer & Kilmer, 1992). Circulation movement within the hotel will separate the various activities relative to public spaces, guest rooms, and back of house. Pathways to different areas must be clearly marked to provide not only good circulation but also relieve congestion and separation of areas (McDonough et al., 2001). Research relative to privacy and separation of the space may provide evidence to improve or inform the design. Additionally, research of appropriate wayfinding methods will be valuable for circulation movement and in relieving congestion.

Public Zone
Public spaces include the entrance, a lobby, corridors, guest elevators, restaurant (**front of house**), exercise, recreation, and transportation.

- Lobby—This includes the front desk, retail shops, concierge, guest arrivals and departures as well as circulation. Administration is included because there is a connection between registration or other services rendered in which employees within administration are involved. However, the public generally does not enter the administration office area.

- Food and beverage—Coffee shops, restaurants, and/or bars are frequently available for the convenience of the traveler.

- Meeting rooms—Hotels frequently have ballrooms, conference rooms, and lounges to accommodate parties and conferences.

- Recreation—Many hotels include amenities such as shops, gyms, swimming pools, and others for the convenience of hotel guests.

- Transportation—An area at or near the entrance is provided for guest to arrive and depart as well as parking for buses, taxis, and cars (Huffadine, 1993).

Concerns for public areas are circulation, accessibility, and efficiency of the space. Research will provide evidence on these issues and will inform the design.

Private Zone
Private areas include guest rooms, administrative offices, back of house, and other spaces for services related to running a hotel.

- Guest rooms—Careful planning of guest rooms involves residential design, but also planning for security and convenience that hotel guests expect such as dead bolts, hair dryers, and Internet connections.

- Administration—Aspects of office design are applied in administration.

- Back of the house—This includes offices for administration and other staff facilities such as housekeeping, laundry, deliveries, disposal, and storage (Huffadine, 1993).

An important aspect of private areas relates to security. Research will provide evidence on security issues. For example, InformeDesign RS "Hotel Design for Seniors" (2003, December 5) summarizes a study that identified factors that compete for senior citizens. One of the issues related to having a sense of security during a hotel stay. Therefore, adapting hotels to meet not only the physical needs of seniors but also psychological needs will gain senior citizens as customers. Designers must carefully plan security methods in the hotel design.

Space Allocation for Hotels: Function and Adjacencies

Designers begin the process of allocating space by examining the basic functions or activities (e.g., housing, guest services, and housekeeping) as well as by examining the adjacency requirements. Spatial configurations, functional allocations, and technical equipment must be analyzed according to the type of hotel. Each type will have different needs and requirements (Huffadine, 1993). Space allocated for guest rooms versus all other function and support spaces will vary depending on the type of lodging. For example, the amount of guest space for a motel (i.e., limited-service hotel) is 90 percent in comparison to 55 percent for a mega resort. Guest rooms may range from 375 square feet for a standard (double bed) room to 1,480 square feet for a luxury two-bedroom suite (Piotrowski & Rogers, 2007, pp. 116–17).

Clearly, depending on the type of hotel (e.g., motel or luxury hotel) and the client, spatial expectations will vary. For example, a designer working on a hotel to accommodate seniors needs to consider accessibility in space allocation, i.e., function and accessibility. A review of literature through InformeDesign, academic journals, or other sources will locate evidence to inform the design related to spatial needs. Pickett's (2007) master's thesis, "A Bed and Breakfast Design Accommodating the Traveling Preferences of the Retired Baby Boomer," addresses travel preferences of retired **baby boomers**.

Security has become an important concern in nearly all design types, and particularly, guests expect provisions for safe and secure environments. However, they do not want to feel imprisoned. Therefore, security must be transparent—exist but invisible—and extensive in luxury and resort hotels. This begins in the lobby with hidden security cameras and continues into the elevator with card access to each level (Piotrowski & Rogers, 2007). Research of existing hotels as well as the literature will provide evidence for best practices and/or in designing for security.

Acoustical control is another concern within hospitality design projects. Particularly, luxury hotels are designed to control and insulate against noise between guest rooms. For example, special plumbing materials and devices can be specified that insulate against noise; service physical plants (e.g., heating and cooling systems) can be acoustically treated; and communication devices such as intercoms can be used to access back of the house areas and eliminate noise for hotel guests. Often background music provided in lobbies, public corridors, public washrooms, and other public areas masks unwanted noise (McDonough et al., 2001). A literature review may reveal studies of acoustical control in hotels and provide evidence to inform the design. Written surveys and interviews of employees as well as observations of clients and employees in the existing hotel or a similar hotel may reveal issues with acoustics and improve the design.

In summary, data collection (facts and new evidence) must include examining the target market, locale, space requirements, security, code research, and more. Specific needs for hotels must accommodate Americans with Disabilities Act (ADA) requirements, egress, sprinkler, and the protection of guests (Kilmer & Kilmer, 1992). Additionally, universal design principles that include appropriate wayfinding need to be applied.

Restaurant Design

Today's mobile society created by modern technology and communications has greatly facilitated traveling to, becoming aware of, and enjoying foods from various cultures (Ryder, 2004). Additionally, eating out has also become an important way to socialize, meet friends, and enjoy good quality food, or to just eat in a hurry. This phenomenon has caused a boom in the restaurant business as well as a change in restaurant design—one of the most creative, innovative designed interiors (Kilmer & Kilmer, 1992; Ryder, 2004).

Various types of restaurant design can be found. Some designs relate to a dining experience in which the customer is served and spends time socializing or being entertained before, during, and after the meal. Others design types include cafeterias, fast food, coffee shops, and family restaurants.

Target Market

The goal of any food and beverage facility from a restaurant to a coffee shop is to provide good food and service as well as an atmosphere that will bring customers back (Piotrowski & Rogers, 2007). Thus, to survive in the restaurant business, it is important to determine the appropriate market by conducting a thorough market analysis (Barabon & Duracher, 2001). A market analysis involves the investigation of four main areas.

- Who are the potential customers?

- What is the competition?

- Where is the best location?

- Will the restaurant be profitable?

To determine potential customers, demographics and the makeup of potential customers need to be identified (Barabon & Duracher, 2001; Piotrowski & Rogers, 2007). This means that the restaurant design must also relate to the potential clients' age and income (Piotrowski & Rogers, 2007) as well as the price they are willing to pay (Kilmer & Kilmer, 1992). There are four categories of diners: eat and run, food connoisseur, comparative diner, and socialite. Eat-and-run types want quick service and usually an inexpensive meal. This type is least concerned with food quality and more concerned with speed and price. Food connoisseurs want excellent food. They are not concerned about the price of the food or speed of service, and desire only quality food. The comparative diners balance price, speed, and quality, and generally dress informally when dining. For the socialite, dining out may be a business event, or an intimate or ceremonial social event. Each expects the price and experience to be different (Kilmer & Kilmer, 1992).

After the target market is determined, the competition must be identified to determine if there is room for another restaurant (Barabon & Duracher, 2001; Piotrowski &

Rogers, 2007). Research will help the owner learn if "there are too many restaurants of a similar kind in the vicinity to support one more" (Piotrowski & Rogers, 2007, p. 156). First, examine the primary competition—those located in close proximity and of similar types; then examine the secondary competition—those located nearby and of different types. Observations of the competition's parking lots and waiting areas will provide important evidence regarding their financial health and the operation's popularity (Barabon & Duracher, 2001).

Next, selecting a location is crucial to the survival of any business, especially a restaurant (Barabon & Duracher, 2001; Piotrowski & Rogers, 2007). The close proximity of the restaurant to its target market makes it more appealing. The design—exterior and interior—is also influenced by location. For example, a restaurant in Chicago will typically differ from one in Santa Fe (Barabon & Duracher, 2001).

Lastly, it is important to consider the economic climate that will influence the longevity of a restaurant venture. Thus, it is best if the design does not follow fads but considers design elements that are of enduring value (Barabon & Duracher, 2001).

"Location, location, location" is stated again and again when discussing a new business, but it is extremely important in the design of a restaurant. With little thought in location as well as the client to be served, the restaurant may not survive. If solid research has been conducted through surveys, interviews, focus groups, and observations, the survival rate of restaurants will increase dramatically. When a decision is made on location and clients, the designer can appropriately design the space and select finishes, furniture, and everything else that is necessary to convey the image the diner will expect.

Spatial Relationships and Organization

As in many design types, restaurants are separated into public and private zones.

Public Zone

The public zone in a restaurant is called the front of house. This includes entry, waiting areas, lounge/bar area, dining areas, service, and restrooms (Kilmer & Kilmer, 1992; Piotrowski & Rogers, 2007). The entry and waiting areas should orient the guest as well as provide visual cues to the various functions such as a host station, waiting area, coat check, and location of cashier. Because more noise is generated from the lounge/bar area, it should be separated from the dining area (Baucom, 1996). A review of literature may provide evidence on reasons for and ways to reduce the impact of noise to occupants. For example, an InformeDesign RS, "Effects of Music on Customers and Employees" (2004, May 28), summarizes an article that provides evidence on the manager's perspective on the influence of music in hospitality settings.

Frequently the dining areas are directed to a view. The view may lead inward toward a focal point, toward others in the dining space, or be centered within for intimate dining accommodations (Kilmer & Kilmer, 1992). Some tables may be in prime locations, and these are considered to be the best in the house; however, according to Piotrowski and Rogers (2007), an effective design is one in which all tables seem to be placed at a prime location.

The design must be well planned in the dining area for good circulation, to meet codes, and to minimize confusion and interference of servers (Kilmer & Kilmer, 1992;

Piotrowski & Rogers, 2007). To accommodate all types of customers, seating arrangements need to be flexible to adjust from one or two persons to large group seating. It should also be arranged to provide areas of privacy as well as maximize socializing within groups (Kilmer & Kilmer, 1992).

Circulation within a restaurant is crucial to not only the customer but also the wait-staff. To create good circulation, transitional spaces occur within a restaurant. A transitional area is needed between the customers' waiting area, but must not interfere with the waitstaff's path. This gives separation from the dining area to provide good circulation as well as anticipation for the dining experience. Another area of transition is between the kitchen and the dining area. These pathways must be unobstructed for the waitstaff, provide acoustical and visual barriers, and give appropriate means of egress (Kilmer & Kilmer, 1992). Ultimately, wait stations are best when they blend into the dining space, are screened or obscured from the diner, and designed for noise reduction (Piotrowski & Rogers, 2007).

Private Zone

The private zone is called the back of house. Along with food preparation, there is space allotted for a manager's office, employee lockers, and restrooms, as well as an area for waste and disposal. The food preparation area is divided into receiving and dry storage; preparation of hot food, cold food, and beverages; serving; and washing (Kilmer & Kilmer, 1992; Piotrowski & Rogers, 2007). Support areas are also important and must be conveniently located near the food pickup area and not visible to the diner (Barabon & Durocher, 1989). This basic planning arrangement for food preparation may vary as much as the meals served, and particularly varies for cafeterias, fast food enterprises, and participatory dining establishments. Most food preparation areas are hidden from customers by doors or halls; however, in some establishments, the preparation and cooking areas are visible; this is particularly the arrangement for participatory cooking centers (Kilmer & Kilmer, 1992).

Space Allocation for Restaurants: Function and Adjacencies

The amount of square footage needed varies with the type of restaurant. The square footage per person varies with the type of service: 11 to 14 square feet for fast food service, 16 to 18 square feet for a cafeteria, 18 to 20 square feet for counter service, 15 to 18 square feet in a hotel restaurant, 10 to 11 square feet for banquet, and 17 to 22 square feet for formal dining (Piotrowski & Rogers, 2007). Many restaurants allow for 16 square feet per person (Kilmer & Kilmer, 1992); however, because of the growth in the older population, designers are expanding this to 18 to 20 square feet per person to provide more accessibility (Baucom, 1996). If the restaurant is located in a hotel, the seating area should allow for approximately 75 percent of the number of guest rooms in the hotel. Seating arrangements should vary with configurations for visual orientation as well as intimate and semi-private groupings (Baucom, 1996). Piotrowski and Rogers (2007) provides greater detail on space allocation for dining areas. A literature review may relate to design elements that include how dining spaces will affect profitability. For example, the InformeDesign RS "Designing

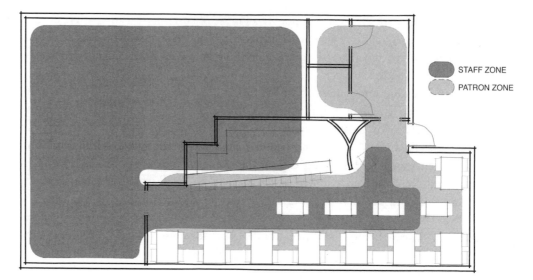

STAFF ZONE

PATRON ZONE

Figure 13.2 This diagram compares the percentage of space needed for a kitchen to dining spaces.

Hotel Restaurants for Profitability" (2002, December 4) notes 10 best practices to aid profitability that include branding and types of dining spaces. Other suggested areas of research would be the examination of human behavior in restaurants to provide evidence to improve space allocation.

Commercial kitchen design is a specialty and should be left to the specialist. However, space must be allocated for a commercial kitchen. "Because of the variation of the type of service and the complexity of any establishment's menu, there is no standard rule for the size of the kitchen as a percentage of the overall size of the facility" (Piotrowski & Rogers, 2007, p. 164). However, one rule of thumb has been one-third size of the dining area (Kilmer & Kilmer, 1992; Piotrowski & Rogers, 2007). Figure 13.2 illustrates the percentage of kitchen needed for a restaurant.

Restaurant Lighting

Lighting in the dining area needs to coincide with the type of dining experience expected, whether it's for a brightly lit room or a dimly lit, intimate environment (Barabon & Durocher, 1989). The type of lighting within each area has its purpose. At the entrance and waiting area, the lighting must be welcoming and well lit for visual recognition. In the dining area, the circulation path should be well lit with lower levels at the tables; however, diners still need to be able to see contrasts, particularly if their eyesight is poor. Adjustable lighting is important to create intimacy and visibility (Baucom, 1996). Locating research studies on age and lighting needs will provide evidence to improve the lighting design within an interior space.

Environmental Conditions

Environmental conditions, such as appropriate seating arrangements and chair size, provide physical comfort for diners (Barabon & Durocher, 1989). The psychological comfort of diners is extremely important so that they will become repeat customers. For example, according to Piotrowski and Rogers (2007), we respond psychologically "to places, things, and events based on our visual impressions. Lighting plays a significant part in promoting the comfort of the guest and providing a successful restaurant experience. Poorly designed lighting can hinder, if not destroy, that experience" (p. 178). Thus, research may focus on locating evidence on the effect of lighting in restaurants as well as other responses to such visual cues as color and textures. All of this will inform the design.

The design of restaurants can be as imaginative as some retail designs. Each has the same underlying principle that the price and service must equal the expectation of the client. Additionally, to be successful and remain in business, eating establishments must generate profits (Kilmer & Kilmer, 1992). Therefore, the furniture, fixtures, and equipment (FF&E) must be chosen to meet the needs of the design for the intended diner.

According to Baraban and Durocher (2001), there is a "direct correlation between the type of restaurant and choice of kitchen equipment" (p. 2). For example, kitchen equipment for a Chinese restaurant will be different than that chosen for a steakhouse. There is also a direct correlation between the type of restaurant and the type of furniture (tables and seating). For example, the tables and chairs in a fast-food restaurant are often made of molded plastic that is easy to clean, whereas hotel dining rooms provides upholstered, comfortable chairs and tables dressed with tablecloths, linens, and flatware.

A literature review should include research on typology, cuisine, target market, space requirements—expected number and ADA—traffic flow, distance, direction, FF&E, wayfinding, universal design and ADA requirements, and code research. Research should also include methods of drawing in the customer. Particularly important is understanding that the square footage needs of both front and back of the house must be considered in research of the target market and expected number of customers. Additionally, research is not limited to literature. Conducting participant observations or the typical observation in hotels are excellent methods of collecting new evidence to inform the design.

> **Ideas for Collecting New Evidence**
>
> Examples of research topics into hospitality design related to restaurants include commercial kitchens and ventilations; consumer or dining satisfaction; ambient influences of food intake and choices; privacy for diners; applications of universal design; work experience for staff; communication among staff as well as between staff and customers; the role of technology; health and safety; appropriate materials; cleanliness; privacy for staff and customers; perceptions of the space; and sustainability.

Application

Topics for research were suggested in Chapter 11; however, more specific research can be conducted within specific design typologies such as hospitality design. A case study of Las Vegas casino hotels uses casual observations for comparison of circulation and wayfinding.

The International Interior Design Association (IIDA) Knowledge Center provides articles related to hospitality design. For example, a Florida State University master's degree thesis (Pickett, 2007), "A Bed and Breakfast Design Accommodating the Traveling Preference of the Retired Baby Boomers," focuses on bed-and-breakfast design and accommodating the traveling preferences of the retired baby boomer. The study considered the authenticity, historic richness, and comfort of a specific type of lodging—the bed-and-breakfast. Another example (Graham, Bernards, Osgood, and Wells, 2006) researched behavior in bars as it relates to the bar design. Results from this research report related to aggressive behaviors and appropriate design of bar interiors.

Examples of InformeDesign research summaries on hospitality concern: hotels providing information on creating loyal customers—"Creating Loyal Hotel Customers" (2004, January 8); specific populations—"Hotel Design for Seniors" (2003, December 5) and "Hotels that Attract Sports Teams (2007, April 9); planning the guest-room floor that will increase profits—"Increase Hotel Profits through Planning" (2003, May 13); and function-space revenue management—"Management Hotel Function Spaces" (2002, December 5). Other InformeDesign RS on hospitality include restaurant design providing information needed for movement and privacy. "How People Move and Behave in Restaurants" (InformeDesign, 2008, January 2) is an example of an RS that examines human factors related to physical and social space by analyzing how people move within a restaurant. Summarizing an article on consumer complaint behavior, the RS "Consumer Complaint Behavior in Restaurants" (InformeDesign, 2003, December 11) examines the relationship between restaurant patrons' demographic characteristics and the complaints these patrons make in response to restaurant service.

In reviewing the InformeDesign RS, it is important to review its Key Concepts and Design Criteria and then use those criteria in informing the design.

Summary

Hospitality design is a blend of commercial and residential design. Hospitality design includes hotels, or lodging, and restaurants, or food and beverage facilities. Each hotel or restaurant attracts a specific target market in its intended location. For both hotels and restaurants, research of the intended location and target market will increase the chances for survival.

Issues related to hotel design that should be researched are circulation, privacy, security, and acoustical control. Careful examination and planning of circulation movement will alleviate congestions. Often, observations will provide evidence to improve and inform the design. Privacy and security are also major concerns. Research through interviews and observations will provide evidence related to security issues. Acoustical control is a concern. Most luxury hotels are designed to control and insulate against noise between guest rooms; however, less expensive hotels may not consider this a priority. Therefore, evidence from research may be needed to convince the hotel client to provide acoustical control.

Several issues relate to restaurant design, such as prime locations and circulation. If the restaurant is well designed, all seating will be placed in prime locations. Additionally, good circulation that does not interfere with waitstaff provides a better dining experience. Examining other restaurants through articles or observations can provide evidence on location and circulation. Other issues that should be researched for evidence are restaurant lighting and environmental conditions (physical comfort). Clearly, whether for a hotel or a restaurant, research for new evidence on various issues will improve and inform the design.

Key Terms

baby boomers

back of house

bed-and-breakfast inn

casino hotel

conference center

extended-stay or all-suite
   facilities

front of house

hostel

limited-service hotel
   (motel)

luxury hotel

resort hotel

THEODORE

Healthcare Design

OBJECTIVES

After reading this chapter, you should be able to:

Understand the areas for data collection and special needs relative to healthcare design

Develop evidence-based design (EBD) for healthcare design.

DRED COURT

Healthcare design includes many types from hospitals and medical offices to nursing homes and assisted living facilities. Each are specialized, but all are involved in providing healthcare. Some healthcare facilities blend together a variety of design categories, e.g., hospitality, residential, and retail design. For example, assisted living facilities blend healthcare with hospitality design (Allen et al., 2004). Nevertheless, the primary focus of healthcare design is the delivery of quality and efficient care within the environment (Cama, 2006). The following is an example of a typology for healthcare design:

- Hospitals
  - Children's hospital
  - Heart hospital

- Physician's medical office or clinic
  - Combination of specialties
  - Orthopedic clinic
  - Pediatric clinic

- Dental-care facilities
  - General dental care
  - Orthodonic office

- Eye-care facilities
  - Optometry office

- Long-term care facilities
  - Nursing home
  - Homes for Alzheimer's patients

- Physical therapy

Healthcare Design

Until the turn of the century, many architects and designers resisted the use of EBD research, believing it would erode the artistic side of the profession by becoming a scientific rather than a design profession (Shepley, 2006). However, realizing that good design is dependent on both art and science (i.e., research), healthcare designers were the first to subscribe to the EBD concept. Design decisions can positively affect quality and safety in the environment, which influences patient health outcomes and creates a positive work experience for staff.

In the new millennium of healthcare, an unprecedented number of hospitals will be built or replaced (Jones, 2007; Henriksen, Isaacson, Sadler, & Zimring, 2007; Ulrich, Zimring, Quan, & Joseph, 2004). These new facilities will accommodate a number of needs that includes population growth, technology changes, efficiency improvements, patient safety, and quality outcomes in healthcare (Clancy, 2008).

EBD in Healthcare Design

A growing number of clients (i.e., healthcare administrators) are well informed, and when working with a professional design team, these clients will expect the application of EBD research to enhance the built environment. Since EBD began in the healthcare industry, healthcare designers have been consciously using EBD to make decisions by applying the current evidence from research and practice to critical design decisions (Hamilton, 2004). As leaders in EBD, healthcare designers realized the natural parallel of EBD to evidence-based medicine and its importance in creating healthy environments (Hamilton, 2007). Healthcare designers began to implement evidence from research into their designs in the 1980s (Ulrich et al., 2008). Interestingly, these designers have no single approach to including EBD in the design; however, they generally begin by (1) developing key goals and objectives for the project, (2) understanding the way that a facility can improve operations with better processes or workflow, (3) enhancing the culture with staff that contributes to and adapts to change, and (4) improving patient care with a safer environment and better quality health outcomes (Zimring, Augenbroe, Mallone, & Sadler, 2008).

Many hospitals across the country are incorporating EBD research into their healthcare projects. The Pebble Project is a joint research effort between the Center for Health Design and selected healthcare providers. The Center for Health Design's **Pebble Project** was created to transform the way healthcare facilities are designed to improve patient outcomes and working conditions for staff. The intent of a Pebble Project was to create change—the pebbles being tossed into a pond—through a ripple effect in the design of healthcare facilities. To date, 44 healthcare facilities have joined and are actively researching design improvements (Pebble Project, 2006). Many other organizations have also adopted EBD, including the Military Health System, the U.S. Agency for Healthcare Research and Quality (Pebble Project, 2006), and Kaiser Permanante, which has a Global Health and Safety Initiative to advance environmental and worker and patient safety (Hampton, 2007).

These projects have become models for EBD with outcomes that have shown these facilities have:

- Improved the quality of care for patients

- Attracted more patients

- Recruited and retained staff

- Increased corporate, community, and philanthropic support

- Enhanced efficiency and productivity in operation (Pebble Project, 2006)

- Improved economics (Zimring et al., 2008)

Using EBD, healthcare facilities have created **therapeutic environments** (Hamilton, 2004) that reduce stress (Marberry, 2006). Ulrich et al. (2008) analyzed more than 1,200 scholarly research articles that show great advances in EBD for healthcare facilities. Additionally, research on **physiological outcomes** has been conducted and applied. These outcomes relate to the effects of light; noise; environment; privacy and control; patient- and family-centered care; safety issues concerning infections, falls, transfers, medical errors, and communication; arts and gardens for **positive distraction**; and healing (Ulrich et al., 2005; Zimring, Ulrich, Quan, & Joseph, 2005).

Research findings support these concepts. For example, because healthcare facilities are stressful environments for families and patients, art and gardens are positive distractions in the healing process (Shepley, 2006; Ulrich. 1999). This indicates that the interior designer must consider ways to incorporate art, gardens, and/or other positive distractions into the design.

EBD Means Better Outcomes

Interior designers play an important role in achieving better outcomes and must understand the impact of their decisions concerning healthcare (Ulrich et al. 2004, 2008). Consider the following:

- Reducing infections may be influenced by materials used for the finishes in patient rooms, such as carpeting, fabrics, ceiling tiles, and wall coverings that may harbor harmful bacteria. The location of sinks and alcohol hand rub dispensers is important to increasing hand washing to prevent infection spread.

- Reducing falls may be aided by considering flooring materials, recognizing wheelchair and heavy equipment traffic in some areas, and wet floors in others such as patient bathrooms, patient rooms, and hallways.

- Reducing stress may be facilitated by providing positive distractions that redirect attention from pain and fear and give the patient a sense of control. Views of nature, music options, and appropriate selection of color and art can impact emotional needs for both patients and staff. Additionally, good wayfinding methods throughout the facility can help reduce stress for patients and visitors (Ulrich et al., 2004; 2008).

Improved sleep is believed to help all patients' natural body rhythms, or **circadian** rhythms, allowing them to heal faster, especially in premature infants (Brandon, Holditch-Davis, & Belyea, 2002). It is important to give attention to light and noise sources and their intensity, such as overhead lights, natural light, noisy equipment, and hard surfaces that reflect noise (Ulrich et al., 2004; 2008).

As evidenced by the previously mentioned examples, interior design decisions impact outcomes. Therefore, research of evidence in these areas will inform the design and develop better patient outcomes. This type of research may be found in the previously cited sources. Other research may be found in research summaries (RS) on InformeDesign, International Interior Design Association's (IIDA) Knowledge Center, and articles from journals in healthcare design. For example, an InformeDesign RS, "Hospital Curtains Harbor Bacteria" (2008, January 2), describes the outbreak and control of antibiotic-resistant bacterial infections in two intensive care units (ICUs) and notes that these types of outbreaks are increasing. Thus, to reduce bacterial infections, various solutions are provided regarding privacy curtains in ICUs: (1) they may be eliminated and other alternatives used to obtain privacy, (2) change curtains twice a week or upon transfer of patients, or (3) implement strict infection control policies. With this information, interior designers can make a decision regarding the specification of privacy curtains as it relates to infection control.

Effect of Color in Healthcare Design

Although scientific evidence of color in healthcare is somewhat subjective, there are psychological connections that have been studied and documented. The color we see with our eyes has associations in our minds that can trigger the healing process. For example, the color blue that we associate with water has a soothing and cooling effect. It, therefore, has healing properties relative to inflammatory diseases. Turquoise, or aqua, has been associated with skin building and used in burn units to help relieve pain. Green is the color most dominant in nature and, as humans, we identify with this color as familiar, safe, and as a retreat, which in turn can help reduce stress and create a calming effect.

For interior designers, it is important to be thoughtful about the amount of color, saturation, and value used within a space. Equally important is the balance of color (i.e., using cool tones and warm tones), and the application of complementary colors or varying shades of color. Newborn babies and the elderly tend to respond more positively to vibrant, bright, bold colors. This is due to the undeveloped eyesight of a baby and the aging eyesight of the elderly. The use of color as it relates to the function and the occupants of the space is critical to consider when designing a healing environment (Andrews, 2001; Marberry & Zagon, 1995).

Bariatric Design

One of the greatest concerns in design spaces is the increase in body size. **Bariatric**, a term related to obesity, has become a field of medicine that provides treatment for individuals who are overweight. Comprehensive programs have been designed to improve an overweight individual's lifestyle through diet and nutrition, exercise, behavior modification, and more. Part of bariatric medicine also involves research into the causes, prevention, and treatment for obesity (MedicineNet, 2008). Thus, in the design of healthcare facilities, space planning, furniture, fixtures, and equipment (FF&E) selection, and other considerations are affected by bariatric patients and/or residents. For example, doorways must be larger, types of bathroom fixtures must be sturdier, and furniture must be larger and able to support the larger body sizes.

Though much of the bariatric research is related to bariatric surgery, some articles and research summaries can be found to provide evidence related to design. Additionally, in some cases, the term obesity is used rather than bariatrics. Articles can be found relative to bariatric furniture and equipment, and because it is an important emerging issue, this will become a highly important research topic. An article by Williams (2008) provides design criteria for the bariatric furniture industry, and these criteria provide evidence for bariatric furniture selection. For example, Williams points out that bariatric furniture is not necessarily bigger or just holds more weight; rather, it is created with a combination of load limit, appropriate dimensions, and design aesthetics to blend with the entire design concept. Then, with this information, the interior designer can use the suggested criteria to select and specify appropriate bariatric FF&E for healthcare facilities.

Spatial Relationships and Organizations

Many community hospitals accommodate a variety of clinical departments, where care is delivered to the patients (e.g., pediatrics, obstetrics, surgery, and general medical care), and support departments, where services are provided to the patients. In general, each department determines the spatial relationship and organization of hospital rooms (Pile, 2003).

Healthcare design provides healthcare services of varying types to patients and their families. Regardless of the type, there are three general areas: administration, clinical patient care, and support services. Within each area, there are distinct spaces and functions that relate to the type of facility and care provided (Kilmer & Kilmer, 1992). These areas may be public, semi-public, or private zones (Cama, 1996). For the interior designer, it is important to research the type of facility and each department and, most importantly, to review current literature for evidence that will inform the design. The reason for this is that the Patient and Family Centered Care philosophy has become the standard of care. This philosophy recognizes the family unit is essential to the patient's life and contributes to the well-being of the patient. It significantly impacts the way care is conceived, organized, and delivered starting in patient rooms and expanding to public spaces.

The public zones include lobbies, front-of-house food service, retail shops, general waiting areas, a chapel, libraries and resource centers, and education and training rooms. The semi-public areas include corridors leading to the patient area and family rooms. The private areas include those in which the administration and staff offices are located, inpatient rooms, family rooms, consultation rooms, exam rooms, treatment and procedure rooms, electronic communication centers, laboratories, private resource centers, volunteer areas, support services, storage, and teaching and conference facilities (Cama, 1996; Kilmer & Kilmer, 1992).

Clarity of circulation within the facility is important and, most importantly, clear signage and wayfinding methods can transform a confusing environment into a user-friendly, easy-to-navigate space. This can be accomplished through appropriate selection of color and art (Huelat, 2007), or through observations of the typical user (e.g., patient, doctor, visitor, nurse, other staff member, or vendors). For example, observations will provide a better understanding of the steps from arrival through treatment, strategies for efficient work process, or a normal visit to the facility, and the relationships of steps for all users. Looking at the spatial relationships and circulation of the users of all spaces will provide a better spatial organization (Pile, 2003).

Medical Office Buildings

A **medical office building** is a facility where physicians and other healthcare professionals see non-hospitalized patients. Medical office buildings may also be referred to as **outpatient clinics** or **ambulatory care centers**. Medical care is increasingly conducted in outpatient clinic settings rather than in more costly hospital settings (Sloane & Sloane, 2003). With new technologies, complex medical treatments that were once provided only in inpatient hospitals are now available in outpatient centers or special outpatient residences with more homelike environments, where family members can assist in providing recuperative care (p. 4).

The reception area and waiting room present the design image for the facility. This concept should project a calming, comforting, and visually appealing space to patients. Positive distractions and connections to natural light and nature are important ingredients. Waiting room furniture must be comfortable and utilize calming colors. Patients should be provided with reading material, coat storage, an area for children to play, and easy access to restrooms and a water fountain. Additionally, a receptionist should have full view and be able to monitor patients and families in the waiting area (Kilmer & Kilmer, 1992).

Each facility contains one or more business offices that hold records. Some may need space for scheduling, billing, insurance records, and clerical work (Kilmer & Kilmer, 1992). However, records are now electronic, which changes the way the medical facility works (Virzi, 2006). Smaller facilities incorporate all business-related functions into one area. Larger facilities may have separate spaces for each function as well as private offices for managers (Kilmer & Kilmer, 1992). Enclosed spaces will also be needed to conduct exams, procedures, lab testing, and X-rays. Testing and X-ray rooms need to be easily accessible to the exam and procedure rooms.

In clinics or medical offices, the doctor's office space should be a minimum of 108 square feet (9 feet by 12 feet) (DeCharia, Panero, & Zelnik, 2001). Examination rooms are approximately 8 feet by 12 feet at a minimum for adults; pediatric exam rooms should be larger to accommodate family members—10 feet by 10 feet at least, and preferably, 10 feet by 12 feet (Malkin, 2002). It is a more generally accepted practice to make exam rooms **same handed** for safety of the patient and convenience of the staff (Cahnman, 2006). These spaces must have the proper furniture, lighting and equipment, e.g., guest chair, physician's stool and writing area, dressing area, exam table, built-in cabinetry with a sink and storage as well as small medical equipment (Kilmer & Kilmer, 1992). The location of a personal computer in the exam room is important; typically, it should be arm-mounted to accommodate the trend of charting within the room, and be visible to the patient. An important consideration is the location of a hand-washing sink, which should be just inside the room and easily accessible to physicians and nurses (Cahman, 2006; Malkin, 2002). Procedure rooms, which are larger than the exam rooms, allow space for equipment to perform minor surgical procedures and to apply casts (Kilmer & Kilmer, 1992). Research of the literature will provide evidence regarding safety or other issues in medical clinics.

Research of the literature provides evidence regarding safety or other issues in medical clinics. For example, InformeDesign RS "Patient and Family Perspectives on Healthcare Facilities" (2003, July 16) summarizes a multiphase study that examined the relationship between the built environment and users of healthcare. The author points out that to better meet users' needs, patients and families (community) should be involved in the design of these facilities. This could be accomplished through community focus groups. Additionally, design criteria were identified to provide a better, more informed design.

Hospitals

Hospitals have similar features of a medical office or clinic, but with expanded services: admitting, emergency, outpatient treatment and inpatient facilities (Pile, 2003). Hospitals designed through evidence-based decisions have become model facilities, i.e., the Pebble Projects noted as follows (Pebble, 2006). In the following discussion of important and emerging hospital features, note that each are areas for evidence collecting for future design projects.

Other aspects of hospital design include the addition of adequate space for clinical services, modern equipment, technologies, i.e., diagnostic and informational, patient rooms, and a variety of amenities to support families and community members (Oland, 2007).

Information technology in room is becoming more advanced and is used by nurses, doctors, and other health professionals to document care in an electronic patient medical record. It also provides a convenient tool for patients to see their medical record, receive instructions and educational programs and materials, and control the environment, such as temperature, lighting, food service, and entertainment.

Increasingly, the use of the electronic medical record has become important in bringing care to the bedside, enabling nurses and doctors to document care at the bedside, provide patient education, and improve patient safety such as reducing medication errors—often called **paper lite** versus paper free (Juett, McIntire, & McIntire, 2005). Paper lite will continue until the community doctors' offices, nursing homes, and insurance companies have all upgraded to electronic medical records, as in one of the Pebble Projects, the new Dublin Methodist Hospital that opened January 2008 (Dezignaré, 2008). It is important to note that Dublin Methodist Hospital is not only the first paper lite facility in Ohio but also incorporated a good portion of EBD in their facility.

Today, patient rooms (approximately 250 to 450 square feet) are designed with zones for patients, staff, and families to coexist comfortably. The patient zones, usually at the center of the room, are patient centered for care and allow for more personal patient control with privacy and confidentiality. Staff work zones (usually the first zone upon entering the room) are designed to provide easy access to the patient, visibility for the patient's care and safety, and efficient functionality. Family zones, usually the far end of the room, offer supportive amenities such as sleeping accommodations and/or workspace that allow families to be present more often and participate in the healing process. Additionally, because of the spatial layout of the room, safety features reduce infections, patient falls, medication errors, and staff injury (Oland, 2007). Figure 14.1 illustrates a patient room layout with all zones—patient, staff, and family.

In the past, nursing stations were centralized, i.e., located in the center of the patient care floors, and served as the center of communication with focus on the patient medical record that all professionals accessed. That has changed due to technology at the bedside and/or in many locations that allow the appropriate doctor, nurse, or allied health professional to access the record as needed from multiple locations. **Centralized nursing stations** are being replaced with **decentralized nursing** alcoves with computer access located just outside the patient room. This increases nurse and patient interactions and helps with safety such as reducing falls and increasing nurse-to-patient communication, resulting in better care and higher patient satisfaction. Nursing substations for pods of 6 to12 rooms provide new spaces for staff interaction to enhance teamwork and provide a location for specific supplies and medication that are not stored in patient rooms (Oland, 2007).

Hospital waiting rooms are areas where family members of patients wait for hospital staff updates. Logically, family members are anxious; however, the design and amenities provided in waiting rooms may provide some relief. Dexter and Epstein (2001) suggest that

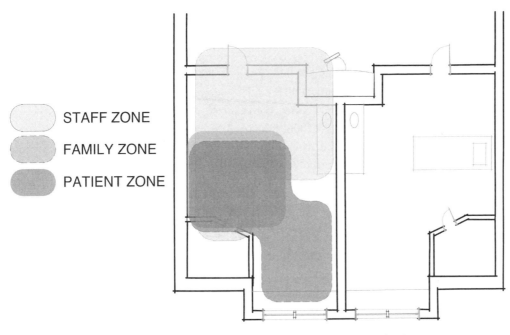

STAFF ZONE

FAMILY ZONE

PATIENT ZONE

Figure 14.1 This drawing shows a patient room layout with patient, staff, and family zones.

waiting room staff be provided not only information technology to update family members but also family members be provided space to wait and receive private, in-person progress reports from hospital staff.

It is important to conduct a review of literature and locate evidence regarding safety, workflow, and efficiency. Additionally, research on patient room and bathroom layout should provide evidence on the proper location of bathrooms to prevent falls, lifts to prevent injuries, sight lines for nurses to monitor patients, and space for family.

Long-Term Care

Long-term care facilities include a variety of facilities for the elderly. Some relate to outpatient care such as **geriatric outpatient clinics** and **adult day care**. Some relate to living arrangements: **assisted living residences, nursing homes/long-term care, dementia/ Alzheimer's care, independent residential living, congregate housing, continuing care retirement community,** and **active adult communities** (Kliment, 2004).

Various philosophies such as **medical model** and **social model** for the design and administration of nursing homes have been used (Eales et al., 2001; Kane, 2001; Thomas, 1996). Medical care has been the main objective of medical model where administrators make decisions for residents, and the atmosphere is institutional. In the last decade, however, the social model, a client-centered model, has been applied that attempts to make the space a more homelike atmosphere (Eales et al., 2001).

However, more recently, the **human habitat model** has emerged; this model was designed to create a homelike environment. With this model, medical services are generally less intensive than the skilled nursing provided in nursing homes and allow the elderly

Ideas for Collecting New Evidence

Examples of research topics into healthcare include advantages of designing single occupancy rooms; designing care around patients by creating three zones—staff, patient, and family—within the room; ways of reducing infections and falls; and improving communication.

more independence and natural lifestyles. Within this type of facility, the atmosphere is of a neighborhood where residents enjoy companionship of humans and animals; choose from a variety of activities such as gardening, cooking, and more; and make decisions in concert with staff (Kane et al. 2007; Thomas, 1996; Thomas, 2002).

Further research of literature will provide evidence for spatial organization that is appropriate for the human habitat model. For example, an InformeDesign RS, "Aesthetics of 'Homelike' Geriatric Facilities" (2006, January 2), summarizes a study that investigated ways that aesthetics of a homelike atmosphere were developed for public spaces in nursing homes and elderly housing. InformeDesign identified design criteria that would include resident preferences and experiences in programming, design, and decorating geriatric residential facilities. However, the interior designer must be concerned that staff perceptions of a homelike environment may not be the same as elderly residents. Additionally, a homelike environment does not mean the inclusion of decorative antique objects and bric-a-brac; rather, the interior designer must base decisions regarding the homelike atmosphere on resident preferences.

The design of facilities for the elderly must be accessible and unobtrusive. Kliment (2004) provides good basic information on space allocations, lighting, wayfinding, and more. Most importantly, a search of literature for new evidence to inform the design must be conducted in these areas. Particularly, suggested areas for research relate to the change in body size—bariatrics, methods of wayfinding for those with dementia or Alzheimer's, and preferences of baby boomers as they age.

Fig. 14.2 Elderly who are able to continue activities they enjoy, such as gardening, feel important and needed.

Much research has been conducted on designing for people with dementia or Alzheimer's. One InformeDesign example, "A Model for Dementia Care Design" (2006, August 2), summarized a review of existing research and design approaches that have been used to care for patients with dementia. It proposed a place-based, multilevel model for patient care with four separate distinct dimensions of special care—individual (people with dementia), social context, physical setting, and organizational context. The social context relates to how people view something based on their surroundings—the physical setting and the organization with its rules and regulations. A diagram of place-based models is included in the article, and can be a framework for the design and development of an Alzheimer's facility.

Because the elderly need long-term care, many prefer to avoid entering nursing homes where care is intensive and very expensive. Rather, more are choosing home healthcare where services are brought to the home or living quarters of the elderly person, such as nurses, aides, and homemakers. This option allows them to stay in their homes where they are comfortable. The greatest challenge with this option is to create an accessible and unobtrusive home. However, if the concept of universal design were applied to all homes, accessibility would not be affected by the occupants' age (Leibrock, 2000).

Design for nursing homes has moved from institutions to neighborhood homes. InformeDesign summarized a case study, "A New Concept for Nursing Home Building" (2007, July 12), in which the Green House concept was implemented. The case study was an innovative design for small residential care homes. The Green House concept is the application of the Human Habitat Model. Design criteria for such homes are provided in the research summary.

Articles or research summaries that discuss universal design are applicable to aging in place. The InformeDesign RS "Difficulties of Aging in Place for the Elderly" (2002, October 12) summarized a study that involved interviewing elderly people to identify their perceptions regarding difficulties when they remained in their homes. Interestingly, many elderly people do not perceive a need for universal design if they are not experiencing difficulty living in their current homes. Clearly, education is needed to improve quality of life. Education is also necessary to help the elderly become aware of support services, housing options, and the physical limitations they may experience. Thus, recognizing the older person's need for independence and familiarity, the designing of new or remodeling of existing homes should involve the use of universal design.

Application

Topics for research were suggested in Chapter 11; however, more specific research can be conducted within specific design typologies such as hospitals, medical offices, nursing homes, or other healthcare types.

The IIDA Knowledge Center provides articles related to healthcare design. Topics include healing environments, wall color of patient rooms, the demand for medical offices, and more.

InformeDesign RS are available on healthcare design. Healthcare categories are numerous such as ambulatory care, assisted living, clinic, emergency room, hospital, laboratory, rehabilitation, wellness center, and more. Summaries include topics such as single-patient rooms, nursing home and senior care facilities, facilities for dementia patients, and more.

In reviewing the InformeDesign RS, it is important to review its Key Concepts and Design Criteria and then use those criteria in informing the design.

Summary

Designers must begin researching the evidence in healthcare design by reviewing the literature to locate the evidence and successful projects, such as the Pebble Projects (2006). These projects are healthcare facilities in which evidence was applied in the design and where ongoing research is being conducted within the completed facility. Other aspects of research must include the staff's work experience, including their work process, culture, and satisfaction; appropriate communication modes between patient and staff; technology-related record keeping and surgical needs; the patient experience, including control, choices, satisfaction, privacy, and health outcome; patient and family involvement in care; safety; infection control; and decentralization versus centralized nurses station. A Pebble Project, the Children's Hospital case study explains how various research methods were used and applied to the design.

A literature review may provide new evidence on design for dementia and Alzheimer's, bariatric needs, single-room occupancy, privacy and control, patient and staff satisfaction, infection control related to materials, and more. Additionally, observations provide evidence that may be insightful related to dementia, Alzheimer's bariatric needs, and workflow or process.

Research articles may also provide evidence on the concern for patient and staff satisfactions, the need for privacy and control for patients, and patients' perceptions of care. Other areas to investigate for evidence include designing for specific age groups—geriatric, adolescent, children, and so on. Designers may also locate evidence to improve spatial organization. In this case, it is important to locate research on staff and the efficiency of workflow—putting nurses at the bedside with technology; centralized versus decentralized nursing stations; and healthcare providers, maintenance personnel, delivery, and other staff and administrative issues.

Research articles may also provide evidence on the effect of light and noise as well as arts and other positive distractions. For long-term care, research may include designing for dementia and Alzheimer's patients. Additionally, observations of people in the spaces as well as being a participant observer and experiencing the space as a patient or resident are excellent methods to inform the design.

Many design firms involve interior designers in the entire process, which includes areas traditionally performed by professionals in other disciplines, such as architecture, landscape, and engineering. This involvement is particularly important in large projects such as healthcare design. The result of incorporating all aspects of the design into the project is an improved final design solution.

Key Terms

adult day care

active adult communities

ambulatory care centers

assisted living residences

bariatric

circadian

centralized nursing station

congregate housing

continuing care retirement
community (CCRC)

decentralized nursing

dementia/Alzheimer's care

geriatric outpatient clinics

human habitat model

independent residential
living

medical model

medical office building

nursing homes or long-
term care

outpatient clinics

paper lite

Pebble Project

physiological outcomes

positive distraction

same handed

social model

therapeutic environments

THEODORE

Retail Design

DRED COURT

According to Piotrowski & Rogers (2007), "retailing is the second largest industry in the United States" (p. 191). How retail space is designed directly impacts the economy of the United States and the world as a whole.

The largest single type of retailer is the grocery store—small grocery stores are located within a small community or section of a city, and are owned by local businesspeople. Superstores (e.g., Walmart and Target) combine groceries with a range of products from personal items to sporting goods. Many retail stores, such as department stores, clothing stores, and automobile showrooms, are continually being built or remodeled. All provide opportunities for design projects.

Retail Design Typologies

The goal in retailing is to entice the customer into the store and then to make the sale. Thus, retailing involves the buying and selling of merchandise and customer service. The goal of retail design is to create a space that encourages increased and continued sales (Piotrowski & Rogers, 2007). Retail spaces can be one of the most exciting places, with their innovative advertising and **visual merchandising** all designed to encourage sales. Examples of various retail design types are department stores, small shops or **boutiques**, shopping malls, showrooms (e.g., automobile dealerships), furniture stores, galleries, and grocery stores (Kilmer & Kilmer, 1992). These retail designs can be placed into four categories: single-store entrepreneurial ownership, chain or **franchise store**, **department store**, and **hypermarket** (i.e., discount and warehouse stores).

An example of retail design typology would be:

- Single-store entrepreneurial ownership (designs controlled by an entrepreneur)
  - Boutiques (noncorporate)
  - Design showrooms
  - Furniture store
  - Appliance store
  - Clothing store

- Specialty store, i.e., computer supply

- Chain or franchise store (designs controlled by corporate owners)
  - Car showrooms
  - Grocery store
  - Office supply
  - Clothing store

- Department store (often an anchor store in a shopping mall and designs controlled by corporate owners)
  - Macy's
  - JCPenney
  - Nordstrom

- Hypermarket, i.e., discount store, warehouse store (large complex with designs controlled by corporate owners)
  - Walmart
  - Target (Piotrowski & Rogers, 2007)

For centuries, merchandise was sold by peddlers or in the marketplace. In some countries, peddlers, also called "hawkers," still travel from village to village to sell their merchandise. However, in these villages, most merchandise is sold in the marketplace. As early as 200 BCE, the retail chain store concept existed in China (Marketing, 2008) with a local businessman operating several retail units (Tarbutton, 1986). However, in 1859, the modern chain store began as a mail-order operation under the name Great American Tea Co., and in the 1860s, retail establishments were opening at which time the name was changed to the Great Atlantic and Pacific Tea Company, Inc. (A&P) (Great A&P Tea Company, 2008). Department stores began in Asia and Europe in the 1600s; these included Bon Marché in Paris, but shopping malls were not developed until the mid-1900s. Shopping malls are common today and provide shoppers with a variety of goods in one shopping area. Some malls also include recreation and entertainment to attract customers (Marketing, 2008).

The Business of Retail

The fundamental activities within retail interiors include buying, selling, and customer service. Retail stores display and sell merchandise to a variety of clients or to specific clientele (Kilmer & Kilmer, 1992; Piotrowski & Rogers, 2007). "The design of retail facilities depends heavily on the designer's ability to understand the retail business and the specific business of the client" (Piotrowski & Rogers, 2007, p. 195). Thus, the designer must learn background information on the target market, which is crucial to a store's profitability (Piotrowski & Rogers, 2007). To draw in the appropriate clientele, the design must meet their needs, whether it is a low-lit, high-end boutique or a bright and open department store. Additionally, circulation is important in retail spaces for movement as well as attracting clients to eye-catching displays (Kilmer & Kilmer, 1992). Other important issues in retail design is the retailer's concern for sufficient space to display merchandise, prevention of shoplifting and internal theft, liability, image of the facility, mix of merchandise, allocation of space, and growth of the business (Piotrowski & Rogers, 2007).

Target Market

Data collection for retail design focuses on the target market, the type of merchandise to be sold, space requirements, ways to draw in the customer, and code research. The way in which the space is designed depends on various criteria; these include target market (or customer profile), location, price, and type of service or product. The design must be sensitive to the type and quality of product being sold (Allen et al., 2004). The design must also target the market to which the product is being sold. Prices range from conservative to high end, and the design, including all aspects of the design such as lighting, can convey the price range. For example:

- Conservative price range = brighter spaces

- High-end price range = low illumination

The way in which the merchandise is displayed also varies based on the type of shopper. For example:

- Younger shopper = playful and stimulating through color, light, and music

- Leisure shopper = good customer service with seating areas

- In-a-hurry shopper = brighter and more efficient layout with good circulation

Location will also affect the design. For example, the design of a store in New York City will be different than one in Springfield, Missouri. In this example, the locations are in different parts of the country, which means that a customer or target market has different expectations. Using various research methods, such as surveys and observations, will provide evidence to design an appropriate interior for a specific area.

The designer should also research shopping preferences related to gender. For example, an InformeDesign RS, "Men's Preferences when Shopping for Clothing" (2003, August 6), summarizes a study conducted to determine men's satisfaction and preferences when shopping for clothing. This research found that most men prefer to shop for clothing in department stores; different clothing brands, styles, and fashion trends should be displayed to attract male shoppers; and male shoppers of different ages have different expectations and needs. Therefore, to attract a specific shopper, the method of displaying merchandise will encourage sales for that target market.

Piotrowski and Rogers (2007) state "retailers have found that when the shopping experience focuses on the senses" (p. 197) consumers are motivated to make a purchase. This means that an atmosphere for buying is created through sight appeal, scent appeal, and theme appeal. For example, sight appeal refers to the size, shape, color, harmony, contrast, and clash within the space. A harmonious space is a more formal environment, whereas a space with contrast and clash is an informal environment that appeals to the younger customer. The scent appeal can be found in bakeries, cosmetics stores, or similar areas within department stores. The scent must entice but not overpower. The theme appeal is used often during various holidays, such as New Year's, Independence Day, Thanksgiving, and Christmas, and around the time of special events, such as the Super Bowl and NASCAR races. Scents and sounds are often included with the theme appeal (Piotrowski & Rogers, 2007). The study summarized in the InformeDesign RS "Themed Retail Environment and Masculinity" (2005, November 9) examines the importance of masculinity in a sports-themed retail environment in Chicago. This study provides suggestions for creating a more masculine environment that will be helpful to inform similar types of design projects.

Research also supports the importance of the store image to attract clients. The InformeDesign RS "Consumer Perception of Store Image" (2004, June 1) reports an exploration of the influence of store image on consumers' store preferences. Various factors such as merchandising, accessibility, reputation, in-store service, store atmosphere, and promotions increase consumer preferences. The key concepts that attract a consumer into a store are (1) store's and consumer's beliefs and values are compatible; (2) stores' attributes act as the external stimuli; and (3) a visit that becomes a recreational activity. An InformeDesign RS, "Consumer's Attraction to Point of Purchase Displays" (2003, September 26), summarizes a study that examined factors that affect aesthetic responses to product displays. These are only two articles that have examined the importance of consumer attraction and making the sale. More may be found on InformeDesign and on International Interior Design Association (IIDA) Knowledge Center.

Other information regarding customer profiles that should also be researched include the age range, geographic distribution, income level, size range especially as it relates to clothing, ethnic influences, and special needs that include size, maternity, and sports insignia (Jerde Partnership, 2004). Research on this type of profile may be through community surveys, interviews, focus groups, and/or observations. Also, articles from American Society of Interior Designers (ASID) or IIDA Knowledge Center and research summaries (RSs) from InformeDesign may provide evidence regarding the implementation of various profiles and the design of a retail space.

Display of Merchandise

The display of merchandise is crucial to making the sales and, ultimately, the success of the store. Clearly, the type of merchandise and customer being attracted to the store influences the planning and designing of the store (Piotrowski & Rogers, 2007). Much of this relates to the behavior of shoppers. Envirosell, a New York-based research and consulting firm, conducts commercial research, particularly with retail design projects by exploring dynamics and patterns of the actual shopping process and influences of purchase decisions. Some of its case studies can be found on its Web site (www.envirosell.com). Though research has been conducted on analyzing shopping behavior that can be used to inform the design, an interior designer can also conduct research by utilizing qualitative methods such as observations, behavior mapping, interviews, and visual recordings.

Visual Merchandising and Design

Another important aspect of display of merchandise is visual merchandising. The purpose of visual merchandising is to encourage a sale. This is accomplished through window displays or displays within the store. Additionally, visual merchandising must display the concept of the space as well as the products (Piotrowski & Rogers, 2007).

Effectively displayed merchandise also is lit appropriately. Thus, the appropriate type of lighting must be selected to display and emphasize the merchandise. Effective lighting, displays, color, and an efficient spatial layout will lure shoppers into the store to buy the merchandise. According to Lisa Heschong (2003) in "Daylight and Retail Sales," a California Energy Commission Technical Report, designers should examine the relationship between monthly sales levels and the presence of daylight in stores. The results indicated that daylight might provide an increase in sales. Additionally, effective and appropriate lighting is discussed in *Designing a Quality Lighting Environment* and *Fundamentals of Lighting* by lighting designer and professor Susan Winchip (2005, 2007). Chapter 7 of this text also discusses some basic fundamental aspects related to lighting design.

Spatial Relationships and Organization

Spatial organization must effectively separate the public from the private zones. The public zones or selling spaces include the entry, merchandise areas, in front of the cashier/transaction areas, and public restrooms. The semi-private areas are dressing rooms, which are shared by customers and sales staff. The private areas, or nonselling spaces, are behind the cashier/transaction areas, product storage and receiving, private restrooms, and offices.

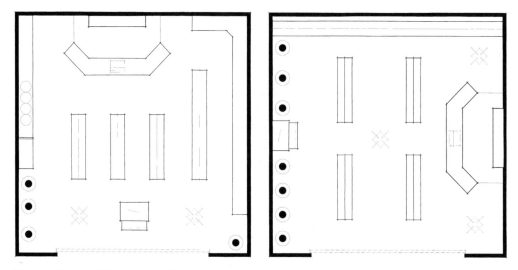

Figure 15.1 *Left*: This drawing illustrates a retail design layout. *Right*: This drawing illustrates an alternative layout for the same space.

Circulation within stores as well as within shopping centers must be unobstructed (Kilmer & Kilmer, 1992; Piotrowski & Rogers, 2007, 2007). With the goal of selling, merchandise must be placed appropriately in order to make the highest number of sales (Piotrowski & Rogers, 2007). Thus, the space allocation and circulation are very important. Figure 15.1 shows two examples of a retail design layout.

Space Allocation

The amount of space needed for circulation and traffic patterns is dependent on the size of the store. Consider the differences between a department store and a boutique. The capability of the store to display and sell products takes priority (Piotrowski & Rogers, 2007). Whether a department store or boutique, the spatial layout for retail design must fit to merchandise, reach, and satisfy the target market, and attract consumers to buy.

There are six basic plans for store layout: coved, varied, straight, pathway, diagonal, and geometric. The **coved plan** is most often used for boutiques, salons, and stores that sell high-end merchandise. It is a creative plan that is more expensive. The **varied plan** is a very functional plan and is best where backup stocks of products are required for immediate access; backup products include shoes and men's shirts. The **straight plan** is an economical plan adaptable to any type of store. The **pathway plan** is applicable to any store, but particularly a store with 5,000 or more square feet on a single level. The **diagonal plan** encourages angular movement to all areas of the store and draws interest to the perimeter. The **geometric plan** is one that allows the designer to create forms and shapes that can be placed at angles to the perimeter. Further information on these plans can be found in *Building Type Basics for Retail and Mixed-Use Facilities* (Jerde Partnership, 2004, p. 47).

A literature review may provide information about appropriately connecting layout to the merchandise and target, designing public spaces for specific age groups, or designing retail spaces that influence shopping behavior, and more. For example, an RS from InformeDesign, "Creating an Entertaining Shopping Experience" (2003), suggests the creation of a store environment that accommodates both pleasure-seeking and utilitarian shopping experiences, organization of stores to facilitate easy product location, and space design with ample room to shop and socialize.

Also critical to the success of the store is the physical layout of displays and fixtures. Piotrowski and Rogers (2007) state that research has been conducted regarding merchandising in the following ways to discover:

- What attracts the customer to the store

- Which traffic patterns within a store are effective

- What height is the merchandise best displayed

- Which materials should be specified to attract the customer through visual, tactile, and audio appeal (p. 202)

Research has indicated that the display of merchandise affects buying. Merchandise should also be grouped into three categories: demand, convenience, and impulse. **Demand merchandise** would be products expected in a particular store. For example, a clothing store would have suits, dresses. These should be placed toward the back of the store to encourage the customer to move throughout the entire space. **Convenience merchandise** would be a product such as hosiery in the example. **Impulse merchandise** would be the unplanned purchases that are decided at the point-of-sale such as jewelry or accessories (Piotrowski & Rogers, 2007).

The InformeDesign RS "Influence of Consumers' Self-Regulation in Retail Settings" (2002, October 13) supports the concept of impulse buying. The authors surveyed shoppers to determine the relationship between shopping emotions and consumer evaluations of their shopping experience. Findings indicated that the design of a retail space that is made to increase time and money spent in the store was harmful in building customer loyalty for action-oriented shoppers. Particularly, impulsive and compulsive shopping can be increased in a retail space that evokes emotions. This study will provide further information and evidence on shopping related to retail store design and merchandising that will inform a retail design project.

Additionally, research also indicated that the manner in which the merchandise is displayed affects sales. An InformeDesign RS, "Merchandise Display Affects Consumer Behavior" (2007, February 22), summarized an investigation of how the coordination and display of retail merchandise influenced consumer behavior when shopping for clothing. The study suggests that coordinating goods to increase the customer's perceived view of quality, such as aesthetic beauty and social desirability, is important.

Shopping Centers or Malls

The shopping center or mall is a destination that houses a variety of boutiques and one or more department stores. Shoppers must be lured to these centers and, therefore, the appeal of the center is just as important as the store and boutiques. There are generally a variety of boutiques, specialty stores, and department stores to bring the customer to shop in more than one store as well as to socialize in coffee shops, food courts, and restaurants. A variety of RSs from InformeDesign provide evidence regarding shopping centers or malls related

Ideas for Collecting New Evidence

Examples of research topics into retail include store image; attracting consumers; consumer behavior; barriers; transaction area design; layout, signage, and lighting; perceptions of spaciousness; work experience for the employees (e.g., culture and satisfaction); technology and communication; training and education of employees; customer needs and desires; safety; accessibility; circulation; aesthetics; and sustainability for retail spaces.

to various situations such as the success of a mall, consumer preferences, wayfinding, and socialization. Some examples include "Anchor Stores Influence Shopping Center Success" (2004, June 17); "Movement through Shopping Malls" (2007, February 1); "Impacts of Shopping Center Location" (2005, September 21); "Consumer Preference for Shopping Center Attributes" (2002, November 25); "Wayfinding in Shopping Malls" (2002, October 30); and "Shopping Mall as Center for Socialization" (2004, December 10).

Application

Topics for research were suggested in Chapter 11; however, more specific research can be conducted within retail design typologies.

The article "A Model for Optimizing Retail Space Allocations" (Costjens & Doyle, 1981), for example, is one example of an article related to retail design.

The IIDA Knowledge Center has sections that relate to specific design types that include retail. The center also has sections listed by topic such as furniture, fixtures, and equipment (FF&E), space planning, and computer technology.

InformeDesign RS are available on retail/store planning. The InformeDesign RS "Best Use of Retail Space Depends on Neighborhood" (2007, January 24), for example, analyzed the impact of neighborhood characteristics to the products being sold.

In reviewing the InformeDesign RS, it is important to examine its Key Concepts and Design Criteria and then use those criteria in informing the design.

Summary

The goal in retailing is to entice the customer into the store and then to make the sale; therefore, the goal of retail design is to create a space that encourages increased and continued sales. This means that the designer must have knowledge of fundamental activities in retail interiors as well as methods used to sell merchandise.

Data collection must focus on the target market, the type of merchandise, space requirements, ways to draw in the customer, and code search. It is, therefore, crucial to research the target market to design for that specific customer. Additionally, the design must also fit the location whether it is New York City or Springfield, Missouri. Data are collected using various methods such as surveys and observations that will provide evidence to design the appropriate interior for a specific location.

With knowledge of the target market and merchandise, space requirements and methods to draw in customers become easier; however, research regarding lighting and retail sales is important. The report on daylight by Lisa Heschong and books on lighting by lighting designer and professor Susan Winchip are excellent resources. Sources such as IIDA Knowledge Center and InformeDesign database provide research articles or summaries on other topics such as display of merchandise, customer types, and more for evidence to improve and inform the design of retail spaces.

Key Terms

boutiques

convenience merchandise

coved plan

demand merchandise

department store

diagonal plan

entrepreneurial ownership

franchise store

geometric plan

hypermarket

impulse merchandise

pathway plan

straight plan

varied plan

visual merchandising

THEODORE

Other Design Categories

After reading this chapter, you should be able to:

Understand the areas for data collection and special needs for other design categories such as institutional, cultural, and recreational facilities

Develop evidence-based design (EBD) for types of design described in this chapter

DRED COURT

There are many more design typologies than can be covered in a single textbook. This chapter provides an overview of some of the other larger design types that were not covered in previous chapters. Institutional facilities, for example, include educational, public, and government spaces. Cultural and recreational facilities include performance halls and **museums**, religious structures, and sports arenas. Of course, there are many more categories within each of these design types. As in other chapters, the examples given here are not to be considered exhaustive but rather intended to demonstrate how designers obtain facts and evidence for various design categories from a variety of sources. Many of these sources are listed at the end of this chapter, but again, these represent the tip of the iceberg of possibilities for the evidence-based designer.

Institutional Facilities

Institutional facilities vary greatly in design typology as well as design needs and requirements. Some facilities are public, whereas others are privately owned. For example, public facilities include schools, government buildings, and libraries; private facilities may also include educational. Some of these facilities are designed for a specific age group such as educational facilities, or for a specific type of user such as the courthouse or prison—both government buildings.

Educational Design

Education has evolved over the centuries from prehistoric and ancient times to the present. Education began with elders and parents teaching their children to learn to survive—hunt, cook, sew, and eventually to draw, letter, or communicate through writing. In the United States, both public and private education is available for students and is required through the age of 16 (Education, 2007). Preschool education as well as elementary has become important to encourage learning at an earlier age. Preschool designs are just as important as any other educational building design.

Examples of typology in educational design may be related to age groups, such as preschool, elementary, high school, and college; or characteristic of study, such as community college, technical institutes, and university; or special circumstances, such as a school for the blind or for the deaf. Libraries and research facilities, laboratories, and studios are parts of these various school types.

Client

In the design of an educational building, there are many clients. A governing body such as a board of directors or regents makes financial decisions. However, parents, students, teachers, and staff are also clients—some as users of spaces, whereas others have a stake through taxes or tuition. Learning from the clients, particularly those who use the spaces daily, should be interviewed and/or observed to understand the workings of all areas and departments.

Spatial Relationships and Organization

Spaces within an educational facility include administration and faculty offices, conference rooms, classrooms, libraries and study areas, computer and/or science labs, a cafeteria and kitchen, a gymnasium with lockers and/or weight rooms, an auditorium with their needed spaces, maintenance closets, and mechanical rooms. These spaces will vary depending upon the type of facility and are also divided into public and private zones. For example, students have access to classrooms, libraries and study areas, labs, a cafeteria, the gymnasium, an auditorium, and a reception desk in administrative offices. However, access to many of these spaces will be at specific times designated by administrators and teachers. Student access to spaces within private zones such as administrative and teacher offices are by invitation. Others are off limits such as the kitchen, maintenance closets, and mechanical rooms.

Safety and Security

Safety and security within educational design has become a major concern. From security cameras to card key entrances, security has tightened because of school violence, particularly to women.

With tightened security, how do students feel about being watched? The InformeDesign RS "Perceptions of School Violence" (2007, July 6) summarizes a study conducted to analyze the perceptions of high school students, teachers, and staff regarding school violence as well as locations where violence was more likely to occur. The author warned of the concern for violence in semi-public areas that did not have constant, direct supervision or were not governed by formal policies. Some areas of concern were school grounds, hallways, cafeterias, gymnasiums and locker rooms, and auditoriums. Would these areas be best served by installing surveillance cameras?

Clearly, safety and security in educational design is very important. The concern is not only in high schools but also within and around preschools to the university campuses. Thus, along with examining new evidence from a literature review, interviews of students, faculty, and staff as well as observations on and around the school's facilities may reveal areas for needed security.

Teaching Methods

Educational design has changed from a teacher-directed approach to the adoption of other methods. Teaching may take place within an open or closed classroom, through **programmed** or **individualized instruction**, or via **distance education** using the Internet or television (Piotrowski, 2007). These varied **teaching methods** are the result of research relating to learning, and because children learn in different ways as they grow (Kolb, 1984), the learning environment should reflect these different ways of teaching. Additionally, the learning environment must stimulate and support the teaching/learning process. In recent years, the design of educational facilities has been influenced by various theories. For example, with the use of **Bloom's taxonomy** in education, educational facilities (i.e., rooms and furniture) are scaled for the children with flexible classroom configurations. Gardner's theory of multiple intelligences suggests personalized learning. Thus, to reinforce the learning experience using this theory, facilities will be more personalized with learning centers (Perkins & Kilment, 2001).

Reggio Emilia theory, which originated in Italy, has been employed in some preschool and toddler educational facilities (Wexler, 2004). The concept behind the theory is viewing the child as a competent learner (Brainy-Child, 2008). Rather than in the **teacher-directed curriculum**, it is the environment that is the teacher (Strong-Wilson & Ellis, 2007) with the child at the center of the curriculum within the space (e.g., **child-directed curriculum**). Therefore, the aesthetics, atmosphere, and organization of the space are crucial to the design of a Reggio Emilia learning environment (Brainy-Child, 2008). Research of literature will provide more information regarding Reggio Emilia theory into the design.

Today, the design of classrooms is more often open than closed. Noise can be an issue. Enmaker and Bomoan (2005) conducted a study to investigate middle school students' and teachers' responses to classroom noise. The authors developed a model to predict teachers' and students' annoyance caused by noise and suggested that individuals should be asked about their perceptions of noise level rather than measuring the levels objectively. Additionally, it was suggested that potential noise sources in the classroom should be identified and use methods of insulation to reduce distracting noises. Using a combination of the Enmaker and Bomoan model as well as conducting observations will inform and improve the design.

Technology

Technology has also changed the educational environment, and particularly, many changes have occurred because of the introduction of computers. This has affected all educational design as well as library design. As desktop computers were introduced into educational facilities, classrooms were designed to accommodate computers, and/or areas or rooms were dedicated specifically to computer usage. However, with the use of laptops in higher education, the need for computer labs is less common. Because technology is continually changing, designing of educational facilities needs to focus on flexibility.

Particularly important is the ergonomics: age of the user from child to adult, size of the classroom, and other special physical needs. An InformeDesign RS, "Virtual Environments and Ergonomics: Needs and Opportunities" (2003, May 13), summarizes a study that conducted a literature review regarding the attributes, capabilities, and side effects in a **virtual environment**. The study identified that side effects related to vision and the muscular system could occur while using the virtual environment; these side effects included disorientation, discomfort, and nausea. The study also suggested that an expert in ergonomics assist with the design and the technology for specific users. In this way, the issues related to vision and muscles could be addressed.

Study Environments

Libraries are resources as well as areas for study. The design of the library can impact student performance. Stone (2001) studied the role of color and design in public and private library environments. Because students frequently use libraries as a place to study, color and design can impact mood, satisfaction, motivation, and performance levels. Therefore, the author suggests providing open plans where less-challenging tasks could be performed, and private areas where more complex tasks could be performed.

Color

Color within educational facilities has changed greatly in the last 50 years, and according to Piotrowski (2007), bright colors used as accessory items in the classroom do not adversely affect children. However, it is particularly important to research current studies in the area to see how children with neurological problems such as **autism** respond to color. Color, because it is related to sensory stimulation, must be carefully selected so that these children will be able to function and learn (Paron-Wildes, 2008). Additionally, the InformeDesign RS "Color Aids Wayfinding for Young Children" (2004, December 15) summarized a study that examined the use of color as a wayfinding method for young children, and suggests that color as visual cues is particularly helpful in a complex environment. However, it is most important to work with and observe the environment to identify routes and spaces for appropriate placement of color as visual cues.

Material Selection

Another issue in education is to create spaces that function appropriately for users' needs. For example, materials must be selected that are safe, resistant to abuse, and easy to maintain. Collecting information on performance criteria for various materials and products is necessary. Additionally, the way spaces are used for teaching purposes will determine the appropriate design and materials. For example, if movies are frequently viewed, appropriate window coverings need to be selected. To collect new evidence, research studies should be located that address concerns for aesthetics relative to appropriate functional choices. Additionally, observations of the way in which students, faculty, and staff use the space will also reveal appropriate choices.

Using a Post-Occupancy Evaluation (POE)

Frequently, the POE provides new evidence that can be applied to the next project. Ornstein (1997) emphasized that the POE can improve educational design. Her study examined the satisfaction level of teachers, students, and staff as well as examining the building performance. She identified several criteria that could be used, such as engaging users in the design process to identify special needs for specific user groups as well as increase and improve the final design. Though the example is from a Brazilian school, the concept of using the POE to improve future projects is important.

Public and Government

Public and government design includes official buildings such as courthouses, capital buildings, police stations, and firehouses. Their designs vary widely based on requirements and needs. Some public and government buildings, such as courthouses and capital buildings, dominate the skyline, whereas others are obscure and tucked away within a downtown area.

Specific facts and details relating to public and government design can be found in the book *Designing Commercial Interiors* by interior designers Christine Piotrowski and Elizabeth Rogers. For evidence to inform the design, research may be conducted through the International Interior Design Association (IIDA) Knowledge Center, InformeDesign, or academic journals. Areas for research that are particularly important relate to security and accessibility as well as circulation, aesthetics, and sustainability.

Ideas for Collecting New Evidence

Examples of research topics into educational design include educational experience and process for teacher, students, and staff; technology usage; safety; accessibility and circulation; aesthetics; sustainability; education in rural areas, for ethnic groups, or for individuals with disabilities; selecting appropriate color for various age groups; and ergonomics for specific age groups or for specific situations, i.e., primary school furniture.

Cultural and Recreational Facilities

Ideas for Collecting New Evidence

Examples of research topics into public and government design include what works and what needs to be improved regarding security concerns and accessibility (for precedents for public and government design); computer monitoring; experience for the employee; visitors' experience; security; accessibility and universal design; circulation; aesthetics; sustainability; and function and user needs of these facilities. (Designers can view tight budgets as an opportunity to be innovative in the design of such buildings.)

Cultural and recreational facilities include a variety of designs. These designs include but are not limited to theaters and other performing arts facilities, museums, religious structures, golf courses, and recreational centers. Each has special needs. Specifically, the designer of a theater or performing arts facility must not only consider the ability to view a performance from all angles but also research technology, lighting, acoustics, and flexibility for the stage design (Hardy & Kliment, 2006). Collecting data from the client, users, site, and documents begins the design process. However, to improve and inform the design, new evidence from journals, research summaries, POEs, and/or other sources must be collected. Particularly, an important area for new evidence would be to examine research on ways to improve viewing the performance.

Museum Design

Museums are facilities "dedicated to preserving and interpreting the material aspects of human activity and the environment" (Museum, 2008, para. 1). Museums may be large or small, and located in a metropolitan area, on a university campus, or in a suburban area. They also educate the public, from children to adults, about the collection exhibited. Collections vary from historic documents to decorative arts and fine arts. In most cases, museums display their **permanent collection** along with **traveling exhibits** (Piotrowski, 2007). "Museum types are classified into five basic types—general, natural history and natural science, science and technology, history, and art" (Museum, 2008, para. 3).

The following is an example of a typology for museum design:

- General: interdisciplinary or multidisciplinary
  - Regional or locality
  - Children's museum

- Natural history and natural science
  - Birds, insects, i.e., butterflies, plants, rocks, and/or fossils
  - Natural history museum

- Science and technology
  - Science museum
  - Air and space museum
  - Railway museum

- History museum

- Art museum
  - Traditional
  - Modern or contemporary

General museums contain collections of a variety of subjects and, thus, are **interdisciplinary** or **multidisciplinary**. Some of these museums serve a region or locality and often **exhibits** relate to local history. Some may serve a specific audience such as a children's museum (Museum, 2008).

Natural history and natural science museums provide **collections** related to the natural world such as specimens of birds, insects, butterflies, plants, rocks, and fossils. Examples include the Smithsonian Institution's National Museum of Natural History in Washington, D.C., and the Natural History Museum in London (Museum, 2008; Piotrowski, 2007). Another example is the Sertoma Butterfly House in Sioux Falls, South Dakota, or the Butterfly Palace in Branson, Missouri. Museums such as the Butterfly House may stand alone, or may be a separate building within a zoological garden, such as the Minnesota Zoo.

Science and technology museums focus on the development and application of scientific ideas and instrumentation. Examples include the Science Museum in London, the National Air and Space Museum in Washington, D.C., the National Railway Museum in York, England, the Museum of Science Industry in Chicago, and Biosphere II in the Arizona desert. The intent is to preserve the heritage related to science and technology.

The history museum also includes a variety of museums with a mass of collections that are exhibited in chronological order (Museum, 2008). Most often, the collections focus on past cultures or a particular culture (Piotrowski, 2007). Examples include Colonial Williamsburg, Virginia; the American History Museum in Washington, D.C.; and the British Museum in London. Visiting various types of museums and observing the users is essential to museum design.

Teamwork

To design a museum, architects and interior designers work as a team along with the museum director and curator. When beginning data collection, the team must examine the focus and mission of the museum as well as the type of collection to be exhibited.

Spatial Relationships and Organization

Within these museums, the basic areas are separated into public and private zones. The public entrance includes the reception area, security guard station, and museum gift shop. Public access is allowed into exhibit **galleries**, public restrooms, and if included, a cafeteria. Semi-private areas may include conference rooms and classrooms. Private areas include a loading dock and receiving, storage, restoration, and offices.

Security

Security is the highest priority in museums. Not only is there security at the entrance but also security guards and surveillance cameras are positioned through the space. Working with the staff and observing visitors in a museum will aid in designing the best location for cameras and guards.

Floor Plan and Circulation

For most museums, floor plans must be both structured and flexible. The structured portion holds the permanent exhibit. However, because there is generally a lack of exhibit space, a portion of the permanent collection is stored. The flexible portion is often for the changing special exhibits. Walls may be movable partitions that can accommodate various exhibit types and sizes. There are also a variety of display methods, such as attached to the wall, display cases, and freestanding.

Ideas for Collecting
New Evidence

Examples of research topics into museum design include visitors' expectations and satisfaction with museums; factors that influence museum visitors; work experience for the employee; visitors' experience; security, crowd control; accessibility and universal design; circulation; aesthetics; sustainability; ethnic communities; art museums; visitors; exhibits; and the varied functions.

Circulating through the space, particularly the exhibits, must be easy. How people move through space can be learned through observations. Research has also been conducted to measure the effects of layout on visitors' spatial behavior in open plan exhibit settings. The InformeDesign RS "How Visitors Move through Open Plan Exhibitions" (2006, December 28) summarizes a study that examined how the layout influences visitors' movement through and interaction with exhibits. Some suggested criteria are to make critical exhibits accessible and visible from many other exhibits to increase visitor engagement, provide information at each exhibit, design exhibits to be encountered in any sequence, and provide wayfinding methods that will also identify themes, that is, labels and colors.

Lighting

Appropriate lighting and its placement are important to effectively view exhibits. Through survey and observation techniques, the InformeDesign RS "Lighting—the Role it Plays in a Museum" (2002, October 12) summarizes a study that investigated the light expectation of museum visitors against that of decision makers. The summary identified strengths and weaknesses in museum light by comparing the museums' current lighting conditions to lighting expectations to identify. From this study, design criteria provide information to improve museum lighting.

Satisfaction of Users

Museums function for the purpose of educating the visitor, who, ultimately, must be satisfied. Research indicates that there is a relationship between visitors' expectations and their satisfaction with the visit. An InformeDesign RS, "Expectation and Satisfaction with Art Museums" (2007, February 21), summarizes a study that notes visitors' expectations may change in the course of a visit and, therefore, creating good circulation and interpretive signage for displays. Additionally, because waiting in line to purchase tickets can be unpleasant, consider using design features that will make the process easier, more pleasant, and comfortable.

Bourdeau and Chebat (2003) studied the influence of location of paintings and signage on visitors' ability to recall titles and paintings after their touring a museum's exhibit space. They suggested that the physical characteristics of the exhibition environment as well as the artwork and its popularity affect learning. For example, exhibits may be placed in three sequences: beginning—when the visitor is learning about the space; middle—when the visitor has optimum attention; and the end—when the visitor is cognitively fatigued. Another consideration is ways to immerse visitors to remember what has been learned. Harvey, Loomis, Bell, and Marino (1998) documented the effects of the museum design that allowed visitors to become immersed in the exhibit. The study revealed that if exhibits drew, engaged, and allowed visitors to become immersed, their learning of the subject matter increased. One of the ways to increase learning would be to have interactive, multisensory stimulation, role-playing prompts, soft lighting, as well as other methods of immersion.

Religious Design

According to Piotrowski and Rogers (2007), a religious facility is a building or a group of buildings where people worship; these include synagogues, mosques, shrines, and temples.

As a general rule, the design of religious structures is based on philosophy or church doctrine. Roberts (2004) notes that each congregation will have specific needs and concerns. As is demonstrated in Case Study 16.1 about the St. Elizabeth Ann Seton School, learning about the particular **religious philosophy** or **doctrine** as well as their specific needs and concerns is vital to the success of the design.

A list of religious typology might include:

- Church (Christianity)

- Synagogue (Judaism)

- Mosque (Islam)

- Shrine (Shinto)

- Temple (Buddhism)

Historically, religious structures were designed with specific layouts. For example, Gothic structures included the narthex, nave, aisles, transept, choir, and apse. Present-day "religious structures reflect not only past architectural styles, but also new forms as building systems have advanced and denominations have required different building formats to meet their needs" (Piotrowski & Rogers, 2007, p. 392). For example, many contemporary churches have incorporated technology, lighting, and acoustics into the design.

Research has been conducted to evaluate how buildings relate to sacredness in architecture. Watson and Kucko (2001) note that sacred architecture is a powerful expression of the human quest for spirituality, and expresses awareness of a higher power. They also point out that to obtain a better understanding of sacred architectural design, designers must analyze the numbers, proportions, symbolism, patterns, materials, and natural rhythms used to design a building.

Collecting evidence for religious design begins by understanding the doctrine; then other means of data collection must take place. The following is a list of data collection methods:

- Learn and understand church doctrine.

- Learn how this doctrine will affect the design.

- Interview individuals and church leaders.

- Conduct focus groups.

- Observe the behavior of parishioners.

Lastly, consider the ethnic culture within the community of the religious structure and its surrounding neighborhood. Will culture affect the design? The InformeDesign RS "Designing Religious Spaces for Ethnic Communities" (2004, July 6) summarized a case study conducted to examine the role of tradition and culture in the design on contemporary religious facilities. The focus was on Native American, West African, and African American community members who are seeking to preserve their culture and identities and yet be part of the contemporary society. From this study, the authors make several suggestions. A few examples are (1) involve community members in the design process; in doing so, designers must be aware of the differences among the ethnic groups; (2) emphasize centrality, i.e., the focus is centered on worship as well as the ethnic groups; (3) interpret traditional forms using modern materials; and (4) determine ways that will address the needs of cultural groups through the process—design and construction.

Recreational Design

Recreational design may combine with various other types of design—office design, hotels, restaurant, or education—or may stand alone. These facility types include the entrance to various activities that may take place indoors, outdoors, or both. These activities may include golf, boating, skiing and other winter sports, aquatics, handball, racquetball, squash, tennis, and equestrian sports. Additionally, fitness and spa facilities as well as dining facilities may be included in many of these types (Diedrich, 2005).

A typology for recreational facilities might include:

- Recreation centers
- Health clubs
- Swimming pools
- Tennis clubs
- Golf clubs
- Bowling alleys

Other Design Categories

There are many different design types. Some include industrial, transportation, and specialized design. Industrial design types generally dominate the skyline in an industrial area—warehouses, automobile manufacturing plants, laboratories, or power plants.

Transportation design includes airplanes and trains as well as cruise ships, motor homes, and terminals. In recent years, there are many concerns related to security at terminals and within the transportation means itself. Also, life safety and accessibility, acoustics, and wayfinding are important areas of consideration in research for evidence (Griffin, 2004).

There are also specialized design types such as kiosks, atriums, greenhouses, churches, theaters, and so on (Allen et al., 2004; Kilmer & Kilmer, 1992). Each category and type has its own special needs and functions.

Application

Topics for research were suggested in Chapter 11; however, more specific research can be conducted within specific design typologies. The St. Elizabeth Ann Seton School case study provides an example of research for an educational and religious facility (see Case Study 16.1).

The IIDA Knowledge Center has sections that relate to specific design types—education, government, religious, and industrial/manufacturing. The center also has sections listed by topic such as FF&E, space planning, and computer technology.

In reviewing the InformeDesign RS, it is important to review its key concepts and design criteria and then use those criteria in informing the design. There are RSs that relate to transportation, correctional facilities, libraries, public facilities, and recreation/community centers as well as school/educational facilities and university/college/institutes. Two examples of InformeDesign RS on transportations are "Airport Waiting Spaces as Shopping Places" (2007, March 5), and "Designing Efficient Airports" (2008, May 13).

Ideas for Collecting New Evidence

Examples of research topics into specialized design include circulation. Questions to explore may be how to address the needs of people with disabilities, and how other buildings or designs have incorporated universal design into their projects.

Summary

This chapter addresses a few of the many design typologies such as institutional, cultural, and recreational facilities. You may further address these examples using your design education, or use them as a springboard to explore others.

Each typology has different concerns and/or needs. For example, acoustics, color, and circulation may be important to facilitate learning in an educational setting. Some decisions may be based on theory, such as Reggio Emilia theory. Security may be the greatest concern in government buildings. Acoustics and lighting may be concerns in cultural facilities. Research through data collection will provide evidence to improve the design.

It is important to use a variety of methods to collect data; these methods include content analysis, surveys, observations, and interviews. This is true as you work within all of the design typologies, including those discussed in previous chapters. Most of all, research should include new evidence located in articles or summaries in order to inform and improve the design project.

Key Terms

Autism

Bloom's taxonomy

child-directed curriculum

collections

distance education

exhibits

galleries

interdisciplinary

multidisciplinary

museums

permanent collection

programmed or
    individualized
    instruction

Reggio Emilia theory

religious philosophy or
    doctrine

teacher-directed curriculum

teaching methods

traveling exhibit

virtual environment

Residential
Spaces

PART
FIVE

THEODORE

Residential Structures: Family and Housing

OBJECTIVES

After reading this chapter, you should be able to:

Recognize the many types of familial structures beyond the nuclear family

Identify and research the different types of housing and understand the needs and concerns for all populations

Develop evidence-based design (EBD) for both residential family structures and the structures that families live in

DRED COURT

Since the late twentieth and early twenty-first centuries, the U.S. population has become more diverse than ever. **Familial structures** have changed with a greater influx of immigrants from Asia, the Middle East, Africa, and other areas of the globe than in previous waves of immigration, which primarily flowed from homogeneous Western European cultures. Additionally, Native Americans view family structure differently than Caucasian Americans of European descent. With more single-parent, blended-family, empty-nester, and other alternative households to the traditional nucleus family household, a plethora of preferences, functional requirements, and economic needs further compound this diversity.

Today, a variety of housing types beyond the single family are available; these include apartments, town houses, Housing and Urban Development (HUD) housing, and condominiums. In recent decades, more emphasis has been given to affordable housing, which may be found in both new and renovated buildings and is intended to accommodate the disabled, elderly, homeless, and working poor—all of whom require assistance finding and maintaining proper housing. Additionally, with an aging population, universal design needs to be implemented into residential spaces. This chapter discusses areas in which to collect data and research new evidence in order to develop EBD for residential spaces.

Familial Structures

Families are composed of individuals. In a **nuclear family**, the individuals are a husband and father, a wife and mother, and one or more children (Lamanna & Riedmann, 2006; Olson & DeFain, 2006). Typically, these families live in single- or multi-family housing types.

The **blended family**, or step family, is one where one or both partners have children from a previous marriage (Olson & DeFain, 2006). Housing for blended families is generally similar to the nuclear family and may be in single- or multi-family housing types.

One of the issues in blended families relates to children who must shuffle between parents. An InformeDesign RS, "Housing and Divorce" (2003, January 28), summarizes a study on this issue and, using surveys and interviews, assessed housing characteristics and perceptions of housing environments as well as the role of the house with marriage, divorce, separation, and the children. Her findings suggest criteria that provide meaning to the homes of divorced families. Examples are to specify flexible furnishings (e.g., sofa beds or futons) that will provide multi-use spaces and ease crowding, create spaces or areas in which children are able to store personal items, and design spaces that provide opportunities for supervision, that is, open plan between kitchen and family room.

Some individuals choose single-hood and create **one-person households**. Though the one-person household can be found at any adult age, it is more common among older people and, especially, older women (Lamanna & Riedmann, 2006). Rather than living alone, some younger singles live with their parents for a period of time or in multi-family housing. The older adult may live in single- or multi-family housing, or possibly in communal or group living units.

A **single-parent family** may be a mother or a father with one or more children (Olson & DeFain, 2006). Single-parent families most frequently reside in single- or multi-family housing. HUD housing is available for low-income single families (Housing, 2007).

The **extended family** frequently blends a married couple or single parent and their children with three or more generations (Olson & DeFain, 2006). Some extended families may develop because of divorce or immigration. Living arrangements will vary and be dependent on the family that absorbs the relative (Lamanna & Riedmann, 2006). Other cultures frequently have extended family situations. Housing for extended families may be single- or multi-family types. The type of spatial layout will depend on cultural preference. For example, Hispanics prefer multiple bedrooms for family members but not large bedrooms (Duell, 2007).

For the **empty nester**, the children are no longer living at home, and the household has reverted back to only the parents (Olson & DeFain, 2006). Empty nesters frequently have more time and disposable income, and many live in single-family housing or move into multi-family housing (e.g., apartments or condominiums) or town houses.

As the senior population increases with the baby boomers' aging, many will choose to remain in their homes. **Aging in place**, for both singles and couples, has become an option instead of moving from the homes in which there has been long-term ownership. If the home has not been designed to accommodate requirements such as the wheelchair, extensive remodeling will be needed (Novelli, 2002). Alternatively, newer homes can be designed to meet future needs, such as wheelchair accessibility, visual impairments, and hearing impairments. Additionally, isolation can be a danger for those aging in place (Pagans, 2007).

One of the many concerns older people have is the cost of renovation. The InformeDesign RS "Residential Adaptation for Aging" (2007, November 12) summarized a study that investigated the feasibility and costs of renovating homes for the older person in lieu of long-term care. Findings determine that financial saving may be incurred by renovating homes compared to costs of long-term care. However, renovation has other drawbacks: bedrooms and bathrooms on a second level are not accessible, and a smaller space may be difficult to adapt for a wheelchair. Thus, a home that is more spacious with a main-level bedroom and bathroom will be the easiest to adapt for accessibility. However, with bedrooms and bathrooms on another level, the installation of a stair lift may be an option.

Today, there is great diversity of family structures. The following are a few examples: parents raising adopted children of a different racial and ethnic background, disabled children, or children adopted at an older than traditional age for adoption; grandparents becoming primary parents for grandchildren; homosexual parents raising children; and foster parents caring for unrelated children (Lamanna & Riedmann, 2006). Housing needs for each of these families may be similar or different from those of the nuclear family. These families live in both single- and multi-family housing.

Housing creates both physical and psychological boundaries. Often individuals within the house have private spaces to call their own, whether a room or a space within a room. Certainly, each individual has a unique identity, but the family shares in functional events, rituals, and an historical past; and gathering areas are needed for shared activities (Lamanna & Riedmann, 2006).

Housing Structures

Housing can be placed into two basic types: single family and multi-family. These housing types are occupied by various familial structures. Table 17.1 lists the housing types with their common name, layout, and common feature(s).

Housing Type	Common Name	Layout	Common Feature(s)
Table 17.1 Housing Types (with Common Name) Related to Layout and Common Features			
Single family	Single detached	With or without garage	
	Duplex attached	Horizontal or vertical layout	Common wall or ceiling/floor
	Triplex attached	Vertical layout	Common ceiling/floor
	Town house	Horizontal layout	Common walls
	Row house	Horizontal layout	Common walls
	HUD low income	With or without garage	
	Habitat for Humanity house	With or without garage	
Multi-family	Big house: multiplex	Horizontal and vertical layout	Common wall or cciling/floor
	Small apartment	Horizontal and vertical layout	Common wall or ceiling/floor
	Low-rise apartment	Horizontal and vertical layout	Common wall or ceiling/floor
	Mid-rise apartment	Horizontal and vertical layout	Common wall or ceiling/floor
	Apartment over commercial	Horizontal and vertical layout	Common wall or ceiling/floor
	Condominium	Horizontal and vertical layout	Common wall or ceiling/floor
	High-rise apartment	Horizontal and vertical layout	Common wall or ceiling/floor
	HUD low income	Horizontal and/or vertical layout	Common wall and/or ceiling/floor

Single-Family Housing

Single-family housing can be found in various configurations. The single **detached** building with or without a garage is the most common. The building is constructed with one to three floors and may be built in dense populated urban areas, in the suburbs, or in the country. The advantage to the single detached building is the flexibility of layout and the ability to develop individual identity and personalization. With larger acreage, the building can be oriented to take advantage of views as well as solar power (Housing Types, 2007). Nuclear families frequently dwell in this type of housing. However, families with different structures may choose this type of housing for homeownership (see Figure 17.1).

The **duplex** has a horizontal or vertical layout with common ceiling or floor systems. The **triplex** has a vertical layout with common ceiling and floor systems. Figures 17.2a

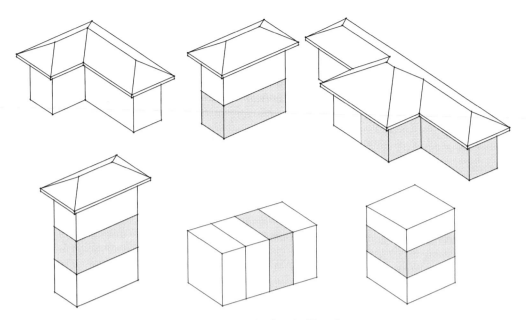

Figure 17.1 *Top left*: This drawing represents single, detached housing.
Figure 17.2a *Top center*: This drawing represents an attached duplex in vertical layout with common ceiling or floor systems. The grayed area represents one unit.
Figure 17.2b *Top right*: This drawing represents an attached duplex in horizontal layout with common wall systems. The grayed area represents one unit.
Figure 17.3 *Bottom left*: This drawing represents an attached triplex in vertical layout with common ceiling and floor systems. The grayed area represents one unit.
Figure 17.4 *Bottom center*: This drawing represents an attached town house or row house. The grayed area represents one unit.
Figure 17.5 *Bottom right*: This drawing represents a stacked row house. The grayed area represents one unit.

and b and 17.3 illustrate a duplex and triplex, respectively. The duplex and triplex are two or three housing units within a detached building. This type of structure can house more people. Each unit has a separate entrance that may be personalized. There are a variety of house designs that can be adapted to a site (Housing Types, 2007). Singles, couples, and small families more often choose this type of housing that has outdoor areas but requires less time spent on yard maintenance. Extended families may find the duplex or triplex acceptable for privacy and shared activities.

The **town house** and **row house** have a horizontal layout with common walls. Figure 17.4 illustrates an attached town house or row house and Figure 17.5 illustrates a stacked row house. These are side **attached** in multiple housing units that are arranged in rows. Units have their own exterior entrance. Features of these types of housing are that each has its own front door, allowing for limited personalization of the entrance. Though each unit is similar from the street, there are many variations found through the country. Outdoor spaces are separate and yet side by side, which may impact privacy. Parking may be on street, off street, or on the ground level of the unit (Housing Types, 2007). Many units are designed for purchase with a homeowner's association. There will also be a greater sense of security with close neighbors, and many units have amenities within the complex or community such as pools, tennis courts, playgrounds, and more (Townhouses, 2007). A variety of familial structure types (singles, couples, empty nesters, etc.) will find this housing type appealing because others are responsible for exterior maintenance and repairs.

Many low-income families have difficulty finding affordable housing. The lack of affordable housing has increased in recent years and has become a hardship for these families (CPD, 2007). In some instances, **HUD low-income housing** and **Habitat for Humanity housing** have provided housing and homeownership for low-income families (Housing, 2007). Some architects and interior designers are working with social services to build affordable housing (Affordable Housing Conference, 2007).

The InformeDesign RS "Housing and Low-Income Women" (2006, January 20) strengthens the importance of participation in construction of low-income housing. The research summary (RS) discusses how participation in a self-help housing program affected low-income women's feelings about their residential environments. It came to light that the main housing concerns were for privacy, safety, and particularly the opportunity to personalize their space. Because of the residents' involvement in the construction and their opportunity to personalize their homes, the residents gained a sense of pride, confidence, and competence. As noted in Chapter 3, concerns have been raised related to income, diversity, and housing types (InformeDesign, 2006, December 6). Disparity in these areas can increase the separation of housing related to diversity and income levels.

Multi-Family Housing

There are many types of **multi-family housing**—big house multiplex, various types of apartment buildings, and condominiums. The big house **multiplex** has a horizontal and vertical layout with common walls and/or common ceilings/floors. The multiplex is four or more housing units within a detached building. Units may be single- or multilevel with private exterior entrances. Some may have shared entrances; however, this creates privacy and maintenance concerns. Figure 17.6a–c illustrates an attached multiplex in a big house.

Housing Types (2007) suggests several other challenges with the multiplex. These include:

- Ability to personalize units and yet maintain the big house feel is another challenge

- Impact of outdoor shared spaces on privacy and function for individuals

- Limited access to sunlight and ventilation from the outside

- Possibility for on-street parking only

Most frequently singles or young couples live in these buildings. Singles may share or live alone, and young couples may find these units convenient to a workplace or university.

Apartment buildings are various sizes from small, **low rise**, and **mid rise** to **high rise**.

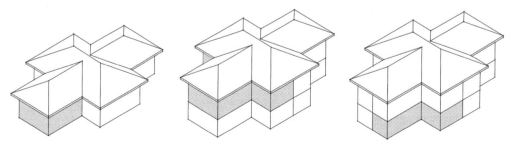

Figure 17.6a–c These drawings represent an attached multiplex in a big house. The grayed area represents one unit.

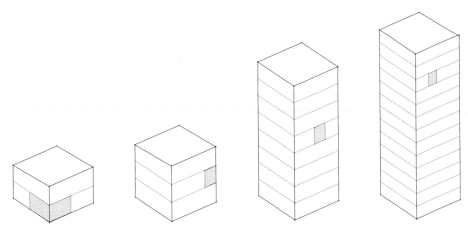

Figure 17.7a–d These drawings illustrate the differences among these various size apartment buildings: small, low rise, mid rise, and high rise. The grayed area represents one unit.

Some are located over commercial spaces. Figure 17.7a–d illustrates the difference between these various size apartment buildings: small, low rise, mid rise, and high rise.

Many small and low-rise apartment buildings are designed with central hallways. These hallways may be directly or indirectly accessible from the street, are the shared space access to units, and often contain windows for light and air on opposite ends. Though the layout and design of each unit may be the same, occupants are able to personalize the interior. Occupants of lower levels often have less privacy and lack a view the upper-level units may have. Low-rise apartments may have private outdoor spaces limited to a balcony or patio; however, most outdoor spaces are shared. Comparing small versus low-rise apartments, low-rise apartments may be designed with a variety of configurations with more flexibility of form, may be oriented to natural or built features with consideration to a site orientation, and are produced with maximum unit count. For the small apartment building, parking is most often on the street and becomes the greatest challenge. For the low-rise apartment, parking may be off street and/or underground (Housing Types, 2007).

As building sizes increase to mid rise, a greater number of features and amenities may be found. For example, the design of a mid-rise apartment may be shaped to respond to surroundings. Interiors become more critical to livability and should be more carefully designed to maintain privacy. Private outdoor spaces may be limited to balconies and to rooftops; however, ground-level outdoor spaces may still be shared. Thus, designers must carefully design public and private spaces. Security is important, but can be a challenge for units at the ground level where there is direct access to the street. For upper-level units, elevators provide easier access. For the mid-rise apartment, parking is most often above or below ground; security must be carefully considered for parking areas (Housing Types, 2007).

High-rise apartment buildings have advantages over the smaller, low-rise, and mid-rise apartments; these advantages include greater privacy, views, varied forms, and security. For example, even with shared hallways, the building can be designed to create a more private entrance to each unit. Each unit may have private outdoor spaces as balconies and/or private roof gardens; however, there are spaces that are shared such as outdoor spaces on the roof or grounds around the building as well as the entrance, elevators, staircases, or hallways or corridors (Housing Types, 2007). Corridors in high-rise buildings may be configured as

single loaded or **double loaded**. Single-loaded corridors are on one side of the building; double-loaded corridors are designed with units on both sides of a central corridor. Double-loaded corridors are most common (DeVido, 1996) because with fewer corridors, there are more units and a greater income for the owner. Additionally, the variety of forms and characteristics of the high rise may provide greater differences in shape, size, and design of units. As in other apartments, the ability to personalize units is limited to entries and personal furnishings; however, an amenity of the high-rise apartment is the possible uninterrupted views. For the high-rise apartment building, there is often greater security at the entrance and with parking garages that are probably underground (Housing Types, 2007).

Apartments over commercial spaces have advantages and disadvantages. The interior may provide a more loft feeling, which can be an advantage; however, the space must be livable—plumbing, heating, and ventilation. The ability to design safe and secure access is important and must be carefully evaluated. Shared spaces—similar to small and low-rise apartment buildings—include entrances, hallways, elevators (if available), and staircases. Access may be the greatest disadvantage—street frontage and walk-up only. Careful planning is needed to separate and integrate access for pedestrians, parking, and trash pickup. Parking is the greatest disadvantage because of the commercial space below and daytime parking may be different than evening parking (Housing Types, 2007). Figure 17.8 illustrates an apartment over a commercial space.

The concept of **condominiums**, or **condos**, refers to apartment, or unit, ownership. Many apartments have been converted into condos in which ownership is confined to the interior walls, floors, and ceilings. Repairs and maintenance within the condo are the responsibility of the owner. However, all owners are partners through the condo association to which owners pay a monthly fee that covers general repairs and maintenance of common areas of the complex as well as build cash reserves for future needs. It also covers normal maintenance of grounds (shoveling snow, cutting grass, and maintaining a pool). In some cases, a special assessment may also be attached for major repairs or maintenance such as a new roof (Condominiums, 2007). Singles, couples, and nuclear families frequently purchase units.

Condominiums are a type of **housing cooperative**, or **co-op housing**, in which each resident owns a unit in the building. Conversely, members of co-op housing "own a share in a corporation that owns or controls the building and/or property in which they live" (National Association of Housing Cooperatives [NAHC], n.d.). Shareholders may occupy a unit and have voting rights in the corporation. This type of housing comes in all shapes and sizes: single family, student housing, senior housing, town houses, garden apartments, mid- and high-rise apartments, and mobile home parks. Though not common in rural America,

Figure 17.8 An apartment may be located over a commercial space. The upper grayed area represents one unit; the lower area represents the commercial space.

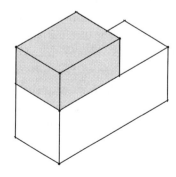

this is common in many large metropolitan areas such as New York City, Chicago, Miami, Minneapolis, Detroit, Atlanta, San Francisco, and Washington, D.C. (NAHC, n.d.).

Any type of family may live in these apartment types. However, income level may vary with the building type or management. HUD low-income multi-family housing is most often similar to small or low-rise apartment living. The layout may be horizontal (i.e., one level) or vertical (i.e., two levels) with common walls and/or ceiling-to-floor connections. On the other hand, families with greater incomes more frequently occupy high-rise buildings or condominiums.

There are many types of residential structures, and various types of familial structures may occupy them. In some instances, interior designers may work with developers, or they may work with individual families to design a residence. A literature review may provide evidence on multi-housing and occupant types, ways of designing quality affordable housing, housing of the future, and more.

Connections: Family and Housing

Studies have connected family structure with housing types. Vanderford, Mimura, Sweaney, and Carswell (2007) examined the relationship between household compositions and the variables of tenure status and residential housing types. Households examined included various family compositions, such as a couple with or without children, or a single person with or without children. The study also included families with extended family members, an unmarried partner, and other unrelated individuals. The housing types included in their study were single-family site-built, multi-family site-built, and manufactured housing. Though all family compositions are found in all three housing types, a greater number of couples with or without children resided in single-family housing, and a single person without children resided in multi-family housing. A greater number of couples with or without children followed by women without children resided in manufactured housing. This information helps designers know households most commonly resided in specific types of structures, and in some cases, manufactured homes are more often in the affordable housing category.

Affordable Housing

Developing good affordable housing is a concern in many countries including the United States. This issue raises many concerns, such as the accommodation of children's needs in tight quarters. An InformeDesign RS, "Children and Housing Design" (InformeDesign, 2004, January 16), summarized a study conducted in Cyprus that compared children's preferences of their housing to housing norms—the large, single-family detached houses with a yard, two bathrooms, and one bedroom for each child. Though conducted in Cyprus, many of the findings are applicable to designs in the United States. Findings that may be evidence for a residential design project include the following:

- Places should be created for children to play in and outside of apartment buildings.

- Design of kitchens and living rooms should be large enough to accommodate larger groups of people, especially to accommodate families that have taken in displaced relatives.

Ideas for Collecting New Evidence

Examples of research topics into housing include features of home and family identity; issues in multifamily housing (i.e., cleanliness, children, daylighting, personal living space, the future of this type of housing, recycling, indoor air quality, mold, and affordable housing design); and issues in single-family housing (i.e., children, sustainability, indoor air quality, expression of personal identity, and affordable homes).

- Bedrooms should be large enough to accommodate up to two children.

- Adequate storage for clothes, toys, and other personal or household items should be provided.

- In housing developments, entertainment and exercise facilities should be included.

- Low-income housing can be designed to fit the norms of society.

The results of this study will help designers, architects, policy makers, and planners understand housing needs and preferences for children and, thus, are able to design child-friendly housing.

The Not So Big House

Architect Sarah Susanka (2001) coined the phase "the not so big house" and wrote a book with an eponymous title. Her inspiration for writing *The Not So Big House* sprang from a concern for houses filling suburbs that were becoming "bigger than ever" (p. 7), but without character and lacking psychological warmth. She suggests "a house is more than square footage and the number of beds and baths" (p. 7). In other words, a house should express the owner's personality. This book and others by Susanka provide ideas for detached housing for a variety of familial structures.

Housing of the Future

What will housing be like in the future? The InformeDesign RS "Visions of Future Homes" (2004, June 16) summarizes a study that explored society's vision of homes in the future and how they will be linked with technology, society, and culture. Findings recognize that homes of the future will have social and functional implications of technology. Today, most homes reflect the values of their occupants. However, the manner in which the media projects newer homes can preserve or change homes of the future. For example, new uses of technology can impact the way we interact and function within the home; thus, technology may change the occupants' values and what has been important in the past. So, the question still remains: what will housing be like in the future? Additionally, how will technology change the way homes are designed and built in the future?

Application

This chapter provides background information regarding familial structures and housing as well as related ideas to help you begin your quest for new evidence to apply to a project.

When beginning the initial discussion with a client, consider their family structures and ask the question: What is the family structure, and how will it affect the design project? Next, consider the type of housing in which they live or plan to live. What does the literature say regarding this family structure and housing type, i.e., multi-family? What are some of the issues that may arise and/or must be addressed?

Some of the research topics may include various familial structures, housing types, affordable housing, homes of the future, aging in place, and appropriate housing.

The International Interior Design Association (IIDA) Knowledge Center, along with a link to residential types, contains several research projects. For example, "An Exploratory Study of Disabled Tenants' Level of Satisfaction Under the Fair Housing Amendments Act (FHAA)," which evaluates the adequacy of the FHAA in protecting the rights of disabled people to accessible multi-family housing (Johansen, 2007).

InformeDesign (2005) contains hundreds of RSs related to residential design. Topics related to multi-family residence may include one or more of the following: daylighting design, future housing, housing cooperatives, and urban renewal programs. Topics related to affordable housing may include one or more of the following: property values or influencing in locations this type of housing.

Summary

There are many types of familial structures, each of which may live in any number of housing types. To design a residence, questions may arise from personal and/or cultural needs for residents. For example, will the housing unit be sufficient for the family as it is presently structured? Will aging in place be a concern for the future? Will extended family members or a caregiver need housing and affect the choice and design?

Knowledge of familial and housing structures, along with evidence gathered through research and data collection, will bring on a new understanding of possible issues that may emerge for you as a designer, and for the world that we all live in together in our many and diverse ways.

Key Terms

aging in place

attached

blended family

condominiums (condos)

detached

double loaded

duplex

empty nester

extended family

familial structure

Habitat for Humanity housing

high-rise

housing cooperative (or co-op housing)

HUD low-income housing

low rise

mid rise

multi-family housing

multiplex

nuclear family

one-person households

row house

single-family housing

single loaded

single-parent family

town house

triplex

THEODORE

Data Collection for Residential Design

OBJECTIVES

After reading this chapter, you should be able to:

Understand that there are many types of familial structures beyond the nuclear family

Identify the occupants—all family members, including children and extended family—as clients

Collect appropriate data for residential design

DRED COURT

W hether designing for a family in a single-family housing, a couple in a condo located in a high-rise building, or a single person in an apartment located in a mid-rise building, designers must collect information to understand the special needs and lifestyle of the occupants. Information or facts collected from the client along with research of new evidence will improve the design.

This chapter explores the process of data collection for residential design. Designers must first identify the users of their residential design. Data collection will then focus on protection and security, status, occupants, location (including climate and orientation), space allocation, and preferences (both aesthetic and functional), as well as additional data specific to each unique project.

Identification of the User

To identify the client, the designer must include all users, or occupants, including head of household, parents, partner, children, members of the blended or extended family, caregiver, and others who live in the same housing unit. Therefore, when data are collected, all occupants must be included in the design. For example, adolescent males and females typically differ in their preferences for bedroom design and decoration. Also, some adolescents are influenced by other family members or friends, whereas others are not (Jones, Taylor, Dick, Singh, & Cook, 2007). For this reason, all occupants must be involved in the design process. At the same time, it is wise to work through the final solution with the individual(s) who handle the finances.

Data Collection

People need housing for shelter (DeVido, 1996), but also to meet individual needs and to reflect occupants' personalities and values. Because the average American moves every six years, the structure itself may not be a reflection of the owner; however, the landscaping, lifestyles, interior finishes, and objects usually act as indicators (Ireland, 2007). Therefore, interior designers must collect data related to preferences and individual responses to color, style, function, finishes, and lighting.

Protection and Security

Houses are designed to protect the occupants from climatic conditions characteristic of the region (Ireland, 2007). For example, a home in the upper Midwest must protect against winter winds and snow as well as rain and hot sun in the summer, whereas a home in Arizona must protect against the hot sun during most of the year.

Houses also provide security from intruders by means of locks as well as security systems. Thus, houses must be constructed with materials appropriate to the specific location and include security systems. Some residences are more vulnerable to crime than others. An InformeDesign RS, "Assessing Residential Vulnerability" (2003, October 27), summarized a study conducted to examine features of **defensible space theory** that help police officers assess vulnerability. The researchers also examined the differences between an officers' perspective of susceptibility and that of burglars and residents. If, for example, police officers have a different view than burglars, residents may have been misadvised and homes may not be safe. As a result of this study, the author suggests shrubbery, tall fences, and other barriers intended to reduce visibility from the street may, unfortunately, increase the vulnerability to burglary. To deter burglars when designing a home, both internal and external visibility should be considered. Also, when considering various security methods, it is important to realize that the value of the home is the driving force for burglars; this means that more expensive homes are more vulnerable than inexpensive homes.

Status

After protection and security issues are met, individuals are concerned about their place in society. Status is represented in different ways, such as the location where a house is built, both the site itself and its area, and the materials used. The size of the house and number of amenities and luxuries increase the level of status.

Occupants

The clients' names, complete address, contact information, and occupations are important general information. It is important to collect data about all occupants of the residence. Data include information about all individuals who occupy the space, such as their ages and any special needs they may have; information about pets—kind, size, and their special needs; and information regarding an overnight or extended-stay guest who will occupy the space. See Appendices N through U for residential surveys. Additionally, questions should be asked regarding the composition of the household. Will it change in the near future, and, if so, how and when (Allen et al., 2004)?

Aging in Place

Because more people, as they age, are choosing to age in place, issues need to be addressed in designing homes for accessibility and safety. An InformeDesign RS, "Housing Design Influences Ability to Age in Place" (2003, April 25), summarizes a study of the low-income elderly person's perceptions of home features that hindered and helped those aging in place—accessibility and safety. The basic accessibility needs must be addressed, but findings suggest that the environment must also promote safety. Thus, a low-maintenance house should be designed that is not only accessible but also safe by avoiding stairs and steps and providing handrails, rails in bathtubs or walk-in showers, raised toilet seats, and more. Yards and outdoor areas should be level for easy maintenance as well as to prevent falls. For more information, these issues are further addressed in the research summaries (RSs) found in InformeDesign.

Location, Climate, Orientation

Designers must also collect data regarding the location, climate, temperature, and orientation (e.g., view). Each area should be described so that the designer may determine or research how these will affect the design.

Space Allocation

In residential design, **social zones** include gathering spaces such as the entry, living rooms, eating areas, family rooms, and recreation areas. **Work zones** include the kitchen, laundry, offices, and dens. Although kitchens are included in work zones, they have also become gathering spaces for many families and even guests. **Private zones** include bedrooms, bathrooms, and other spaces that are used only by family members. Though the bathroom may be part of the private zone, at least one must be accessible to guests (Allen et al., 2004; Kilmer & Kilmer, 1992).

Space allocation relates to building type (e.g., apartment or single-family dwelling), familial structure (e.g., nuclear or single-parent family), occupant numbers, physical needs (e.g., accessibility), and spatial needs (e.g., function and adjacencies). Data collected from the client clearly affects the final design. To help understand these needs, questions must be designed to learn how the client's lifestyle will affect each room's function and requirements. The designer will learn about the number who will occupy each room, the frequency of use, the formal versus informal use, adjacencies and location preferences, questions specific to each type of room, and requirements such as furniture, flooring, and cabinetry. Additionally, any multifunctional spaces must be included in the collected data.

Space planning is an important part of housing design, and with the change in family lifestyles, concern to create universal design, and needs for special populations—aging and disabled—must be incorporated into space planning. The InformeDesign RS "Rethinking Residential Space Planning" (2003, June 2) summarized a study that provided a perspective for residential space planning with the following criteria to address the concerns: house orientation, entryways, work areas, storage, plumbing, privacy, and persons with physical challenges. Particularly important is to design flexible floor plans that meet changes that may occur over a longer period of time. The research summary (RS) will provide further details that will address concerns for a specific client.

Technology has affected home design. Individuals in many households use wired or wireless computers for personal communication. This may include the home office (Slotkis, 2006). Home offices are more common, and design for home-based business involves the use of technology. Intille and Larson (2005) studied how to create computer environments at home. They "are developing technologies and design strategies that use context-aware sensing to empower people with information by presenting it at precisely the right time and place." This coincides with the "just-in-time" way of working (see Chapter 12). Additionally, computers are now used to manage and control heating, ventilation, and air conditioning (HVAC) systems, security systems, and audiovisual media" (Slotkis, 2006, p. 395).

Storage is essential for individuals' as well as household needs. Individually, each person should have at least 4 feet of closet space. Collectively, storage is needed in the kitchen, laundry rooms, bathrooms, as well as the garage. Particularly, the kitchen needs adequate counter space to work and cabinet space for storage. Adequate closet space is needed for maintenance (brooms, vacuums, cleaning supplies, etc.), coats for guests, and for dead storage (off season, such as the lawn mower) (Kilmer & Kilmer, 1992). Thus, specific storage needs by room as well as separate storage areas should also be noted.

It is also important to collect information about hobbies and activities—who is involved and where the activity or hobby takes place. With a greater use of electronics, data must be collected regarding communication modes, equipment needs, and location for each.

Family Interaction

Families need places to interact with each other. An InformeDesign RS, "Family Interaction and Home Design" (2004, July 13), summarizes a study that evaluated how residential spaces can be designed for the optimal family interaction. Some residents may envision a more idealized space that will not reflect actual use and living situations. Flexible space can be designed to support multiple activities that can occur simultaneously and will facilitate interaction throughout the children's lives.

Indoor Air Quality

During the building or remodeling process, all products and materials should be carefully selected to obtain good indoor air quality (IAQ). There are several research studies to aid this quest for evidence. Nussbaumer (2004) investigated the effects of IAQ on persons with multiple chemical sensitivity (MCS). To lessen possibilities of symptoms, this author suggests specifying products and materials that limit emissions of toxic chemicals, and also suggests resources for more information. InformeDesign (2005, October 4) summarized a study that proposed ventilation rates for new homes based on an analysis of existing toxin levels, i.e., formaldehyde. The authors also suggest investigating ways to reduce or eliminate toxic emissions from new construction material by considering alternative materials and assembly procedures. For more information on IAQ, RSs can be located on the InformeDesign database.

Recycling Convenience

Recycling is important and areas to deposit recycling should be included in the design. An InformeDesign RS, "Designing for Household Recycling" (2004, July 6), summarizes a study that analyzed design factors that would increase household recycling as well as develop behaviors toward recycling. To accomplish this, the authors make the following suggestions:

- Kitchens should be designed with a door that enters into the garage or is near the garage. This serves a dual purpose—removal of recyclable goods is made easier and groceries are not carried through the house.

- A specific recycling area should be designed adjacent to or within the kitchen with a minimum area of 9 square feet. See Figure 18.1a–f for various layouts.

- Kitchens should also be designed so the sink is in or near the recycling area. This will facilitate rinsing items for recycle, even reusing items, and removing and disposing of lids, caps, and so on into a trash container. When recycling is made easier, attitudes developed will positively impact recycling rates.

Preferences—Aesthetic and Functional

Everyone responds in some way to aesthetics. For example, the organization of a space or the lack thereof will create different responses. Individuals respond differently to different colors, have preferences for style, and so on. Color responses are affected by psychological and cultural backgrounds; style preferences may be idealistic or based on educated knowledge (Ireland, 2006). Also, cultural preferences may relate to the ethnic background,

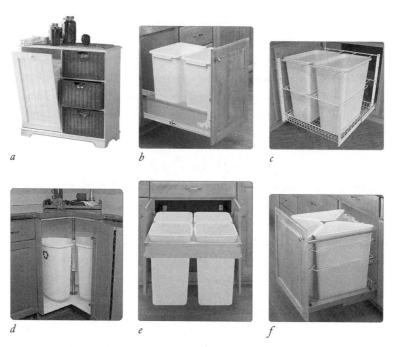

Figure 18.1 These drawings illustrate different cabinetry designs for recycling: (a) a furniture piece with a recycle bind; (b) a double-bin pull-out; (c) a side-by-side double-bin pull-out; (d) recycling bins in a lazy Susan configuration; (e) 4-bin recycling pull-out; and (f) a variation of the 4-bin recycling pull-out.

memorabilia from travel, and/or other educated knowledge. Design for a particular residence is also related to individual or family values—preference for type of atmosphere, need for separation or interaction, and so on (Kilmer & Kilmer, 1992). Designers must collect background information from the client to learn about such responses and preferences.

Everyone wants to feel comfortable, and when designing a home, clients expect to feel comfortable in their new or newly redesigned home. Often, to accomplish this, people focus on the floor plan and square footage—building more rooms and more space. Instead they should focus on the quality of the spaces rather than on quantity. "A house is so much more than its size and volume, neither of which has to do with comfort" (Susanka, 2001, p. 10).

Additional Data to Collect

Questions may also be added relative to human factors, such as health concerns, anthropometric data, and lighting needs. These are discussed in Chapter 7 (e.g., lighting) and Chapter 9. Frequently, clients prefer to use some existing furniture, fixtures, and equipment (FF&E); therefore, an inventory must also be conducted. Further information on taking an FF&E inventory can be found in Chapter 6. Table 18.1a–e provides an FF&E inventory form for residential spaces.

When designing in an existing building, two interior assessments must be conducted: a material/finish assessment, and an interior architecture assessment. A room-by-room

Table 18.1

FF&E Inventory for Residential Design

A. Furniture Inventory

Room	Type	Size	Color	Finish	Condition	Refinishing	Reupholstering

B. Finishes (Background) Inventory

Room	Type	Size	Color	Finish	Condition	Refinishing	Reupholstering

C. Fixtures (Cabinetry) Inventory

Room	Type	Size	Color	Finish	Condition	Refinishing	Plumbing/Electrical

D. Fixtures (Plumbing) Inventory

Room	Type	Size	Color	Finish	Condition	Refinishing	Plumbing/Electrical

E. Equipment (Appliances) Inventory

Room	Type	Size	Color	Finish	Condition	Cabling	Plumbing

material/finish interior assessment should include the following: room name, period/style, wall color(s), wall texture/finish, ceiling color, ceiling system, floor covering type/color, floor finish, window treatment, exterior shading devices, and special collections. A room-by-room interior architecture assessment should include the following: room name, significant architectural elements, lighting-enhanced architecture, noteworthy exterior views, security concerns, safety concerns, energy/environmental concerns, circulation concerns, luminaires appropriate style/size, universal design concerns, and acoustical concerns (Winchip, 2005, 2008).

Using interior assessments to collect facts is important; however, to develop evidence to inform the project, a literature search must take place. For example, a family room is probably the most used room in many households. Therefore, the furniture chosen must meet performance criteria that meet family needs. However, according to an InformeDesign RS, "Interiors Influence Perceptions of Age, Class, and Family Status" (2008, May 7), sitting behavior is the most detrimental to posture over a period of time. In this summary, the study developed a model to determine the stability of posture and explain sitting behavior. Their study revealed that sitting behavior affects posture. Thus, a designer could use their model to determine the chair that best suits the client.

Materials chosen in residential design are based on the design and physical attributes of a space. However, the InformeDesign RS "Interiors Influence Perceptions of Age, Class, and/or Family Status" (2004, July 20) summarizes that preferences may be based on social attributes—age, class, and/or family status—that the homeowner assigns to a space. For example living rooms that are sparsely furnished and covered with wood floors and a rug may be associated with younger, lower-middle-class, single adults; contemporary furnishings along with pastel colors and carpeting rather than wood are associated with middle age, middle-class couples, and families; traditional furnishings, rich colors along with expensive ornamentation and collectibles, pictures, paintings, portraits, and books may be associated with older, upper-class families or widows. With this information, the designer can assist the client in identifying very important social and personal values and allow for personalization and presentation of artifacts that are important to the client.

Economics

Economics is always a factor in all families. In nearly 30 percent of families, two parents work outside the home on a full-time basis (Olson & DeFain, 2006). Some earn dual incomes in order to make ends meet, others to provide extra income. Interior designers will work with clients both on tight budgets and with greater disposable income.

For tight budgets, the concept of affordable housing will be important. Using World War II housing innovations, a study, summarized by the InformeDesign RS "Flexible, Affordable Homes Meet Residents' Needs" (2003, April 10), applied them to present housing needs. From this research, criteria were developed. The following are a few examples (other criteria can be found on the InformeDesign database):

- Combined living and dining areas

- Attic spaces used for bedrooms

- Multipurpose designed for various uses

- Upper floors or basements can be left without partitions to allow for future expansions

- A **mechanical core** will reduce plumbing costs

Ideas for Collecting New Evidence

Examples of research topics into residential design include bedrooms for adolescents; daylighting design for high-rise buildings; individuality and identity in suburbia; kitchen appliances; meeting family needs in small, affordable housing; the second home; relocation or adaptation for older adults or elderly; and creating a sense of community.

Though this information may not be surprising, today's homes are more often large and seem to be the most desirable. However, not every client can afford the large, spacious home, and ways to create an affordable home are even more desirable for the majority of clients.

All homes should be designed for good IAQ. Therefore, research related to affordable housing and indoor air quality will be important in designing healthy homes regardless of income. Particularly, manufactured homes have been considered more prone to volatile organic compounds (VOCs) than site-built homes. However, the InformeDesign RS "Sources of VOCs in New Houses" (2004, June 14) summarizes that a study conducted to measure VOCs in newly manufactured homes and site-built houses found different results. Their results indicated that VOC concentration levels were similar. They also identified and suggested materials with lower VOC levels as substitutes or means of reducing emissions. Another InformeDesign RS, "Wood Products and Residential VOC Emissions" (2004, February 16), determines primary sources of VOC emissions in newly manufactured homes. The study focused on wood products and provided suggestions for substitutes or means of reducing emissions for residential spaces. Thus, whether a manufactured house (sometimes associated with affordable housing) or site-built house, IAQ can be affected by interior materials and products used in building and furnishing houses.

Application

Research topics may include spatial relationships and organization, related to familial structures and housing types, adjacencies, multi-use spaces, and the design of affordable housing.

International Interior Design Association (IIDA) Knowledge Center with a link to residential types contains several research projects. Examples of articles are as follows. "Bathing for Older People with Disabilities" examines the safety aspects of bathing, and studied the safety and accessibility needs for older people and their caregivers. The study provides design directives (Mullick, n.d.). "Beyond Walls" describes how designers are pushing spatial boundaries as they search for new ways to address changing human needs (Rewi, 2004). Other articles that may provide evidence for a design project can be found on the IIDA Web site (http://knowledgecenter.iida.org/Research.aspx). Other examples are as follows: "A Grass-Roots Effort to Grow Old at Home," "Million-Dollar Home and Wealth in the United States," "A Review of Methods for the Manufacture of Residential Roofing Materials," and "A Study of Outdoor Space Planning in Apartment Housing" (IIDA, 2008).

American Society of Interior Designers (ASID) Knowledge Center (2008) provides a link to aging and accessibility and then aging in place connects to "Aging in Style: Design for an Aging Population." This site (http://asid.org/designknowledge) links to a variety of articles written by ASID members. Examples of articles include: "Remove Barriers to

Improve Quality of Life," "Is Aging in Place Design Right for You?," and "Aging in Place and Green Design: They're More Alike Than You Think!"

InformeDesign (2005) contain hundreds of RSs related to residential design. Some RS examples were listed in the previous chapter. Some RSs relate to color responses and preferences, appearance of color in a room, and many more. Others may relate to sustainability. These examples are only a few illustrations of literature that can provide evidence to inform the design.

Summary

Data collected from users of residential spaces provide information on special needs and lifestyles. With information or facts collected from the client, research for new evidence related to the design will improve the outcome of any design project. Use the Ideas for Collecting New Evidence throughout this book to begin the process of locating evidence, brainstorming new ideas, and uncovering evidence appropriate to every specific client and project.

Key Terms

defensible space theory	private zones	social zones
mechanical core	public zones	work zones

Drawing Conclusions

PART
SIX

Putting to Practice
Evidence-Based Design

OBJECTIVES

**After reading this chapter and previous chapters,
you should be able to:**

Apply knowledge from the previous chapters into a design project

Organize data into a programming document

Determine areas where evidence will inform and improve the design

Integrate facts and evidence to inform and improve the design

Use design theory or theories to apply and/or analyze a design

DRED COURT

To develop an understanding of evidence-based design (EBD), we have examined methods of data collection, considered various topics and design types, and explored tools and approaches to stimulate research. Throughout the book, each chapter has supplied us with examples that apply specific knowledge. This chapter concludes with a recap of the application of EBD.

Drawing Conclusions

At the beginning of the programming phase, designers collect data from their clients and sites through a variety of methods, including interviews, questionnaires, observations, and focus groups. Examples of the documents are included in the appendices. Designers record this information in a program document—either for nonresidential or residential (see Appendices A and B).

To determine areas that need further research, designers review the facts. These areas may be the site, structural needs, contextual needs (e.g., lighting and furniture, fixtures, and equipment, or FF&E), human factors (e.g., territoriality and crowding), and the specific design type (e.g., patient safety in healthcare). Research may also include diversity in order to apply feng shui concepts to a design or to create a hospital meditation room that meets all spiritual needs. Various resources are available to locate evidence to inform the design. Sources include books; periodicals; academic journals; research summaries such as those found at InformeDesign, International Interior Design Association (IIDA), and American Society of Interior Designers (ASID) Knowledge Centers; as well as observations and post-occupancy evaluations (POEs).

Historic precedents research is used to analyze past structures and concepts from precedents that may be applied or provide insight for a design project. Resources include books on the history of architecture and interiors, architectural precedents, or the study of architecture and/or interiors. Design precedents research will stimulate conceptual ideas, locate trends, and show recent design examples. Trade magazines, designers' online portfolios, and observations are excellent resources for such evidence.

Data and evidence can be organized into a chart with the criteria on the left and columns for facts and evidence (see Table 19.1). The last column on the right is used to explain a plan or ways to integrate facts and evidence into the design. Then a narrative with bulleted points for each criterion is written to document the findings.

Table 19.2 lists data and/or evidence to include in this document. Some research areas may be fact finding only (e.g., structural—fire code search); some areas are best researched for new evidence (e.g., human factors, sustainability); and some areas may or may not be important in every design project. Table 19.2 provides a recap of suggested research to assist in locating facts and evidence. This recap is not all inclusive, but can be used to stimulate further inquiry.

When this information is organized and documented in a written format, one or two design theories may be chosen to analyze findings. Theories may be chosen relative to what is important to the design project. Table 2.1 in Chapter 2 provides application suggestions.

With programming documents, research documents, and a design theory analysis completed, designers can then revise program requirements. Clearly, designers not only collect facts but also locate and use evidence that will inform the design. Therefore, the evidence that has been collected can inform the design and otherwise change the direction of any or all aspects of the project; this is the way that you create evidence-based design.

Table 19.1
Chart to Organize the Integration of Evidence into Design

Research Areas	List of Facts Gathered	List of Evidence Researched	Plan or Ways to Integrate Evidence into Design
Structural Needs			
Contextual Needs			
Sustainability Needs			
Human Factors			

Client Needs
  Commercial spaces
  Residential spaces			

Specific Design Type			
Diversity			
Historic Precedents			
Design Precedents			

Table 19.2
Charts Recapping Suggested Research to Locate Facts and Evidence

Research Areas or Topics	Recap of Suggested Research
Structural Needs	• Research zoning for possible location • Consider orientation of building to site • Analyze site in a graphical presentation • Use Table 3.1 as a site analysis checklist • Use Table 3.2 for site analysis questions • Examine structural materials and systems • Search fire and building codes applicable to design
Contextual Needs	• Research possible source of energy • Determine appropriate HVAC system • Determine method of heating • Examine ways to create quality lighting • Consider the various methods of communication (Internet, phones, etc.) • Consider improvements in plumbing system for conservation • Determine acoustical system, if applicable • Plan for a sprinkler system, if applicable

(continued)

Table 19.2

Charts Recapping Suggested Research to
Locate Facts and Evidence *(continued)*

Research Areas or Topics	Recap of Suggested Research
Sustainable Needs	• Examine possibilities for preservation, restoration, renovation, and adaptive reuse • Consider energy conservation methods • Examine every material to promote good IAQ • Research plants that will promote good IAQ
Human Factors	• Evaluate workstations for good ergonomics • Use Table 6.2 to conduct ergonomics evaluation • Examine proxemics: distance zones, crowding, territoriality, etc. • Consider the application of universal design • Examine possible wayfinding methods

Client Needs:
Commercial Spaces
	• Examine the organizational documents
	• Examine the following:
	  • Communication modes
	  • Space allocation
	  • FF&E, color, art, etc.
	  • Economics (productivity)
	• Use Table 7.1 to gathering information
	• Research must include all users and customers

Client Needs: Residential Spaces	• Determine needs for protection and security • Consider each client with his/her individual needs • Research universal design for all ages, especially aging in place
Specific Design	• Examine issues that relate to specific designs • Refer to individual chapters for suggested facts and evidence
Diversity	• Research diverse cultures with various spiritual needs and apply to design as appropriate; i.e., meditation room in a hospital • Before applying diverse designs, thoroughly research to properly apply • Research other aspects of diversity
Historic Precedents	• Select an historic building or buildings for inspiration • Evaluate architectural and interior criteria • Evaluate theoretical criteria • Determine applicable data to apply to a project
Design Precedents	• Examine precedents for a specific design type in the trade publication and/or actual project • Interview a design firm that worked on a specific design type • Locate and observe conceptual ideas in a similar design type • Examine brands, trends, conceptual ideas, or new innovative ideas that may be significant in future design projects • Determine knowledge that may be applied to another project

Case Study 12.1

Las Vegas Chamber of Commerce

When reading the following case study, focus your attention on the research process, organizational profile, open versus closed office, and data collection methods. The following information was provided through interviews with and approved by Craig Galati, principal and architect, and Rosemary D'Amato, registered interior designer and Leadership in Energy and Environmental Design Accredited Professional (LEED AP). Additional information located at www.lgainc.com.

The CC's goals were to update their brand to remain the ultimate business organization in southern Nevada; create spaces and amenities that would increase retention and attract quality businesses; and change the corporate culture and environment to serve the CC members and employees.

To accomplish their goals and by mutual agreement of executives and employees, the designers concluded that more open workspace was needed to enhance interaction and communications. The opportunity to relocate into a new, upscale, mixed-use development—the Town Square Las Vegas—allowed for growth and the needed improvements.

In their old facilities, employees were segregated into private offices, causing territoriality. To encourage the needed collaboration, a multifunctional open office environment was designed. The new office environment brought people together and proved conducive to productivity. The open office plan was arranged at angles and provides access to window views and natural lighting. The break area is on the interior—the only area without natural light. This area has become a hub of activity—a place to interact and connect.

Even with the open-office systems, employees can personalize and privatize their spaces. That included the opportunity to select an office chair through a chair survey. Staff members were given nine chairs from which to choose (three manufacturers, three types, and three equivalents). In this manner, they were educated on the value of ergonomics of the chair for the individual as well as the opportunity to select their own chairs—all of which were ergonomically correct.

Size and placement of offices were also carefully considered. For example, accounting executives spend most of their time in the field; therefore, their offices were smaller. Offices for the accounting department were located at "dead ends" to increase privacy and minimize traffic flow. Where private offices were needed, they were incorporated into the open environment. Figure Case Study 12.1.1 shows the open office plan.

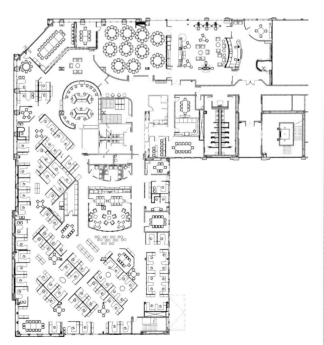

Figure Case Study 12.1.1 Las Vegas Chamber of Commerce open floor plan. *(Drawn by Lucchesi Galati)*

Because the vision and mission of Las Vegas CC is to be an advocate for Nevada business, their new location in Town Square allowed space for a visitor's center, conference center, and post office. The Visitor's Center provided space for businesses to display business cards and flyers or brochures and a state-of-the-art conference center for meetings. The space also includes an onsite U.S. Post Office for the convenience of area businesses and visitors. The Visitor's Center is also a space where CC members could meander. However, though visitors could not enter CC's business operation section, CC employees could visit with the public and make an important connection with them. Figure Case Study 12.1.2 shows the business-center area for people to meet.

With the project completed, the CC is now relocated in a new, upscale, mixed-use development—the Town Square Las Vegas. At this location, Lucchesi Galati was able to create an environment that enhanced and develop the organizational culture and their new brand.

It is an open office with open communication and yet spaces that allow for privacy where needed. Thus, with thorough research of the organization and staff, the resulting project was a success.

Figure Case Study 12.1.2 Las Vegas Chamber of Commerce business center. *(Tom Craig, Opulence Studios)*

Case Study 13.1

Comparison of Las Vegas Casino Hotels

As you read through this case study, focus your attention on wayfinding, circulation, and observational research methods. Interior design student Michelle Ralston assisted in the writing.

Hotel guests and visitors like to be able to easily maneuver through large public spaces and find their destination. To accomplish this, good wayfinding methods and circulation paths are extremely important for successful designs.

Casino hotels are generally large complexes that include a casino area as well as entrances, registration, concierge, ticket sales, shops, coffee shops, restaurants, bars, lounge areas, and pathways to other hotels. To maneuver through these spaces, good wayfinding methods

such as signage, maps, electronic maps, and color coding help guests find their destinations. Additionally, in any hotel, the registration area can easily become congested with larger groups, especially during the standard check-in time. Areas such as a concierge desk, ticket sales, and cafeterias may also become congested with waiting lines. Providing a definitive difference between a casino and other public areas, ceiling heights often vary. For example, casino areas often have lower ceilings in comparison to the high ceilings of other public areas.

Observations of various casino hotels provided insight into areas that were in need of improvement and those that worked well. This type of observation can improve the design of future hotels.

Luxor

The exterior of the Luxor is impressive, and marketing for the property is what brings in guests. However, when inside, the feeling is completely different. To register at the Luxor at the busiest time of the day, guests stand in long lines with roped stanchions leading to the registration desk. The wait is long and frustrating for guests, who are most likely exhausted from their travels. Additionally, the registration lines block portions of the main walk area that circulate through the hotel. To add to the confusion, the concierge, ticket sales, and baggage storage are also located near the front entrance of the Luxor. Figure Case Study 13.1.1 shows the congestion in the registration area. Additionally, finding one's way around the Luxor is a challenge. Signage is at a minimum and hard to see, which creates a wayfinding issue.

Figure Case Study 13.1.1 This photograph of the Luxor Hotel and Casino registration area, shot at a slower time of the day, shows the congestion of a major circulation path. *(Linda Nussbaumer)*

Paris

The exterior of Paris is also impressive. However, the interior is in direct contrast to the Luxor. Paris's registration area has been separated from the main circulation

Figure Case Study 13.1.2 This photograph shows the lack of congestion in the registration area in the Paris Casino Hotel. *(Linda Nussbaumer)*

area. Lines may form, but stanchions are not present nor do lines block or interfere with main circulation. The concierge is located at the edge of the registration area for convenience and does not interfere with either registration or the main traffic flow. Figure Case Study 13.1.2 shows Paris's registration area.

Paris uses street circulation paths that are wide and clearly visible. Paris uses street signs with arrows to aid guest wayfinding (see Figure Case Study 13.1.3). Signage is located at various intervals and/or intersections for ease of wayfinding. However, although the signage is adequate, larger and clearer lettering would be advantageous.

Figure Case Study 13.1.3 The Paris Casino Hotel uses street signs as a wayfinding method. *(Linda Nussbaumer)*

Bellagio and Wynn

Of all the hotels on the strip, Bellagio and Wynn have the best space layout and are easily maneuvered spaces. The registration area of the Bellagio is along one side of the lobby. On the opposite side is the entrance to the casino floor (see Figure 13.1.4). This design left plenty of space in the middle for large groups waiting for check-in and at no time in our observation was there a major congestion problem. However, a better solution would have been to create a greater separation between the registration area and a main circulation path.

The design of Wynn's registration area is similar to that of Paris. The area is a separate space with good acoustical control and a polished, refined, and sophisticated feeling to greet those who enter. This space is even more efficient than Paris's because it is larger and has its check-in and concierge services on both sides. The wayfinding techniques appear to be the same in both of the hotels. Their lighted signs, adjacent to the pathways, are spaced often enough to eliminate any confusion.

Figure Case Study 13.1.4 The Bellagio Casino Hotel experiences little or no congestion based on its design. *(Linda Nussbaumer)*

Conclusion

Wayfinding and circulation were analyzed through observations, and problems and benefits were noted in each hotel. From the data collected, this data collection method provides evidence that can inform a design, whether a casino hotel or another heavily traveled public space.

Case Study 14.1

The Children's Hospital, Denver, Colorado

As you read through this case study, focus your attention on various data collection methods to inform the design—benchmarking, shadowing, focus groups, and literature reviews. With permission, this case study is a summarized article that appeared in the May 2008 issue of *Healthcare Design* magazine.

According to the design team at Zimmer Gunsul Frasca (ZGF) Architects, the design of the Children's Hospital (TCH) in Denver was heavily based on research and evidence-based design principles that informed the design process. The methods used were benchmarking tours; shadowing; focus groups; and a review of literature.

Benchmarking involved touring 12 peer facilities. These tours provided evidence on how other facilities managed program elements such as patient room amenities, food services, signage, and finish materials, as well as ways to help improve healing environment elements, such as location of caregivers, flow and floor adjacencies, patient room layout, and organization of operating rooms. Tours also helped to compare single-level and stacked, multilevel organization of space.

Shadowing involved the design team's attempt to actively place themselves into the minds of children who were patients, families who supported the children, and physicians and staff who provided care. Seven designers from ZGF Architects spent two weeks shadowing and interviewing families, patients, and more than 250 staff members in 27 different departments. This research provided evidence regarding conditions within the facilities such as noise, congestion, travel distance, crowding, storage issues, inadequate sleeping accommodations, and more. This method of research helped the team understand these issues and gained a sense of empathy for all users. This evidence impacted the design of in-patient nursing units, patient rooms, the surgery department, and the emergency department.

Focus groups were conducted with patient and family groups, a cultural focus group, and local community groups. Groups were asked to discuss their experiences in the existing TCH hospital and their desires for a new children's hospital. Questions related to parking, wayfinding, patient rooms and amenities, family amenities, cafeteria services, emergency services, safety and security, intensive care and neonatal intensive care units, overall atmosphere, and general services. The most common requests were as follows:

- Expanded accommodations for parent—sleeping quarters, showers, and ability to stay in child's room

- Parental assistance with activities and distractions

- Respite spaces for parents and siblings of the sick child

- A 24-hour cafeteria

- More storage space and lockers for personal belongings

- Internet access including data ports and computer terminals

The cultural focus group was particularly important given the many Spanish speakers, Native Americans, and those of other cultures who reside in Denver. This group was especially interested in bilingual wayfinding and kiosks as well as accommodations for larger families.

Research of literature was conducted to locate evidence regarding healing properties of color. Using various sources on color theory, the design team carefully determined the amount, intensity, and value of color that would be used throughout the hospital. They learned that blue is beneficial for burn victims because of its association with cool, refreshing water; green is beneficial for relieving tension and lowering blood pressure; and children are most responsive to lime green. Their study also aided the creation and application of five color palettes:

1. Social palette
   a. Bright, rich colors—oranges, reds, yellows, and greens; includes Colorado imagery
   b. Applied to active, energetic areas such as the cafeteria

2. Tranquil palette (a soothing atmosphere)
   a. Pastel colors—sky blue, mint green, butter yellow, and lavender
   b. Applied in such areas as intensive care units, respite areas, and chapel

3. Spirited palette
   a. Bold tropical colors—turquoise, magenta, apple green, and sunflower yellow
   b. Applied to clinic spaces and in-patient floors

4. Community palette
   a. A combination of all color palettes with strong accent colors against a neutral backdrop
   b. Applied to circulation areas including the atrium

Each palette was applied in specific areas most appropriate for a psychological need. Figure Case Study 14.1.1 shows one example of the community palette.

Research was also conducted on the benefits of natural light and connections to nature. The team learned

Figure Case Study 14.1.1 Community palette. *(Photo by Eckert & Eckert, Courtesy of Zimmer Gunsul Frasca Architects LLP)*

Figure Case Study 14.1.2 Artwork at the Children's Hospital. *(Photo by Basil Childers, Courtesy of Zimmer Gunsul Frasca Architects LLP)*

that bright natural light is beneficial in reducing depression and agitation, improving sleep and circadian rhythms, reducing pain, lessening the need for pain medication, and shortening the hospital stay. Thus, in their design of TCH, windows and light wells were used to bring in natural light to enhance the space and maximize the amount of daylight flowing into the space.

Because art provides a positive distraction as well as a sense of discovery, it would be an integral part of the design at TCH. Particularly, art was used to reinforce a connection with nature and especially to the Colorado Mountains. Because art is "ageless," it appealed to children as well as adults. Art can be found through the hospital with specific types of art found on different levels. This becomes a wayfinding tool, e.g., snowflakes, skaters, trout, and so on that may be found in glass panels, wall panels, or within the floor design. Figure Case Study 14.1.2 presents example of artwork in TCH.

This hospital is one of the Center for Health Design's Pebble Projects that applies research into its design and is conducting research to determine if this facility meets and/or surpasses the main object: to promote healing, aid recruitment, retain staff, and reduce operating costs. This in-process research project measures and assesses the following:

1. Family satisfaction

2. Staff satisfaction

3. Infection rates

4. Private versus semi-private rooms and clinical outcomes

Since TCH opened in October 2007, it appears that there is greater satisfaction with service and an increase in staff. It seems that EBD positively affected an organization and, most likely, the bottom line.

For further details, the article may be accessed from *Healthcare Design* magazine, or online from http://www.healthcaredesignmagazine.com (Zacharakis, Van der Meulen, & Johnson, 2008).

Case Study 16.1

St. Elizabeth Ann Seton School, Las Vegas, Nevada

As you read through this case study, focus your attention on how the research focus fits the client. The following information was provided through interviews with and approved by Craig Galati, principal and architect. For more on Lucchesi Galati, go to www.lgainc.com.

Craig Galati, principal and architect at Lucchesi Galati, in Las Vegas, Nevada, states that when designing a church, the research "starts with the people." This must begin by understanding its purpose—to worship and to teach—as well as the doctrine of the church. It can be explained as three concentric circles, which begin in the center with spiritual, organizational, and physical at the outer circle.

1. Spiritual—research theological and pastoral doctrine

2. Organizational—determine the needs and goals that must be achieved

3. Physical—function and requirements that relate back to the organization and spiritual

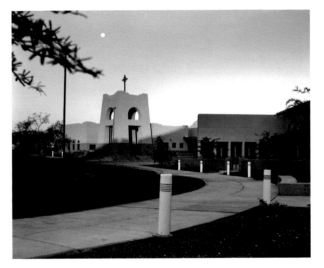

Figure Case Study 16.1.1 St. Elizabeth Ann Seton Church and School exterior, designed by Lucchesi Galati. The design of the church and school are seamlessly connected to existing buildings. *(Opulence Studios, Las Vegas)*

The St. Elizabeth Ann Seton School designed by Lucchesi Galati included a new kindergarten through grade 8 school and parish (see Figure Case Study 16.1.1). Particularly important was fitting buildings on their existing property as well as providing parking, playgrounds, and athletic fields. An important part of the design process was to bring together the parish's concepts of faith, values, education, and community. This relates to understanding the client as well as conducting research on doctrine. At the beginning of the project, the design firm determined what was important to the project, and with this project, this included creating spaces designed (1) to be flexible and multiple use, (2) for lifelong learning, (3) with integrated technology, and (4) to reflect their image and pride.

The completed project includes an elementary school, a lifelong learning center, a community center, classrooms, kitchen, administrative offices as well as outdoor courtyards. Figure Case Study 16.1.2 is an example of a classroom in the school. An important aspect of programming was the involvement of more than 20 parishioners, and with their participation, the parish's needs were developed and integrated into the design. Truly, the project exemplifies research of the client, their reason for existence, spiritual foundation, and organizational needs and goals that culminated in a functional space that fulfills their requirements.

Figure Case Study 16.1.2 The St. Elizabeth Ann Seton elementary school is designed for 500 students. This photo is an example of one classroom. *(Cava Photography, Las Vegas)*

Appendices

Appendix A
Program Document: Nonresidential

Human Ecosystem Programming Model
Problem Statement:
Project Goals:
Project Objectives:

Programming for Nonresidential Space
Human Organism
Client and User Needs
Profile Clients:

1. Determine desired corporate culture and image/formality for business and for individuals or special ranks.
2. Determine status markers for individuals or specific ranks.
3. Identify specific psychological needs of each employee or user (territory, crowding, isolation, privacy, security).
4. Identify the anthropometric measurements.
5. Identify issues related to ergonomics within each design type.
6. Identify the number, destination, and frequency of visitors.

7. Consider any special needs of user groups or their activities.
8. Identify mid- and long-range plans. (Is the client likely to grow, shrink, or diversify?)
9. Identify goods or services provided by the client.
10. Determine if new technology will impact this business in the future.

Economic Needs

Establish budget range:

1. Price furniture and extend out as necessary.
2. Determine if build-out costs are included.
3. Determine if maintenance costs are built in.
4. Determine if post-occupancy evaluation is included.

Designed Environment

Contextual Assessment

Develop site analysis:

1. Identify the exterior architectural style of the existing building (if applicable) and surroundings.

Building Needs

Assess existing building or develop needs assessment for new structure:

1. Describe the interior architecture of the existing building (if applicable).
2. Inventory existing HVAC, acoustical, lighting, electrical, and plumbing conditions and special or unusual needs.
3. Inventory existing fixed-in-place furnishings and fixtures or equipment and unusual spatial needs.
4. Identify signage needed.
5. Document foreseeable needs and technology.

Safety Needs

Address physical and air quality safety issues:

1. Log any existing unusual health-related conditions or special needs of the user.

Furniture/Equipment Needs

Assess existing or proposed furnishings:

1. List existing furnishings and measurements.
2. List specific furniture, fixture, and equipment needs or requests and their measurements.
3. Identify ambient, feature, task safety, and security lighting needed for each area and/or workstation.
4. Identify any necessary special surface treatment.

Natural Environment

Climatic Needs

Determine the impact of the environment on the interior of the building:

1. Identify site conditions: temperature, wind direction, precipitation, humidity levels, and quantity of sunlight for all four seasons in relationship to the building.
2. Consider windows relative to status within the organization.
3. Consider temperature control by placement.
4. Consider daylighting and artificial temperature controls.

Geographic Needs

1. Identify topography and vegetation conditions in relationship to the interior of the building.
2. Note daylighting and artificial lighting relative to vegetation levels throughout the year.

Environmental Needs

Consider health risks of location:

1. Test area for existing health risks such as radon, lead, etc.
2. Assess proximity to environmental risk/hazards.

Social Environment

Physical Needs

Research building restrictions:

1. Identify buildings' regulatory constraints such as: zoning, fire safety, and ADA codes.
2. Find nature of variances, special permits, and current and pending use control.
3. Identify neighborhood covenants.
4. Identify written and unwritten policies of the business.

Psychological Needs

Identify individual and group needs:

1. Define territory and spatial needs of the work groups and/or departments.
2. Identify markers for sense of arrival, invitation to enter, sense of place.

Social Needs

Evaluate internal social relationships, role in community:

1. Identify decision-making hierarchy.
2. Identify the hierarchical structure (include organizational chart).
3. Define the cultural, historic, religious, social, or political elements influencing this business.

4. Identify client, user, and visitor activities and length of stay.
5. Gather personnel data—number of employees in various work groups or team, in departments, job classifications, job titles; functions, activities, and duration of each.
6. Identify primary activities of individual employees, work groups, and departments.
7. Identify functional relationships between individual employees, work groups, and departments.

Based on ideas from Miller & Zborowsky (1995).

Appendix B
Program Document: Residential

Human Ecosystem Programming Model
Problem Statement:
Project Goals:
Project Objectives:
Programming for Residential Space
Human Organism
Client and User Needs
Profile Clients:

1. Determine image/formality desired for whole family and individual members.
2. Determine status marker for individual family members.
3. Identify specific psychological needs of individual family members (territory, crowding, isolation, privacy, security).
4. Identify the anthropometric measurements applicable to these users.
5. Identify the number and frequency of visitors.
6. Determine any special needs of the visitors or their activities.
7. Identify mid- and long-range plans that are likely to outgrow this space.

Economic Needs
Establish budget range:
1. Price furnishings and extend out as necessary. 2. Determine if build-out costs are included. 3. Determine if maintenance costs are built in. 4. Determine if post-occupancy evaluation is included.
Designed Environment
Contextual Assessment
Develop site analysis:
1. Identify the exterior architectural style of the existing building (if applicable) and of surrounding buildings.
Building Needs
Assess existing building or develop needs assessment for new structure:
1. Document the interior architecture of the existing building (if applicable). 2. Inventory existing HVAC, acoustical, lighting, electrical, and plumbing conditions, and special or usual needs inventory existing fixed-in-place furnishings and fixtures or equipment and unusual spatial needs. 3. Document foreseeable needs and technology. 4. Log any existing unusual health-related conditions or special needs of user.
Safety Needs
Address physical and air quality safety issues:
1. Log any existing unusual health related conditions or special needs of user.
Furniture/ Equipment Needs
Assess existing or proposed furnishings:
1. List existing furnishings and measurements. 2. List specific furniture, feature, and equipment needs or requests and their measurements. 3. Identify ambient, feature, task, safety, and security lighting needed for each area. 4. Identify any necessary special surface treatments.
Natural Environment
Climatic Needs
Determine the impact of the environment on the interior of the building:
1. Identify site conditions: temperature, wind direction, precipitation, humidity levels, and quantity of sunlight for all four seasons in relationship to the building. 2. Note views and sight lines.

3. Consider temperature control by room placement.
4. Consider daylighting and artificial lighting.

Geographic Needs

1. Identify topography and vegetation conditions in relationship to the interior of the building.
2. Note daylighting and artificial lighting relative to vegetation levels throughout the year.

Environmental Needs

Consider health risks of location:

1. Test area for existing health risks such as radon, lead, etc.
2. Assess proximity to environmental risks/hazards.

Social Environment

Physical Needs

Research building restrictions:

1. Identify the building's regulatory constraints such as zoning, fire safety, and ADA codes.
2. Find nature of variances, special permits, and current and pending use control.
3. Identify neighborhood covenants.
4. Identify written and unwritten policies of neighborhoods.

Psychological Needs

1. Define territory and spatial needs of the individual users.
2. Identify markers for sense of arrival, invitation to enter, and sense of place.

Social Needs

Evaluate internal social relationships, role in community:

1. Identify decision-making route of the household.
2. Identify main activities of individuals and the family group.
3. Define the cultural, historic, religious, social, or political elements influencing this individual or family.
4. Determine what type of entertaining the family does, as well as type, length of stay, and formality level.

Based on ideas from Miller & Zborowsky (1995).

Appendix C
Commercial Programming Questionnaire: General Client Information

Project: Location:

Name: Role (owner, employee, customer):

What is the business/organization's profile and structure?

Business-Related Data

Purpose of the business/organization:

Mission/goals/objectives of the business/organization:

Image of the business/organization:

Elements contributing to profits and return on investment (ROI):

Energy and environmental conservation policies and practices:

Current critical issues related to the industry:

Current social events affecting the business/organization:

Anticipated changes in personnel:

Anticipated changes in activities:

Demographic profile of employees (gender, age, ethnic, and cultural background)

Where is the property location, and what are property needs and anticipated changes?

Property Data

Geographic location:

Building owned or leased:

Anticipated changes in space needs:

Anticipated renovation:

Anticipated furniture changes:

Anticipated changes in interior elements (floor coverings, wall coverings, ceilings, window treatments):

Source: Winchip (2008).

Appendix D
Individual Survey Questionnaire

Date _____

To prepare for the redesign of _____ (company), the following questions will provide valuable information for the design team. Thank you for your participation.

1. How long have you worked for _____ (company)?
    a. Less than 1 year
    b. 1 to 5 years
    c. 5 to 10 years
    d. 10 to 15 years
    e. 15 years or more

2. In what department do you work?
    a. Executive
    b. Financial
    c. Sales and Marketing
    d. Human Resources
    e. Research and Development
    f. Other

3. What is your job function?
    a. Executive Management
    b. Senior Management

c. Manager

d. Supervisor

e. Nonsupervisory staff

4. Do you work as a team within your organization?

a. Yes

b. Frequently

c. Sometimes

d. Seldom

e. No

5. Does your supervisor listen to your ideas and then pass them on to the management?

a. Yes

b. Frequently

c. Sometimes

d. Seldom

e. No

Rate the following function of the space related to furniture and equipment in your workspace:

6.	Adequate furniture	☐	☐	☐	☐	☐	☐	Inadequate furniture
7.	Well furnished	☐	☐	☐	☐	☐	☐	Poorly furnished
8.	Functional	☐	☐	☐	☐	☐	☐	Nonfunctional
9.	Flexible furniture	☐	☐	☐	☐	☐	☐	Inflexible furniture
10.	Efficient layout	☐	☐	☐	☐	☐	☐	Inefficient layout
11.	Flexible layout	☐	☐	☐	☐	☐	☐	Inflexible layout
12.	Adequate space	☐	☐	☐	☐	☐	☐	Inadequate space
13.	Adequate equipment	☐	☐	☐	☐	☐	☐	Inadequate equipment

Explain what changes need to be made to improve the function of your space.

Rate the following conditions: sound, temperature, air quality, and maintenance.

14. Noisy   ☐   ☐   ☐   ☐   ☐   ☐   Quiet

15.	Cold	☐ ☐ ☐ ☐ ☐ ☐	Hot
16.	Good air quality	☐ ☐ ☐ ☐ ☐ ☐	Poor air quality
17.	No odors	☐ ☐ ☐ ☐ ☐ ☐	Smelly
18.	Dirt	☐ ☐ ☐ ☐ ☐ ☐	Clean

Explain what changes need to be made to improve conditions.

```
┌─────────────────────────────────────────────┐
│                                               │
│                                               │
│                                               │
│                                               │
│                                               │
│                                               │
└─────────────────────────────────────────────┘
```

Rate the following circulation: ability to move through space, locate areas, signage, and symbols.

19.	Easy movement	☐ ☐ ☐ ☐ ☐ ☐	Obstructed movement
20.	Easy to locate areas	☐ ☐ ☐ ☐ ☐ ☐	Difficult to locate areas
21.	Appropriate signage	☐ ☐ ☐ ☐ ☐ ☐	Inappropriate signage
22.	Excellent wayfinding	☐ ☐ ☐ ☐ ☐ ☐	Poor wayfinding

Explain what changes need to be made to improve circulation throughout the facility.

```
┌─────────────────────────────────────────────┐
│                                               │
│                                               │
│                                               │
│                                               │
│                                               │
│                                               │
└─────────────────────────────────────────────┘
```

Rate the following aesthetics and atmosphere:

23.	Color is appealing	☐ ☐ ☐ ☐ ☐ ☐	Dislike color
24.	Pleasant atmosphere	☐ ☐ ☐ ☐ ☐ ☐	Unpleasant atmosphere
25.	Exciting	☐ ☐ ☐ ☐ ☐ ☐	Sterile
26.	Orderly	☐ ☐ ☐ ☐ ☐ ☐	Disorganized
27.	Daylight	☐ ☐ ☐ ☐ ☐ ☐	Artificial light

Explain what changes need to be made to improve the aesthetics and atmosphere.

```
┌─────────────────────────────────────────────────────────────┐
│                                                               │
│                                                               │
│                                                               │
│                                                               │
│                                                               │
│                                                               │
│                                                               │
│                                                               │
└─────────────────────────────────────────────────────────────┘
```

Rate your attitude and mood as a user of the space:

28.	Pleasant	☐	☐	☐	☐	☐	☐	Unpleasant
29.	Like	☐	☐	☐	☐	☐	☐	Dislike
30.	Relaxed	☐	☐	☐	☐	☐	☐	Tense
31.	Inspired	☐	☐	☐	☐	☐	☐	Uninspired
32.	Optimistic	☐	☐	☐	☐	☐	☐	Pessimistic
33.	Motivated	☐	☐	☐	☐	☐	☐	Unmotivated
34.	Bored	☐	☐	☐	☐	☐	☐	Interested
35.	Satisfied	☐	☐	☐	☐	☐	☐	Dissatisfied
36.	Sad	☐	☐	☐	☐	☐	☐	Happy

Explain what changes need to be made that would improve attitudes and moods.

```
┌─────────────────────────────────────────────────────────────┐
│                                                               │
│                                                               │
│                                                               │
│                                                               │
│                                                               │
│                                                               │
│                                                               │
└─────────────────────────────────────────────────────────────┘
```

Based on ideas from Scott-Webber (1998).

Appendix E
Individual Interview Questionnaire

Questions Related to Individual Workspaces

Date: _____

Company: _____

Department:_____ Supervisor: _____

Interviewee: _____

Position: _____

Job Description: _____

Phone: _____ E-mail: _____

Interviewed by: _____

Reviewed by: _____

1. Briefly describe your functions within the department.

2. Briefly describe the functions of your department.

[blank box]

3. Briefly outline the flow of work through your department.

[blank box]

4. List and rank the departments with which you frequently communicate.
   a. Workflow:

[blank box]

   b. Physically:

[blank box]

5. Briefly describe conference facilities needed within your department.

[blank box]

6. List colleagues within your department:

Name:	Titles:	Function

7. List your support requirements: files, storage, supplies.

```



```

8. List the furniture needed to perform work.

```



```

9. List any furniture changes needed.

```



```

10. List and describe special equipment needed to complete your tasks.

```



```

11. Which changes should be made in your workspace? Rank in order of preference: more flexible furniture and layout, more space. Explain.

```
1.

2.

3.
```

12. What changes should be made in working conditions? Rank in order of preference: adjustment to noise levels, individual temperature control, and improvement in air quality. Explain.

1.

2.

3.

13. What changes or improvements should be made in circulation? Rank in order of preference: wayfinding maps, better signage, and easier movement through the space. Explain.

1.

2.

3.

14. What changes should be made in aesthetics and atmosphere? Rank in order of preference: change color to a more exciting work environment, incorporated daylighting, and create a more orderly space. Explain.

1.

2.

3.

15. What changes should be made in attitude and mood for the users of the space? Rank in order of preference: motivating, relaxing, and satisfying. Explain.

1.

2.

3.

Based on ideas from Kilmer & Kilmer (1992), Rayfield (1994), and Scott-Webber (1998).

Appendix F
Site Survey of Existing Conditions

Date: _____

Company: _____

Survey conducted by: _____

1. Determine the orientation of windows relative to natural light.
    - How will the orientation change during various times of day and seasons of the year?
    - Do nearby buildings or the potential for future buildings obstruct natural light?

2. Locate views or obstructions from windows.
    - Are the present views good or are improvements needed?
    - Are there obstructions to the view?
    - What are obstructions that may occur in the future?

3. Examine the quality of the present layout.
    - What are the present shapes of spaces and where are they located?
    - Are the adjacencies organized appropriately or is change needed?
    - Are the storage areas and/or closets adequate or is more space needed?
    - Are the bathrooms and kitchen adequate?
    - Are the elevators and stairs adequate in the building (commercial and/or apartment)?

4. Note any problems (exterior and interior) related to noise.
   - Are there noise issues from outside the building, the elevator, staircase, and/or adjacent spaces?
   - Within the spaces, are there noise and/or privacy issues for the users?

5. Examine elements that should be changed.
   - Location of walls, windows, doors
   - Adequacy of storage and/or closets
   - Improvements needed for bathrooms and kitchens

Based on ideas from Pile (2003).

Appendix G
Post-Occupant Evaluation Survey

We want to conduct a post-occupancy evaluation (POE) of your building or space. The purpose of this evaluation is to assess how well the building or space performs for those who occupy it in terms of health, safety, security, functionality, and psychological comfort. The benefits of a post-occupancy evaluation include: identification of good and bad performance aspects of the building or space; better utilization of the building or space; and feedback on how to improve future, similar buildings or spaces.

Please respond only to those questions of the following survey that are applicable to you. Indicate your answers by marking the appropriate blank with an X.

1.   In an average workweek, how many hours do you spend in the following spaces (specify):

      Space A:

      Space B:

      Space C:

      Space D:

      Space E:

      Space F:

Hours	A	B	C	D	E
0–5					
6–10					
11–15					
16–20					
21–25					
26–30					
31–35					
36–40					
40+					

Answer Questions 2–5 using the following quality ratings: Quality Ratings Key: EX = Excellent quality; G = Good quality; F = Fair quality; P = Poor quality.

2.   Rate the overall quality of the following area in your space.

	EX	G	F	P
A) Space Category A				
B) Space Category B				
C) Space Category C				
D) Space Category D				
E) Space Category E				
F) Space Category F				
G) Other, Specify				

3.   Rate the overall quality of Space Category A in terms of the following:

	EX	G	F	P
A) Adequacy of the space				
B) Lighting				
C) Acoustics				
D) Aesthetics				
E) Odor				
F) Functionality				
G) Security				
H) Flexibility of use				
I) Other, specify				

4. Rate the overall quality of Space Category B in terms of the following:

	EX	G	F	P
A) Adequacy of the space				
B) Lighting				
C) Acoustics				
D) Aesthetics				
E) Odor				
F) Functionality				
G) Security				
H) Flexibility of use				
I) Other, specify _____				

5. Rate the overall quality of Space Category C in terms of the following:

	EX	G	F	P
A) Adequacy of the space				
B) Lighting				
C) Acoustics				
D) Aesthetics				
E) Odor				
F) Functionality				
G) Security				
H) Flexibility of use				
I) Other, specify _____				

6. Rate the overall quality of Space Category D in terms of the following:

	EX	G	F	P
A) Adequacy of the space				
B) Lighting				
C) Acoustics				
D) Aesthetics				
E) Odor				
F) Functionality				
G) Security				
H) Flexibility of use				
I) Other, specify _____				

7. Rate the overall quality of Space Category E in terms of the following:

	EX	G	F	P
A) Adequacy of the space				
B) Lighting				
C) Acoustics				
D) Aesthetics				
E) Odor				
F) Functionality				
G) Security				
H) Flexibility of use				
I) Other, specify _____				

8. Rate the overall quality of Space Category F in terms of the following:

	EX	G	F	P
A) Adequacy of the space				
B) Lighting				
C) Acoustics				
D) Aesthetics				
E) Odor				
F) Functionality				
G) Security				
H) Flexibility of use				
I) Other, specify _____				

9. Rate the overall quality of design of this space:

	EX	G	F	P
A) Aesthetic quality of interior				
B) Amount of space				
C) Environmental quality (lighting, acoustics, temperature, etc.)				
D) Proximity to views				
E) Adaptability to changing uses				

(continued)

	EX	G	F	P
F) Security				
G) Maintenance				
H) Relationship of space/layout				
I) Quality of finish materials				
1) Floors				
2) Walls				
3) Ceiling				
J) Other, specify _____				

10. Select and rank in order of importance equipment of facilities that are currently lacking in this space.

11. Make any other suggestion you wish for physical or managerial improvements in your building.

12. Demographic information:
    a) Your room #/building area:
    b) Your position:
    c) # of years in the present position:

13. Other issues that could be addressed? (IMPORTANT)

Source: Piotrowski (2008).

Appendix H
Department Questionnaire Checklist

Department title:

Department code (if applicable):

Contact person:

Current location:

Department head (chairperson):

Divisions within department listed above:

Divisions within Department/Title	Checkmark represents department questionnaire completed (comment as needed)

Remarks:

Based on ideas from Rayfield (1994).

Appendix I
Equipment Report

Date:

Name	Quantity	Remarks
Equipment		
Computer monitor		
Printer		
Scanner		
Copier		
LAN file server		
Typewriter		
FAX		
Shredder		
Refrigerator		
Microwave		

Name	Quantity	Remarks
Storage		
Letter vertical file		
Lateral files		
Storage cabinets		
Flat files		
Bookcases		
Mailboxes		
Safe		
Work surface		
Desk		
Mail table		

Based on ideas from Rayfield (1994).

Appendix J
Support Area

Date:

Area	Quantity of Areas	Total Square Footage	Remarks (codes, room titles, personnel, equipment, and other information)
Reception Area			
Conference Room			
Resource Room			
Equipment Room			
Workroom			
File Room			
Mail Room			
Storage Room			

Based on ideas from Rayfield (1994).

Appendix K
Adjacency List

Date:

Divisions or Departments within _____ Corporation	Mandatory Adjacency (1)	Same Level (2)	Adjacent Level (3)	Remarks

Based on ideas from Rayfield (1994).

Appendix L
Commercial Programming Questionnaire: Observation Form

Project:

Location:

Observation date:

Observation start date:

Observation finish time:

1. Describe people in the space (number of people, employees, customers, approximate ages, special needs, etc.).

2. Describe activities in the space.

3. Describe the role of lighting in conducting activities.

4. Describe unnatural movement that could be the result of poor lighting (e.g., shielding eyes, hesitations).

5. Describe any modifications or adjustments to the environment conducted by end users that could be the result of poor lighting.

6. Describe any problems associated with lighting and the principles of universal design.

7. Describe any problems associated with acoustics and the principles of universal design.

8. Describe any problems associated with floor finishes and the principles of universal design.

9. Describe any problems associated with circulation and the principles of universal design.

10. Describe any problems with wear related to circulation patterns.

11. Identify preferred area(s).

12. Identify any unoccupied area(s).

Based on ideas from Winchip (2005 and 2008).

Appendix M
Conference Room Requirements

Date:

Number of Participants	Frequency: Number of Days per Month	Duration: (Hours and Number of Days)	Attendees (%)		Scheduled: Time of Day Used	Purpose or Remarks
			Corp	Other		
Other						
Up to 5						
To 10						
To 20						
To 30						
To 40						
To 50						
To 75						
To 100						
To 200						

Based on ideas from Rayfield (1994).

Appendix N
Residential Programming Questionnaire:
General Client Information

Date:

I. General Information

Client name:

Address:

City, state, zip:

Home phone: Work phone:

Occupation:

II. Occupants

Names	Age	Special/Universal Needs

Pets	Kind/Size	Special Needs

Guest	Age	Frequency of Visits

Will the composition of the household change in the near future?

Yes   No   (Circle)

How will it change?

III. Location, Climate, and Orientation: How Will They Affect the Design?

Describe the following issues to determine how each will affect the design:

Issue Categories	Description
Location	
Climate	
Temperature	
Orientation: view	

IV. Housing

Check the type of housing in which the occupants live:

House ( )   Apartment ( )   Town house ( )   Condo ( )   Other ( ):

V. Scope of the Project

What is the scope of the project?

Scope	State Room(s) Included
Entire Home	
1st Floor	
2nd Floor	
Lower Level	

VI. Economics and Time Frame

What are the economic concerns and when does the client require project completion?

Budget	
Price Range	
Time Frame	
Phase	

VII. Lifestyle and Design Preferences

Go to Appendix O.

VIII. Room Requirements

Go to Appendix P.

IX. Human Factors: Special Health Concerns

Go to Appendix Q.

X. Lighting Needs

Go to Appendix R.

XI. FF&E Inventory

Go to Appendix S.

XII. Interior Assessment

Go to Appendix T.

1. Material/Finish Interior Assessment

2. Interior Architecture Interior Assessment

XIII. Anticipated Future Changes

1. Changes in individuals living in the building:

2. Changes in number of rooms:

3. Changes in activities:

4. Anticipated renovations:

5. Furniture changes:

6. Changes in interior elements (floor coverings, wall coverings, ceilings, window treatments):

Based on ideas from Allen et al. (2004) and Winchip, S. (2005 and 2008).

Appendix O
Residential Programming Questionnaire: Lifestyle and Design Preferences Section

In what hobbies and activities do occupants engage?

Activity	Family Member(s)	Location of Activity
Computer		
Television		
Stereo		
Reading		
Piano playing		
Other instruments		
Model building		
Crafts		
Sewing		
Board games		
Cooking together		
Children's play area		
Collections		

What communication modes and equipment are necessary?

Communication Mode	Equipment Needs	Location
Phone		
Security system		
Audio system		
Other		

What are the occupants' design preferences relative to design?

Preference Categories	Description of Preferences
Color(s)	
Mood	
Light	
Style	
Other	

Based on ideas from Allen et al. (2004) and Winchip, S. (2005 and 2008).

Appendix P
Residential Programming Questionnaire: Room Requirements Section

How does the client's lifestyle affect each room's function and requirements?

Details	Comments

Living or Great Room

Type of   Formal __ _____

entertaining   Informal __ _____

Number of people _____ (max) _____

Frequency of use _____/month _____

Adjacent to _____ / Location _____

Storage Needs   Requirements (FF&E)

_____   _____

Dining Room

Type of dining   Formal   __   _____

                  Casual   __   _____

                  Both   __   _____

Number of people _____ (max)   _____

Frequency of use _____/month   _____

Adjacent to _____ /   Location _____

Storage Needs   Requirements (FF&E)

_____   _____

Breakfast Room/Area

Number of people _____ (max)   _____

Frequency of use _____/week   _____

Adjacent to _____ /   Location _____

Storage Needs   Requirements (FF&E)

_____   _____

Snack Bar

Number of people _____ (max)   _____

Frequency of use _____/week   _____

Adjacent to _____ /   Location _____

Storage Needs   Requirements (FF&E)

_____   _____

Kitchen

Cooking   Simple   __   _____

              Casual   __   _____

              Elaborate   __   _____

              Gourmet   __   _____

Number of people _____ (max)   _____

Frequency of use _____/week   _____

Adjacent to _____ /   Location _____

Storage Needs   Requirements (FF&E)

_____   _____

Family Room

Adjacent to _____ / Location _____

Requirements (FF&E) & Storage Needs

_____

Bedrooms

Adjacent to _____ / Location _____

#	Who	Requirements (FF&E) & Storage Needs
1	_____	_____
2	_____	_____
3	_____	_____
4	_____	_____

Bathrooms

Adjacent to _____ / Location _____

#	Who	Requirements (FF&E) & Storage Needs
1	_____	_____
2	_____	_____
3	_____	_____

Other Rooms—as required by client

Laundry

Number of people _____ (max) _____

Ages of people _____ _____

Frequency of use _____/day _____

Adjacent to _____ / Location _____

Storage Needs   Requirements (FF&E)

_____   _____

Office or Study

Number of people _____ (max) _____

Ages of people _____ _____

Frequency of use _____/day _____

Adjacent to _____ / Location _____

Storage Needs   Requirements (FF&E)

_____   _____

Music Room

Type of Music   Formal __   _____
                     Casual __   _____
                     Both   __   _____

Number of people _____ (max)   _____

Frequency of use _____/week   _____

Adjacent to _____ / Location _____

Storage Needs   Requirements (FF&E)

_____   _____

Playroom

Number of people _____ (max)   _____

Ages of people _____   _____

Frequency of use _____/day   _____

Adjacent to _____ / Location _____

Storage Needs   Requirements (FF&E)

_____   _____

Hobby Room

Number of people _____ (max)   _____

Ages of people _____   _____

Frequency of use _____/week   _____

Adjacent to _____ / Location _____

Storage Needs   Requirements (FF&E)

_____   _____

Workshop

Number of people _____ (max)   _____

Ages of people _____   _____

Frequency of use _____/week   _____

Adjacent to _____ / Location _____

Storage Needs   Requirements (FF&E)

_____   _____

Garage

Number of cars _____ (max)

Other vehicles

Adjacent to _____ / Location _____

Storage Needs   Requirements (FF&E)

_____   _____

Other

Number of people _____ (max)

Frequency of use _____/week

Adjacent to _____ / Location _____

Storage Needs   Requirements (FF&E)

_____   _____

Storage Needs

Adjacent to _____ / Location _____

Based on ideas from Allen et al. (2004).

Appendix Q
Commercial or Residential Programming Questionnaire: Human Factors

Health Concerns (e.g., Dementia, Alzheimer's Disease, SAD, Cognitive Processing, and Hearing): Anthropometric Data

1. How will the health of the occupant(s) affect the design?

Visual Impairment	Yes	No
Cataracts		
Glaucoma		
Diabetic retinopathy		
Difficulty seeing contrasts		
Difficulty with visual acuity		
Difficulty detecting motion		
Difficulty with depth perception		
Reduced field of vision		
Color blindness		
Problems with glare		
Problems with flickering lights		

Impairment	Yes	No
Walking with assisting device and type		
Difficulty standing		
Difficulty sitting		
Hearing loss		
Reaction time		
Cognitive impairment		
Other (explain)		

2. Anthropometric data—please provide measurement (in inches or millimeters) in a range for:
   a) Distance (in inches or millimeters) from seat to eye level
   b) Distance from floor to eye level
   c) Reach distance

Source: Winchip (2008).

Appendix R
Commercial or Residential Programming Questionnaire: Lighting Needs

1. Lighting Needs: Activity Assessment by Room

Room	Location in Room	Activity	Special Lighting Needs	User(s)	Day(s) of Week	Time of Day	Duration	Technology	Furniture	Luminaire(s)

2. Perceptions of Lighting Assessment in Existing Spaces*

Client:

Room:**

Lighting Method:

Perceptions of Lighting	Yes	No	Details
Appropriate level of illumination			
Appropriate mood and atmosphere for activities			
Appropriate amount of daylight			
Appropriate energy conservation			
Appropriate environment conservation			
Appropriate accent lighting for artwork or special collection			
Problems with distribution of light on a task			
Problems with glare			Time of day: Time of year
Problems with shadow			Time of day: Time of year
Problems with reflections on task surface			
Problems with flickering			
Problems with color accuracy			
Problems with apparent color of room			
Problems with seeing objects ___ people ___			
Problems with reaching controls			
Problems with manipulating controls			
Problems with heat from lamp			
Problems with electrical outlets			
Problems with the apparent size of the room			
Problems with safety			
Problems with security			
Additional comments			

* to be completed by the assistance of a lighting designer
** repeat for each room

Source: Winchip (2008).

Appendix S
Furniture, Fixtures, and Equipment Inventory

A. Existing Furniture Inventory

Item No.	Type	Size W × L × D	Color	Finish	Condition	Refinishing	Reupholstering

B. Existing Fixtures Inventory

Item No.	Type	Size W × L × D	Color	Finish	Condition	Refinishing	Other Information

C. Existing Equipment Inventory

Item No.	Type	Size W × L × D	Built-in Freestanding Work Surface	Finish	Power Required	Heat Release	Acoustic	Cabling	Special Requirements

Based on ideas from Rayfield (1994).

Appendix T
Commercial or Residential: Interior Assessment

1. Material/Finish Interior Assessment

Room	Period/ Style	Wall Color(s)	Wall Texture/ Finish	Ceiling Color	Ceiling System	Floor Covering Type/Color	Floor Finish	Window Treatment	Exterior Shading Devices	Special Collections

2. Interior Architecture Interior Assessment

Room	Significant Architectural Elements	Lighting Enhanced Architecture	Noteworthy Exterior Views	Security Concerns	Safety Concerns	Energy/ Environmental Concerns	Circulation Concerns	Luminaires Appropriate Style/Size	Universal Design Concerns	Acoustic Concerns

Source: Winchip (2005 and 2008).

Appendix U
Commercial or Residential: Interior Assessment for Lighting

Room:

Lighting method:

Lighting	Yes	No	Details
General Lighting Concerns			
Appropriate level(s) of illuminations			
Appropriate layers of lighting			
Appropriate amount of daylight			
Appropriate mood and atmosphere for activities			
Appropriate luminaire to promote the desirable image and value			
Appropriate balance of illumination between rooms			
Appropriate balance of illumination between zones			
Appropriate patterns of light, shade, and shadow			

Lighting	Yes	No	Details
Appropriate luminaires/lighting methods for the geometry of the space			
Appropriate flexibility of lighting in multifunctional spaces			
Appropriate lighting for special needs, such as video-conferencing, audiovisual presentations, medical procedures			
Appropriate illumination in transitional areas			
Problems with patterns of light			
Dark areas or corners			
Adequate perimeter lighting			
Appropriate consideration for axial planning			
Appropriate environment for light art			
Luminaires/Lamps			
Appropriate style/size of luminaires			
Problems with size/style of luminaire dominating the interior			
Problems with distribution of light on a task			
Appropriate relationship among the user, task light source, and furniture dimensions			
Appropriate localized lighting			
Appropriate lighting for visual art and special collections			
Problems with glare			
Problems with exposed lamps			
Problems with heat from lamps			
Problems with lamps/luminaire maintenance			
Problems with fading			
Problems with ceilings appearing dirty			
Problems with shade or shadows			

(continued)

Lighting	Yes	No	Details
Undesirable striations or scallops on walls			
Potential ergonomic problems due to lighting			
Problems with veiling reflections			
Problems with flickering			
Problems with color accuracy			
Problems with the apparent color of a room			
Problems with the appearance of facial features of skin tones			
Lighting Systems Control			
Problems with location of controls			
Problems with manipulating controls			
Problems with noise from controls			
Problems with how controls are calibrated			
Problems with the location of controls for detecting motion			
Convenient switching arrangement			
Safety, Security, Energy			
Adequate illumination for egress during an emergency			
Emergency lighting calibrated to allow enough time to leave a space and building during an emergency			
Emergency lighting mounted in a variety of locations			
Location of electrical outlets in compliance with ADA regulations			
Location of switches in compliance with ADA regulations			
Problems with luminaires interfering with people or architectural elements such as door swings			

Lighting	Yes	No	Details
Location of luminaires in compliance with ADA regulations			
Problems with safety including stairways, bathrooms, and kitchens			
Problems with faulty wiring, frayed cords, or overloaded circuits			
Lamp type and wattage comply with manufacturer's specifications			
Appropriate luminaires for wet conditions			
Luminaires interfere with viewing emergency fixtures and signage			
Safety, Security, Energy			
Appropriate lighting for emergency personnel who are trying to help people exit a building during an emergency			
Adequate lighting at security checkpoints			
Appropriate transitional lighting in areas around elevators			
Problems with lighting systems swaying in a tall building			
Problems with seeing signage			
Problems with energy efficiency			
Additional comments			

Based on ideas from Winchip (2005 and 2008).

Appendix V
Space Planning Program

Company name or type:

Definition of space:

Room name:

Function	Approx. Size	Approx. Area
_____ room		
Mechanical and Electrical		

Function	Approx. Size	Approx. Area
Plumbing		
HVAC		
Other		

Appendix W
Building and Fire Code Research Chart

Chapters below refer to IBC book chapters. Using the International Building Code (IBD) book, conduct a code search for your project.

Chapter 3: Use and occupancy classification

- Determine occupancy type

Chapter 4: Special detailed requirements based on use and occupancy

- Determine if your occupancy type applies to this chapter

Chapter 5: General building heights and areas

- Table 503: Allowable height and building areas

- Section 506: Area modifications (frontage increase and sprinkler)

- Section 507: Unlimited area

- Section 508: Mixed use and occupancy
  - Table 508.2: Incidental use area (hint: determine sprinkler first)

- Section 508.3.1: Accessory occupancies (10% rule)

- Section 508.3.2: Non-separated occupancies (most restrictive applies to all)

- Section 508.3.3: Separated occupancies (sum of ratios less than one)

Chapter 6: Types of construction

- Section 602: Construction classification (describes types of construction)
  - Table 601: Fire-resistance rating requirements for building elements (determine rating of individual building components)
  - Table 602: Fire-resistance rating requirement for exterior walls based on separation distance (if applies)

Chapter 7: Fire-resistance rated construction

- Section 705: Fire walls (describes where and when used and how constructed)
  - Table 705.4: Fire wall fire-resistance rating (describes fire rating based on occupancy)

- Section 706: Fire barriers (describes where and when used and how constructed)
  - Table 706.3.9: Fire-resistance rating requirements for fire barrier assemblies or horizontal assemblies between fire areas (describes fire rating based on occupancy type)

- Section 707: Shaft enclosures (where and when required)

- Section 708: Fire Partitions (describes where and when used and how constructed)
  - Table 715.4: Fire door and fire shutter fire protection ratings
  - Table 715.5.3: Limiting sizes of wired glass panels

- Section 717: Concealed spaces (restricts potential spread of fire behind finishes within floor/wall construction, etc.)

- Section 715.5.7.2

Chapter 8: Interior Finishes

- Section 803: Wall and ceiling finishes (803.1 delineates classification)
  - Table 803.5: Interior wall and ceiling finish requirements by occupancy

- Section 804.4.1: Delineates floor finish requirements

- Section 806: Decorative materials and trim (describes allowable and quantity of surface decorations and trim)

Chapter 9: Fire protection systems

- Section 903: Automatic sprinkler systems (determine if sprinkler system is required based on occupancy type)

- Section 906: Portable fire extinguishers (Rule of thumb: provide in close proximity to all major exits and within every 150 lineal feet within an exit system.)

Chapter 10: Means of egress

- Define egress pathway system (exit access, exit, and exit discharge)

- Section 1004: Occupant load
  - Table 1004.1.1: Maximum floor area allowance per occupant (determine occupant load of overall building)
  - Table 1005.1: Egress width per occupant served
  - Table 1007: Accessible means of egress (must provide accessible means of egress)

- Section 1007.2.1: Elevators required (four stories or more)

- Section 1007.3.1: Exit stairways (accessible means of egress must have 48" clear width between handrails)

- Section 1007.6: Areas of refuge (where required, size, and two-way communication)

- Section 1008: Doors, gates, and turnstiles

- Section 1008.1.2: Door swing (shall swing in direction of travel when serving an occupant load of 50 or more)

- Section 1008.1.4: Floor elevation (there shall be a floor or landing on each side of a door)

- Section 1008.1.6: Thresholds (height restrictions)

- Section 1008.1.7: Door arrangement (space between two doors in a series)

- Remainder of 1008 (hardware and signage requirements)

- Section 1009: Stairs

- Section 1009: Stairways (stairway width must not be less than 44"; see exceptions)

- Section 1009.2: Headroom (80" minimum)

- Section 1009.3: Stair treads and risers

- Section 1009 also applies to curved and spiral stairways

- Section 1010: Ramps

- Section 1010.2: Slope (1:12)

- Section 1010.3: Cross slope (not steeper than 2% [1:50])

- Remainder of section deals with design/layout of ramps

- Section 1012: Handrails

- Section 1013: Guards

- Section 1014: Exit access (addresses exit access arrangement)

- Section 1014.2: Egress through intervening rooms

- Section 1014.3: Common path of egress travel (shall not exceed 75 feet in non-hazard occupancy)

- Section 1014.4: Aisles (defines aisle widths within tables, etc.)

- Section 1015: Exit and exit access doorways
  - Table 1015.1: Space with one means of egress

- Section 1015.2.1: Two exits or exit access doorways (minimum distance apart)

- Section 1015.2.2: Three or more exits (minimum distance apart)

- Section 1016: Exit access travel distance
  - Table 1016.1: Exit access travel distance

- Section 1017: Corridor

- Section 1017.2: Corridor width (minimum width allowable)

- Section 1017.3: Dead ends
  - Table 1017.1: Corridor fire-resistance rating

- Section 1017.5: Corridor continuity

- Section 1019: Number of exits and continuity
  - Table 1019.1: Minimum number of exits for occupant load
  - Table 1019.2: Buildings with one exit

- Section 1020: Vertical exit enclosures (read exceptions, particularly 8 and 9)

- Section 1025: Assembly

- Section 1025.4: Foyers and lobbies (encroachment restriction)

- Section 1026: Emergency escape and rescue (emergency escape and rescue for R and I-I occupants)

- Section 1026.2: Minimum size (of openings)

- Section 1026.3: Maximum height above floor (of opening)

- Section 1026.5: Window wells

Chapter 11: Accessibility

- Accessibility requirements are listed in this chapter.

Chapter 29: Plumbing systems

- Table 2902.1: Determine minimum number of plumbing facilities.

- Plumbing facility count is determined by use and occupancy load total for the interior space you are designing. (Remember: divide occupancy load by two to account for total women and total men to determine number of people who will use space. Use total occupant count (men and women combined) to determine drinking fountain and service sink requirements. Urinal/water closed ratios in men's 1:3 ratio in assembly and business occupancies; 1:2 for all others.

* Areas to figure, complete, etc., as well as underlined portions

Glossary

accretion traces Changes or additions made to an environment that relate to behavior.

active adult communities A life-stage housing in communities for those ages 55 and over that contains health clubs, college classrooms, and computer labs.

active solar energy system The use of mechanical equipment to collect solar radiation that is converted into thermal energy.

ADA Acronym for the American Disabilities Act.

adaptive reuse The adaptation of old structures for new purposes and while preserving the shell or structure.

adult day care Care and companionship for seniors who need assistance and/or supervision during the day, as is the "adult day care center."

aging in place Remaining in one's home while growing old and modifying the home to accommodate the aging process.

ambulatory care center A medical office building that may also be called an outpatient clinic.

analysis The study of the parts (e.g., data) and their interrelationships in making up a whole.

anthropometrics Measurements of the size, weight, and proportions of the human body.

assisted living residences Residential settings for elderly or senior adults where help may be provided for individuals to keep them independent. These facilities offer choices in personal care and health-related services; the occupants must be able to care for themselves to a greater degree than the nursing home.

attached housing Houses or apartment units connected by common walls and/or floors.

autism A conditions that disrupts perceptions and relationships.

baby boomers The largest population group, born between 1946 and 1964.

back of house The private zone where employees and staff are allowed.

bariatric A term related to obesity. Products and treatment for individuals who are overweight.

bed-and-breakfast inn A hotel of limited rooms where breakfast is included with the stay.

behavior mapping Collecting data through an observational technique where activities of an individual or a group occupying a space are recorded on a plan of the space (behavior map).

blended family A family that includes children of a previous marriage of one spouse or both.

Bloom's taxonomy Benjamin Bloom developed a taxonomy or classification of different objectives and skills that educators set for students.

boutique Small store that often sells specific products such as women's clothing.

boutique hotel A hotel with an intimate, unique concept.

bullpen The main workforce located in the center of the building and in desks placed in rigid rows.

CADD The acronym for Computer Aided Drafting and Design.

case study An in-depth investigation of a single site (c.g., office, residence, hotel), behavior, or individual.

casegoods Furniture that provides interior storage space and are frequently made of wood or wood products.

casual observation A quick visual inspection or observation of activities or the space.

centralized nursing station Nursing station located in the center of a floor to control and monitor patient rooms.

chain Several businesses under one management or ownership.

change theory A theory that examines various factors (e.g., economy, technology, resources) that affect change.

chi Energy, or the "duality of **yin** (negative, feminine, dark) and **yang** (positive, masculine, light) that guides universal life."

child-directed curriculum Curriculum where the child is at the center within the space.

chinoiserie A style of art and design that reflects Chinese influence in American or European cultures.

circadian Natural body rhythms such as sleep patterns.

closed-ended questions Questions designed for possible responses.

CMU Acronym for concrete masonry units; also called concrete blocks by consumers.

collections A group of items or objects; several different works such as paintings or decorative art pieces grouped together in a museum.

color rendering index (CRI) Color of artificial lamps compared to natural light.

communication modes Ways in which the firm communicates.

concept (or schematic) development phase The phase of the design process is the ideation phase where ideas for details, sections, elevations, and plans are sketched. It is also the phase where preliminary design decisions and documents are prepared.

condominium (condo) An individually owned home within an attached complex; the owner pays a monthly or yearly charge to maintain common areas such as landscaping, recreation, fitness facilities, and more.

conference center A hotel that is designed for conferences.

conduction Transferring thermal energy (e.g., heat) directly through matter (or material).

congregate housing Similar to independent living except that the facility usually provides conveniences and support services (e.g., meals, housekeeping, and transportation).

content analysis A research technique used to analyze text (e.g., books, Web sites, newspaper articles, speeches, paintings, laws) for the presence of a particular word(s) or phrase; objectively and systematically identifying the form and content of written or spoken material.

continuing care retirement community (CCRC) A community that offers several levels of assistance; these include independent living, assisted living, and nursing home care.

contract administration phase Administration of a design project takes place during this phase of the design process and involves the execution of the project, ordering, constructing, installing, and supervising a project to completion.

contract document phase Contract documents are prepared and approved by the client during this phase of the design process.

convection Transference of thermal energy (e.g., heat) through the atmosphere by the movement of cool or warm air currents.

convenience merchandise Additional merchandise to accompany.

convenience selection Subjects are selected based on availability rather than other means such as chance or random selection.

coved plan A creative plan that is more expensive; most often used for boutiques, salons, and stores that sell high-end merchandise.

cradle to cradle (c2c) A product life cycle ends with a new beginning through reuse or recycling.

cradle to grave A product life cycle ends with disposal to a landfill.

crowding Crowded situations that bring psychological feelings of insecurity and confinement or provide security and stability.

cultural intelligence The ability to interpret a culture other than one's own.

decentralized nursing Nursing that takes places just outside a patient room to increase nurse and patient interaction.

defensible space theory A range of mechanisms that are combined to allow residents to be in control of their environment.

demand merchandise Products expected in a particular store; for example, a women's clothing store would have suits, dresses, etc.

dementia/Alzheimer's care A specialized skilled nursing care for an individual with dementia/Alzheimer's.

design development phase Final design decisions for plans, specifications, and preparation of final presentation documents are made during this phase of the design process.

design precedents (also called precedents studies or case studies) A similar or an earlier occurrence in design (office, retail, etc.) that serves as an example or model.

design process A systematic, logical step-by-step process by which a design is executed.

detached housing A house that is completely separate from neighboring houses.

diagonal plan A plan that encourages angular movement to all areas of the store and draws interest to the perimeter.

direct data Responses to direct questions.

distance education Education delivered through electronic means such as the Internet or television.

dome A hemispherical roof or ceiling.

double-loaded corridors A corridor with rooms, units, or apartments on both sides.

duplex Most frequently, it is a house divided into two living units or residences—each with separate entrances.

eco-effectiveness The guiding principle of eco-effectiveness is waste equals food; industrial systems emulate the healthy abundance of nature.

emissions Discharge of something (e.g., gases) into the air.

empty nester A parent whose children are grown and have left home.

entrepreneurial ownership Owning, organizing, operating, and assuming the risk for a business venture.

environmental design Designs that demonstrate a concern for and apply design with low impact on the ecological systems.

environmental press The pressure of an environment; it can be a positive or negative pressure.

ergonomics The applied science of equipment design that reduces operator fatigue and discomfort to maximize productivity.

erosion traces Deterioration or wear that provides patterns of use.

evaporation To convert or change into a vapor.

evidence-based design (EBD) A process for the conscientious, explicit, and judicious use of current best evidence or findings from research and practice to making critical decisions.

evidence Objects and information that are helpful in forming a decision; results, or findings from research or investigation.

exhibits A display such as art or other works.

existing conditions The condition of the environment when data are collected.

experiment A research procedure carried out to determine the effect of an independent variable (an action or treatment) on a dependent variable (a behavior) under controlled conditions; experiments are usually conducted in a laboratory setting.

extended family A family group that consists of parents, children, and other close relatives living in close proximity under the same roof or geographically.

extended-stay or all-suite facilities A hotel where customer stay for a longer period of time; rooms may include a kitchenette.

fact finding Locating a piece of information.

familial structure The makeup of a family.

feng shui Literally means "wind and water." A system of orientation that uses "chi—the earth's natural forces or energy—to balance the yin and yang to achieve harmony."

FF&E An acronym for furniture, fixtures, and equipment.

fixed-feature space A fixed element that controls human behavior; the building, the permanent walls, and equipment or fixed furnishing.

franchise store Chain store.

free address See *hoteling*.

front of house The public zone where customers or clients are allowed.

functionalism A theory that examines basic function relative to its fit in the environment and to satisfy users' needs.

fusuma Screens used to separate rooms.

galleries The place for an exhibition of art or other works.

geodesic dome A domed or vaulted structure of straight elements that form interlocking polygons or triangular forms.

geometric plan This plan create forms and shapes that can be placed at angles to the perimeter.

geothermal Heating and cooling systems that use internal heat from the earth as the source.

geriatric outpatient clinics Medical facilities that treat elderly or older adult patients and do not require an overnight stay.

Gestalt theory The whole is greater than the sum of its parts. It employs a visual perception of putting components together.

golden mean Classical proportions of division; i.e., division of a wall into one-third/two-thirds is a pleasing proportion.

golden rectangle A rectangle with a ratio of 23 (golden section).

golden section Classical proportions of geometric relationships 12, 23, 35, 58, and so on.

green design Designs that use products and services that reduce use of nonrenewable resources and minimize the ecological or environmental impact.

groin vault An arrangement of arches that forms a double barrel vault.

guesting See *hoteling*.

Habitat for Humanity housing Housing built through the nonprofit organization Habitat for Humanity. Houses are built in partnership with community and families in need.

high-rise apartment An apartment building that is eight or more stories on a small footprint.

historical precedents A similar or an earlier occurrence in architecture—exterior and interior that serves as an example or model.

hostel Inexpensive lodging for travelers, particularly young travelers; frequently found in European cities.

hot-desk See *hoteling*.

hoteling Also called free address, just-in-time, guesting, or hot-desk. It is an unassigned office approach—no personally assigned office, workstation, or desk. The employee calls ahead for a work area or desk and is assigned a work area or desk upon arrival.

housing cooperatives (or co-op housing) People join together to form a cooperative; the group owns or controls the housing.

HUD low-income housing HUD (Housing and Urban Development) offers apartments for individuals with low income.

human factors The study of the way humans relate to the world around them; concerned with improving performance and safety.

human habitat model Designed to create a home environment where medical services are generally less intensive than the skilled nursing provided in nursing homes and allow the elderly more independence and natural lifestyles.

HVAC The acronym for Heating Ventilation Air Conditioning.

hypermarket Discount store and warehouse store.

ikebana A special floral arrangement placed alone in the tokonoma.

impulse merchandise Products located near the cash register to entice last minute, impulse purchasing.

independent residential living Residential living setting for elderly or senior adults that may or may not provide hospitality or support services.

indirect data Hidden or less obvious information conveyed through behaviors such as body language, gestures, or direct or lack of eye contact.

indoor air quality (IAQ) The content or quality of indoor air that could affect the health of building occupants.

informal (nonfixed) space People to people; relates to human interaction within the spatial experience.

InformeDesign A research and communication tool for designers that summarizes research articles from a large variety of journals.

interdisciplinary Within the discipline or field such as within the field of interior design.

interior ecosystem model A theory that encompasses the relationship of the human to each environment—natural, social, and designed.

interview Collecting data with a survey instrument that utilizes verbal questions.

interviewer-administered The interviewer asks questions and records responses.

Islam A Muslim religion; a monotheistic religion based on the word of God revealed to Muhammad during the seventh century.

just in time See *hoteling*.

kelvins (K) Measurement for color temperature that indicates the degree of red or blue from a light source (natural or artificial).

Leadership in Energy and Environmental Design (LEED) A third-party certification program that is a nationally accepted benchmark for the design, construction, and operation of a green building.

life-cycle assessment The assessment or evaluation of products through its life cycle (extraction or production to disposal).

limited-service hotel A hotel designed for quick, easy-to-reach service, and convenient parking.

loosely coupled office No one particular office setting. The setting could be at home, in a neighborhood work center, in a car or on an airplane, or at the central office; the setting varies from week to week or even day to day.

low-rise apartment An apartment building that is up to four floors and contains 12 or more units.

luxe-oriented boutique hotel A hotel that combines the concept of luxury and boutique.

luxury hotel A hotel with larger rooms and suites with many amenities.

meaning of place The concept of meaning that place has to each individual.

mechanical core The area of a building in which mechanical systems are integrated.

medical model Medical care has been the main objective of medical model and administrators make decision for residents, and the atmosphere is institutional.

medical office building Also referred to as outpatient clinics or ambulatory care centers.

mid-rise apartment An apartment building that is five to eight floors.

mission statement A statement of purpose or reason for a firm's existence.

mock-ups Assimilation of real situations to test a theory.

multi-family housings A building that contains multiple separate housing units.

multidisciplinary Among different disciplines or fields.

multiple chemical sensitivity (MCS) An illness in which the individual becomes sensitive to numerous chemicals at low concentration levels and affects multiple organ systems.

multiplex An apartment with multiple units.

museum A place where important objects are preserved.

nonrenewable resources Resources such as petroleum or a mineral that cannot be replaced.

nuclear family A family that consists of husband, wife, and children.

nursing homes or long-term care Facilities that provide round-the-clock skilled nursing care for the elderly or ailing adults.

observation Watch or view in a casual or methodical manner.

one-person households One person living within a housing unit.

open planning Removal of walls within an office (including executive offices) that creates an open plan.

open-ended questions Questions are designed so that possible answers are unknown.

organizational chart A diagram, table, or map that displays positions of each job within the business.

organizational culture A group of people who share similar interests or purpose (e.g., business) and use similar practices to conduct business.

organizational profile A visual representation that show the manner in which management leads the firm.

outpatient clinic A medical office building that may also be called an ambulatory care center.

paper lite Electronic method for medical records.

participant observation Researcher or observer becomes part of the environment or people being studied.

passive solar energy system Natural or passive means of collecting solar radiation or energy with little or no mechanical equipment.

pathway plan Applicable to any store but particularly a store with 5,000 or more square feet on a single level.

Pebble Project A joint research effort between the Center for Health Design (a nonprofit research and advocacy organization) and selected healthcare providers. The work is intended to create a ripple effect within healthcare communities by presenting research and examples of healthcare facilities whose designs have positively altered their quality of care and economic performance.

permanent collection A collection that stays within a museum or similar facility.

person-centered maps Studying and mapping people's tasks, activities, and movement through a space.

person-environment theory A theory that connects the individual and his or her environment and person-to-person relationships within the environment.

photoelectric Concerned with the electric or electronic effects caused by light or other electromagnetic radiation.

photovoltaic Solar cells that convert sunlight into electric energy.

physiological outcomes Results or consequences of the functioning of the physical body.

place attachment The formation of an emotional bond with the immediate social and physical environment.

place identity People identify or incorporate a place into the larger concept of their own identities.

place-centered maps Mapping how people use a space.

pool Also called a secretarial bay; an area within a large firm that groups together the support staff.

population An entire group of people, events, or things under study.

positive distraction Distractions such as gardens or artwork that are psychologically positive during the healing process.

post-occupancy evaluation (POE) After a building is completed and occupied, a systematic method of assessing the performance of a building during a site visit.

post-test Test conducted after the treatment in the experimental method.

pre-test Test conducted before the treatment is performed in the experimental method.

precedents Similar or earlier occurrences that are used as examples or models.

preservation Maintaining the original structure, materials, and form so that it does not deteriorate.

private zones Areas within a home that are distinctly private, such as bedroom or bathroom.

program document A document that organizes data collected and is used as to begin working through the design process to the solution.

programmed or individualized instruction Instruction that is designed for the individual; a teaching method that involves sequences of controlled steps that a student must learn before moving on to the next step.

programming phase The information-gathering phase of the design process.

proxemics The study of the cultural, behavioral, and sociological aspects of spatial distances between humans.

public zones Areas where the public is allowed.

qualitative Involves various methods, analysis, and data based on non-numerical observations or qualitative inquiry that is intended to describe meaning and patterns of relationships.

quantitative Expressed in quantity; involves the numerical measurement of observations, surveys, and more.

questionnaire A (written) formal set of questions used to collect information for a subject.

radiation Energy that radiates or is transmitted as rays or waves.

randomized selection Subjects are select at random (e.g., every nth person on a list); each subject has an equal chance of being selected.

Reggio Emilia theory An educational theory for preschoolers and toddlers that views the child as a competent learner; child-directed curriculum.

religious philosophy or doctrine Rules, principles, or ideas taught as truth for a particular religious sect.

renewable resources Resources that are inexhaustible or replaceable by new growth.

renovation Upgrading or altering an existing building to increase its useful life and function.

research To study something through scholarly or scientific investigation or inquiry.

research summaries (RS) Summary of a scholarly or scientific investigation or inquiry found on InformeDesign.

resort hotel A hotel located in a destination spot that may include a beach, golf courses, fishing, and/or other recreational activities.

restoration The state of being restored; restoring something to its former or original condition, place, etc.

roof pond Requires thermal mass similar to Trombe wall, but is located on the roof.

row house One of a series of houses connected by common walls and forms a continuous group of houses.

same handed Patient room layouts that are exactly the same (e.g., doors, bed in the same side of the room).

sample selection The manner in which the sample for the study is selected. The method may be a randomized selection or a convenience selection. The process of measuring certain conditions in the environment.

sample (1) A portion, piece, or segment of something that is a representative specimen of the larger whole. (2) A section or subgroup of a population that is measured by some method.

schematic (or concept) development phase The ideation phase of the design process where ideas for details, sections, elevations, and plans are sketched. It is also the phase where preliminary design decisions and documents are prepared.

secretarial bay Also called a pool; an area within a large firm that groups together the support staff.

self-administered Respondent answers questions that may be mailed or provided at some event.

semifixed-feature space Movable objects, furniture, furniture arrangement, or the ability to move furniture from place to place.

sense of place A sense of belonging occurs when there is a feeling of comfort and safety within a place.

shibui A Japanese approach to design that expresses the connection to nature.

shoji Screens used at the windows and may be used as room dividers.

single-loaded corridors Rooms located on only one side of a corridor.

single-parent family Family that consists of one parent (either mother or father) and children.

single-family housing type A dwelling that is generally occupied by one family.

sink The absorption of chemicals or energy into materials and later released back into the air.

site planning A process of planning for a proposed building to a particular site. Planning will examine possible building configurations, legal boundaries, topography, natural elements, noise and traffic, prevailing winds, view, etc.

social zones Areas within a home for social interaction. These zones may be formal or informal areas.

socioeconomic status Different levels of status based on household income level, household type, race, age, and housing ownership.

sociofugal Keeping people apart.

sociopetal Bringing people together.

solar energy Radiant energy that is derived from the sun.

straight plan An economical plan adaptable to any type of store.

strategic plan A document that shows the direction the business plans to go. It is a written vision and the future plans for a firm.

structured (focused) interview Interview questions have been pre-designed for interview.

subject A single member of a sample; multiple members of a sample.

survey A systematic method for studying behavior that cannot be observed or used as an experiment; method often used to gather data about people's beliefs, attitudes, values, and behaviors. Usually consists of written or verbal questions.

systematic observation Systematically planning observations and recording data.

target market A segment of the population to which a product will be marketed.

tatami a 3-foot by 6-foot mat that covers the floor.

teacher-directed curriculum The teacher is at the center and creates and directs the curriculum.

teaching methods A way of teaching.

telecommuting Work that involves the use of a computer or telephone. Employees may be located in a work center or may work from home.

territoriality A behavior pattern that consists of controlling, defending, and showing ownership of an area.

theory A set of interrelated principles, ideas, or relationships; an assumption based on limited information; a conjecture.

therapeutic environments Healing environments.

thermosiphoning A method of passive heat exchange that pumps liquid and/or heat is transferred without the use of a conventional liquid pump.

third place theory Place attachment through the concept of community building such as a social place, meeting place, or public space.

tokonoma An alcove found on the interior of Japanese dwellings in which an ikebana (floral arrangement) is placed.

town house Generally, a single-family house of two or sometimes three stories that is often connected to a similar house by a common wall.

toxins A substance that is produced by living cells or organisms; it is capable of causing illness when introduced into the body.

trace observation Observing physical traces by looking at the physical environment for earlier activities such as worn carpet or stacks of paper that have not been filed.

traveling exhibit An exhibit that is shipped and displayed in various locations.

treatment An activity or event used tests a theory.

triplex An apartment building that contains three units.

Trombe wall A sun-facing wall built from material that acts as thermal mall (stone, concrete, metal, adobe, or water tanks). It combines air space, insulated glazing, and vents to form a large solar thermal collector.

typicals A space that is similar to another, e.g., all guest suites with a queen bed will be similar to each other.

typology (typologies) A system of groupings that are identified by specific attributes (characteristics) or similarity of use. For example, an art museum is a type of museum design or a department store is a type of retail design.

universal design Well-planned spaces that meet the needs of every user without drawing attention to people with disabilities.

unstructured interview Interview that uses open-ended questions.

user survey Collecting information for users of a space.

Vaastu Shastra Literally means "dwelling" or "site." Concept that governs the site, building orientation, and placement of every detail, including the proportions of all spaces.

validity The extent to which an instrument or procedure measures what it is intended to measure (internal validity). The ability to generalize the results to another population (external validity).

variable Property that takes on different values (e.g., gender male, female). Independent variable(s)—property that is changed or manipulated to determine the effect on the dependent variable (e.g., amount of study time). Dependent variable—the property that is affected by the change of an independent variable (e.g., grades).

virtual environment An environment generated by the computer.

virtual office The office of the future that instantly responds to occupant's arrival.

visual and content analysis Analysis of visual, written, and spoken material used in research.

visual merchandising Displaying store merchandise to encourages sales.

volatile organic compounds (VOCs) Organic chemical compounds that vaporize when they enter the atmosphere.

wayfinding A process of navigating through unfamiliar territory.

work zones Areas in which tasks are performed, such as food preparation or office workroom.

yang The positive, masculine, and light of chi. Also see *yin*.

yin The negative, feminine, and dark of chi. Also see *yang*.

zoning districts Division or areas divided into zones with similar characteristics.

zoning law Laws that governs zoning.

zoning A term used in urban planning for a system of land-use regulation in various parts of the world. The word originates from the practice of designating permitted uses of land based on mapped zones that separate one set of land uses from another.

References

Chapter 1: Introduction to Evidence-Based Design

Allen, P. S., Jones, L. M., & Stimpson, M. F. (2004). *Beginnings of interior environments* (9th ed.). Upper Saddle River, NJ: Pearson Education.

American Society of Interior Designers (ASID). (2005). Knowledge Center. Retrieved on January 8, 2008, from http://asid.org/knowledge/Home.htm

Duerk, D. P. (1993). *Architectural programming: Information management for design*. New York: Wiley.

Farlex, Inc. (2008). *The free dictionary*. Retrieved on September 9, 2008, from www.thefreedictionary.com

Geboy, L., & Keller, A. B. (2004). Research in practice: The design researcher's perspective. *Implications, 4*(11). Retrieved on September 16, 2008, from www.informedesign.umn.edu/Newsletter Archive.aspx

InformeDesign. (2005). Glossary of terms. University of Minnesota. Retrieved on August 15, 2007, from www.informedesign.umn.edu/Glossary.aspx

International Interior Design Association (IIDA). (2007). IIDA Knowledge Center. Retrieved on January 7, 2008, from knowledgecenter.iida.org

Kilmer, R., & Kilmer, W. O. (1992). *Designing interiors*. Orlando, FL: Holt, Reinhart, and Winston.

Malkin, J. (2008). *A visual reference for evidence-based design*. Concord, CA: The Center for Healthcare Design.

Malkin, J., & Guerin, D. A. (2005). A business case for creating a healing environment. *InformeDesign Webcast*. Retrieved on August 1, 2007, from www.informedesign.umn.edu/Webcast.aspx

Martin, C. S., & Guerin, D. A. (2006) Using research to inform design solutions. *Journal of Facilities Management, 4*(3), 167–180.

Pena, W. M., & Parshall, S. A. (2001). *Problem seeking: An architectural programming primer* (4th ed.). New York: Wiley.

Piotrowski, C. M. (2002). *Professional practices for interior designers* (3rd ed.). New York: Wiley.

Preiser, W. F. E. (1995). Post-occupancy evaluation: How to make building work better. *Facilities, 13*(11), 19–28.

Stichler, J. F., & Hamilton, D. K. (2008). Evidence-based design: What is it? *Health Environments Research & Design Journal* (*HERD*), *2*(2), 3–4.

Chapter 2: Design Theories

Bartuska, T. J., & Young, G. L. (Eds.). (1994). *The built environment: Creative inquiry into design and planning.* Menlo Park, CA: Crisp Publications.

Blumer, H. (1986). *Social interactionism: Perspectives and method.* Berkeley, CA: University of California Press.

Boeree, C. (2000). *The history of psychology.* Retrieved on April 13, 2008, from www.ship.edu/%7 Ecgboeree/historyofpsych.html

Gestalt Psychology. (2008). In Encyclopædia Britannica. Retrieved April 13, 2008, from Encyclopædia Britannica Online: www.britannica.com/EBchecked/topic/232098/Gestalt-psychology

Goffman, E. (1959). *The presentation of self in everyday life.* New York: Bantam Doubleday Dell Publishing.

Golant, S. M. (1998). Changing an older person's shelter and care setting. In R. J. Scheidt & P. G. Windley (Eds.), *Environment and aging theory: A focus on housing* (pp. 33–60). Westport, CT: Greenwood Press.

Guerin, D. A. (1992). Interior design research: A human ecosystem model. *Home Economics Research Journal, 20*(4), 254–263.

Heuberger, B. F., & Special, K. W. (1997). A conceptual framework for critical review: The Aronoff Center for the Arts. *Journal of Interior Design, 23*(1), 11–26.

Holbeche, L. (2006). *Understanding change: Theory, implementation, and success.* Burlington, MA: Butterworth-Heinemann.

Howell, S. C. (1980). *Designing for aging: Patterns of use.* Cambridge, MA: MIT Press.

InformeDesign. (2003, November 1). *Place attachment of residents of all-black towns.* Retrieved on June 2, 2008, from www.informedesign.umn.edu/Rs_detail.aspx?rsId=1492

InformeDesign. (2005). Search InformeDesign. *University of Minnesota.* Available online at www .informedesign.umn.edu/

InformeDesign. (2005, December 14). *Religious symbolism and place attachment.* Retrieved on June 2, 2008, from www.informedesign.umn.edu/Rs_detail.aspx?rsId=2221

InformeDesign. (2007, March 14). *Physical and social aspects of coffee shops.* Retrieved on June 2, 2008, from www.informedesign.umn.edu/Rs_detail.aspx?rsId=2722

International Interior Design Association (IIDA). (2007). *IIDA Knowledge Center.* Available online at http://knowledgecenter.iida.org/

Kopec, D. (2006). *Environmental psychology for design.* New York: Fairchild Books.

Lang, J. (1987). *Creating architectural theory.* New York: Van Nostrand Reinhold.

Lawton, M. P. (1986). *Environment and aging.* Albany, NY: Center for the Study of Aging.

Lawton, M. P. (1998). Environment and aging: Theory revisited. In R. J. Scheidt & P. G. Windley (Eds.), *Environment and aging theory: A focus on housing* (pp. 1–31). Westport, CT: Greenwood Press.

Lawton, M. P., Altman, I., & Wohlwill, J. F. (1984). Dimensions of environment-behavior research: Orientation to place, design, process, and policy. In I. Altman, M. P. Lawton, & J. F. Wohlwill (Eds.), *Elderly people and the environment,* New York: Plenum Press.

Lawton, M. P., & Nahemow, L. (1979). Social science methods for evaluating the quality of housing for the elderly. *Journal of Architectural Research, 7,* 5–11.

Leupen, B., Grafe, C., Kornig, N., Lampe, M., & deZeeuw, P. (1997). *Design and analysis.* (Netherlands: Rotterdam, Trans.). New York: Nostrand Reinhold. (Original work published 1993.)

Lewin, K. (1951). *Field theory in social science.* New York: Harper.

Loustau, J. (1988) A theoretical base for interior design: A review of four approaches from related fields. *Journal of Interior Design, 14*(2), 3–8.

Pegasus. (n.d.) Retrieved on September 11, 2007, from http://pegasus.cc.ucf.edu/~janzb/place/place sense.htm

Pile, J. (2000). *History of interior design.* New York: Wiley.

Schaie, K. W., & Willis, S. L. (1999). Theories of everyday competence and aging. In V. L. Bengston & K. W. Schaie (Eds.), *Handbook of theories of aging.* New York: Springer Publishing Co.

Smith, A. (1911). *The theory of moral sentiments.* Ed. by E. G. West. Indianapolis: Liberty Classics.

Worster, D. (1982). *Dust bowl: The Southern Plains in the 1930s.* New York: Oxford University Press.

Chapter 3: Methods of Data Collection

Berg, B. L. (1989). *Qualitative research methods for the social sciences.* Needham, MA: Allyn & Bacon.

Cama, R. (1997). Programming. In S. O. Marberry (Ed.), *Healthcare design in healthcare and senior living design.* New York: Wiley.

Duerk, D. P. (1993). *Architectural programming: Information management for design.* New York: Wiley.

Groat, L., & Wang, D. (2002). *Architectural research methods.* New York: Wiley.

Guerin, D., & Dohr, J. (2005) Research 101—Part III: Research Methods. *A research tutorial by InformeDesign.* Retrieved on November 23, 2007, from http://informedesign.umn.edu/Page .aspx?cId=182

InformeDesign. (2005). Home page. *University of Minnesota.* Retrieved on November 20, 2007, from http://www.informedesign.umn.edu/Default.aspx

Pena, W. M., & Parshall, S. A. (2001). *Problem seeking: An architectural programming primer* (4th ed.). New York: Wiley.

Pile, J. F. (2003). *Interior design* (3rd ed.). Upper Saddle River, NJ: Prentice Hall.

Piotrowski, C. M. (2002). *Professional practice for interior designers* (3rd ed.). New York: Wiley.

Piotrowski, C. M. (2008). *Professional practice for interior designers* (4th ed.). New York: Wiley.

Preiser, W. F. E. (1995). Post-occupancy evaluation: How to make building work better. *Facilities, 13*(11), 19–28.

Rayfield, J. K. (1994). *The office interior design guide: An introduction for facilities managers and designers.* New York: Wiley.

Scott-Webber, L. (1998). *Programming: A problem solving approach for users of interior spaces.* Houston, TX: DAME.

Sommer, R., & Sommer, B. B. (2001). *Behavior guide to behavioral research: Tools and techniques.* New York: Oxford University Press.

Vockell, E. L., & Asher, J. W. (1995). *Educational research* (2nd ed.). Englewood Cliffs, NJ: Prentice Hall.

Wang, D. (2004). Diagramming research methods. *Journal of Interior Design, 33*(1), 33–43.

Winchip, S. (2005). *Designing a quality lighting environment.* New York: Fairchild Books.

Chapter 4: Historic Precedents

Allen, P. S., Jones, L. M., & Stimpson, M. F. (2004). *Beginnings of interior environments* (9th ed.). Upper Saddle River, NJ: Prentice Hall.

Ching, F. (2007). *Architecture: Form, space, order* (3rd ed.). New York: Wiley.

Clark, R. H., & Pause, M. (2004). *Precedents in architecture* (3rd ed.). New York: Wiley.

Harwood, B., May, B., & Sherwood, C. (2002). *Architecture and interior design through the eighteenth century.* New York: Prentice Hall.

InformeDesign. (2005). Search InformeDesign. *University of Minnesota.* Available online at www .informedesign.umn.edu/

InformeDesign. (2008, May 7). *Meaning and identity behind Egyptian architecture.* Retrieved on May 23, 2008, from www.informedesign.umn.edu/Rs_detail.aspx?rsId=2851

International Interior Design Association (IIDA). (2007). *IIDA Knowledge Center.* Available online at http://knowledgecenter.iida.org/

Ireland, J. (2007). *Residential planning and design.* New York: Fairchild Books.

Kostof, S. (1985). *History of architecture: Settings and rituals.* New York: Oxford University Press.

Pile, J. (2006). *Architecture and interior design from the eighteenth century to present.* New York: Prentice Hall.

Precedent. (2007). In Encyclopædia Britannica. Retrieved September 28, 2007, from Encyclopædia Britannica Online: www.britannica.com/eb/article-9001153

The College of William & Mary (WM). (2008). Construction at William and Mary: Design Guidelines. *William and Mary.* Retrieved on May 23, 2008, from www.wm.edu/construction/design guidelines.php

Watson, S. A., & Kucko, J. K. (2001). Thorncrown and the Mildred B. Cooper Chapels: Sacred structures designed by Fay Jones. *Journal of Interior Design, 27*(2), 14–25.

Chapter 5: Design Precedents

Benschneider, B. (2008, February). Healthcare: A beacon of healing. *Interior Design, 79*(2), 97–100.

Cannon, R. R. (2007, October). Holt Renfrew's luxe look. *Interior Design, 78*(12), 298–307.

Clean Lines. (2007, October). Clean Lines. *Interior Design, 78*(12), 155–156.

Fisher, T. (2008, March/April). Abstract regionalism. *Architecture Minnesota, 34*(2), 28–31, 57.

Hagberg, E. (2008, April). Behind the curtains. *Metropolis: Architecture + Design,* 138–144.

Kaufman, S. (2008, May). Island jewel. *vmsd.Experience Retail Now, 139*(5), 52–53.

Kilmer, R., & Kilmer, W. O. (1992). *Designing interiors.* Orlando, FL: Harcourt Brace Jovanovich.

LeFevre, C. (2008, May/June). The HGTV effect. *Architecture Minnesota, 34*(3), 54–59.

Lincoln, B. (2007, October). Dining in style. *Interior Design, 78*(12), 284–289.

Potts, K. (2008, May/June). Green goes the neighborhood. *Architecture Minnesota, 34*(3), 48–53, 81, 83.

Tamarin, N. (2008a, May). Rafael Viñoly Architects to design NYPD Stationhouse. [Electronic Version] *Interior Design, 78*(7).

Tamarin, N. (2008b, May). Wing Luke Asian Museum to open in Seattle. [Electronic Version] *Interior Design, 78*(7).

Tisch, C. (2008a, March). Advances in healthcare by design. *Interiors & Sources, 15*(2), 40–48.

Tisch, C. (2008b, May). Creative vision. *Interiors & Sources, 15*(4), 42–49.

Chapter 6: Structural Needs

Allen, P. S., Jones, L. M., & Stimpson, M. F. (2004). *Beginnings of interior environments* (9th ed.). Upper Saddle River, NJ: Prentice Hall.

Ballast, D. K. (2007). *Interior construction & detailing for designers and architects* (4th ed.). Belmont, CA: Professional Publications.

Binggeli, C. (2007). *Interior design: A survey.* New York: Wiley.

Carlson, E. J. (2008, March). Human behavior and life safety: Learning from past tragedies. In R-AISON D'ETRE: Reason for Being. *Conference Presentations 2008* Interior Design Educators Council, Montreal, CA (pp. 177–189). Indianapolis, IN: IDEC.

Center for Universal Design (CUD). (1997). *The principles of universal design, version 2.0.* Raleigh, NC: North Carolina State University. Retrieved on February 5, 2008, from www.design.ncsu .edu/cud/about_ud/udprinciples.htm

Color Rendering. (2007). Energy federation. Retrieved on November 13, 2007, from www.efi.org/ factoids/cri.html

DeVido, A. (1996). *House design: Art and practice.* New York: Wiley.

Harwood, B., May, B., & Sherman, C. (2008). *Architecture and interior design from the 19th Century, Vol. 2.* New York: Wiley.

InformeDesign. (2005). Search InformeDesign. *University of Minnesota.* Retrieved on November 1, 2007, from www.informedesign.umn.edu

InformeDesign. (2006, April 26). *Alternative suburbs for desert metropolitan areas.* Retrieved on November 20, 2007, from www.informedesign.umn.edu/Rs_detail.aspx?rsId=2391

InformeDesign. (2006, February 22). *Using neighborhood history to shape neighborhood future.* Retrieved on November 15, 2007, from www.informedesign.umn.edu/Rs_detail.aspx?rsId=2313

InformeDesign. (2006, May 10). *Legal issues and managed growth.* Retrieved on November 20, 2007, from www.informedesign.umn.edu/Rs_detail.aspx?rsId=2403

InformeDesign. (2006, December 6). *Can zoning facilitate diversity?* Retrieved on November 20, 2007, from www.informedesign.umn.edu/Rs_detail.aspx?rsId=2628

InformeDesign. (2007, August 8). *Moisture permeability in building materials.* Retrieved on November 20, 2007, from www.informedesign.umn.edu/Rs_detail.aspx?rsId=2842

InformeDesign. (2007, August 21). *Trees improve neighborhoods near retail environments.* Retrieved on November 15, 2007, from www.informedesign.umn.edu/Rs_detail.aspx?rsId=2281

InformeDesign (2007, October 3). *Post-occupancy evaluation of hospital accessibility and fire safety.* Retrieved November 20, 2007, from www.informedesign.umn.edu/Rs_detail.aspx?rsId=2876

InformeDesign. (2007, October 31). *Strawbales can make good wall building material.* Retrieved on November 20, 2007, from www.informedesign.umn.edu/Rs_detail.aspx?rsId=2901

International Interior Design Association (IIDA). (2007). *IIDA Knowledge Center.* Available online at http://knowledgecenter.iida.org

Ireland, J. (2007). *Residential planning and design.* New York: Fairchild Books.

Kicklighter, C. E. (1984). *Architecture: Residential drawing and design* (7th ed.). South Holland, IL: Goodheart-Willcox.

Kilmer, R., & Kilmer, W. O. (1992). *Designing interiors.* Orlando, FL: Holt, Reinhart, and Winston.

Mazumdar, S., & Geis, G. (2003, Autumn). Architects, the law, and accessibility: Architects; approaches to the ADA in arenas. *Journal of Architectural and Planning Research, 20,* 199–220. Abstract Retrieved on November 7, 2007, from IIDA Knowledge Center database.

Nielson, K. J., & Taylor, D. A. (2007). *Interiors: An introduction* (4th ed.). New York: McGraw-Hill.

Noise Reduction Coefficients (NCRs). (1998). *Sound absorption.* Norlite Corporation. Retrieved on November 12, 2007, from www.norliteagg.com/maps/sound.htm#nrc

Olympiapark München. (2008). *The Olympic Park: Olympic Games 1972.* Retrieved on August 11, 2008, from www.olympiapark-muenchen.de/index.php?id=olymp_spiele_1972&L=1&L=1

Pile, J. F. (2003). *Interior design* (3rd ed.). Upper Saddle River, NJ: Prentice Hall.

Rupp, W., & Friedmann, A. (1989). *Construction materials for interior design: Principles of structure and properties of materials.* New York: Whitney.

Scott-Webber, L. (1998). *Programming: A problem solving approach for users of interior spaces.* Houston, TX: DAME.

Site Analysis & Building Placement. (2007). University of Florida. Retrieved on November 15, 2007, from www.cce.ufl.edu/current/green_building/site.html

Slotkis, S. J. (2006). *Foundations of interior design.* New York: Fairchild Books.

Spence, W. P. (1993). *Architectural working drawings: Residential & commercial buildings.* New York: Wiley.

Zoning. (2007). In Encyclopædia Britannica. Retrieved November 7, 2007, from Encyclopædia Britannica Online: www.britannica.com/eb/article-9078441

Chapter 7: Contextual Needs

Allen, P. S., Jones, L. M., & Stimpson, M. F. (2004). *Beginnings of interior environments* (9th ed.). Upper Saddle River, NJ: Pearson Prentice Hall.

American Society of Interior Designers (ASID). (2008). *ASID Design Knowledge: Universal design.* Available online at www.asid.org/designknowledge/aa/universal

Ballast, D. K. (2007). *Interior construction & detailing for designers and architects* (4th ed.). Belmont, CA: Professional Publications.

Binggeli, C. (2007). *Interior design: A survey.* New York: Wiley.

Boni, J., & Koltai, R. (2000). Exit Sings. *DELTA Snapshots, 8.*

Center for Universal Design (CUD). (1997). *The principles of universal design, version 2.0.* Raleigh, NC: North Carolina State University. Retrieved on February 5, 2008, from www.design.ncsu .edu/cud/about_ud/udprinciples.htm

Color Rendering. (2007). Energy federation. Retrieved on November 13, 2007, from www.efi.org/ factoids/cri.html

DeVido, A. (1996). *House design: Art and practice.* New York: Wiley.

InformeDesign. (2003, June 3). *Fire exits and instruction facilitate safe evacuation.* Retrieved on January 15, 2008, from www.informedesign.umn.edu/Rs_detail.aspx?rsId=1333

InformeDesign. (2003, July 22). *Hospitality building design and materials impact fire safety.* Retrieved on January 15, 2008, from www.informedesign.umn.edu/Rs_detail.aspx?rsId=1401

InformeDesign. (2005). Search InformeDesign. *University of Minnesota.* Available online at www .informedesign.umn.edu

InformeDesign. (2005, March 1). *Evaluating the quality of the office environment.* Retrieved on January 10, 2008, from www.informedesign.umn.edu/Search.aspx?sVal=evaluating%20the%20quality% 20of%20the%20office%20environment

InformeDesign. (2005, March 10). *Fire alarm levels in senior care facilities.* Retrieved on January 15, 2008, from www.informedesign.umn.edu/Rs_detail.aspx?rsId=1889

InformeDesign. (2005, April 2). *Beach-going habits of coastal residents.* Retrieved on January 15, 2008, from www.informedesign.umn.edu/Rs_detail.aspx?rsId=1905

InformeDesign. (2005, July 15). *Mechanical lifts in healthcare facilities.* Retrieved on January 15, 2008, from www.informedesign.umn.edu/Rs_detail.aspx?rsId=2002

InformeDesign. (2005, December 21). *Unequal restroom waiting.* Retrieved on January 15, 2008, from www.informedesign.umn.edu/Rs_detail.aspx?rsId=2241

InformeDesign. (2006, August 23). *Researching lighting quality in offices with images.* Retrieved on January 10, 2008, from www.informedesign.umn.edu/Rs_detail.aspx?rsId=2520

InformeDesign. (2006, September 20). Emotional reactions to threatening natural encounters. Retrieved on January 15, 2008, from www.informedesign.umn.edu/Rs_detail.aspx?rsId=2552

InformeDesign. (2007, October 3). *Post occupancy evaluation of hospital accessibility and fire safety.* Retrieved January 20, 2008, from www.informedesign.umn.edu/Rs_detail.aspx?rsId=2876

International Interior Design Association (IIDA). (2007). *IIDA Knowledge Center.* Available online at http://knowledgecenter.iida.org

Ireland, J. (2007). *Residential planning and design.* New York: Fairchild Books.

Kicklighter, C. E. (1984). *Architecture: Residential drawing and design* (7th ed.). South Holland, IL: Goodheart-Willcox.

Kilmer, R., & Kilmer, W. O. (1992). *Designing interiors.* Orlando, FL: Holt, Reinhart, and Winston.

Madsen, J. J. (2006, July). Acoustics: Absorb, block, and cover. *Buildings.* www.buildings.com/articles/ detail.aspx?contentID=3182

Nielson, K. J., & Taylor, D. A. (2007). *Interiors: An introduction* (4th ed.). New York: McGraw-Hill.

Noise Reduction Coefficients (NCRs) (1998). *Sound Absorption.* Norlite Corporation. Retrieved on November 12, 2007, from www.norliteagg.com/maps/sound.htm#nrc

Norton, P., & Christensen, C. (2006, July). Cold-climate case study for affordable zero energy homes. *National Renewable Energy Laboratory: Innovation for our Energy Future.* Solar 2006 Conference, Denver, CO: July 9–13, 2006.

Pile, J. F. (2003). *Interior design* (3rd ed.). Upper Saddle River, NJ: Pearson Prentice Hall.

Rupp, W., & Friedmann, A. (1989). *Construction materials for interior design: Principles of structure and properties of materials.* New York: Whitney.

Scott-Webber, L. (1998). *Programming: A problem solving approach for users of interior spaces.* Houston, TX: DAME.

Site Analysis & Building Placement. (2007). University of Florida. Retrieved on November 15, 2007, from www.cce.ufl.edu/current/green_building/site.html

Slotkis, S. J. (2006). *Foundations of interior design.* New York: Fairchild Books.

Spence, W. P. (1993). *Architectural working drawings: Residential & commercial buildings.* New York: Wiley.

Suttell, R. (2006, February) Security: A blueprint for reducing risk. *Buildings.* www.buildings.com/articles/detail.aspx?contentID=2945. Retrieved on September 16, 2008, from IIDA.org research database.

Will, A., & Baker, K. (2007). The performance of remodeling contractors in an era of industry growth and specialization. *Joint Center for Housing Studies.* Abstract retrieved on November 15, 2007, from IIDA Knowledge Center database.

Winchip, S. (2005). *Designing a quality lighting environment.* New York: Fairchild Books.

Winchip, S. (2008). *Fundamentals of lighting.* New York: Fairchild Books.

Chapter 8: Sustainability Needs

Allen, P. S., Jones, L. M., & Stimpson, M. F. (2004). *Beginnings of interior environments* (9th ed.). Upper Saddle River, NJ: Pearson Prentice Hall.

Binggeli, C. (2007). *Interior design: A survey.* New York: Wiley.

Center for Universal Design (CUD). (1997). *The principles of universal design, version 2.0.* Raleigh, NC: North Carolina State University. Retrieved on February 5, 2008, from www.design.ncsu.edu/cud/about_ud/udprinciples.htm

InformeDesign. (2004, August 31). *Preserving traditional housing in Beijing.* Retrieved on January 25, 2008, from www.informedesign.umn.edu/Rs_detail.aspx?rsId=1758

InformeDesign. (2005). Search InformeDesign. *University of Minnesota.* Available online at www.informedesign.umn.edu

InformeDesign. (2005, November 2) *Plants reduce air pollution.* Retrieved on January 25, 2008, from www.informedesign.umn.edu/Rs_detail.aspx?rsId=2154

InformeDesign. (2007, May 24). *Bringing daylight into underground spaces.* Retrieved on January 25, 2008, from www.informedesign.umn.edu/Rs_detail.aspx?rsId=1666

InformeDesign. (2006, July 17). *Architecture in historic districts.* Retrieved January 25, 2008, from www.informedesign.umn.edu/Rs_detail.aspx?rsId=2269

InformeDesign. (2007, November 7). *Achieving sustainability by reusing buildings.* Retrieved January 25, 2008, from www.informedesign.umn.edu/Rs_detail.aspx?rsId=2905

International Interior Design Association (IIDA). (2007). *IIDA Knowledge Center.* Available online at http://knowledgecenter.iida.org

Ireland, J. (2007). *Residential planning and design.* New York: Fairchild Books.

Kilmer, R., & Kilmer, W. O. (1992). *Designing interiors.* Orlando, FL: Holt, Reinhart, and Winston.

Nussbaumer, L. L. (2004). Multiple chemical sensitivity: The controversy and related to interior design. *Journal of Interior Design, 30*(2), 51–65.

Nussbaumer, L. L. (2005 April). Multiple chemical sensitivity (MCS). *Implications 3*(4). Retrieved on January 25, 2007, from www.informedesign.umn.edu

Nash, J. (2001). Chemical sensitivity: Complaining can be a good thing. *Occupational Hazards, 63*(10), 21. Retrieved April 20, 2003, from InfoTRAC database.

National Park Service. (n.d.). Introduction. Retrieved on April 25, 2008, from www.nps.gov/dsc/dsgncnstr/gpsd/ch1.html

Pilatowics, G. (1995). *Eco-interiors: a guide to environmentally conscious design.* New York: Wiley.

Pile, J. F. (2003). *Interior design* (3rd ed.). Upper Saddle River, NJ: Pearson Prentice Hall.

Scott-Webber, L. (1998). *Programming: A problem solving approach for users of interior spaces.* Houston, TX: DAME.

Slotkis, S. J. (2006). *Foundations of interior design.* New York: Fairchild Books.

Spector, S. (2003, August). Creating school and strengthening communities through adaptive reuse. [Abstract available from IIDA Knowledge Center database.] *National Clearinghouse for Educational Facilities.*

United States Green Building Council (USGBC). (2008). *LEED rating system.* Retrieved on August 12, 2008, from www.usgbc.org/DisplayPage.aspx?CMSPageID=222

Chapter 9: Human Factors

Allen, P. S., Jones, L. M., & Stimpson, M. F. (2004). *Beginnings of interior environments* (9th ed.). Upper Saddle River, NJ: Pearson Prentice Hall.

Binggeli, C. (2007). *Interior design: A survey.* New York: Wiley.

Center for Disease Control and Prevention (CDC). (2000a). *Computer workstation ergonomics.* Retrieved on November 3, 2007, from www.cdc.gov/od/ohs/Ergonomics/compergo.htm

Center for Disease Control and Prevention (CDC). (2000b). *Ergonomic checklist.* Retrieved on November 2, 2007, from www.cdc.gov/od/ohs/Ergonomics/compergo.htm

Cocci, S., & Bordi, N. M. (2005, September). An investigation of ergonomic design and productivity improvements in foodservice production tables. *Foodservice Research International, 16,* 53–59. Retrieved on February 5, 2007, from IIDA Knowledge Center database.

DeChiara, J., Panero, J., & Zelnik, M. (1991). *The time-saving standards for interior design and space planning.* New York: McGraw-Hill.

Dreyfuss Associates, H. (2002). *The measure of man & woman* (2nd ed.). New York: Wiley.

Ergonomic Details! (a). Ergonomics . . . Consider these ergonomic principles. *AFD Contract Furniture.* Retrieved on November 3, 2007, from www.ergonomicdesign.com/html/ergo-principles.html

Ergonomic Details! (b). Ergonomics . . . What is it? *AFD Contract Furniture.* Retrieved on November 3, 2007, from www.ergonomicdesign.com/html/ergo-principles.html

Hall, E. T. (1966). *The hidden dimension.* New York: Doubleday.

Human-factors Engineering. (2007). In Encyclopædia Britannica. Retrieved November 3, 2007, from Encyclopædia Britannica Online: www.britannica.com/eb/article-9106309

InformeDesign. (2003, June 2). *Age affects perceptions of workplace design.* Retrieved on February 5, 2008, from www.informedesign.umn.edu/Rs_detail.aspx?rsId=1326

InformeDesign. (2004, February 9). *Kitchens for older people.* Retrieved on February 5, 2008, from www.informedesign.umn.edu/Rs_detail.aspx?rsId=1584

InformeDesign. (2005). Search InformeDesign. *University of Minnesota.* Available online at www.informedesign.umn.edu

InformeDesign. (2005, July 25). *Breaking cultural barriers in the workplace.* Retrieved on February 5, 2008, from www.informedesign.umn.edu/Rs_detail.aspx?rsId=2024

InformeDesign. (2005, September 30). *Hospital spaces affect nurses*. Retrieved on February 5, 2008, from www.informedesign.umn.edu/Rs_detail.aspx?rsId=2097

InformeDesign. (2007, June 13). *Individual responses to casino design*. Retrieved on February 5, 2008, from www.informedesign.umn.edu/Rs_detail.aspx?rsId=2801

InformeDesign. (2007, July 6). *Evaluating nursing home environments*. Retrieved on February 10, 2008, from www.informedesign.umn.edu/Rs_detail.aspx?rsId=2622

International Interior Design Association (IIDA). (2007). *IIDA Knowledge Center*. Available online at http://knowledgecenter.iida.org

Kilmer, R., & Kilmer, W. O. (1992). *Designing interiors*. Orlando, FL: Holt, Reinhart, and Winston.

Komac Ltd. (2005). Ergonomics. Retrieved on November 3, 2007, from www.komac.co.uk/index.php?id=ERGONOMICS

Nielson, K. J., & Taylor, D. A. (2007). *Interiors: An introduction*. New York: McGraw-Hill.

Panero, J., & Zelnik, M. (1979). *Human dimension & interior space*. New York: Whitney.

Pile, J. F. (2003). *Interior design* (3rd ed.). Upper Saddle River, NJ: Pearson Prentice Hall.

Salmi, P. (2007). Wayfinding design: Hidden barriers to universal access. *Implications 5*(8). Retrieved on February 5, 2008, from www.informedesign.umn.edu

Slotkis, S. J. (2006). *Foundations of interior design*. New York: Fairchild Books.

Winchip, S., Inman, M., & Dunn, P. C. (1989). Stress due to crowding in multifamily dwelling interior spaces. *Home Economics Research Journal, 18*(2), pp. 179–188.

Chapter 10: Diversity in Design

African Architecture. (2008). In Encyclopædia Britannica. Retrieved May 20, 2008, from Encyclopædia Britannica Online: www.britannica.com/eb/article-9384737

African Art Museum. (1999). History of African visual arts. *African Art Museum*. Retrieved on May 20, 2008, from www.zyama.com/a.help.pages/history.html

Allen, P. S., Jones, L. M., & Stimpson, M. F. (2004). *Beginnings of interior environment* (9th ed.). Upper Saddle River, NJ: Pearson Education.

American Indian Culture Research Center. (n.d.). *The four directions*. Retrieved on May 20, 2008, from www.bluecloud.org/21.html

Anthony, K. H. (2001). *Designing for diversity: Gender, race, and ethnicity in the architectural profession*. Urbana and Chicago: University of Illinois Press.

Arya, R. (2000). *Vaastu: The Indian art of placement*. Rochester, Vermont: Destiny Books.

Begay, R. K. (2004a). Early structures. *Navajo Architecture Concepts & Design*. www.members.tripod.com/rkbegay/id2.htm

Begay, R. K. (2004b). Conceptual schemes. *Navajo Architecture Concepts & Design*. www.members.tripod.com/rkbegay/id3.htm

Begay, R. K. (2004c). Color material texture. *Navajo Architecture Concepts & Design*. www.members.tripod.com/rkbegay/id4.htm.

Binggeli, C. (2007). *Interior design: A survey*. New York: Wiley.

Callahan, K. L. (n.d.). *An introduction to Dakota culture and history*. Retrieved on May 20, 2008, from www.geocities.com/Athens/Acropolis/5579/dakota.html

Cox, K. M. (2000). *Vastu living: Creating a home for the soul*. New York: Marlowe & Company.

Finney, D. (n.d.). *Native American Housing*. Retrieved on May 20, 2008, from www.greatdreams.com/native/nativehsg.htm

Gelil, N. A. (2006). A new *mashrabiyya* for contemporary Cairo: Integrating traditional latticework from Islamic and Japanese cultures. *Journal of Asian Architecture and Building Engineering, 5*(1), 37–44. Retrieved from IIDA Knowledge Center database.

Harwood, B., May, B., & Sherman, C. (2002). *Architecture and interior design through the eighteenth century*. New York: Wiley.

Hinduism. (2008). In Encyclopædia Britannica. Retrieved May 20, 2008, from Encyclopædia Britannica Online: www.britannica.com/eb/article-9105952

India. (2008). In Encyclopædia Britannica. Retrieved May 22, 2008, from Encyclopædia Britannica Online: www.britannica.com/eb/article-9111197

InformeDesign. (2003, February 10). *Color, meaning, culture, and design.* Retrieved on May 20, 2008, from www.informedesign.umn.edu/Rs_detail.aspx?rsId=1248

InformeDesign. (2005). Search InformeDesign. *University of Minnesota.* Available online at www.informedesign.umn.edu

InformeDesign. (2005, April 2). *Culture informs color.* Retrieved on May 19, 2008, www.informedesign.umn.edu/Rs_detail.aspx?rsId=1913

InformeDesign. (2005, July 27). *Breaking cultural barriers in the workplace.* Retrieved on May 20, 2008, from www.informedesign.umn.edu/Rs_detail.aspx?rsId=2024

InformeDesign. (2006, July 26). *Cultural sustainability in design.* Retrieved on May 20, 2008, from www.informedesign.umn.edu/Rs_detail.aspx?rsId=2494

InformeDesign. (2006, September 20). *Beliefs that underlie feng shui.* Retrieved on May 19, 2008, from www.informedesign.umn.edu/Rs_detail.aspx?rsId=2546

InformeDesign. (2005, October, 27). *Religion and climate impact tradition housing in Iran.* Retrieved on May 20, 2008, from www.informedesign.umn.edu/Rs_detail.aspx?rsId=2150

InformeDesign. (2006, December 6). *Can zoning facilitate diversity?* Retrieved on November 20, 2007, from www.informedesign.umn.edu/Rs_detail.aspx?rsId=2628

InformeDesign. (2007, September 12). *Meaning and symbolism in Arab-American Muslim home interiors.* Retrieved on May 20, 2008, from www.informedesign.umn.edu/Rs_detail.aspx?rsId=2863

InformeDesign. (2008, May 7). *Housing design for Somali immigrants.* Retrieved on May 20, 2008, from www.informedesign.umn.edu/Rs_detail.aspx?rsId=3027

International Interior Design Association (IIDA). (2007). *IIDA Knowledge Center.* Available online at http://knowledgecenter.iida.org

Kannikeswaran, K. (2008). Indian temples. *The Templenet Encyclopedia.* Retrieved on May 20, 2008, from www.indiantemples.com/arch.html

Nielsen, K. J., & Taylor, D. A. (2007). *Interiors: An introduction* (4th ed.). New York: McGraw.

Smithsonian Institution. (n.d.). Explore the collection. *National Museum of African Art.* Retrieved on May 20, 2008, from http://africa.si.edu/collections/index.htm

Young, D., & Young, M. (2006). *Spontaneity in Japanese art and culture.* Retrieved on May 19, 2008, from http://japaneseaesthetics.com/index.html

Vaastu International. (2000). *A multi disciplinary approach to Vaastu energy.* Retrieved on May 20, 2008, from www.vaastuinternational.com/vastushastra.html

Chapter 11: Data Collection for Commercial Spaces

Aiman-Smith, L. (2004). What do we know about developing and sustaining a culture of innovation. Retrieved on December 22, 2007, from http://cims.ncsu.edu/documents/WDWK_culture.pdf

Allsteel. (2008). *Knowledge Center.* Retrieved on October 1, 2007, www.allsteeloffice.com/Allsteel Office/Knowledge+Center

American Society of Interior Designers (ASID). (2008). *ASID design knowledge.* Available online at www.asid.org/designknowledge

Binggeli, C. (2007). *Interior design: A survey.* New York: Wiley.

Cama, R. (1997). Programming. In Marberry, S. O. (Ed.), *Healthcare design in healthcare and senior living design.* New York: Wiley.

Cameron, K., & Quinn, R. (2006). *Diagnosing and changing organizational culture.* New York: Wiley.

Ching, F. (2007). *Architecture: Space, form, and order* (3rd ed.). New York: Wiley.

Clark, J. E. (2007). *Facility planning: Principles, technology, guidelines.* New York: Pearson Prentice Hall.

Farren, C. D. (1988). *Planning and managing interior projects.* Kingston, MA: R. S. Means Company.

Haworth. (2007). Changing nature of work. *Haworth: Change by design.* Retrieved on January 10, 2008, from www.haworth.com/Brix?pageID=1233

Hierarchical (2007). In *Merriam-Webster's Collegiate Dictionary.* Retrieved on September 30, 2007, from www.britannica.com/dictionary?book=Dictionary&va=hierarchical%20&query=hierarchical

Hierarchical Organization (2007). In *Marketing power, Inc.* Retrieved on September 30, 2007, from www.marketingpower.com/mg-dictionary.php?Searched=1&SearchFor=hierarchical%20 organization

InformeDesign. (2004, March 15). *Specifying seating for the elderly.* Retrieved on March 5, 2008, from www.informedesign.umn.edu/Rs_detail.aspx?rsId=1611

InformeDesign. (2004, March 30). *Job analysis in organizations without boundaries.* Retrieved on March 5, 2008, from www.informedesign.umn.edu/Rs_detail.aspx?rsId=1630

InformeDesign. (2004, July 20). *Organizational culture influences employee performance.* Retrieved on February 25, 2008, from www.informedesign.umn.edu/Rs_detail.aspx?rsId=1739

InformeDesign. (2005). Search InformeDesign. *University of Minnesota.* Available online at www.informedesign.umn.edu

InformeDesign. (2005, July 15). *Task chair preferences.* Retrieved on February 15, 2008, from www.informedesign.umn.edu/Rs_detail.aspx?rsId=2003

InformeDesign. (2007, August 29). *Obesity and the designed environment.* Retrieved on February 15, 2008, from www.informedesign.umn.edu/Rs_detail.aspx?rsId=2853

International Interior Design Association (IIDA). (2007). *IIDA Knowledge Center.* Available online at http://knowledgecenter.iida.org

Kilmer, R., & Kilmer, W. O. (1992). *Designing interiors.* Orlando, FL: Holt, Reinhart, and Winston.

Marberry, S. O., & Zagon, L. (1995). *The power of color: Creating healing spaces.* New York: Wiley.

Piotrowski, C. M. (2002). *Professional practices for interior designers* (3rd ed.). New York: Wiley.

Piotrowski, C. M. (2007). *Professional practices for interior designers* (4th ed.). New York: Wiley.

Piotrowski, C. M., & Rogers, E. A. (2007). *Designing commercial interiors* (2nd ed.). New York: Wiley.

Rayfield, J. K. (1994). *The office interior design guide: An introduction for facilities managers and designers.* New York: Wiley.

Salmi, P. (2007). Wayfinding design: Hidden barriers to universal access. *Implications, 5*(8). Retrieved February 5, 2008, from www.informedesign.umn.edu/NewsletterArchive.aspx#

Scott-Webber, L. (1998). *Programming: A problem solving approach for users of interior spaces.* Houston, TX: DAME.

Slotkis, S. J. (2006). *Foundations of interior design.* New York: Fairchild Books.

Steelcase. (2008). *Research.* Available online at http://steelcase.com/na/Research.aspx?f=17554

Tharp, B. M. (2005). Four organizational culture types. In Knowledge+Research, Haworth, Inc. Retrieved on September 30, 2007, from http://haworth.com/Brix?pageID=413

Veitch, J. A., Farley, K. M. J., & Newsham, G. R. (2002, April). Environmental Satisfaction in Open-Plan Environments: 1. Scale Validation and Methods.

Zhao, T., & Tseng, C. L. (2007, June). Flexible facility interior layout: A real options approach. *Journal of the Operational Research Society, 58*(6), 729–739. Retrieved from the Ingentaconnect database.

Chapter 12: Office Design

Allen, P. S., Jones, L. M., & Stimpson, M. F. (2004). *Beginnings of interior environments* (9th ed.). Upper Saddle River, NJ: Pearson Prentice Hall.

American Society of Interior Designers (ASID). (2005). *Knowledge center.* Available online at http:// asid.org/knowledge

Becker, F., & Steele, F. (1994). *Workplace by design.* San Francisco: Jossey-Bass.

Center for Universal Design (CUD). (1997). *The principles of universal design, version 2.0.* Raleigh, NC: North Carolina State University. Retrieved on February 5, 2008, from www.design.ncsu .edu/cud/about_ud/udprinciples.htm

InformeDesign. (2005). Search InformeDesign. *University of Minnesota.* Available online at www .informedesign.umn.edu

InformeDesign. (2008, April 30). *Designing workplaces for flexibility.* Retrieved on May 15, 2008, from www.informedesign.umn.edu/Rs_detail.aspx?rsId=2456

International Interior Design Association (IIDA). (2007). *IIDA Knowledge Center.* Available online at http://knowledgecenter.iida.org

Jones, H. (2007, November 28). 2008 Industry Forecast: Keeping pace in '08. *Construction Today.*

Kilmer, R., & Kilmer, W. O. (1992). *Designing interiors.* Orlando, FL: Holt, Reinhart, and Winston.

Levitch, G. (2003). *BlueSpace: The office of the future has a mind of its own.* Steelcase, Inc. Retrieved on May 15, 2008, from www.steelcase.com/na/bluespace_the_office_of_the_f_Research.aspx?f =19242

Piotrowski, C. M., & Rogers, E. A. (2007). *Designing commercial interiors* (2nd ed.). New York: Wiley.

Rayfield, J. K. (1994). *The office interior design guide: An introduction for facilities managers and designers.* New York: Wiley.

Salmi, P. (2007). Wayfinding design: Hidden barriers to universal access. *Implications, 5*(8). Retrieved on February 5, 2008, from www.informedesign.umn.edu/NewsletterArchive.aspx#

Slotkis, S. J. (2006). *Foundations of interior design.* New York: Fairchild Books.

Chapter 13: Hospitality Design

Allen, P. S., Jones, L. M., & Stimpson, M. F. (2004). *Beginnings of interior environments* (9th ed.). Upper Saddle River, NJ: Pearson Prentice Hall.

Baraban, R. S., & Durocher, J. F. (1989). *Successful restaurant design.* New York: Van Nostrand Reinhold.

Baraban, R. S., & Durocher, J. F. (2001). *Successful restaurant design* (2nd ed.). New York: Van Nostrand Reinhold.

Baucom, A. H. (1996). *Hospitality design for the graying generation.* New York: Wiley.

De Chiara, J., Panero, J., & Zelnik, M. (2001). *Time-saving standards for interior design and space planning* (2nd ed.). New York: McGraw-Hill.

Graham, K., Bernards, S., Osgood, D. W., & Wells, S. (2006, November). Bad nights or bad bars? Multi-level analysis of environmental predictors of aggression in late-night large-capacity bars and clubs. *Addiction, 101,* 1569–1580. Abstract retrieved from IIDA Knowledge Center database.

Huffadine, M. (1993). *Project management in hotel and resort development.* New York: McGraw-Hill.

InformeDesign. (2002, December 5). *Managing hotel function spaces.* Retrieved on March 18, 2008, from www.informedesign.umn.edu/Rs_detail.aspx?rsId=1186

InformeDesign. (2002, December 4). *Design elements can increase hotels' bottom line.* Retrieved on March 19, 2008, from www.informedesign.umn.edu/Rs_detail.aspx?rsId=1181

InformeDesign. (2002, December 4). *Designing hotel restaurants for profitability.* Retrieved on March 19, 2008, from www.informedesign.umn.edu/Rs_detail.aspx?rsId=1182

InformeDesign. (2003, May 13). *Increase hotel profits through planning.* Retrieved on March 19, 2008, from www.informedesign.umn.edu/Rs_detail.aspx?rsId=1318

InformeDesign. (2003, December 5). *Hotel design for seniors.* Retrieved on March 18, 2008, from www.informedesign.umn.edu/Rs_detail.aspx?rsId=1517

InformeDesign. (2003, December 11). *Consumer complaint behavior in restaurants.* Retrieved March 20, 2008, from www.informedesign.umn.edu/Rs_detail.aspx?rsId=1521

InformeDesign. (2004, January 8). *Creating loyal hotel customers.* Retrieved on March 18, 2008, from www.informedesign.umn.edu/Rs_detail.aspx?rsId=1550

InformeDesign. (2004, May 28). *Effects of music on customers and employees.* Retrieved on March 18, 2008, from www.informedesign.umn.edu/Rs_detail.aspx?rsId=1670

InformeDesign. (2005). Search InformeDesign. *University of Minnesota.* Available online at www.informedesign.umn.edu

InformeDesign. (2006, July 12). *Business or leisure: How it affects hotel choice.* Retrieved March 19, 2008, from InformeDesign database www.informedesign.umn.edu/Rs_detail.aspx?rsId=2475

InformeDesign. (2007, April 9). *Hotels that attract sports teams.* Retrieved March 19, 2008, from www.informedesign.umn.edu/Rs_detail.aspx?rsId=2581

InformeDesign. (2008, January 2). *How people move and behave in restaurants.* Retrieved on March 19, 2008, from www.informedesign.umn.edu/Rs_detail.aspx?rsId=2949

International Interior Design Association (IIDA). (2007). *IIDA Knowledge Center.* Available online at http://knowledgecenter.iida.org

Jones, H. (2007, November 28). 2008 Industry Forecast: Keeping pace in '08. *Construction Today.*

Kilmer, R., & Kilmer, W. O. (1992). *Designing interiors.* Orlando, FL: Holt, Reinhart, and Winston.

McDonough, B., Hill, J., Glazier, R., Lindsay, W., & Sykes, T. (2001). *Building type basics for hospitalities.* New York: Wiley.

Pile, J. F. (2003). *Interior design* (3rd ed.). Upper Saddle River, NJ: Pearson Prentice Hall.

Piotrowski, C. M., & Rogers, E. A. (2007). *Designing commercial interiors* (2nd ed.). New York: Wiley.

Pickett, M. M. (2007). A bed and breakfast design accommodating the traveling preference of the retired baby boomers. (Master's Thesis, Florida State University.) Abstract retrieved from http://etd.lib.fsu.edu/theses/available/etd-07032007-202751

Slotkis, S. J. (2006). *Foundations of interior design.* New York: Fairchild Books.

Tse, E. C., & Ho, S. (2006). Targeting sports teams: How hotels can get into the game. [Research summary: Hotels that attract sports teams.] *Cornell Hotel and Restaurant Administration Quarterly, 47*(1), 49–60. Retrieved from InformeDesign database.

Chapter 14: Healthcare Design

Allen, P. S., Jones, L. M., & Stimpson, M. F. (2004). *Beginnings of interior environments* (9th ed.). Upper Saddle River, NJ: Pearson Prentice Hall.

Andrews, T. (2001). *How to heal with color.* St. Paul, MN: Llewellyn Publications.

Brandon, D. H., Holditch-Davis, D., & Belyea, M. (2002). Preterm infants born at less than 31 weeks' gestation have improved growth in cycled light compared with continuous near darkness. *The Journal of Pediatrics, 140*(2), 192–199.

Cahnman, S. F. (2006, August). Key considerations in patient room, part 2: The same-handed room. *Healthcare Design Magazine.* Available online: www.healthcaredesignmagazine.com/Current_Issue.htm?ID=5164 (1 of 12) 8/2/2006

Cama, R. (1997). Programming. In Marberry, S. O. (Ed.), *Healthcare Design in Healthcare and Senior Living Design*. New York: Wiley

Cama, R. (2006). The opportunity is now. In Marberry, S. O. (Ed.), *Improving Healthcare with Better Building Design*. Chicago, IL: Health Administration Press.

Center for Universal Design (CUD). (1997). *The principles of universal design, version 2.0*. Raleigh, NC: North Carolina State University.

Clancy, C. M. (2008). Designing for safety: Evidence-based design and hospitals. *American Journal of Medical Quality, 23*(1), 66–69.

De Chiara, J., Panero, J., & Zelnik, M. (2001). *Time-saving standards for interior design and space planning* (2nd ed.). New York: McGraw-Hill.

Dexter, F., & Epstein, R. H. (2001). Reducing family members' anxiety while waiting on the day of surgery: Systematic review of studies and implications of HIPPA health information privacy rules. *Journal of Anesthesia, 13*(7), 478–481

Dezignaré. (2008 January). OhioHealth opens doors to next generation hospital: Natural design elements, all-digital technology and "paperless" environment make it among the first of its kind. *Interior Design Industry News*. Retrieved on February, 26, 2008, from www.dezignare.com/whatshot/08/jan/08.pebbleproject.html

Hamilton, D. K. (2004). Four levels of evidence-based design. *Healthcare Design, 3*, 18–26.

Hampton K. (2007). Hospitals and clinics go green for health of patients and environment, *Journal of the American Medicine Association (JAMA), 298*, 1625–1529.

Henriksen, K., Isaacson, S., Sadler, B. L., & Zimring, C. M. (2007). The role of the physical environment in crossing the quality chasm.

InformeDesign. (2002, October 12). *Difficulties of aging in place for the elderly*. Retrieved on March 25, 2008, from www.informedesign.umn.edu/Rs_detail.aspx?rsId=1061

InformeDesign. (2003, July 16) *Patient and family perspectives on Healthcare facilities*. Retrieved on March 25, 2008, from www.informedesign.umn.edu/Rs_detail.aspx?rsId=1389

InformeDesign. (2005). Search InformeDesign. *University of Minnesota*. Available online at www.informedesign.umn.edu

InformeDesign. (2006, January 2). *Aesthetics of "homelike" geriatric facilities*. Retrieved March 25, 2008, from www.informedesign.umn.edu/Rs_detail.aspx?rsId=2290

InformeDesign. (2006, August 2). *A model for dementia care design*. Retrieved on March 25, 2008, from www.informedesign.umn.edu/Rs_detail.aspx?rsId=2501

InformeDesign. (2007, July 12). *A new concept for nursing home building*. Retrieved on March 25, 2008, from www.informedesign.umn.edu/Rs_detail.aspx?rsId=2827

InformeDesign. (2008, January 2). *Hospital curtains harbor bacteria*. Retrieved on March 25, 2008, from www.informedesign.umn.edu/Rs_detail.aspx?rsId=2945

International Interior Design Association (IIDA). (2007). *IIDA Knowledge Center*. Available online at http://knowledgecenter.iida.org

Juett, S., McIntire, P. E., & McIntire, M. (2005 September). Designing for the new communications technology. *Healthcare Design*. Retrieved on February 27, 2008, from www.healthcaredesignmagazine.com

Kilmer, R., & Kilmer, W. O. (1992). *Designing interiors*. Orlando, FL: Holt, Reinhart, and Winston.

Kiment, S. A. (Ed.). (2004). *Building type basics for senior living*. New York: Wiley.

Kohn, L. T., Corrigan, J. M., & Donaldson, M. S. (Eds.). (2000). *To err is human: Building a safe health system*. Institute of Medicine. Washington, D.C.: National Academy Press.

Marberry, S. O. (Ed.) (2006). *Improving healthcare with better building design*. American College of Healthcare Executives Management Series. Chicago, IL: Health Administration Press.

Marberry, S. O., & Zagon, L. (1995). *The power of color*. New York: Wiley.

REFERENCES

MedicineNet, Inc. (2008). Definition of Bariatrics. *MedicineNet, Inc.* Retrieved on April 4, 2008, from www.medterms.com/script/main/art.asp?articlekey=23437

Oland, C. S. (2007). Environment of care: Investing in design. Unpublished manuscript.

Pebble Project. (2006). *The center for health design.* Retrieved on October 9, 2007, from http://health design.org/research/pebble

Pile, J. F. (2003). *Interior design* (3rd ed.). Upper Saddle River, NJ: Pearson Prentice Hall.

Salmi, P. (2007). Wayfinding design: Hidden barriers to universal access. *Implications, 5*(8). Retrieved on February 5, 2007, www.informedesign.umn.edu/NewsletterArchive.aspx#

Shepley, M. M. (2006). The role of positive distraction in neonatal intensive care unit settings. *Journal of Perinatology, 26*(3), 34–37.

Shepley, M. M. (2006). Evidence-based design and architecture. In Wagenaar, C. (Ed.), *The Architecture of Hospitals.* NHI Publishers.

Sloane, D. C., & Sloane, B. C. (2003). *Medicine moves to the mall.* Baltimore, MD: John Hopkins University Press.

Slotkis, S. J. (2006). *Foundations of interior design.* New York: Fairchild Books.

Spellman, D. B., & Franke, D. (March, 2007). The heArt of healing. *Healthcare Design, March 2007.*

Ulrich, R. S. (1999). Effects of gardens on health outcomes: Theory and research. In Marcus, C. C. & Barnes, M. (Eds.), *Healing Gardens: Therapeutic Benefits and Design.* New York: Wiley.

Ulrich, R., Zimring, C., Quan, W., & Joseph, A. (2004). *The role of the physical environment in the hospital of the twenty-first century: A once-in-a-lifetime opportunity.* Concord: The Center for Health Design.

Ulrich, R., Zimring, C., Quan, W., & Joseph, A. (2005). The impact on stress. In Marberry, S. O. (Ed.), *Improving Healthcare with Better Building Design.* Chicago, IL: Health Administration Press.

Ulrich, R., Zimring, C., Zhu, Z, DuBose, J, Seo, H, Choi, Y, Quan, W., & Joseph, A. (2008). A review of the research literature on evidence based healthcare design. *Health Environmnets Research & Design Journal* (HERD), *1*(3), 61–125.

Virzi, A. M. (2006). *Electronic medical records: Charting Mayo Clinic's progress.* Retrieved on February 18, 2008, from www.baselinemag.com/c/a/Projects-Processes/Electronic-Medical-Records-Charting-Mayo-Clinics-Progress

Williams, D. S. (2008). Design with dignity: The design and manufacturing of appropriate furniture for the bariatric patient population. *Bariatric Nursing and Surgical Patient Care, 3*(1), 39–40.

Zacharakis, S., Van der Meulen, S., & Johnson, T. (2008, May). The process of design—Informing the building of a "healing environment" at The Children's Hospital in Denver, Colorado. *Healthcare Design Magazine.*

Zimring, C. M., Ulrich, R., Quan, W., & Joseph, A. (2005). The environment's impact on safety. In Marberry, S. O. (Ed.), *Improving Healthcare with Better Building Design.* Chicago, IL: Health Administration Press.

Zimring, C. M., Augenbroe, G., Mallone, E. B., Sadler, B. (2008). Implementing healthcare excellence: the vital role of the CEO in evidence-based design. *Health Environments Research and Design Journal* (HERD), *1*(3).

Assistance provided by the following:
Charisse Oland, Oland Consulting in Sioux Falls, SD
Nancy Fishman, Sharron van der Meulen, and Terri Johnson, Principal Interior Designers, Zimmer Gunsul Frasca Architects LLP in Portland, OR
Susan Zacharakis, Director of Clinical Planning, the Children's Hospital in Aurora, CO

Chapter 15: Retail Design

Allen, P. S., Jones, L. M., & Stimpson, M. F. (2004). *Beginnings of interior environments* (9th ed.). Upper Saddle River, NJ: Pearson Prentice Hall.

Center for Universal Design (CUD). (1997). *The principles of universal design, version 2.0.* Raleigh, NC: North Carolina State University.

Costjens, M. & Doyle, P. (1981). "A Model for Optimizing Retail Space Allocations," *Management Science, 27*(7), 822–833.

De Chiara, J., Panero, J., & Zelnik, M. (2001). *Time-saving standards for interior design and space planning* (2nd ed.). New York: McGraw-Hill.

Great Atlantic & Pacific Tea Company, Inc. (2008). In Encyclopædia Britannica. Retrieved August 14, 2008, from Encyclopædia Britannica Online: www.britannica.com/EBchecked/topic/242870/Great-Atlantic-Pacific-Tea-Company-Inc

Heschong, L. (2003, October). Daylight and retail sales. *Technical report: CA Energy Commission.* New Buildings Institute. Retrieved on March 22, 2008, from www.new buildings.org

InformeDesign. (2002, October 13). *Influence of consumers' self-regulation in retail settings.* Retrieved on March 25, 2008, from www.informedesign.umn.edu/Rs_detail.aspx?rsId=1086

InformeDesign. (2002, October 30). *Wayfinding in shopping malls.* Retrieved on March 26, 2008, from www.informedesign.umn.edu/Rs_detail.aspx?rsId=1118

InformeDesign. (2002, November 25). *Consumer preference for shopping center attributes.* Retrieved on March 26, 2008, from www.informedesign.umn.edu/Rs_detail.aspx?rsId=1141

InformeDesign. (2003, August 6). *Men's preferences when shopping for clothing.* Retrieved on March 25, 2008, from www.informedesign.umn.edu/Rs_detail.aspx?rsId=1428

InformeDesign. (2003, September 22). *Creating an entertaining shopping experience.* Retrieved on September 16, 2008, from www.informedesign.umn.edu/Rs_detail.aspx?rsId=1452

InformeDesign. (2003, September 26). *Consumers' attraction to point of purchase displays.* Retrieved on March 25, 2008 from www.informedesign.umn.edu/Rs_detail.aspx?rsId=1455

InformeDesign. (2004, June 1). *Consumer perception of store image.* Retrieved on March 25, 2008, from www.informedesign.umn.edu/Rs_detail.aspx?rsId=1679

InformeDesign. (2004, June 17). *Anchor stores influence shopping center success.* Retrieved on March 26, 2008, from www.informedesign.umn.edu/Rs_detail.aspx?rsId=1708

InformeDesign. (2004, December 10). *Shopping mall as center for socialization.* Retrieved on March 26, 2008, from www.informedesign.umn.edu/Rs_detail.aspx?rsId=1846

InformeDesign. (2005). Search InformeDesign. *University of Minnesota.* Available online at www.informedesign.umn.edu

InformeDesign. (2005, September 21). *Impacts of shopping center location.* Retrieved on March 26, 2008, from www.informedesign.umn.edu/Rs_detail.aspx?rsId=2070

InformeDesign. (2005, November 9). *Themed retail environments and masculinity.* Retrieved on March 25, 2008, from www.informedesign.umn.edu/Rs_detail.aspx?rsId=2169

InformeDesign. (2007, January 24). *Best use of retail space depends on neighborhood.* Retrieved on March 25, 2008, from www.informedesign.umn.edu/Rs_detail.aspx?rsId=2665

InformeDesign. (2007, February 1). *Movement through shopping malls.* Retrieved on March 26, 2008, from www.informedesign.umn.edu/Rs_detail.aspx?rsId=2678

InformeDesign. (2007, February 22). *Merchandise display affects consumer behavior.* Retrieved on March 25, 2008, from www.informedesign.umn.edu/Rs_detail.aspx?rsId=2697

International Interior Design Association (IIDA). (2007). *IIDA knowledge center.* Available online at http://knowledgecenter.iida.org

Marketing. (2008). In *Encyclopædia Britannica.* Retrieved August 14, 2008, from Encyclopædia Britannica Online: www.britannica.com/EBchecked/topic/365730/marketing

Jerde Parnership, The. (2004). *Building type basics for retail and mixed-use facilities.* New York: Wiley.

Kilmer, R., & Kilmer, W. O. (1992). *Designing interiors.* Orlando, FL: Holt, Reinhart, and Winston.

Pile, J. F. (2003). *Interior design* (3rd ed.). Upper Saddle River, NJ: Pearson Prentice Hall.

Piotrowski, C. M., & Rogers, E. A. (2007). *Designing commercial interiors* (2nd ed.). New York: Wiley.

Slotkis, S. J. (2006). *Foundations of interior design.* New York: Fairchild Books.

Tarbutton, L. (1986). *Franchising: The how-to book.* New York: Prentice Hall.

Chapter 16: Other Design Categories

Allen, P. S., Jones, L. M., & Stimpson, M. F. (2004). *Beginnings of interior environments* (9th ed.). Upper Saddle River, NJ: Pearson Prentice Hall.

Brainy-Child. (2008). Reggio Emilia approach. Retrieved on May 10, 2008, from www.brainy-child .com/article/reggioemilia.html

Center for Universal Design (CUD). (1997). *The principles of universal design, version 2.0.* Raleigh, NC: North Carolina State University.

De Chiara, J., Panero, J., & Zelnik, M. (2001). *Time-saving standards for interior design and space planning* (2nd ed.). New York: McGraw-Hill.

Diedrich, R. J. (2005). *Building type basics for recreational facilities.* New York: Wiley.

Griffin, K. W. (Ed.). (2004). *Building type basics for transit facilities.* New York: Wiley.

Hardy, H., & Kliment, S. A. (Eds.). (2006). *Building type basics for performing arts facilities.* New York: Wiley.

InformeDesign. (2003, May 13). *Virtual environments and ergonomcs: Needs and opportunities.* Retrieved on May 10, 2008, from www.informedesign.umn.edu/Rs_detail.aspx?rsId=1314

InformeDesign. (2004, July 6). *Designing religious spaces for ethnic communities.* Retrieved on May 10, 2008, from www.informedesign.umn.edu/Rs_detail.aspx?rsId=1718

InformeDesign. (2004, December 15). *Color aids wayfinding for young children.* Retrieved on May 9, 2008, from www.informedesign.umn.edu/Rs_detail.aspx?rsId=1841

InformeDesign. (2005). Search InformeDesign. *University of Minnesota.* Available online at www .informedesign.umn.edu

InformeDesign. (2006, December 28). *How visitors move through open plan exhibitions.* Retrieved on May 10, 2008, from www.informedesign.umn.edu/Rs_detail.aspx?rsId=2575

InformeDesign. (2007, February 21). *Expectations and satisfaction with art museums.* Retrieved on May 10, 2008, from www.informedesign.umn.edu/Rs_detail.aspx?rsId=2687

InformeDesign. (2007, March 5). *Airport waiting spaces as shopping places.* Retrieved on May 12, 2008, from www.informedesign.umn.edu/Rs_detail.aspx?rsId=2703

InformeDesign. (2007, July 6). *Perceptions of school violence.* Retrieved May 9, 2008, from www.informe design.umn.edu/Rs_detail.aspx?rsId=2621

InformeDesign. (2008, May 14). *Designing efficient airports.* Retrieved on May 14, 2008, from www .informedesign.umn.edu/Rs_detail.aspx?rsId=3038

International Interior Design Association (IIDA). (2007). *IIDA Knowledge Center.* Available online at http://knowledgecenter.iida.org

InformeDesign. (2002, October 12). *Lighting—The role it plays in a museum.* Retrieved on May 10, 2008, from www.informedesign.umn.edu/Rs_detail.aspx?rsId=1041

Kilmer, R., & Kilmer, W. O. (1992). *Designing interiors.* Orlando, FL: Holt, Reinhart, and Winston.

Kolb, D. A. (1984). *Experiential learning: Experience as the source of learning and development.* New York: Prentice Hall.

Museum, types of. (2008). In Encyclopædia Britannica. Retrieved May 13, 2008, from Encyclopædia Britannica Online: www.britannica.com/eb/article-9117299

Neuman, D. J. (2003). *Building type basics for community and university facilities.* New York: Wiley.

Paron-Wildes, A. J. (2008). Sensory stimulation and autistic children. *Implications, 6*(4). Retrieved on May 1, 2008, from www.informedesign.umn.edu/Newsletter.aspx

Perkins, L. B., & Kilment, S. (2001). *Building type basics for elementary and secondary schools.* New York: Wiley.

Pile, J. F. (2003). *Interior design* (3rd ed.). Upper Saddle River, NJ: Pearson Prentice Hall.

Piotrowski, C. M., & Rogers, E. A. (2007). *Designing commercial interiors* (2nd ed.). New York: Wiley.

Roberts, N. W. (2004). *Building type basics for places of worship.* New York: Wiley.

Rosenblatt, A. (2001). *Building type basics for museums.* New York: Wiley.

Slotkis, S. J. (2006). *Foundations of interior design.* New York: Fairchild Books.

Strong-Wilson, T., & Ellis, J. (2007). Children and Place: Reggio Emilia's Environment as Third Teacher. *Theory Into Practice, 46*(1), 40–47. Retrieved May 11, 2008, from www.informaworld.com/10.1080/00405840709336547

Von Naredi-Rainer, P. (2004). *Museum building: A design manual.* Basel, Switzerland: Birkhauser.

Wexler, A. (2004). A theory for living: walking with Reggio Emilia. *Art Education, 57*(6), 13–19. Retrieved May 11, 2008, from http://eric.ed.gov/ERICWebPortal/custom/portlets/recordDetails/detailmini.jsp?_nfpb=true&_&ERICExtSearch_SearchValue_0=EJ740171&ERICExtSearch_SearchType_0=no&accno=EJ740171

Chapter 17: Residential Structure: Family and Housing

Affordable Housing. (2007, 19 June). Personal notes. *Affordable Housing Symposium.* St. Paul, MN. June 19, 2007.

Community Planning & Development (CPD). (2007). Affordable housing. *Homes & Communities.* U. S. Department of Housing and Urban Development. Retrieved on October 21, 2007, from www.hud.gov/offices/cpd/affordablehousing/index.cfm

Condominiums. (2007). *Home buyer's information center.* Retrieved on October 21, 2007, from www.ourfamilyplace.com/homebuyer/condo.html

DeVido, A. (1996). *House design: Art and practice.* New York: Wiley.

Duell, J. D. (2007). Home builders cater to cultural differences. *Professional Builder.* Retrieved on October 18, 2007, from www.housingzone.com/probuilder/article/CA6421687.html

Housing. (2007). FHA single family housing. *Homes & Communities.* U. S. Department of Housing and Urban Development. Retrieved on October 18, 2007, from www.hud.gov/offices/hsg/sfh/hsgsingle.cfm

Housing Types. (2007). *Housing types fact sheets.* Retrieved on October 18, 2007, from www.designcenter.umn.edu/reference_ctr/factsheets/FS_housing_types.html

InformeDesign. (2003, January 28). *Housing and divorce.* Retrieved on May 15, 2008, from www.informedesign.umn.edu/Rs_detail.aspx?rsId=1242

InformeDesign. (2004, June 16). *Visions of future homes.* Retrieved May 15, 2008, from www.informedesign.umn.edu/Rs_detail.aspx?rsId=1702

InformeDesign. (2004, January 16). *Children and housing design.* Retrieved May 15, 2008, from www.informedesign.umn.edu/Rs_detail.aspx?rsId=1559

InformeDesign. (2005). Search InformeDesign. *University of Minnesota.* Available online at www.informedesign.umn.edu

InformeDesign. (2006, December 6). *Can zoning facilitate diversity?* Retrieved on November 20, 2007, from www.informedesign.umn.edu/Rs_detail.aspx?rsId=2628

InformeDesign. (2006, January 20). *Housing and low-income women.* Retrieved from on May 15, 2008, from www.informedesign.umn.edu/Rs_detail.aspx?rsId=2272

InformeDesign. (2007, November 12). *Residential adaptation for aging.* Retrieved on May 15, 2008, from www.informedesign.umn.edu/Rs_detail.aspx?rsId=2484

International Interior Design Association (IIDA). (2007). *IIDA Knowledge Center.* Available online at http://knowledgecenter.iida.org

Johansen, T. H. (2007). An exploratory study of disabled tenants' level of satisfaction under the Fair Housing Amendments Act. *Journal of Interior Design, 32*(2), 28–41. Abstract available online at http://knowledgecenter.iida.org

Lamanna, M. A., & Riedmann, A. (2006). *Marriages & families: making choices in a diverse society* (9th ed.). Independence, KY: Thomson Wadsworth.

National Association of Housing Cooperatives (NAHC). (n.d.). About NAHC & housing co-ops. Retrieved on May 30, 2008, from www.coophousing.org/about_nahc.shtml

Novelli, W. D. (2002). Baby boomers: Helping aging boomers to age in place. *AARP.* Retrieved on October 18, 2007, from www.aarp.org/about_aarp/aarp_leadership/on_issues/baby_boomers/helping_aging_boomers_to_age_in_place.html

Olson, D. H., & DeFrain, J. (2006). *Marriages & families: Intimacy, diversity, and strengths* (5th ed.). New York: McGraw.

Pagans, C. (2007). How to find a village: Shifting the focus of retirement living from independence to interdependence. *Guide to Retirement Living.* Retrieved on October 18, 2007, from www.guidetoretirementliving.com/article.asp?aid=211

Susanka, S. (2001). *The not so big house.* Newtown, CT: Taunton Press.

Townhouses. (2007). *Home buyer's information center.* Retrieved on October 21, 2007, from www.ourfamilyplace.com/homebuyer/townhouse.html

Vanderford, S. E., Mimura, Y., Sweaney, A. L., & Carswell, A. T. (2007). An analysis of tenure and house structure type by household composition. *Family and Consumer Sciences Research Journal, 36*(2), 93–109.

Chapter 18: Data Collection for Residential Design

Affordable Housing. (2007, June). Personal notes. *Affordable Housing Symposium.* St. Paul, MN. June 19, 2007.

Allen, P. S., Jones, L. M., & Stimpson, M. F. (2004). *Beginnings of interior environments* (9th ed.). Upper Saddle River, NJ: Pearson Education.

DeVido, A. (1996). *House design: Art and practice.* New York: Wiley.

Holtzschue, L. (2002). *Understanding color.* New York: Wiley.

InformeDesign. (2003, April 10). *Flexible, affordable homes meet residents' needs.* Retrieved on May 10, 2008, from www.informedesign.umn.edu/Rs_detail.aspx?rsId=1282

InformeDesign. (2003, April 25). Housing design influences ability to age in place. Retrieved on May 15, 2008, from www.informedesign.umn.edu/Rs_detail.aspx?rsId=1295

InformeDesign. (2003, June 2). *Rethinking residential space planning.* Retrieved on May 15, 2008, from www.informedesign.umn.edu/Rs_detail.aspx?rsId=1328

InformeDesign. (2003, October 27). *Assessing residential vulnerability.* Retrieved on May 10, 2008, from www.informedesign.umn.edu/Rs_detail.aspx?rsId=1482

InformeDesign. (2004, February 16). *Wood products and residential VOC emissions.* Retrieved on May 10, 2008, from www.informedesign.umn.edu/Rs_detail.aspx?rsId=1592

InformeDesign. (2004, June 14). *Sources of VOCs in new houses.* Retrieved on May 10, 2008, from www.informedesign.umn.edu/Rs_detail.aspx?rsId=1696

InformeDesign. (2004, July 6). *Designing for household recycling.* Retrieved May 15, 2008, from www.informedesign.umn.edu/Rs_detail.aspx?rsId=1715

InformeDesign. (2004, July 13). *Family interaction and home design.* Retrieved on May 15, 2008, from www.informedesign.umn.edu/Rs_detail.aspx?rsId=1726

InformeDesign. (2004, July 20). *Interiors influence perceptions of age, class, and family status.* Retrieved on May 15, 2008, from www.informedesign.umn.edu/Rs_detail.aspx?rsId=1741

InformeDesign. (2005). Search InformeDesign. *University of Minnesota*. Available online at www
.informedesign.umn.edu

InformeDesign. (2005, October 4). *Proper ventilation can reduce indoor formaldehyde levels*. Retrieved
on May 15, 2008, from www.informedesign.umn.edu/Rs_detail.aspx?rsId=2091.

InformeDesign. (2008, May 7). *Sitting positions and posture*. Retrieved on May 10, 2008, from www
.informedesign.umn.edu/Rs_detail.aspx?rsId=3028

International Interior Design Association (IIDA). (2007). *IIDA Knowledge Center*. Available online
at http://knowledgecenter.iida.org

Intille, S. S., & Larson, K. (2005). Designing and evaluating home-based, just-in-time supportive
technology. *Studies in Health Technology and Informatics, 118*, 79–88. Abstract retrieved from
IIDA Knowledge Center database.

Ireland, J. (2007). *Residential planning and design*. New York: Fairchild Books.

Jones, R. M., Taylor, D. E., Dick, A. J., Singh, A., & Cook, J. L. (2007). Bedroom design and decoration: gender differences in preference and activity. *Adolescence, 42*(167), 539–53. Retrieved
from IIDA Knowledge Center database.

Kilmer, R., & Kilmer, W. O. (1992). *Designing interiors*. Orlando, FL: Holt, Reinhart, and Winston.

Mullick, A. (n.d.). Bathing for older people with disabilities. *Center for Inclusive Design and Environmental Access*. [Abstract retrieved from IIDA Knowledge Center database.] Article available
online: www.ap.buffalo.edu/idea/publications/Bathing%20for%20Older%20People.htm

Nussbaumer, L. L. (2004). Multiple chemical sensitivity: The controversy and related to interior
design. *Journal of Interior Design, 30*(2). 51–65.

Olson, D. H., & DeFrain, J. (2006). *Marriages & families: Intimacy, diversity, and strengths* (5th ed.).
New York: McGraw.

Rewi, A. (2004, Winter). Beyond Walls. *Perspective*, 10–15.

Susanka, S. (2001). *The not so big house*. Newtown, CT: Taunton Press.

Slotkis, S. J. (2006). *Foundations of interior design*. New York: Fairchild Books.

Winchip, S. (2005). *Designing a quality lighting environment*. New York: Fairchild Books.

Winchip, S. (2008). *Fundamentals of lighting*. New York: Fairchild Books.

Appendices

Kilmer, R., & Kilmer, W. O. (1992). *Designing interiors*. Orlando, FL: Holt, Reinhart, and Winston.

Miller, N., & Zborowsky, T. (1995). Unpublished paper. University of Minnesota.

Pile, J. F. (2003). *Interior design* (3rd ed.). Upper Saddle River, NJ: Pearson Prentice Hall.

Piotrowski, C. M. (2008). *Professional practices for interior designers* (4th ed.). New York: Wiley.

Rayfield, J. K. (1994). *The office interior design guide: An introduction for facilities managers and
designers*. New York: Wiley.

Scott-Webber, L. (1998). *Programming: A problem solving approach for users of interior spaces*. Houston,
TX: DAME.

Winchip, S. (2005). *Designing a quality lighting environment*. New York: Fairchild Books.

Winchip, S. (2008). *Fundamentals of lighting*. New York: Fairchild Books.

Resources for Research and Programming

A variety of resources will inform your research into programming and data collection. Along with the references documented throughout this book, the following is a list of recommended resources from books, periodicals, and the Internet. Note that Internet sites are often updated or removed; however, this list should inspire you to look for other sites as well.

Chapter 3: Data Collection Methods

Books

Sommer, R. (1969). *Personal space: The behavioral basis of design.* Englewood Cliffs, NJ: Prentice-Hall.

Periodicals and Journal Articles

Becker, F., & Carthey, J. (2007). Evidence-based design: key issues in a collaborative process. *Center for Interdisciplinary Built Environment Research.* University of Newcastle, Hunter Valley, NSW, Australia.

Online Resources

Vanguard Vista (for do-it-yourself surveys and examples): www.vista-survey.com

Case Study 4.1: The Role of Historic Precedents in Contemporary Design

Carter, R. (1966). *Breakthrough: The saga of Jonas Salk.* New York: Trident Press.
Latour, A. (Ed.) (1991). *Louis I Kahn: Writings, lectures, interviews.* New York: Rizzoli.
Steele, J. (1993). *Architecture in detail: The Salk Institute.* London: Phaidon Press.

Wiseman, C. (2007). *Louis I. Kahn: Beyond time and style, A Life in Architecture*. New York: W. W. Norton & Company.

Ronner, H., & Jhaveri, S. (Eds.). (1987). *Louis I. Kahn: Complete works 1935-1974*. Basel, Switzerland: Birkhauser.

Chapter 5: Design Precedents

Books

Bell, J. (2005). *Penthouse living*. New York: Academy Press.

Curtis, E. (2007). *Fashion retail*. New York: Wiley.

Peyton, J. (2006). *Pub scene*. New York: Academy Press.

Ryder, B. (2007). *New restaurant design*. London: Laurence King Publishing.

Susanka, S. (2001). *Creating the not so big house: Insights and ideas for the new American home*. Newtown, CT: Taunton Press.

Susanka, S. (2007). *Inside the not so big house: Discovering the details that bring a home to life*. Newtown, CT: Taunton Press.

Susanka, S. (2002). *Not so big house solutions for your home*. Newtown, CT: Taunton Press.

Susanka, S. (2001). *The not so big house*. Newtown, CT: Taunton Press.

Thomas-Emberson, S. (2008). *Airport interiors: Design for business*. New York: Academy Press.

Periodicals

Interior Design magazine: residential and commercial

Interiors and Sources magazine: commercial

Metropolis: Architecture + Design magazine: residential and commercial

vmsd.Experience Retail Now magazine: visual merchandising and store design

Online Resources

Buildings: http://www.buildings.com

Contract magazine: http://www.contractmagazine.com

Interior Design magazine: http://interiordesign.net

Interiors & Sources magazine: http://www.isdesignet.com

Metropolis: Architecture + Design magazine: http://metropolismag.com

National Association of Home Builders (NAHB): http://www.nbnnews.com: articles on building industry trends such baby boomers' expectations or single women buying real estate, and more

vmsd.Experience Retail Now magazine: http://www.vmsd.com

Chapter 6: Structural Needs

Books

Ramsey, C. G., & Sleeper, H. R. (1993). *Architectural graphic standards* (8th ed.). New York: Wiley.

Periodicals

Building Design + Construction magazine

Environmental Design + Construction magazine

Healthcare Building Ideas magazine

Hospitality Construction magazine

Retail Construction magazine

Online Resources

Building Design + Construction magazine: http://www.bdcnetwork.com

Environmental Design + Construction magazine: http://www.edcmag.com

Healthcare Building Ideas magazine: http://www.healthcarebuildingideas.com
Hospitality Construction magazine: http://www.hospitalityconstruction.com
Retail Construction magazine: http://www.retailconstructionmag.com
Site analysis: http://www.cce.ufl.edu/current/green_building/site.html
Structural systems: http://www.b4ubuild.com/links/hvac.shtml

Chapter 7: Contextual Needs

Books

Spence, W. P. (1993). *Architectural working drawings: Residential & commercial buildings.* New York: Wiley.

Online Resources

Site analysis: http://www.cce.ufl.edu/current/green_building/site.html
Various mechanical systems: http://www.b4ubuild.com/links/hvac.shtml mechanical systems and links

Chapter 8: Sustainability Needs

Books

Barnett, D. L., & Browning, W. D. (1995). *A primer on sustainable building.* Snowmass, CO: Rocky Mountain Institute.
Bower, John. (1999). *Healthy house building for the new millennium: A Design & Construction Guide.* Unionville, IN: The Healthy House Institute.
McDonough, W., & Braungart, M. (2002). *Cradle to cradle: Remaking the way we make things.* New York: North Point Press.
McLennan, J. F. (2004). *The Philosophy of sustainable design.* Kansas City, MO: EcoTone.
Mendler, S. F., & Odell, W. (2002). *The HOK guidebook to sustainable design.* New York: Wiley.

Periodicals

Environmental Building News magazine
Environmental Design + Construction magazine: Also on online: http://www.edcmag.com/

Journal Articles

Hodgson, A. T., Beal, D., & McIlvaine, J. E. R. (2002). Sources of formaldehyde, other aldehydes and terpenes in a new manufactured house. *Indoor Air, 12*(4), 235–242.
Moussatche, H., and Languell, J. (2002). Life Cycle Costing of Interior Materials for Florida's Schools. *Journal of Interior Design* 8(2), 37–49.
Rehwagen, M., Schlink, U., & Herbarth, O. (2003). Seasonal cycle of VOCs in apartments. *Indoor Air, 13*(3), 283–291.
Tremblay, K. R., Peng, L., Kreul-Froseth, S. A., & Dunbar, B. H. (1999). Perceived effects of carpet on indoor air quality. *Housing and Society, 26*(1–3), 16–25.

Online Resources

Evidence Based Environmental Design: http://muhc-healing.mcgill.ca/english/Speakers/ulrich_p.html
Green Building Resource Guide: http://www.greenguide.com
Green Builders: http://www.greenbuilder.com
Green Guard: http://greenguard.org
Green Home: http://www.greenhomeliving.com
Green Seal: http://greenseal.org

IIDA Knowledge Center: http://knowledgecenter.iida.org
InformeDesign database: http://www.informedesign.umn.edu
Minnesota Sustainable Design Guide: http://www.sustainabledesignguide.umn.edu
Rocky Mountain Institute: http://www.RMI.org
Sustainable Architecture Building and Culture: http://www.sustainableabc.com
United States Green Building Council: http://www.usgbc.org
World Watch Institute Newsletter: http://www.worldwatch.org/index.php

Chapter 9: Human Factors

Online Resources
Anthropometrics, ergonomics, and more:
http://www.anthrotech.net
http://www.hf.faa.gov/Webtraining/HFModel/Variance/anthropometrics1.htm
http://www.ergonomicdesign.com/html/ergo.html
http://design-technology.info/anthropometrics
http://www.ergonomics.org

Chapter 10: Diversity in Design

Books
Butler-Biggs, J., with Daniels, A. (2000). *The feng shui directory.* New York: Watson-Guptill.

Online Resources
American Indian Culture Research Center: http://www.bluecloud.org/21.html
ASID Design Knowledge: http://www.asid.org/designknowledge/aa/universal/
IIDA Knowledge Center: http://knowledgecenter.iida.org
InformeDesign database: http://www.informedesign.umn.edu/
Islamic history: http://islamicity.com/education/culture/#Culture
Navajo Architecture: http://www.members.tripod.com/rkbegay/index.htm
Vaastu International: http://www.vaastuinternational.com/vastushastra.html

Chapter 11: Data Collection for Commercial Spaces

Periodicals
Contract magazine
Interior Design magazine
Interiors and Sources magazine
Metropolis magazine

Online Resources
Interior Design magazine: http://interiordesign.net
Interiors & Sources magazine: http://www.isdesignet.com
Journal of Interior Design: http://www.idec.org
Knoll: http://www.knoll.com
Metropolis magazine: http://metropolismag.com

Chapter 12: Office Design

Online Resources
Buildings magazine: http://www.buildings.com
Contract magazine: http://www.contractmagazine.com
Fast Company: http://www.fastcompany.com

Haworth—contract furniture and textiles: http://haworth.com
Interior Designers of Canada (IDC): http://www.interiordesigncanada.org
Implications: http://www.informedesign.umn.edu
IIDA Knowledge Center: http://knowledgecenter.iida.org
Interior Design magazine: http://interiordesign.net
Interiors & Sources magazine: http://www.isdesignet.com
Journal of Interior Design: http://www.idec.org
Knoll—contract furniture, textiles, and modern classic furniture: http://www.knoll.com
Metropolis magazine: http://metropolismag.com
Steelcase—contract furniture and textiles: http://steelcase.com
Universal design: Center for Universal Design: http://www.design.ncsu.edu/cud

Chapter 13: Hospitality Design

Books
Studio GAIA. (2006). *Hotel, restaurant, bar, club design.* New York: HarperCollins International.

Online Resources
American Institute of Wine & Food (AIWF): http://www.aiwf.org
Association of American magazine: http://www.club-mgmt.com
Food and Drink Magazine: http://www.fooddrink-magazine.com
Hospitality Design Magazine: http://www.hdmag.com
Hotel Business magazine: http://www.hotelbusiness.com
Implications: http://www.informedesign.umn.edu
Lodging magazine: http://www.lodgingmagazine.com
National Restaurant Association (NRA): http://www.restaurant.org
Restaurant Design: http://www.restaurantdesign.com
Restaurant Hospitality: http://www.restaurant-hospitality.com

Chapter 14: Healthcare Design

Books
Brawley, E. (2005). *Design innovations for aging and Alzheimer's.* New York: Wiley.
Brawley, E. (1997). *Designing for Alzheimer's disease: Strategies for creating better care environments.* New York: Wiley.
Leibrock, C. (1999). *Design details for health: Making the most of interior design's healing potential.* New York: Wiley.
Malkin, J. (2002). *Medical and dental space planning: A comprehensive guide to design, equipment, and clinic procedures.* New York: Wiley.
Malkin, J. (2008). *A visual reference for evidence-based design.* Concord, CA: The Center for Health Design.

Periodicals
Healthcare Design magazine
Journal of Healthcare Design
Health Environments Research & Design Journal (*HERD Journal*)

Online Resources
American Association of Retired Persons: http://www.aarp.org
Arts and Healing Network: http://www.artheals.org/start.html
ASID Design Knowledge: http://www.asid.org/designknowledge

Center for Health Design magazine: http://www.healthdesign.org/resources
Center for Health Design magazine—The Pebble Projects: http://healthdesign.org/research/pebble
Dental Economics: http://www.de.pennet.com
Design for Senior Environments magazine: http://www.nursing-homesmagazine.com
Dublin Hospital: http://www.dezignare.com/whatshot/08/jan/08.pebbleproject.html
Healthcare Design magazine: http://healthcaredesignmagazine.com
Hospital and Health Networks: http://www.hhnmag.com
Implications: http://www.informedesign.umn.edu
IIDA Knowledge Center: http://knowledgecenter.iida.org
InformeDesign database: http://www.informedesign.umn.edu
Journal of the American Dental Association: http://www.ada.org
Journal of the American Medical Association: http://www.ama-assn.org
Medical Economics Magazine: http://www.pdr.net/memag/index
New England Journal of Medicine: http://www.content.nejm.org
Universal design: Center for Universal Design: http://www.design.ncsu.edu/cud
Veterinary Economics Magazine: http://www.vetecon.com
Veterinary Hospital Design: http://www.hospitaldesign.net

Chapter 15: Retail Design

Books
Curtis, E. (2007). *Fashion retail.* New York: Wiley.
Lopez, M. J. (1995). *Retail store planning & design manual* (2nd ed.). New York: Wiley.

Periodicals
Retail Construction magazine
vmsd.Experience Retail Now magazine: Visual merchandising and store design

Online Resources
InformeDesign database: http://www.informedesign.umn.edu
Institute of Store Planning (ISP): http://ispo.org
National Association of Store Fixture Manufacturers: http://nasfm.org
National Retail Federation: http://www.nrf.com
Retail Council of Canada: http://www.retailcouncil.org
Retail Industry: http://retailindustry.com
Retail Construction magazine: http://retailconstruction-mag.com
vmsd.Experience Retail Now: http://www.vmsd.com

Chapter 16: Other Design Categories

Books
Lueder, R., & Berg Rice, V. J. (2008). *Ergonomics for children . . . Designing products & places for toddlers to teens.* New York: Taylor & Francis.
Thomas-Emberson, S. (2008). *Airport interiors: Design for business.* New York: Academy Press.

Online Resources
American Jewish Congress: http://www.ajcongress.org
Center for Universal Design: http://www.design.ncsu.edu/cud
Chicago Art Institute: http://www.artic.edu
Church Resource Guide: http://www.churchresourceguide.com
Crystal Cathedral: http://www.crystalcathedral.org

Getty Center: http://www.getty.edu
International Council for Christians and Jews: http://www.iccj.org
Metropolitan Museum of Art: http://www.metmuseum.org
Museum of Modern Art: http://www.noma.org
National Golf Foundation: http://www.ngf.org
Public libraries: http://www.publiclibraries.com
St. Patrick's Cathedral: http://www.ny-archdiocese.org

Chapter 17: Residential Structures: Family and Housing

Books

Ireland, J. (2007). *Residential planning and design.* New York: Fairchild.

Susanka, S. (2001). *Creating the not so big house: Insights and ideas for the new American home.* Newtown, CT: Taunton Press.

Susanka, S. (2007). *Inside the not so big house: Discovering the details that bring a home to life.* Newtown, CT: Taunton Press.

Susanka, S. (2002). *Not so big house solutions for your home.* Newtown, CT: Taunton Press.

Susanka, S. (2001). *The not so big house.* Newtown, CT: Taunton Press.

Periodicals

Interior Design magazine

Perspective magazine

Online Resources

Condominiums: http://www.ourfamilyplace.com/homebuyer/condo.html

Housing and Urban Development (HUD): http://www.hud.gov/offices/cpd/affordablehousing/index.cfm and http://www.hud.gov/offices/hsg/sfh/hsgsingle.cfm

Housing types fact sheets: http://www.designcenter.umn.edu/reference_ctr/factsheets/FS_housing_types.html

Professional Builder magazine: http://www.housingzone.com/probuilder/article/CA6421687.html

Chapter 18: Data Collection of Residential Design

Books

Binggeli, C. (2007). *Interior design: A survey.* New York: Wiley.

Susanka, S. (2001). *Creating the not so big house: Insights and ideas for the new American home.* Newtown, CT: Taunton Press.

Susanka, S. (2007). *Inside the not so big house: Discovering the details that bring a home to life.* Newtown, CT: Taunton Press.

Susanka, S. (2002). *Not so big house solutions for your home.* Newtown, CT: Taunton Press.

Periodicals

Interior Design magazine

Perspective magazine

Illustration Credits

4.1e	Dean Isham
4.2	Dean Isham

Chapter 5

5.1	Photography by Richard Johnson
5.2	Courtesy Rockwell Group
5.3	Courtesy Bluprint Chicago
5.4	Photography by Jim Roof Creative
5.5	© Eric Laignel
5.6	Courtesy of Hugh Boyd, Architect
5.7	Courtesy Rafael Viñoly Architects

Chapter 6

6.1	Dean Isham
6.2	Dean Isham

Chapter 8

8.1	Courtesy Drayton Hall
8.2	Minnesota Historical Society
8.3	Linda Nussbaumer
8.4	Dean Isham

Chapter 9

9.1	Dean Isham
9.2	Dean Isham
9.3	Dean Isham
9.4	Dean Isham
9.5	Dean Isham

Chapter 10

10.1	Dean Isham
10.2	iStockPhoto
10.3	Dean Isham
10.4	© The Trustees of The British Museum/Art Resource
10.5	Dean Isham
10.6	Courtesy ATSA.com

Chapter 11

11.1	Dean Isham
11.2	Dean Isham
11.3a	Dean Isham
11.3b	Dean Isham

11.3c	Dean Isham
11.3d	Dean Isham
11.4a	Dean Isham
11.4b	Dean Isham
11.4c	Dean Isham
11.4d	Dean Isham
11.5	Dean Isham

Chapter 12

12.1	Dean Isham
12.2	Dean Isham

Chapter 13

13.1	Getty Images
13.2	Dean Isham

Chapter 14

14.1	Dean Isham
14.2	iStockPhoto

Chapter 15

15.1a	Dean Isham
15.1b	Dean Isham

Chapter 17

17.1	Dean Isham
17.2a	Dean Isham
17.2b	Dean Isham
17.3	Dean Isham
17.4	Dean Isham
17.5	Dean Isham
17.6a	Dean Isham
17.6b	Dean Isham
17.6c	Dean Isham
17.7a	Dean Isham
17.7b	Dean Isham
17.7c	Dean Isham
17.7d	Dean Isham
17.8	Dean Isham

Chapter 18

18.1a–f	Courtesy of Kitchensource.com

Index

Page numbers in italics refer to figures or tables

mechanical systems (*continued*)
  heating, ventilation, and air conditioning
    (HVAC), 102–3, 165
medical office buildings, 202–3
mission statements, 159
museum design, 84–85, 226–28

Native American design, 148–49
noise reduction coefficient (NRC), 109
nursing homes
  human habitat model, 205–6
  medical model, 205
  social model, 205
  see also long-term care facilities
nursing stations, 204

observation, 15
observation of behavior, 45–48
  structured observations, 47–48
  unstructured observations, 45–47
office design, 77
  color, 168
  data collection, 178–79
  financial institutions, 179–80
  history, 174–76
  spatial relationships and organization:
    departments, 178; private zones, 177–78;
    public zones, 176–77
open-ended questions, 44
organizational charts, 159, *160–62*
organizational culture types
  adhocratic, 161
  clan, 161
  hierarchical, 160
  market, 160
organizational profiles, 159–62
outpatient clinics. *See* medical office
  buildings

paper lite, 204
Parthenon, 57
participant observations, 46
passive solar energy, 118
Pebble Project, 199
permanent collections, 226
person-environment theory, 26–28
photoelectric, 118
photovoltaic, 118
physiological needs
  anthropometrics, 126–28
  ergonomics, 126, 128–30
physiological outcomes, 199
place attachment, 31
place identity, 31
plumbing, 108

pool or secretarial bay, 177
populations, 16
positive distraction, 200
post-occupancy evaluations (POEs), 7, 13
  in educational design, 225
precedents, 10
  design: educational design, 83–84; healthcare
    design, 80–82; hotel design, 78, *79*; museum
    design, 84–85; office design, 77; public and
    government design, 84; residential design,
    85–86; restaurant design, 78–80; retail
    design, 82–83
  historic: analysis criteria, 56–57; architecture
    and interior design criteria, 57–64; final
    analysis, 69–70; sacred spaces analysis, 72–73;
    theoretical criteria, 64–69; Villa Capra (La
    Rotonda) analysis, 70–72
preservation, restoration, renovation, and adaptive
  reuse, 115–17
problem statements, 50–51
program documents, 40
  goals, 51
  objectives, 51
  problem statements, 50–51
programming, 4–5, 7–8
  programming goal and objective example, 8
  See also data collection; research
proxemics, 130–35
public and government design, 84, 225
punch list, 7
psychological and sociological needs
  anthropology of space: fixed-feature space,
    131; informal, or nonfixed, space, 133;
    semifixed-feature space, 131–33
  crowding, 134–35
  distance zones, 133–34
  proxemics, 130–35
  territoriality, 135

qualitative research
  definition, 15
quantitative research
  definition, 15
questionnaires, 41, 42

radiation, 119
recreational design, 230
recycling, 251
Reggio Emilia theory, 224
religious design, 228–30
research
  data collections methods, 40–50; commercial
    spaces, 158–69
  distinction between fact finding and, 8
  new evidence application, 16–17